Praise for

JUSTICE IN KELLY COUNTRY

'Strahan brings to life a lost world of rural Victoria in the era of gold-seeking, free selection and bushranging. The book climaxes in the pursuit of the Kelly Gang, the moment when Anthony steps briefly into national history. But this is above all the story of an Irish migrant who makes his way in colonial Victoria by pursuing the hard life of a country policeman. It is also a family history: in tracing the life and times of Anthony, Lachlan is also learning something more about his own father, Frank, an archivist, historian and radical who admired the rebel and folk hero – Ned Kelly – and despised a man of the law, his own relative, who had helped bring a killer to justice.'
— Frank Bongiorno, Professor of History at the Australian National University and author of *The Sex Lives of Australians*

'A brilliant and original window into the Kelly outbreak – of the hunter rather than just the hunted.'
— Janet McCalman AC, Emeritus Redmond Barry Distinguished Professor at the University of Melbourne and author of *Vandemonians*

'This compelling and intimate history offers a new perspective on a national legend – the infamous Kelly Gang – and a vivid picture of the life of a policeman on the colonial Victorian frontier ... The book evokes the frugality and hardship of bush life as well as the moral and practical challenges of remote policing. Strahan's career takes us constantly into the dark side of the colonial world, into the rough, vain and violent underside of a frontier society ... It is also a beautiful meditation on history and memory and the power of family storytelling. This is a fascinating and original history, taut and suspenseful, written with subtlety and flair.'
— Tom Griffiths, Emeritus Professor of History at the Australian National University and author of *The Art of Time Travel*

JUSTICE IN KELLY COUNTRY

The story of the cop who hunted
Australia's most notorious bushrangers

LACHLAN STRAHAN

MONASH
UNIVERSITY
PUBLISHING

Published by Monash University Publishing
Matheson Library Annexe
40 Exhibition Walk
Monash University
Clayton, Victoria 3800, Australia
publishing.monash.edu

Monash University Publishing: the discussion starts here.

Copyright © Lachlan Strahan 2022
Lachlan Strahan asserts his right to be known as the author of this work.

All rights reserved. Apart from any uses permitted by Australia's *Copyright Act 1968*, no part of this book may be reproduced by any process without prior written permission from the copyright owners. Enquiries should be directed to the publisher.

9781922633507 (paperback)
9781922633514 (pdf)
9781922633521 (epub)

 A catalogue record for this book is available from the National Library of Australia

Design by Les Thomas
Cover design by Les Thomas
Typesetting by Jo Mullins
Maps by Alan Laver
Author photograph by Lily Petkovska
Letter by Anthony Strahan reproduced with kind permission from Public Records Victoria
Certificate of appreciation to Anthony Strahan reproduced with kind permission from the Rutherglen Historical Society Collection

Printed in Australia by Ligare Book Printers

For Lily and our children,
Joschka and Katya, with love.

CONTENTS

Prologue ix
Introduction xiv

PART I: DEFENDING THE THIN BLUE LINE
1   The Boy from Timolin 3
2   Ordered Out Like a Dog 18
3   Swindle 33
4   Tragedy and Vice 47
5   The Convict Stain 61
6   Saucy Jack 80

PART II: THE OUTRAGE AND THE JUNCTION
7   Something Wicked This Way Comes 93
8   Chain Reaction 105
9   Judgement Day 126
10 Loose Ends 137
11 A Master of His Own Domain 150

PART III: THE KELLY OUTBREAK
12 The Greta Mob 171
13 Over the Edge 184
14 A Few Words 202
15 Stringybark Creek 219
16 The Endless Chase 230
17 One Last Stand 244
18 Rutherglen Days 261
19 A Terror to Evil-Doers 279

Coda 300

Acknowledgements 303
Notes 306
Bibliography 313
Index 316
About the Author 327

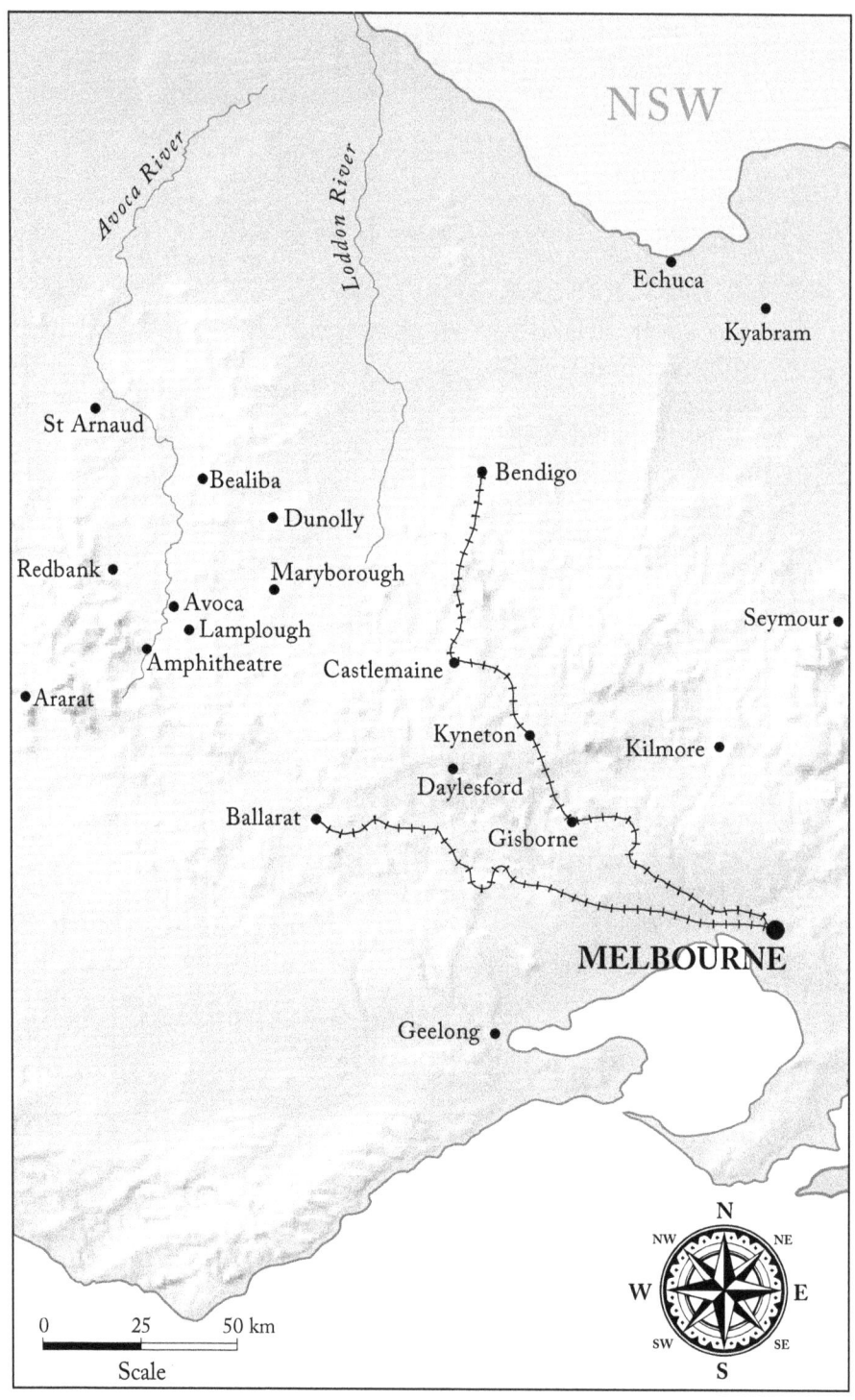

PROLOGUE

An unforgiving southerly was blowing on Tuesday 15 October 1878 as Senior Constable Anthony Strahan and Senior Constable Edward Shoebridge of the Victoria Police rode towards the bridge over the Ovens River, near Moore's Pioneer Hotel, not far from Wangaratta. The two police officers had worked together on and off since the early 1870s and knew they could rely on each other if trouble came – though Shoebridge sometimes marvelled at his companion's fiery Irish temper.

Strahan and Shoebridge were close to the end of another gruelling patrol. During their long ride – first north to Eldorado, before turning south, past Oxley and Milawa, to Moyhu and Edi in the King Valley – the two had been sleeping rough and eating paltry rations. They were looking forward to a warm meal and a bed when they arrived home.

This patrol had come to nothing, like so many others over recent months. The Kellys were elusive, almost like ghosts. True, it was easy enough to hide in the dense countryside that covered parts of the northeast, but it seemed some locals were doing their best to keep the Kellys out of gaol, tipping them off as the police patrols scoured the district.

Six months before, magistrates had issued a warrant to arrest Ned Kelly for the attempted murder of Constable Alexander Fitzpatrick. The incident had occurred at the Kelly home near Greta, a township to the south of Wangaratta, where Strahan was stationed. Another warrant followed – this to arrest Ned's mother, Ellen, for aiding and abetting her son in the act. The Kelly boys, Ned and his younger brother Dan, had taken to the bush to evade capture, and it was up to the Victoria Police to find them and bring them to justice.

All the trouble with the Kellys had started in the area around Moyhu. It was here that the two brothers and their accomplices had stolen horses in late 1877 from squatters and selectors, setting off a train of events that had resulted in the colony's biggest manhunt. At least the land approaching Wangaratta was mostly flat farming country, a welcome respite from the foothills, gullies and ridges of the previous days. As their exhausted horses approached the Ovens River Bridge, Strahan and Shoebridge fell into an almost sullen silence, each man hunched down in his coat and preoccupied with his thoughts in the cool wind and fading light. Strahan was frustrated. He knew this patrol party should have been larger. He and Shoebridge were hunting armed culprits who had shot and wounded one of their own. But the Victoria Police was stretched thinly across the colony, and the district commander in Benalla, Superintendent John Sadleir, had said he could spare no more officers. Towns such as Oxley didn't even have a single constable on duty.

Strahan's head snapped up at the sound of a horseman crossing the bridge from the other side of the river. He reached for his Webley revolver but already knew that he wouldn't be able to pull it out in time. The Victoria Police's standard-issue holster was notoriously cumbersome at the best of times, and this wasn't that.

'Bail up! Throw up your hands or I'll blow your brains out,' yelled Ned Kelly.

As he pulled up his horse, Strahan gasped in a mixture of disbelief and irritation. He and Shoebridge hadn't been able to find the Kellys – but now the Kellys had found them. Ned held a rifle at his shoulder, the barrel pointed straight at the two policemen. Strahan could see Dan to Ned's left, astride his horse with his own rifle levelled. Two other horsemen were further down the track, both wielding rifles. In the deepening gloom, the sun dipping below the horizon, he couldn't pick them out, though there was something familiar about the look of one of them.

'Strahan, I hear you've been strutting around the district blathering about how you'll bring me and my brother in,' Ned shouted across the bridge.

'Yeah, Strahan, you've got a big mouth,' Dan added.

'I'm just doing my bloody job, Ned. You and Dan started this mess. You could end it here. You're already in trouble. Just come into town with us. Don't make things worse for yourselves,' Strahan shouted back.

PROLOGUE

Sitting in his saddle just behind Strahan, Shoebridge was alarmed. *Here we go again*, he thought. He had seen his old colleague dig in his heels before, almost spoiling for a row, but now was not the time to argue the point. 'Anthony, for heaven's sake, be careful. I don't want to die out here,' he said in a low voice.

'I've got a mind to finish you off right here,' declared Ned, leaning forward in his saddle, tightening his grip on the rifle.

'Shoot the bugger,' yelled Dan, seemingly even more intent than his older brother on shedding blood. His ill-fitting clothes emphasised his diminutive stature, and his contorted expression made his threat somehow both comical and sinister.

'So, you'd just shoot me like a dog, would you? In cold blood? Would you, Ned?' Strahan responded, keeping his hands in the air, well away from his hips, showing that he was making no move to unholster his revolver.

'Well, it was you and that other rotten trap, damn Sergeant Steele, who dragged my mother out of her hut in the middle of the night. With my baby sister! And it was you, Strahan, who put her in your lock-up in Greta. Now that bastard judge has sent her away to Pentridge for three years! She never hit that lying Fitzpatrick! I let Fitzpatrick go and I swore I'd never let another trap go,' shouted Ned, shaking with righteous anger.

Strahan didn't back down. 'Are you really telling me that Fitzpatrick wasn't at your ma's place? That she didn't smash him over the head with a shovel? Do you take me for a fool?'

'Tell me why, for the love of God, I shouldn't blow your brains out?' bellowed Ned. He raised his rifle higher and put a finger on the trigger.

Strahan realised that he had gone too far. He had a wife and five children back in Greta. Now was not the time to die. Certainly not for riling up Ned Kelly.

'Look, Ned. I was doing my duty and following orders when I took your ma in. I had no choice. You know my wife looked after her while she was in my lock-up. Marion made sure Ellen and little Alice were warm and comfortable, had proper food, could get some rest. There was no way we were going to make a mother and her child suffer. And I was out here looking for you when Justice Barry sentenced your mother. I had nothing to do with that. I didn't testify. I've got my own wife and children,' said Strahan, his tone calm but with the hint of a plea.

Ned didn't lower his rifle, but he paused. All four men had fallen quiet. Two police officers and two men on the run, on a lonely bridge.

'Alright, Strahan. You and your wife did right by my mother. I won't deny that,' Ned said eventually. 'You're a lucky bastard because I'm going to let you go home to your bed tonight. But mark my word, this will only happen once. If we cross paths again, I won't hesitate. I'll put a big hole right there.' He pointed to Strahan's head.

With a final glare, the Kelly brothers turned their horses around, joined their shadowy companions down the track and galloped off. Strahan and Shoebridge looked at each other, shaking with relief. That had been close.

Something very much like this could have happened to my great-great-grandfather, Senior Constable Anthony Strahan, a mounted officer in the Victoria Police who had already served in eight stations across central and northeast Victoria by the time this meeting allegedly took place. I use 'allegedly' because I'm relying on a family memory passed down from generation to generation to sketch this apparently fateful encounter. Anthony was certainly entangled in the Kelly Outbreak, right to its heart, but I've been unable to find any verifiable sources, oral or written, to back up this dramatic story. We know that memory is imperfect, the stories it produces partial and prone to elaboration, especially when told across the decades. This particular tale, as I inherited it, is thin: the Kelly Gang ambushed Senior Constable Anthony Strahan on a bridge, but let him go because he and his wife, Marion, had looked after the family's adored matriarch, Ellen Kelly, in the lock-up at the Greta police station. That's it. Nothing more. The story doesn't say when or exactly where this apparent incident took place. So I've chosen as the setting one of the many smaller bridges of the day near Wangaratta and invented the heated conversation, weaving in elements of the known history and including the kind of phrases that Ned and Anthony used in their own accounts.

But that's as far as this fiction will go. The story that follows is based on sources from the time. Written sources aren't unimpeachable – far from it. The written record of the time is patchy and patterned with silences, gaps, misperceptions, bias and outright lies. And many events and people aren't captured, having slipped from sight, lost forever. But a historian can't tell an authentic story by playing with figments and scraps, inventing things, pretending to know what he doesn't. I won't play fast and loose with you. I'll tell the tale of Anthony Strahan's life and his long career in the Victoria Police as plainly as I can. I'll tell you when I'm engaging in speculation, trying to fill in some of the gaps or divine his motives. I'll leave you to judge if I've seen my ancestor with a clear eye. But as you'll find, I don't need to embroider events or take imaginative leaps because the story the records reveal is dramatic enough. At times, life is more interesting, less expected and certainly more complicated than fiction, and the story of Anthony Strahan is one such case.

INTRODUCTION

We saw two men at the logs they got up and one took a double barreled fowling-piece and fetched a horse down and hobbled him at the tent. We thought there were more men in the tent asleep those being on sentry we could have shot those two men without speaking but not wishing to take their lives we waited McIntyre laid the gun against a stump and Lonigan sat on the log I advanced, my brother Dan keepin McIntyre covered which he took to be constable Flood and had he not obeyed my orders, or attempted to reach for the gun or draw his revolver he would have been shot dead but when I called on them to throw up their hands McIntyre obeyed and Lonigan ran some six or seven yards to a battery of logs insted of dropping behind the one he was sitting on, he had just got to the logs and put his head up to take aim when I shot him that instant or he would have shot me as I took him to be Strachan the man who said he would not ask me to stand he would shoot me first like a dog.

'… *he would shoot me first like a dog.*' What are a few words? Some would say words are fleeting, easily contradicted by yet other words, unable to change the course of events, let alone draw blood.

An old adage attests that sticks and stones may break your bones but words will never hurt you. Yet while we might tell our children this is so, shielding them from being wounded or provoked, we know that words can indeed inspire strong emotions, evoking love, inspiring courage and loyalty, or engendering hatred, whipping up intolerance and inflicting pain. Words matter. They aren't inconsequential, for they can be harnessed for good or ill and bear so potently on our sense of identity and character. Across cultures and time, they have become entwined with notions of honour and dignity. Often, they can't be retracted or forgotten once said. Sometimes they can't be forgiven and become the spark for retribution and revenge.

Can a person be judged by a few words, especially if uttered on the spur of the moment, in anger, frustration, disappointment or even despair? Perhaps those hasty words were no more than a reaction to other stinging, hot, angry words. Can that person be held to account for how those words are heard and then interpreted by another, often at second- or third-hand – almost always distorted, magnified and made more definitive and irrevocable by the telling and the retelling? Words can assume a life of their own, a larger meaning. They can become totemic, the fulcrum of a narrative, the trigger that propels events in one direction or another. Such words might be praised or condemned more keenly if they have become immortalised due to the events that followed them.

My forebears, the Strahans, had a way with words. At times, it seems this gift of the gab, this facility with language, was a boon: a way of connecting with others; a method for winning friendship, creating trust, wooing, sealing a deal or selling a product; a means of entertaining and charming. But this gift of the gab could also get Strahans into trouble.

It was my great-great-grandfather, Senior Constable Anthony Strahan, who found himself, with a few alleged harsh words, at the centre of one of Australia's most colourful national stories, the Kelly Outbreak. Just two or three days before the notorious events at Stringybark Creek in Victoria's High Country on 25 October 1878, when Ned Kelly and his gang shot dead three policemen, Anthony Strahan had a heated argument with one of the young outlaw's uncles, the notoriously shifty Patrick Quinn. Several months later, Ned gave his account of that exchange in his famous self-defence, a long rambling document taken down by his mate and fellow gang member, Joe Byrne, which later became known as the Jerilderie Letter. In it, Ned accused Anthony Strahan of saying he would shoot him as if he were a dog.

Anthony's pithy apparent threat has been memorialised over the decades in history books, newspaper articles and even an ironic novel by Peter

Carey. Mostly he has been pegged in this great national story as a villain. He has been blamed by many, at the time and later, for causing much of the trouble that unfolded during the Kelly Outbreak.

It is hard to be related to a villain. All of this was even more confronting because my father, Frank Strahan, a passionate archivist of Australian history, was a staunch Kelly partisan. He had a natural inclination to defend the underdog, and impoverished Irish battler and rebel Ned Kelly seemed the epitome of this. But who was Anthony Strahan? Was he really the heartless law enforcement officer who saw Ned Kelly as little more than a dog? Or was there more to the story?

As I began to dig into the past to get a fix on my great-great-grandfather, to understand how and why he had become a central figure in a national legend, I realised that his life was more complex than the standard narrative.

Anthony's policing career up until 1878 had left no significant trace in Australian historical scholarship or literary and popular mythology. Even the Wooragee Outrage – in which Anthony captured two marauding bushrangers, and which engendered an uproar throughout colonial Victoria at the time – has been all but forgotten. I was able to tell Anthony's story to this point in time by drawing on extensive information in contemporary official files and press coverage, but nothing more. In one sense, this was an advantage because I dealt with a clean historical slate, assembling the elements of his life from original sources, unassisted but also unencumbered by an existing historical narrative.

Yet when my research turned towards his posting in Greta, my journey into Anthony's life entered different terrain. Tracing the next phase of his career could not have been more different, for I was grappling with the fact that he was an identifiable, if hazy, figure in a great Australian story: the Kelly Outbreak. I soon realised I would have to navigate a highly charged body of writing about Ned Kelly, which has almost invariably cleaved into fiercely opposed pro-Kelly and anti-Kelly camps. Aside from the occasional contribution by a woman writer, such as Clare Wright's excellent article on the women in Ned's life,[1] all the main Kelly writers are blokes. In part, they are playing out different narratives about Australian masculinity, inevitably saying something along the way about their own sense of being an Australian man.

One side of this debate is prone to taking Ned Kelly largely at his word. It casts him as a social bandit and a rebel fighting an unjust order, placing him in the pantheon of Australian heroes. In this version of the past, anyone who resisted or didn't support the Kellys – a teacher, a stationmaster or a humble farmer, let alone a police officer – is cast as part of 'the establishment'. The other side of the debate sees Ned Kelly as a fabulist and a liar, with a talent for obfuscation. The Jerilderie Letter, which refers to Anthony by name, is considered little more than a rambling, self-justifying statement from a criminal.

One side tends to downplay, explain away or ignore some of the violence committed by Ned and his associates. It overstates the level of popular support he enjoyed and tends to represent the police in solely dark colours. The other side veers towards the reverse.

To me, Anthony's place in Kelly history does not align neatly with either camp. To some extent, he was the victim of happenstance – he ended up in a particular place at a particular time and became caught in a complicated series of events at a crucial moment in Australia's history. However, so much about Anthony's life – all those circumstances and events that fashioned his character and shaped the way he saw the world around him and the decisions he made – helped to bring him to that moment when he became entangled with Australia's most infamous bushranger. More than mere happenstance was at play. Even his origins on the other side of the world had started him on a path that led all the way to an isolated and wild part of the bush in the Australian colonies.

Perhaps many who have researched and written about the Kelly Outbreak have not been willing enough to acknowledge that a chain reaction of events, with its own logic and momentum, pushed all the players along, one thing triggering another. This isn't to say we should absolve the participants in the Outbreak on both sides, including Anthony, of personal responsibility for what they believed and did. Rather, it's to see that sometimes people end up in places they didn't foresee or entirely choose.

The Kelly Outbreak has loomed so large that it has tended to blot out much else that happened – before, at the time and later – reducing complex events to a one-dimensional narrative with an almost inexorable trajectory. Anthony's story has been sucked up into this. To the extent that he is remembered at all in history books, he is defined by the Kelly story. It's as though nothing else mattered, or even took place, in his life. Yet the three years or so of the Kelly Outbreak, dramatic as they were, accounted for less than 10 per cent of his thirty-two years as a bush policeman. As I unpicked Anthony's role in the hunt for the Kelly Gang, I realised that so much else occurred in his life that revealed who he was and how colonial society worked.

Anthony made a critical decision during the Kelly Outbreak: he set out to bring Ned to justice. He felt he had no other choice; he was doing his sworn duty as a policeman. But, in so doing, he helped feed a national story about the oppressive power of the state, the Australian larrikin ethos and a working-class family's sense of social injustice. His life forever intersected with Ned's, and he became ensnared in the Kelly legend.

This book is about resuscitating Anthony from the weight of the Kelly legend and recovering his story, in all its gritty, moving and sometimes confronting detail, as he tried to build a life in a frontier society while undertaking a tough and often thankless job. My great-great-grandfather was a complex and, in some ways, flawed man: committed to upholding justice but prone to letting his temper get the better of him; guided by firm, even unyielding, principles yet at times guilty of hypocrisy; capable of both compassion and hardness, cool judgement and rash action. By this book's end, readers will appreciate what it was like, as a bush police officer, to chase a hardened criminal through dense bush for days on end, to defend the honour of a woman who has been shunned by small-minded folk, to search for a man who has walked into a raging river in despair, to close down a sly grog shanty, to stand up to a tyrannical superior, to treat a woman bitten by a black snake in the middle of nowhere, to apprehend a man who has just killed his wife's lover and burned down the family home, to nab a dodgy squatter who has been stealing his neighbour's sheep, to become embroiled in a bitter feud with a local publican, to pin down a shyster who has been passing counterfeit bank notes around town, and to still find time to raise a family, own a racehorse and work a small farm.

Anthony Strahan was driven by an admirable sense of justice which could at times be inflexible. In his policing career and his personal life, he could be kind, but also severe. Above all, Anthony Strahan was compelling.

PART I

DEFENDING
THE THIN BLUE LINE

 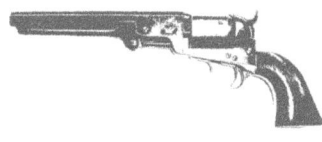

IRELAND

1

THE BOY FROM TIMOLIN

There is a family myth that dominated my childhood, and a good proportion of my adulthood.

Dad, or Franko as we called him, was a radical Australian nationalist, ever determined to stand up for what he thought was right and dispatching misconceptions about what had moulded and defined Australia. He was decidedly anti-English. He saw the English as the colonial oppressors who had held back the emerging Australian nation, imposing a rigid class system, preserving structures of privilege and deference and mutating our economic development. He was proud our family origins distanced us from the Poms. He always told his three sons with some defiance and a deep sense of righteousness that we came from good Scottish, not English, stock. Dad knew intellectually that in some ways this distinction was artificial – he in fact liked and respected many things about England and had dear English friends – but he held on to it nonetheless. In 1982 I was watching Granada Television's superb rendition of Evelyn Waugh's *Brideshead Revisited* with my mother, Lynne, when Dad came into the room and snorted, 'Why are you watching that Brit shit?' Dad's anti-English sprays were always a mixture of genuine feeling and performance – even when the stalls were only occupied by his wife and sons.

But in 2016, long after Dad's death, as I was investigating Anthony Strahan's past, I made a discovery: a key part of Dad's Strahan family story was wrong. In 1997 I had spent several weeks with Dad and my wife, Lily Petkovska, in Scotland scouring through shops to find the clan origins of the Strahans, to no avail. As I sifted through records in Melbourne and

Dublin nearly two decades later, I realised why. Our Strahan forebears came to Australia from Ireland, not Scotland. As I reviewed the records, the unknown, hidden contours of the Irish origins of my Strahan forebears slowly emerged, filling in gaps and correcting misconceptions in my immediate family's sense of self.

The more common version of our family name, Strachan, does harken back to the lands of Strathaen and Strathachan in Kincardineshire, a shire on Scotland's east coast, south of Aberdeen. Like so many names, 'Strachan' originated in the landscape, 'strath' meaning valley and 'aen' or 'aven' meaning river. Some of the Strachans of Kincardineshire adopted a family motto, *'Non Timeo Sed Caveo'* ('I am not afraid but I beware'). It is clear our spelling of the name is known in Scotland – but it is more common in Ireland and England.

In the records I came across many Scottish ancestors, but I also found plenty of English forebears, the occasional Welsh man or woman and lots of Irish. And those Irish blood lines were crucial in shaping Anthony Strahan. The family origins of the Strahans are more complicated than Dad's emotional, almost guttural, Scottish pride let his sons believe. Had Dad known, he likely would have celebrated our Irish origins, for in his cosmos, no one had suffered more under the English heel than the Irish.

Yet Dad was partly right, if wide of the mark by some generations. In an unpublished family history – given to me by one of my second cousins from Bendigo, Alan Strahan – a distant relative, Robin Denholm, writes that two Strachan brothers moved from Scotland to Ireland at some point between 1689 and 1694, during the reign of William III (better known as William of Orange), one settling in Belfast and the other in Dublin. He doesn't offer a source for this contention, likely relying on family folklore.

A significant number of English and Scottish Protestants did settle in Ireland in the years after William defeated James II at the Battle of the Boyne on 1 July 1690. But Protestants had been settling in Ireland since Henry VIII had rejected the authority of the Papacy in the early 1530s and created the Church of England. Henry's government dissolved the Irish monasteries and established the Church of Ireland as the state, Anglican, church in 1537, beginning a long period of Protestant ascendancy. During the first forty years of the seventeenth century, as many as 100,000 people from Britain, mostly Protestants, moved to Ireland, settling predominantly in the north and the east. The political and military domination of the Protestant minority was powerfully reinforced when Oliver Cromwell's New Model Army vanquished the Confederate forces in the early 1650s. By the 1670s, Ireland was home to around 300,000 Protestants; 200,000 English, mostly Anglicans; and 100,000 Scots, mostly Presbyterians, together constituting around 20 per cent of the population. The Protestant presence was strong in Dublin, Ulster and the eastern counties of Wicklow, Carlow, Wexford and parts of Kildare. This Protestant bulwark lived alongside a Catholic Gaelic majority and a much older Anglo-Norman minority that remained loyal to Catholicism. So the Strachan brothers could have come to Ireland in the 1690s or at any earlier point in the seventeenth or even the sixteenth century.

Whenever the first Strachans in my family settled in Ireland, it seems fairly certain that two brothers, my fourth great-grandfather, Edward, born in 1765, and his younger brother, Isaac, were living at Bolton Hill in southern County Kildare and Belair in County Wicklow respectively in the late eighteenth century. If Denholm is right, they were likely descendants of the Strachans who had settled in Dublin in the 1690s. They dropped the 'c' from their name, perhaps following an English way of softening 'Strachan'.

By the late eighteenth century, the sectarian divide in Ireland had become starker and the Strahan family was decidedly Protestant by faith and cultural identification. Isaac, though, crossed this religious, social and political boundary and married a Catholic. According to one account, written by a family member in the nineteenth century, his married life proved unhappy: 'His wife is said to have set fire to his bed while he slept. He left the country. She remained and brought up her sons as Catholics, and their descendants continue in that religion.'

The other Strahans of eastern Ireland perhaps took Isaac's sorry tale as yet another confirmation that Catholics could not be trusted. Generation after generation, they remained members of the Church of Ireland and married inside the Protestant community. From the very beginning, the

Strahans of County Kildare were entwined with the long and often terrible conflict between Catholics and Protestants in Ireland. As we shall see, even when they moved to the other side of the globe, the Strahans continued to be embroiled in this ongoing sectarian battle.

While his brother had seemingly become entangled in an unhappy and even violent relationship with a Catholic, Edward settled down as a farmer in Kildare and married a Protestant woman called Deborah. Unfortunately, my efforts to determine Deborah's surname or any information about her family of origin have come to nothing. This is sadly a common experience for those trying to piece together aspects of Ireland's history, for a swathe of its national records, including all census data from between 1821 and 1851 and many parish papers, were destroyed in a fire that engulfed the Irish Public Record Office during the civil war, when Free State forces bombarded their republican opponents sheltering in the adjacent Four Courts on 28 June 1922. Nonetheless, it is almost certain Deborah was the daughter of another Protestant farmer.

Edward's home at Bolton Hill, a gently rolling part of Kildare, was close to Timolin, a town that became important to the Strahans over several generations. Harkening back to a monastery established by St Moling of Ferns in the seventh century, Timolin was long known by its Gaelic names, Tigh Moling and Tigh Mo Linne. Like so much of Ireland, it had a turbulent and often bloody history. Edmond le Boteler burned down the Church of Moling in 1328 and the Marquess of Ormonde took the local castle during the reign of Charles I, executing its garrison. The town was the scene of an infamous massacre during the Irish Confederate Wars (1641–53). However, by the early nineteenth century Timolin was a quiet village on the mail coach road between Dublin, just over 70 kilometres to the north, and Carlow, the principal town of County Carlow, 26 kilometres to the south. In 1837, it boasted no more than thirty-four households, 288 residents and one church, St Mullins, a Church of Ireland congregation. Built in 1832, the church was an austere building with no external ornaments. The Quakers had a meeting house at Ballitore, just to the north, while the nearby Catholic chapel was a plain but spacious structure. Local quarries supplied sandstone and pebble limestone, the latter being burnt for manure, while peat came from the nearby bog of Narraghmore. The Timolin area had one parish school and three private schools, which accommodated 300 children in 1839. A fair was held in the town centre twice a year. Athy, to the west, was the nearest town of any size, with a population of 4500 in 1837. Long a garrison for British troops, Athy was seen as a loyalist stronghold. Another larger town, Baltinglass, which encompassed 256 households in 1837, lay further afield to the southeast, in Wicklow.

Edward and Deborah had three sons: Robert in 1788, Anthony in 1799 and Richard in 1804. The long gaps between these birthdates suggest that Edward and Deborah likely had more children, who probably died in infancy. The youngest surviving son, Richard, was christened at St Mullins in Timolin in April 1805, underlining the Strahan family's close links with the Church of Ireland.

Edward and his family occupied an intermediate position in the class structure of rural Ireland in the early nineteenth century. A powerful Anglican elite owned the majority of the country's land, wielding considerable political, economic and social power. Indeed, a good two-thirds of the country's landmass was owned by only 2000 people, and fewer than 800 possessed half of that land. Many of these powerful Anglican landowners were absentee landlords, meaning their links to any given locality were tenuous. Catholics constituted just over 80 per cent of the population but owned little land, with many Catholic farmers renting marginal holdings. Wealthy Catholic landowners were few, and some converted to the Church of Ireland to save their property. Edward was a member of the class of middle-sized and larger-scale Protestant farmers who leased their land from the powerful Anglican landowners, often in turn sub-letting some of their holdings to small-scale farmers.

Edward was leasing land in the 1820s around Timolin from George Drake Esquire. With substantial holdings stretching across the parishes of Timolin and Portersize, Drake was a member of the Protestant landed gentry. He did not live on his Timolin–Portersize estate, residing instead at New Ross, a town in southwest Wexford. Edward's holdings were not confined to the immediate locality around Timolin, however, for he leased additional land a few kilometres south of Timolin at Belan from Mason Gerard Stratford, the Fifth Earl of Aldborough. The Stratfords were an old English family from Warwickshire who had likely settled in Ireland around 1660, first purchasing land near Baltinglass. They boosted their political and social stocks by supporting William of Orange and became part of the Protestant landowning elite in Kildare and Wicklow. From his fields in Belan, Edward could see the seat of the Stratford family, Belan House, just down the road. Built in 1743 by the first Earl of Aldborough, Belan House was an imposing three-storey gabled house with a grand granite stairway at its front. Reputedly built from the remains of a castle destroyed in 1641, it boasted large stables, extensive parklands, fishponds, a classical temple, a chapel, a theatre, tea rooms and a fruitery. By the 1820s, the house had fallen quiet, with Mason Gerard preferring to stay at Stratford Place in London or Aldborough House in Dublin. One visitor in the 1830s found a striking but eerie building: 'Though uninhabited for fully ten years, the house was in perfect repair, no trace of damp or decay and to all appearances might have been lived in a week before.'

The Stratfords' fortunes had declined by the 1820s, in part because Gerard Mason was a hopeless spendthrift and a bigamist. When he was short of funds, he reputedly did the rounds of the London moneylenders with a gun and threatened to shoot himself until he was given some cash. Belan House became heavily mortgaged and gradually fell into disrepair. When I visited Belan in April 2018 with one of my cousins, Laura Daly, to see Edward's fields, Belan House had disappeared entirely, aside from the old stone gate, an obelisk standing forlornly in a field and the stables. Laura and I drove along a muddy track, skidding from side to side, almost becoming bogged, to examine the stables, which were largely intact but dilapidated and overgrown.

In the 1820s and 1830s, the empty Belan House would still have reminded Edward about where he stood in Kildare's social and economic hierarchy. But the Strahans were by no means destitute, as was evident in the career choices of Edward's sons. The eldest, Robert, and the youngest,

Richard, settled in Dublin and became cabinet-makers. Robert joined the family firm, Robert Strahan and Co., which had been established by an earlier Robert Strahan in Dublin in 1776. By the mid-nineteenth century, Strahan and Co. Furniture and Upholstery had become prosperous, with premises on Chancery Lane and two workshops. It manufactured high-quality, functional furniture for the Office of Public Works, better-off Dublin families and some of the great Irish country houses. Several Strahan pieces were more elaborate, with the firm showing an ornate walnut table at the second London International Exhibition in 1862. Robert and his family became urban people, members even of the wider social and economic elite of Dublin. Less is known about Robert's young brother, Richard, though he too lived in Dublin until he died in 1872.

Although Edward stayed in touch with his eldest and youngest sons in the city, his bond was much stronger with his middle son, Anthony, my third-great-grandfather. Unlike his Dublin-dwelling brothers, Anthony settled in Timolin and became a farmer. He remained grounded in his small rural community, farming the Strahan acres in Timolin and Belan with his father. Anthony married a Protestant, Anne Giltrap, in Dublin in 1829; he was thirty and she only seventeen. Like other farmers from somewhat prosperous backgrounds, he had delayed getting married to help his father work the family farm. It is likely Edward played some role in selecting his son's bride, since marriages for the stronger farming families were carefully arranged, with each union building new kinship networks of benefits and obligations. The extended Giltrap family worked farms in three counties, Kildare, Carlow and Wicklow, indicating that Anne came from another rural family of solid means who leased land from the major Protestant landowners such as Sir Robert Paul, in turn sub-letting some of their holdings.

Edward died in December 1854 at ninety-nine, an astoundingly ripe age for the nineteenth century. He was buried in the graveyard at the old abbey in Baltinglass, fittingly only 20 metres or so from the imposing granite tomb of the Earls of Aldborough. Deborah likely predeceased him by some years, but they were not buried together, suggesting she may have been laid to rest in her own family's home town, Hollywood in Wicklow. By the time his father died, Anthony had built up a decent farm, leasing 17 acres at Belan from the sixth and last Earl of Aldborough and 29 acres around Timolin from George Drake, meaning his total holding was close to 50 acres, placing him among the more affluent tenant farmers. The boundaries of some of the Strahan fields in Timolin remain unchanged to this day, though any sign of the family home or other farm buildings has long since vanished. Underscoring the Strahan family's long links with agriculture in Kildare, another Anthony Strahan, a descendant of my third great-grandfather, was farming land around Timolin as late as the early 1960s.

Timolin was a large rural parish in the mid-nineteenth century and supported a substantial agricultural economy, with land both tilled for crops such as wheat, barley and oats and used as pasture to rear and fatten livestock. It is likely Edward and Anthony devoted their holdings to a combination of tillage and pasture: their comparative wealth would have allowed them to invest in purchasing animals. Their holdings dwarfed those of the impoverished Catholic tenant farmers, the majority of whom eked out miserable existences on tiny plots – many of Timolin's tenant farms were smaller than 5 acres. In 1854, Anthony was paying a sizeable £40 in rent every year to George Drake and the Earl of Aldborough. However, he was renting houses and land to seven tenants in Timolin and Belan, with each paying 10 shillings per year. It is likely some of these tenants were quite humble, even impoverished, for just over half of the country's dwellings in 1841 were no more than mud cabins with only one room.

It was a good thing that Anthony was able to draw on solid means, for he and Anne were to have thirteen children. The first, Edward, arrived in 1830, when Anne was only eighteen, and the last, Elizabeth, came in 1855, when she was forty-three. Anne must have been a strong woman constitutionally to survive so many births over twenty-five years and live to an old age. Surprisingly, given the high infant mortality rate of the time, twelve of the thirteen children survived into adulthood. All were christened in St Mullins, reaffirming the strong Strahan link with Timolin.

So many children could not make a living from the family farm; they would have to marry into other local families, find different occupations or move. This irresistible mathematics explains at least in part why seven of Anthony's children migrated to Australia. Their cousins in Dublin did not join this wave of migration, presumably because they had become established in the furniture-making business.

It was Edward, the eldest son, who first opted to migrate to the Australian colonies. He was likely attracted, like so many others, by the opportunities the colonies seemed to offer in abundance, especially given the tough conditions in Ireland. When he boarded the *Eliza* at Plymouth on 30 November 1852, the two countries presented a stark contrast. The Great Famine, which had ravaged Ireland between 1845 and 1852, killing up to a million people through starvation, malnutrition and disease and inducing another million to emigrate, had only just ended. Meanwhile, the goldrush had started in the Australian colonies, first in New South Wales and then in Victoria, less than eighteen months before.

The Famine had been much more severe in the western and southern parts of the country, where subsistence farming dominated. Eastern counties such as Kildare and Wicklow, and Ulster in the north, fared better. It is not known how the Strahans coped during the harsh Famine years, but it is revealing that Anthony and Anne had four children between 1846 and 1851, all of whom lived to an advanced age. Labourers and small-scale farmers were hit hardest by the Famine and the Strahans were no doubt protected to a significant degree by their social standing. In his history of Ireland, R. F. Foster notes that large-scale farmers (with 30 acres or more) 'not only escaped almost unscathed but in fact strengthened their position during the Famine years'. But even if Anthony Strahan and his family had come through the Famine without privation, they would have been affected by it. The prospect of inheriting land dwindled after the Famine as more landholders decided not to subdivide their land between their offspring. The traumatic impact of such widespread hardship exacerbated the longstanding structural weaknesses that were holding back the Irish economy, not least the failure to industrialise beyond pockets such as Ulster.

Emigration offered the chance of a better life, a new beginning. By 1890 three million Irish-born were living overseas, stripping many young people from counties around the country.

It is telling that Edward decided to migrate even though he was the eldest son and might have expected to inherit his father's land holdings. His relatively high level of education compared to his siblings and most other young people in Ireland might have been a factor in persuading him to look outwards. Although the rate of primary-school education was high in Ireland in the mid- to late nineteenth century, few students went on to secondary school. It seems he was brought up in part by his grandfather, Edward, perhaps because he was the firstborn, and attended the Grammar School in Athy. Family tradition long held that he should also complete a Master of Arts at Dublin's prestigious university, Trinity College, but this was not the case. His education was enough to launch him on a professional career, though, for he apparently worked as a schoolteacher in Somerset before leaving for the colonies. Perhaps one post-Famine trend, the Catholic devotional revolution, had helped to induce Edward to emigrate, for he was a devout Protestant, even contemplating at one point becoming a minister of the Church of Ireland. He had a way with words, but he was decidedly serious-minded, even stern, and he was not the sort of man who would get himself into trouble with fiery outbursts. As we shall see, some of his brothers shared his facility for language but not his earnest moderation.

Why did Edward choose Victoria? A passage to the Australian colonies cost four times that across the Atlantic to the United States or Canada. Edward likely followed a regional pattern, however, for the Irish Midlands had strong migration links with Australia. He became part of a significant stream of young Irish who travelled to the other side of the world to find a new life in the Australian colonies: between 1845 and 1860, nearly 250,000 emigrated to Australia. In *A New History of the Irish in Australia*, Elizabeth Malcolm and Dianne Hall divide Irish immigrants to Australia into three groups: members of the Protestant Anglo-Irish elite, which had close social, cultural and political ties with England; middle-class Protestant and Catholic men who were employed in the armed forces, the professions and the civil service; and Catholic men and women from poor rural backgrounds, who made up the largest group. But they overlook a fourth group. Edward Strahan did not belong to the Anglo-Irish elite, and although he was educated, he was not a member of the Irish Protestant middle class, which was drawn overwhelmingly from the cities and towns of Ireland. Rather, the Strahans were part of that intermediate rural class of larger tenant farmers who were members of the Church of Ireland. Malcolm and Hall note that 25 per cent of the Irish who migrated to Australia were Protestant, yet their wide-ranging and insightful study focuses almost entirely on the Catholic immigrants, leaving the Irish Protestant experience in Australia out of the picture for the most part.

When he set out for Victoria in 1852, less than three weeks before his twenty-second birthday, Edward was in many respects a typical Irish migrant. He was young, fit and single, though his education likely set him apart from many of his fellow travellers. He voyaged as an assisted emigrant, meaning his journey was sponsored, most likely by the colonial authorities in Australia. Edward's passage on the *Eliza*, a refitted vessel built in 1838, was arduous, lasting 131 days – far longer than usual – due to bad weather. This gruelling voyage took a toll, with forty-one of the 371 passengers, including twenty-nine children, dying en route from various scourges, pneumonia, enteritis, tuberculosis, cholera and typhus. Edward helped to nurse the ill passengers and was commended at the end of the voyage. He arrived in Portland, western Victoria, unscathed on 9 April 1853. The oldest permanent European settlement in Victoria, settled by the Henty family in 1834, Portland was a well-established community by the mid-1850s, even aspiring to be the Liverpool of Victoria.

As Malcolm and Hall demonstrate eloquently, the Irish came to Australia with significant cultural baggage in tow: 'For centuries, the English perceived the Irish as primitive, treacherous, violent, lazy and stupid.' Reflecting this entrenched pattern, nineteenth-century Australian popular culture harboured 'a dazzling array of visual and aural stereotypes' about the Irish, including those concerning their distinctive brogue and their allegedly ugly physical features, from heavy jaws to sloping foreheads.

These stereotypes were directed mainly at Catholic Irish immigrants, often personified in a figure of ridicule, Paddy, who was variously dumb, lazy and heavy-drinking, or truculent, cunning and criminal. But Irish Protestants were not entirely exempted from such prejudice. If Edward had to contend with such bigotry when he arrived in Portland, his education and faith likely provided some protection. He did not linger long on the coast and went to work for a pastoralist at Audley, 50 kilometres to the north of Portland. Edward showed some prowess as a farmer and became a manager at a second farm, a run of some size boasting 600 cattle and 4000 sheep.

Chain migration was common in Ireland in the mid-nineteenth century, and Edward was the pathfinder for his siblings. The next oldest son in the family, Robert, born in 1832, arrived in Victoria in 1854 or 1855, while Edward was still working at Audley. Setting what would become a family pattern, Robert joined the Victoria Police in May 1855. His choice of profession was not accidental. The Irish faced discrimination in the colonial job market, with some advertisements expressly preferring English or Scottish applicants, though this was aimed mainly at excluding Catholics. The force provided a welcoming and secure career for many Irish immigrants, Catholic and Protestant. Robert entered what was still an emerging institution, for the *Police Regulation Act 1853* had created one consolidated force less than three years earlier. The massive influx of men during the goldrush had engendered a complex law-and-order challenge, and the Victoria Police sensibly replaced a motley collection of seven autonomous and mostly ineffective policing bodies. In this, Victoria was a trailblazer for New South Wales, which would not forge a united police force until a decade later.

Some thought the Victoria Police should use the Royal Irish Constabulary (RIC), a paramilitary force formed by Robert Peel in Ireland in 1814, as a model, believing it was better suited to policing in rural areas – as most of Victoria outside Melbourne was in the 1850s. RIC personnel wore rifle-green uniforms, carried carbines and lived in barracks; they performed policing functions but also suppressed civil disorder and dissent, often with considerable violence. In the end, although it adopted some RIC operational procedures, the Victoria Police was deliberately established as a civilian policing entity, employing civilian ranks and terminology. Many Irishmen with RIC experience joined up, meaning some RIC habits and preconceptions exerted a certain influence, but the force adopted its own, more community-based method of policing.

The requirements for enlisting in the Victoria Police were straightforward. A recruit had to be 'of a sound constitution, able-bodied, and under the age of 45 years, of good character for honesty, fidelity and activity, and unless circumstances shall render it necessary to dispense with this qualification in any case, he shall be able to read and write'. Further, he could not have been convicted of any felony, nor have worked as a bailiff, a sheriff's bailiff, a parish clerk, a hired servant or an innkeeper. Robert Strahan fitted the bill. Five-foot nine with hazel eyes and brown hair, he was twenty-three in 1855, fit and able-bodied. He was literate, more so than many of his fellow constables. On his enlistment form, Robert gave farrier as his occupation and declared his allegiance to the Church of England.

The force Robert joined was big, perhaps too big, with more than 1600 officers. It would not develop a more coherent and professional structure for decades, long lacking both a formal means for assessing aspiring recruits and a proper system of promotion, which was determined by patronage. It did not have even a rudimentary training program, and constables were expected to learn on the job by trial and error. This was troubling because the nascent Victoria Police was heavily armed. In 1854, at the height of the turbulent goldrushes, the force's 1639 officers had 2207 firearms, 932 swords and bayonets, and 1000 batons.

With his younger brother embarking on a policing career, Edward left Audley for the diggings at Avoca, in central Victoria. But he had no luck and went to work on another cattle farm in Gippsland, where he stayed for eighteen months. In mid-1857, deciding that he did not want to make a life as a farmer, he moved to Melbourne to take up again as a teacher, securing a position at an Anglican school attached to St Peter's Eastern Hill. St Peter's was already a Melbourne institution – the foundation stone had been laid in 1846 by Charles Joseph La Trobe, the superintendent of the Port Phillip district. Edward embarked on a respectable life as a professional man.

The brothers stayed in touch. On 11 June 1857, Edward married Sarah Ann Campbell, a Presbyterian who had arrived from Scotland in 1853 with her parents. Robert signed the register as a witness. Although he taught for many years at St Peter's, Edward attended the Presbyterian Church, in deference to his wife's faith.

Some months later, the Strahan contingent in Melbourne doubled when two sisters in the family, Mary, aged twenty-four, and Deborah, twenty-one, arrived in Melbourne on the *Shakespeare* in December 1857. Several decades earlier, it would have been unusual for two young women to travel across the world unaccompanied by a male relative. The Strahan sisters were part of a new trend following the Great Famine, where young, single Irish women migrated without male travelling companions. The Australian colonies still faced a shortage of single women in the 1850s, and unmarried women like Mary and Deborah were in high demand as servants and brides. As the daughters of a well-established farmer, they qualified to travel as assisted emigrants – the 1853 regulations prioritised several categories, including 'respectable young women trained for domestic or farm service'. The sisters travelled on the *Shakespeare* in the quarters reserved for single women, located at the opposite end of the vessel from the quarters of the single men. The ship's surgeon-superintendent was charged with supervising the assisted emigrants on board, including looking after the morals of the single women and ensuring they didn't mix with the crew or male passengers.

The sisters would have been reassured during the long journey to Melbourne by the knowledge that they were travelling to a city where two of their older brothers were living. Deborah joined Edward's household soon after arriving. Reflecting a practice common in middle-class households, Deborah never married and stayed with her brother's family for the rest of her life, helping to care for the children and maintaining the house. Edward and Sarah's children became fond of their 'Aunt Debbie'. Mary married William Young in 1860, quickly having two children. Like her sister, she remained in Melbourne throughout her life.

In August 1860, a fifth member of the family decided to join his siblings in Victoria. Boarding the 800-tonne *Lord Raglan* in Liverpool in August 1860 as an unassisted migrant, the twenty year old confirmed his name on the passenger log: *Anthony Strahan*. My great-great-grandfather.

Anthony was no doubt aware that the long journey between Britain and the Australian colonies was dangerous and sometimes resulted in terrible shipwrecks. Nearly 1000 people had perished when three vessels sank on their way to Australia between 1854 and 1857. Less than two months before the *Lord Raglan* left Liverpool, the *Royal Charter* sank off the Welsh coast on 26 October 1859, on its way back from Melbourne, with the loss of 427 lives. The tragedy was covered extensively in the British press, but Anthony was undeterred. A new life beckoned.

Given his family's means, Anthony may have undertaken the journey as a second-class passenger, affording him a small cabin. Third-class travel was a much harsher experience. Whatever class Anthony travelled, some challenges faced all passengers alike: boredom, storms, the threat of various diseases, monotonous meals of poor quality and the enervating humidity of the tropical climes along the route. It seems his journey was less eventful than Edward's seven years earlier, as his voyage was shorter and he was not called on to care for sick passengers. Like the other ships that plied the route across the Atlantic and Indian Oceans between Britain and the Australian colonies, the *Lord Raglan* came south with much-needed supplies, docking in Fremantle on 9 November 1860 to unload a cart horse, a blood horse and fourteen Sturgeon merino sheep before heading east.

Anthony arrived in Melbourne less than three weeks later, on 25 November. On the ship's manifest, he described himself as a labourer. He was four months shy of twenty-one and, like his siblings, never to see Ireland again. Some migrants did return, either because they were wealthy enough to visit or because they had given up on the colonies. The Strahans came to Victoria to stay; failure was not an option.

2

ORDERED OUT LIKE A DOG

When Anthony descended the gangplank, Melbourne was the biggest city in the Australian colonies, with a population between 120,000 and 140,000. It had come a long way in only twenty-five years, its growth supercharged by the goldrushes and the booming wool industry. Just two days before the *Lord Raglan* dropped its anchor, two vessels left Melbourne carrying 28,303 ounces of gold and nearly 4500 bales of wool.

Although he had seen Liverpool and likely Dublin on his way to Australia, Anthony had never lived in a town, let alone a city. Melbourne boasted a university, a museum, a general post office, a town hall, botanical gardens, gas street lighting, and myriad shops, banks and manufacturing premises. Underlining Victoria's links to the rest of the Empire, the public library had just received a donation of firearms removed from members of the failed Sepoy Mutiny in India. The populace could choose to follow the affairs of the day by reading three daily newspapers and ten weeklies. Residents were still gripped by excitement because Burke and Wills had left Royal Park only three months earlier, with 15,000 spectators cheering on their ultimately ill-fated expedition to reach the Gulf of Carpentaria. Melbourne could also lay claim to a lively cultural scene, with one gallery displaying paintings by Nicholas Chevalier and Eugene von Guérard in late November. Dr Charles Perry presided over the affairs of Anthony's faith as the Lord Bishop of the United Church of England and Ireland. In the week that Anthony arrived, the governor opened the new session of the Legislative Assembly, which was due to consider bills on postal reform, land titles, the goldfields, district councils, water supply and insolvency. Richard Heales, a teetotalling former wheelwright and coachbuilder, became the chief secretary a day or so after Anthony came ashore, demonstrating that men of humble origins could aspire to high office.

But the city also had a darker side. Melbourne faced significant public health challenges, with measles and scarlet fever having taken the lives of 309 children over the previous year. Debate about the city's sanitary conditions was lively. Crime was a growing problem. The Supreme Court had convened on 16 November to hear a slew of larceny charges, including against an embezzler who had been found in a drunken slumber in the Black Boy Hotel. On Anthony Strahan's first evening in the city, Samuel Cherry and Benjamin Long were arrested while playing cards in a brothel on Little Lonsdale Street and charged with robbery under arms.

It is not known what Anthony did in Melbourne over the next two years, though he presumably drew upon the assistance of his siblings. At heart a country lad, he probably didn't find urban living agreeable. Melbourne offered many strange things, including kangaroo sausages and Australian rules football. But one thing seems certain: he came to Victoria fully intending to follow his older brother Robert into the Victoria Police. Like many Irishmen, he had served with the RIC at home to enhance his chances of being accepted as a policeman in the colonies. Anthony had joined the RIC in November 1859, at nineteen, recommended by the vicar who had christened him at St Mullins in Timolin, the Reverend Latham Coddington. He resigned only four months later, in February 1860, just enough time to complete the initial training program.

It is likely Anthony applied to enter the Victoria Police soon after reaching Melbourne, for many recruits in the early 1860s had to wait as long as fifteen months before being accepted. He joined the force as a foot constable on 12 September 1862, aged twenty-two. A competent rider due to his time on his family farm and later in the RIC, Anthony had applied to become a mounted constable, but the mounted service had no vacancies. On his enlistment form, the force declared my great-great-grandfather 'tolerably intelligent and smart', noting his complexion as 'fresh'. Five-foot nine with brown hair and blue eyes, he declared the Church of England as his faith.

Anthony entered a force different from that Robert had joined nearly seven years earlier. With the peak of the goldrush passed, the Victoria Police had been reduced to 1200 men. Successive cuts had seen a constable's pay fall from 10 shillings per day in the late 1850s to only 7 shillings sixpence in 1861, the same wage as railway labourers. This left the men of the Victoria Police, writes Robert Haldane in his history of the force, in an indeterminate social position between unskilled labourers and tradesmen. Unlike soldiers, Victoria's policemen were not clothed and fed by the government. Constables had to purchase their uniform, except for the hats shako and a few other small ancillary items, usually placing them in debt for their first year in the service. They worked long hours for their modest pay, much longer hours than many other workers in the colony. By 1856, most stonemasons were working an eight-hour day in Victoria, setting a historic precedent. Carpenters, bricklayers and plasterers followed suit a few years later, and in 1870 the Victorian government mandated an eight-hour day for any men hired to construct railways, government buildings and schools. Not so the colony's policemen, who worked twelve hours a day, seven days a week. They were obliged to rise at 5.30am (6.30am in winter) and only permitted a paltry twelve days off per year. Overtime did not exist. Haldane notes that the line between being on and off duty was barely perceptible: 'Policing was not just a job but a way of life, and the men in blue serge whose duty it was to superintend the lives of others were themselves closely supervised and controlled.' Officers received considerably better pay and benefits, including the attentions of a personal batman. But as ordinary constables, Anthony and Robert occupied a much lower rank in the colony's social hierarchy than their teacher brother.

Anthony and Robert were both typical Victorian policemen in that they were Irish. Many early police forces in England, Scotland, Canada and the United States in the nineteenth century were heavily Irish in composition, but the Irish contingent of the Victoria Police was out of all proportion to the Victorian population. The new *Police Regulation Statute of 1873* required all officers to re-swear their oaths in January 1874, revealing that 867 of the force's 1060 men – a staggering 82 per cent – were Irish. At that time, the Irish only accounted for 12 per cent of the state's overall population. A paltry 3 per cent of personnel, only thirty men, were born in Australia, even though 45 per cent of Victoria's population was Australian-born at that time. Such a glaring discrepancy exacerbated a sense among some in the community that the police were a foreign force, imposed from above and outside.

Most of the 867 Irish-born officers in the Victoria Police in 1874 were Catholic, with 556 men declaring a Catholic faith and 311 a Protestant affiliation. Nearly half of these 867 had served in the RIC. Changes in Ireland had reinforced this trend. In the latter part of the 1850s and into the early 1860s, 6000 men resigned from the RIC, due to low pay, poor living conditions and tough marriage rules. RIC personnel could only marry after seven years of service and if they could provide 'evidence of solvency considered appropriate to a married state'. Victorian policemen required permission to marry, but this was rarely refused. The service records of the RIC indicate that many officers resigned in the 1850s and 1860s to emigrate, primarily to the United States or Australia, often to join local police forces.

In Australia, the late nineteenth century found those of Irish extraction on both sides of the law in high numbers. Sometimes tensions and animosities from Ireland, communal and personal, were transposed to Victoria. It has often been argued that people of Irish extraction numbered disproportionately among those who ran afoul of the law in the Australian colonies. A.M. Topp, an English-born businessman and a lead writer for *The Argus*, drew on Victorian government statistics to claim in 1881 that the Irish were particularly prone to resorting to 'personal violence' instead of 'calling in the aid of the law or of public opinion'. Venting long-held English prejudices, he argued that the Irish tendency towards acts of violence was 'an obvious characteristic of an imperfectly civilized race … one that has never been taught to respect the law, but only to resort to brute force'. Malcolm and Hall establish convincingly that Topp manipulated the statistics to make his case, leaving out some data and twisting others. After re-examining the statistics, they conclude that people of Irish stock were no more likely to be convicted of serious crimes than other ethnic groups. Of the 151 men and one woman who were executed in Victoria between 1842 and 1891, 27.6 per cent were Irish, roughly equivalent to the Irish share of the population. But the Irish did make up a bigger proportion (nearly 42 per cent) of those executed between 1865 and 1879, when Anthony Strahan's career was at its peak. As we shall see, although the overall rate of serious violent crimes fell sharply during the 1870s, he came to play a leading role in several notable cases where Irish offenders were charged with capital offences.

The Irish were also over-represented in other crime statistics. By the 1880s, Victoria had a wide range of public-order offences: drunkenness, riotous or offensive behaviour, abusive language, having no visible means of support, begging, cruelty to animals, illegal gambling, lunacy. The Victoria Police used the vagrancy laws to clear the streets of unwanted characters, from drunks, prostitutes and beggars to the homeless, hawkers and the poor. Malcolm and Hall observe that 'most Irish and Catholic arrests were for non-violent offences against public order, often involving drunkenness, not for violent crimes against the person', though they note that most Protestant arrests were for similar offences. Those who were arrested for these less serious offences were brought before magistrates, not judges in higher courts, and generally given light forms of punishment – small fines or short prison sentences – or released. Given the high arrest rate for public-order crimes, Anthony inevitably encountered many Irish offenders, mostly Catholics, across the course of his career.

Since members of the force policed a wide range of criminal offences, they often had to negotiate complex situations. This was not easy, especially in a state undergoing significant change as the frontier conditions of the first thirty years of white settlement became more ordered and the goldrushes receded. But the force lacked any training program in the early 1860s, even as its officers were being asked to keep watch over a sprawling colony with complicated law-and-order issues. The Chief Commissioner, Captain Frederick Standish, regarded training as a waste of time.

Born in Lancashire in 1824, the son of a government officer who was once a companion of the prince regent, Standish served in the British Army with the artillery between 1843 and 1852, working for a time for the lord lieutenant of Ireland and retiring with the rank of captain. Accumulating debt after heavy betting losses at the race track, he sold up and migrated to Victoria in 1852, spending a period on the gold diggings. He secured a series of government appointments, first as the Assistant Commissioner of the diggings at Sandhurst (Bendigo) in 1854, then as the Chinese Protector and finally as the third Chief Commissioner of the Victoria Police in 1858, even though he had no prior policing experience.

Standish has justly received a good deal of criticism over the years for his dissolute bachelor lifestyle, including heavy gambling and drinking, which affected his management of the force. He resided at the Melbourne Club from 1873, setting himself apart from his officers, most of whom lived in humble circumstances. Some of this criticism is a product of the Kelly myth, projected backwards, at times distorting or obscuring aspects of Standish's career. J. S. Legge observes that Standish demonstrated 'considerable intellectual administrative skill' when he was in the full vigour of health. But it is incontrovertible that the man who would preside over the Victoria Police for twenty-two years had a significant, often predominating, impact on the character of the force. His preferences, strengths and shortcomings shaped how policing was conducted in Victoria across the 1860s and 1870s. He influenced Anthony Strahan's career profoundly at key junctures.

Standish believed constables were made, not born, and should learn on the job. For Anthony, four months with the RIC was hardly adequate preparation for a demanding role in a colony on the other side of the world. But he was young and ambitious, and he would make the most of it.

When Anthony joined up in 1862, the Victoria Police's 1200 men were stretched thinly across more than 250 stations scattered around the colony. Many of these stations were in remote localities, staffed by only one or two constables. Without formal training, policemen were required to learn bushcraft as well as basic policing as they went about their duties. Their work was often lonely and dangerous. They traversed rough bush tracks through unsettled terrain in all weather conditions. Searing heat, prolonged droughts, storms and swollen rivers were constant threats.

It was these angry elements that took the life of Anthony's older brother, Robert. On 4 April 1863, when he was stationed at Seymour, Robert escorted a prisoner from the lock-up down to the Goulburn River to empty the night-tub. Taking his life into his own hands, the prisoner bolted into the river, swollen by heavy rains, and swam across to the other bank. Robert alerted his commanding officer, Senior Constable Dennis Deasy, and crossed the river in a boat in pursuit. Deasy took a faster route, crossing the river at a nearby ford. By the time Robert reached the other bank, Deasy had already nabbed the daring escapee. Perhaps stung by his failure to recapture the prisoner who had been in his charge, Robert didn't wait a few more minutes to catch a boat back to Seymour, unwisely opting to cross the river on a passing dray at the ford. This burst of impatience had fatal consequences. The dray overturned when the horses got into trouble in the surging water and both Robert and the driver, Smale, drowned. Robert's body was not found for two days. He was only thirty.

Anthony was one of the twelve jurors at the inquest at the Royal Hotel in Seymour. He identified Robert's body.[1] It must have been confronting for him, just twenty-three years old and less than a year into his service with the force, to look down at his brother's cold, bloated corpse. Robert was unmarried and childless. His older brother, Edward, was the sole executor of his will, underscoring the strong bonds between the Strahan siblings. Robert left £250, a substantial sum, to his parents in Timolin.

While Robert's tragic death must have cut Anthony deeply, it didn't deter his younger brother from continuing his career in the Victoria Police. And Anthony's life was about to change in more ways than one. After a stint at the depot on Swanston Street in Melbourne, he was posted to Redbank, a goldmining settlement in the Pyrenees district of central Victoria, 200 kilometres northwest of Melbourne. Avoca was the nearest town of any size, 22 kilometres to the south. Although the Redbank goldrush had peaked in 1860–61, mining continued near the town in fits and starts, and the district's population was just under 5000 at the end of 1862. Much of the land around the town had been sold off to farmers. Like other mining towns, Redbank had more than enough pubs, always a source of trouble, especially with many footloose young men around.

Anthony had his work cut out for him. The force was under strain as it maintained law and order across the unruly colony. Police policy stated it was 'highly desirable that many of the police should reside among and identify themselves with the citizens'.[2] Placing police in small towns ensured the force had a visible presence, which was appreciated by the community. The local police constable was the most important and sometimes the only public official around. This gave young men in the force social standing and considerable authority and responsibility. But it could be uncomfortable, even dangerous, if a policeman was not accepted by the community, or worse, ended up at odds with some locals.

Anthony tried to establish himself in the Redbank community without being overbearing. He took the job seriously. His superior rated him as 'well-conducted and smart' in August 1864. The young constable from Timolin had made a promising start to his career.

But he faltered shortly after securing this assessment.

Over the next few weeks, Anthony had two altercations with a superior that revealed an abrasive side to his character. The first was minor: in mid-August 1864, Anthony was cautioned by the Avoca superintendent, Hugh Ross Barclay, for 'using improper language' to Sergeant Bryan Coleman. Altercations between officers and their superiors were not uncommon. Policing was physically and emotionally demanding, and the dynamics in stations could become tense, with officers taking exception to what they saw as unreasonable or harsh instruction. Egos left plenty of scope for conflict. Even so, this incident revealed that Anthony Strahan, the 24-year-old son of a Kildare farmer, was tenacious and strong-willed, unafraid of engaging in a stoush – especially if he was convinced he had done nothing wrong.

The second incident was more telling. It was unfortunate that Anthony was sent from Redbank on 20 October to the station in St Arnaud, a goldmining town on the road between Ballarat and Mildura, under the command of the very same Sergeant Coleman. Putting the two men together only months after they had clashed was going to end badly. Anthony likely went to St Arnaud bristling about the cautioning and ready for another round. The row that ensued indicated that Anthony might be the sort of man to nurse a grudge, that he perhaps found it hard to forgive and forget. This hot-tempered streak, which Ned Kelly captured in his Jerilderie Letter, would forever come to define Anthony in the national imagination.

Superficially, Anthony and his new superior had much in common: they were both Irish, the latter hailing from County Monaghan, and they had both served in the RIC before migrating to Victoria. But other factors divided them. Although neither was seemingly devout, Coleman was Catholic and Anthony Protestant. Coleman was fourteen years older than Anthony, a far more experienced policeman. After six years in the RIC, Coleman was steeped in its stern paramilitary practice. He likely looked down on Anthony's fleeting four months of service. And having served in the Victoria Police for a decade, he was accustomed to expecting obedience.

In August 1864, Coleman was rated 'a most trustworthy and efficient sergeant'. But his record was not unblemished. Posted to the Melbourne suburb of Footscray upon enlisting, he was reprimanded twice, once in 1855, for not reporting a death until two days after the event, and again in 1856, for not reporting an accident. Infractions in his next assignment in Gippsland said more about his character. He was reprimanded in Sale in 1860 twice, first for improperly addressing an inspecting superintendent while seated in a public vehicle and then for vindictiveness in binding a Mrs Jameson to keep the peace in relation to himself and his wife.[3] The first reprimand suggested Coleman did not appreciate being counselled, perhaps taking offence too readily. The second revealed he had a mean streak. His superiors decided that his ill-treatment of Mrs Jameson was sufficiently serious to transfer him from Sale to suburban Richmond.

On 29 October 1864, Anthony wrote to the new superintendent in Avoca, Joseph Mason, to lodge three misconduct complaints against

Coleman. First, he contended that Coleman delivered his orders in a 'disagreeable and overbearing manner which … was most tyrannical'. He said he had entered the station's office on 24 October to ask what task he should do that day, only to be 'ordered by Sergeant Coleman to leave the room the same as you would a dog'. Second, Coleman had accepted an invitation to have a drink at the St Arnaud Hotel while on duty on 23 October, ignoring an intoxicated customer who was causing 'a rough'. Anthony insisted that it was 'the general opinion of the St Arnaud people that Sergeant Coleman takes no notice of liquor being sold on Sunday in the St Arnaud Hotel'. Third, he alleged that he had been forced to remain at the station's stables between 6am and 8am on 26 October because Coleman had 'not got out of bed'.

Other policemen faced more serious misconduct allegations, but Anthony's complaints could not be shrugged off. His reputation impugned, Coleman responded swiftly. Anthony's report had been 'concocted through vindictive motives', he claimed in a letter to Mason. He denied 'in toto' any overbearing or tyrannical conduct, stating that he remembered well the circumstances of 24 October. He had ordered Anthony and Constable Thomas McInerney to get about carting gravel into the yard: 'Constable Strahan came into the office in a very excited manner to know why the Sergeant should order him to his work. He was told in reply that so long as he was at the St Arnaud station he should consider himself under the control of Sergeant Coleman, at the same time in consequence of his insolent language he was ordered to leave the office and go to his work.'

Coleman denied being on duty on the night of 23 October. He claimed he had availed himself of the invitation to have a drink in the St Arnaud Hotel to 'ascertain who was in the house, as the new Publicans Act does not authorise Sergeants or Constables to demand admittance unless specially authorised'. On entering the hotel, he had found only the owner and 'a bona-fide lodger', who was talkative, but not rowdy. Coleman stated 'without fear of contradiction' that the colony did not have 'a more orderly kept hotel'. As for the last complaint, Coleman conceded that he might have been 'a few minutes late at stables' because he had been 'up in charge of a prisoner in the lock-up during the greater portion of the night'.

To ascertain the truth, Mason convened an inquiry at the St Arnaud station on 23 November. In addition to the protagonists, he questioned three other policemen, Constables Thomas McInnerney, John Gaggin and John Kilbride, the hotel owner and his barman. It quickly became apparent the St Arnaud station was divided.

If he had little in common with Coleman, Anthony was almost bound to get on with Gaggin. Not only were they both Irish, but they were also single, close in age and Protestant. Gaggin had a similarly fiery temperament. In 1861 he was fined 10 shillings for fighting with another officer on the public road between Kyneton and Woodend. While he was stationed in Heathcote in 1864, his superior rated his conduct and efficiency as good. However, transferred shortly afterwards to St Arnaud, Gaggin was reported by Coleman for improperly releasing a prisoner. He received a reprimand. Gaggin had his own score to settle with his sergeant.

Born in County Clare in 1829, McInnerney was eleven years older than Anthony, much closer in age to his sergeant. Like Coleman, he was Catholic and married. He had come to Victoria after serving for ten years with the British Army's 47th Lancashire Regiment, including in the Crimean War. The two older policemen might have been brought together by their previous service, but perhaps an old tension between the army and the police lurked, for McInnerney and Anthony were united by their dislike of their sergeant.

John Kilbride was another Catholic, and the oldest of the quartet, born in 1827. He was also the most experienced policeman, having served for eleven years with the RIC and twenty months with the Dublin Police before migrating to Victoria. He joined the Victoria Police as a foot constable in February 1858, days after disembarking in Melbourne. He had been a policeman his entire adult life. In August 1864, Barclay judged Kilbride 'a steady ordinary constable – conduct always good'. But his record was not untarnished. Kilbride became a senior constable in January 1859 less than a year after joining up, yet his elevation was short-lived. Soon after being promoted, he was found guilty of using government forage to feed a private horse and demoted to constable. And there he stayed for the rest of his career. He kept out of trouble for the next five years, until just before the inquiry into Coleman. On 5 November, he returned to the station from duty at the St Arnaud races under the influence of liquor. Reported by Coleman, he pleaded guilty and received a reprimand from Mason. So Kilbride, too, had his reasons for resenting his sergeant.[4]

The three constables split ranks on Coleman's manner. Two insisted Coleman gave his orders harshly and disagreeably. Gaggin admitted he would have reported Coleman on other occasions if he could have substantiated the charges. McInnerney agreed it was the duty of a non-commissioned officer to correct subordinates' mistakes but said he sometimes felt aggrieved at the way Coleman remonstrated with him. Kilbride didn't appear to resent his sergeant for reprimanding him after the races; having served in the force for twenty years, he readily accepted an authoritarian style of leadership. He told the inquiry he didn't think it necessary for a sergeant to 'use complimentary terms in giving orders to the men under his charge … any man in charge of a station [might] sometimes speak in a sharp or excited manner'.

The allegation of accepting a drink while on duty was potentially damning. Drunkenness was entrenched in the police, reflecting a wider pattern across the colony, especially among the lower classes. Heavy drinking prevented some constables from discharging their duties, undermining the effort to maintain law and order, even though police regulations strictly prohibited imbibing alcoholic beverages. Given the scale of the problem, the Victorian government had made it a criminal offence for publicans to 'permit any constable to become intoxicated on his premises or to be supplied with fermented or spirituous liquors whilst intoxicated or on duty'.[5] Anthony did his best to make the charge stick, implying his superior was playing favourites, accepting a drink from one publican while hawkishly watching the others. He insisted that Coleman had done nothing to deal with a rowdy customer. But the owner of the St Arnaud Hotel, Thomas Donaldson, and his barman claimed that Coleman was not in the habit of drinking at the hotel on a Sunday, though they did not deny he had accepted a drink on this occasion. Kilbride defended his superior: he was 'not aware that Sergeant Coleman shows any favour or affection for the proprietor of the St Arnaud Hotel more than any other hotel as Mr Donaldson keeps his house as respectable as any other in the colony'. He noted that he had never had occasion to report the St Arnaud Hotel since Donaldson had been the proprietor.

Mason dealt swiftly with the charge of arriving late at the station's stables. Anthony admitted he did not know what time Coleman had gone to bed on 25 October; nor did he know that the sergeant had been attending to a prisoner in the lock-up. He conceded Coleman might have said when he had arrived at the stables that he had overslept, asking the constables why they hadn't roused him.

Mason wrote to Chief Commissioner Standish on 25 November to set out his findings. He considered 'the first charge is proved as the evidence given by Constables Strahan, Gaggin and McInnerney go to show that the Sergeant is in the habit of giving his orders in an overbearing and disagreeable manner and I have no reason to doubt the Constables' evidence as I believe they are truthful men'. Constable Kilbride's evidence had favoured the sergeant, but Mason noted that his duties brought him less often into direct contact with Coleman than the others. Mason dismissed the second charge. He agreed that Coleman should not have accepted a drink but said the sergeant might have had good reasons for entering the premises, including to observe who was there on a Sunday. Coleman had remained inside for no more than five minutes. Mason noted that the St Arnaud Hotel was 'a well conducted and orderly establishment and the there is no favour shown to it by Sergeant Coleman more than any of the other licensed hotels at St Arnaud'. He dismissed the third charge, arriving late at the stables, as 'paltry and vexatious'. Any man could oversleep, especially if he had been up all night.

Standish concurred with Mason. While the second and third charges could be seen as frivolous, Coleman 'indulged' – a telling word – 'in a rough and overbearing manner to his subordinates'. He directed Mason to caution Coleman to 'adopt a more courteous and conciliatory manner' when directing the constables serving under him: 'It is of vital importance to the interests of the Police Force that all members of the Department should be civil, obliging and courteous.' If constables saw their superior officers conduct themselves in a disagreeable manner, it was probable that they would 'take the cue from them and thus bring discredit on the service'. Constables were more likely to 'obey orders cheerfully and willingly when spoken to properly than hectored and bullied'.[6]

Anthony was vindicated. The charge of bullying had always been the most important. What does his run-in with Coleman tell us? Anthony was willing to stand up to what he saw as a tyrannical exercise of power. Doing so was bold. He was only a junior constable, taking on an officer several grades higher. The Victoria Police was a tight-knit organisation and its members scorned conspiring against their own. Lagging, dobbing in a fellow officer, was usually regarded with contempt – though the police records show numerous conflicts between officers ending up in inquiries and disciplinary action. Accusing Coleman of misconduct was risky: it might lead to retribution. But fear of incurring the wrath of a vengeful superior didn't restrain Anthony, especially as he had the backing of two other constables. He had already demonstrated in the discharge of his duties that he was organised and chased down details; he had catalogued Coleman's apparent indiscretions with the same rigour. Was Anthony right to act this way? Given he was only on temporary duty in St Arnaud for two weeks, he could have tolerated Coleman's boorish behaviour. But one senses he was not a man to let such matters lie.

Although he had escaped serious punishment, Coleman must have been stung at being cautioned by the Chief Commissioner himself. He likely took umbrage at being brought to book by what he saw as an impudent upstart. His family circumstances made an already stressful experience more difficult – Coleman was providing for a wife, Mary, and five young children. He could not afford to lose his job or pay a fine, especially as Mary was heavily pregnant. Coleman resigned from the force in May 1865, six months after Mason's inquiry, to take up the lease for a pub in St Arnaud – somewhat controversially, given Anthony's accusations. He and his family left their home at Darkbonee and moved into town to reside on Napier Street.[7] Perhaps he had already been planning to leave the force, but the bruising, even humiliating, experience of being brought to heel by a younger colleague might well have accelerated his decision to take up a different occupation.

Anthony was probably pleased when he heard that his foe had resigned. For the first time but not the last, he had bested his opponent.

3

SWINDLE

Buoyed by the official response to his complaint about Coleman's bullying, Anthony felt his stock had risen. He was soon transferred to Bealiba, another small town in the central goldfields – the force could move officers at short notice, without any right of appeal, sometimes across large distances and at their own expense. Not long after arriving, Anthony applied again to join the mounted division, commonly known as the O'Shays because it had so many Irish officers. He wrote directly to Superintendent Mason in December 1864 to say that it had always been his wish to become a mounted constable. He affirmed that if he were accepted into the mounted division he would demonstrate by 'attention to and zeal in the performance of his new duty' that he was worthy of being redeployed.

Mason sent a positive recommendation to Standish, noting that Anthony was well accustomed to horses, rode well and was a light man. The last factor was important because the force had a weight requirement for becoming a mounted constable. Importantly, Mason noted Anthony was 'steady and active in the execution of his duty'.

Unfortunately, Mason had made a mistake. He sent a follow-up memo to Melbourne in January 1865 to admit Anthony's 'peculiar compact build' had deceived him into underestimating his weight. He had thought Anthony could not weigh more than 11 and a half stone, around the threshold for joining the mounted division, but he weighed 12 stone 8 pounds. Standish was unimpressed, chastising Mason for making a recommendation without ascertaining Anthony's weight. He wrote, somewhat huffily, that he would wait for clarity on whether kit had been issued: 'It would be hard to dismount the man without a fair trial, if he had been put to the expense of [acquiring a new mounted officer's] uniform.' Mason admitted on 26 January that kit had already been given to Anthony but pointed out that Senior Constable Michael O'Donnell had reported favourably on Anthony's conduct as a mounted constable. He thought it only fair that Anthony be given a trial of a few months.[1]

And so Anthony triumphed and became a mounted constable two and a half years after joining the force. His heftier build appeared not to impede his horsemanship, for he was to remain a mounted officer for the next two decades. Anthony wore white trousers, white gloves, a serge blue tunic with an open collar, a large belt diagonally across his chest, calf-length boots and a shiny black hat. He carried a sword as well as firearms.

In his new role, Anthony brought to bear that tenacity and attention to detail he had deployed against Coleman and was soon chalking up convictions. On 8 October 1865, a carrier named William Worm was camping near Bealiba when a thief stole a parcel of draping worth £20 from his wagon. Anthony suspected George Bachelor as the culprit, given his fidgety manner. Disguising himself in plain clothes, he trailed Bachelor. Anthony had already come to understand that effective policing involved waiting and watching. His patience paid off, for he caught Bachelor in the act of removing his booty from his house. He arrested the thief, recovering £12 worth of the stolen property. Bachelor pleaded guilty in Maryborough and was sentenced to nine months' imprisonment with hard labour.

The Bachelor case serves as a reminder that many crimes in the colony involved prosaic matters, with humble offenders stealing small items from equally humble victims. Still, Mason thought Bachelor's arrest demonstrated great tact, perseverance and efficiency, and recommended on 27 November that Standish grant Anthony a £2 reward. Established in 1849, the Police Reward Fund was housed in the colonial government's central accounts. Half of all fines were channelled into the fund and the monies used either to reward officers for meritorious conduct or to compensate them for injuries or working excess hours.[2] The fund became controversial: some wondered if it encouraged policemen to rack up convictions for pecuniary reasons.

Whether or not they created a perverse incentive, the rewards supported a better standard of living by supplementing the modest incomes of the rank-and-file police. Standish approved the reward, agreeing the Bachelor case was 'very creditable'. Constable Strahan had showed 'a very commendable amount of judgment' by opting to watch Bachelor rather than putting him on his guard by immediately accusing him of committing theft.

By late 1866, four years into his career, Anthony was developing a reputation as an industrious and effective officer, winning the respect of his superiors, including the Chief Commissioner. It was important he develop a strong relationship with Senior Constable O'Donnell, his boss in Bealiba, after his bitter falling-out with Coleman. O'Donnell was another Irishman. A Catholic born in County Clare in 1829, he had served with the RIC for six and a half years before migrating to Victoria in 1857. He had joined the force in 1858, becoming a Senior Constable in 1862. When Anthony arrived in Bealiba, O'Donnell was living in the town with his wife, Bridget, and their infant daughter. The O'Donnells were an agreeable family and Anthony felt at ease in their company.

Anthony kept racking up arrests. In August 1866, he was attending the police court in Dunolly when he heard that William Rogers, alias Bill the Butcher, had stolen a gold ring. Rogers was a habitual criminal, dealing in fake jewellery and committing other offences, including assaulting Senior Constable Thomas Shanklin seven months earlier. Riding back to Bealiba, Anthony overtook a man on the track. Engaging him in conversation, he realised he was Rogers and placed him under arrest. Rogers resisted vigorously. Holding Anthony at bay with one arm, he reached into his trouser pocket with his free hand and threw the ring into the bush. Anthony took note of where Rogers pitched his plunder, returning once the culprit was incarcerated to retrieve the ring. In November, the Dunolly general sessions put Rogers back behind bars, this time for one year with hard labour. Mason recommended Anthony for another £2 reward. Standish agreed.[3]

Anthony must have felt his career was on the up and up. But then Mason received an angry letter of complaint from John Cook, the owner of the International Hotel on Bealiba's main street, about the inappropriate conduct of one Mounted Constable Strahan.

People know too much about each other in small towns. Privacy is hard to come by when residents encounter one another daily; issues can escalate easily, building into grudges and worse. And so it was between the publican and the policeman.

Cook wrote that Anthony had arrived at his hotel on 21 November 1866 at 9pm and began playing a billiards game called swindle. With closing hour approaching, Cook had asked his patrons to depart, but Anthony and the other billiards players replied that they would play one more game and go. They 'then played till 6am the following morning when Constable Strahan left considerably the worse for liquor'. When Anthony had called at the hotel the next day to settle the bill, he had disputed the 11 shillings total. Cook alleged that Anthony had called him 'some opprobrious epithets, also telling me he would find a way to humble me … evidently meaning he would find some trivial cause to summons me to the Police Court'. Anthony had summonsed him once before for not keeping his lamp burning at night. When issuing the summons, Anthony had apparently told Cook it was 'the way to bring me to heel because I ordered him out of my public house some time previous'. With witnesses to verify his complaint, Cook trusted that Mason would not allow 'a constable to make use of his position to tyrannise over and oppress the public'.

Anthony's summonsing of the publican was not surprising. It was common, notes historian Doug Morrissey, for citizens in nineteenth-century Victoria to settle all manner of differences, trifling and serious, in a court of law. The 'number of charges and counter-charges laid could be bewildering', sometimes leading magistrates to dismiss cases because the evidence presented was so contradictory.[4] Throughout his career, Anthony would spend a good deal of time summonsing others and being summonsed in return. But Cook had opted not to summons Anthony. He wanted the force to sanction him.

Mason convened an inquiry at the Bealiba station on 1 December. This was Anthony's second in two years, though this time he was in the dock, facing three charges: playing billiards in the International Hotel from 9pm on Wednesday 21 November to 6am on Thursday 22 November; using insulting language to John Cook; and being under the influence of liquor. He pleaded guilty to playing billiards but denied the other charges.

Cook testified first. He said Constable Strahan had come to his hotel at 9pm in uniform. Anthony had racked up a bill of 13 shillings and sixpence for cigars and ten glasses of gin and peppermint, paying 2 shillings and sixpence as he departed, but leaving a bill of 11 shillings standing. Insisting he had seen Anthony drink all ten glasses, Cook said the young policeman was the worse for drink. His appearance was flushed and he was striking the billiard balls badly. Strahan had called on his hotel on 22 November, Cook continued, and asked for the bill. When told he owed 11 shillings, Strahan declared that he would not be swindled out of his money. He had returned on the evening of 23 November. Cook had repeated the total, whereupon Strahan had called him 'a damned swindler' and 'a damned coward', saying he would find a way to humble him. Two patrons had been present during this incident.

Anthony used his chance to question Cook to impugn him. He accused the publican of using abusive language. Cook denied describing Anthony as 'the damnedst bastard' and 'a two-faced bloody bastard', though he admitted calling him 'a two-faced man'. Anthony charged that Cook had said he would have him removed from the Bealiba station. Cook denied this too. Anthony accused the publican of saying he would get his head punched by a dozen men were it not for his 'bloody jacket'. Cook abjured making any threats. Revealing the rancour between the two men stretched back some time, he declared that Anthony had got him fined for using abusive language towards him previously. 'I was also fined at your insistence for allowing billiards to be played in my licensed house on a Sunday. I did say that if you were not removed from [Bealiba] you would have me up before [the courts again before] the Christmas holidays were over.' By this point, Anthony's anger was emanating from the pages of the inquiry transcript.

Cook was a German immigrant, having arrived in the Australian colonies from Prussia in 1849 as Johann Wilhelm Koch, the son of a shipwright. After spending eighteen months in South Australia, he was naturalised in 1851, anglicising his name as John Cook. Anthony and Cook were from different cultural worlds, the more so because one was Protestant and the other Catholic. Cook was old enough to be Anthony's father. Cook had married an Irishwoman, Margaret Connell, in 1857. In 1866 she was thirty-one, much closer in age to Anthony (who was twenty-five) than her husband (forty-seven). Margaret was from a realm Anthony knew well, for she was born in western Wicklow, not far from Timolin.

Several participants in the night-long billiards game testified that Anthony had been sober. A miner, George Bisson, said Anthony had played fifteen games of swindle, only losing three, suggesting that my great-great-grandfather was pretty handy with a cue.

By contrast, farmer Hamilton Todd gave a quite different account. He claimed he had arrived at the hotel at 8pm and stayed until 6:30am, when he had retired to sleep in one of the rooms. He had had a good many drinks himself, as had Anthony – he testified that he and the constable had drunk glass for glass. He had gone to bed drunk and considered Anthony to have been under the influence too. Yet he admitted he could not say whether Anthony had drunk all the rounds of gin brought to him. Anthony said he had thrown some into the fireplace and asked if Todd had seen him do so; Todd had not. 'I judged you being under the influence of liquor from you playing the last game unsteady and Mr Melville beating you easy,' he said. Todd claimed Melville had won the last game by 20 points, though he quickly admitted he didn't understand how swindle was scored. He insisted nonetheless that he knew when a man played well.

Denis Kelly, another miner, had been in the bar when Anthony came into the hotel the next day, asking for Margaret Cook. Mr Cook had entered the bar with his wife, and Anthony had asked how much he owed. 'I cannot recollect what Mr Cook said but Constable Strahan disputed five drinks of the account and called Mr Cook a swindler,' Kelly recounted. Cook had retorted that he had never swindled a man and called Anthony a scoundrel for what he'd done while Cook was absent from the hotel.

Anthony had asked Cook what he meant. When Cook had replied 'You know what I mean,' Anthony had called Cook a coward.

The police manual specified that members of the force had to exercise their powers with 'great caution and prudence'. It was 'essential that they keep under complete control their private feelings'.[5] This was often easier said than done, especially in heated situations, and Anthony had obviously failed to keep his feelings under control in the hotel on multiple occasions. He was determined to prove that he had been both provoked and threatened with violence. He pushed Kelly for more. The miner admitted that he had 'heard Mr Cook say if it was not for your jacket you would get your head punched. I heard Mr Cook say that Hamilton Todd would punch your head if not for your jacket.'

Neither Kelly nor Anthony explained what Anthony had done while Cook was away, but it had clearly incensed the publican. Had Anthony had in an improper liaison with Margaret Cook? Margaret was two months pregnant in November. Could Anthony have been the father? Though perhaps Anthony had only asked for her on 23 November because he believed he would get a better hearing because she was Irish.

Cook had good reason to be protective of Margaret. The couple had survived a hideous year. Margaret had given birth to three children in 1865: twins, Margaret and Charles Louis, and a son, Charles. All had died soon after birth. Cook would not have wanted his wife drawn into his conflict with Anthony, worrying about her health.

By this stage of the inquiry, several points were incontrovertible. When Anthony arrived at the hotel on 21 November, he and Cook already disliked each other intensely. Given the charges that Anthony had brought against Cook, turning up at the hotel had been a provocative act. Cook had probably served Anthony through gritted teeth and resented not being able to turn him away because he was an on-duty policeman. Anthony and Cook were both hot-tempered and good at dishing out insults. Todd and Cook were close friends. They were a good twenty years older than Anthony; like his mate, Todd saw Anthony as a cocky, pushy young copper who took advantage of his uniform. In threatening to punch Anthony, was he not only backing up his friend, but also defending the honour of a woman he held in high estimation? And even if he had not been drunk, Anthony had stayed in a hotel all through a night in uniform. Surely this was inappropriate?

Senior Constable O'Donnell, Anthony's commanding officer, was the last witness. He had instructed Anthony to go to the hotel to monitor a suspect individual. He admitted the idea had originated with Anthony himself but added that he had concurred. O'Donnell said he had called into the hotel at 10:30pm, leaving Anthony there on duty. He had next seen Anthony at the police stables at 7:30am the next day. 'He had his horse groomed and the stables cleaned out at that hour. I spoke to him. He seemed drowsy but was perfectly sober.' Anthony had come straight from the hotel after being up all night, so drowsiness was to be expected. Whether drunk or simply exhausted, he had still reported for duty.

Anthony had the last word. He testified that a squatter residing near Bealiba had told him he suspected that William Morris, a butcher, had stolen thirteen of his sheep, spiriting them away over some days. Morris had been at the hotel throughout the night of 21–22 November, joining the game of swindle. Anthony said he had also been watching Morris the previous two nights. Such conduct was consistent with Anthony's reputation for being a dogged, patient and observant policeman.

Mason wrote to Standish, concluding that Anthony had been playing billiards in the execution of his duty with the knowledge of his senior constable. 'I must confess that the course adopted by the Constable to watch the supposed offender is one that I do not approve of and I think some other course might have been adopted for watching Morris's movements during the night,' he wrote. Nonetheless, if it was deemed necessary to 'remain in the house where the suspected person was amusing himself', it 'would not have answered the Constable's purpose to sit quietly all night without entering into the spirit of the game as that course would naturally arouse the suspicion of a guilty person, whereas the Constable taking part in the game would lead to the supposition that he was there only for amusement'. Yet he deemed the weight of evidence established that Anthony had used insulting language towards Cook. The last charge, being under the influence of liquor, 'must I think fall to the ground as the weight of the evidence is decidedly in favour of the Constable being sober'. In conclusion, Mason stressed that Anthony 'has conducted himself soberly and steadily since he entered the police force'. He was efficient, and his record sheet showed but one charge, using improper language to Sergeant Coleman. John Cook 'entertained an ill feeling' towards Anthony because the policeman had prosecuted him on two occasions.

Although he had written up a fair summation of the allegations, Mason's willingness to give Anthony the benefit of the doubt was expected given they had been working together in the district for several years. Indeed, Mason had recommended his subordinate be rewarded for diligent and effective police work.

Standish was committed, as he had demonstrated in the Coleman case, to enforcing firm and proper standards. He thought O'Donnell more at fault than Anthony for Anthony's presence in a public house while on duty. Having received his superior's consent, Strahan could 'hardly be blamed for having adopted the very questionable methods of watching a suspected person by sitting up the whole night in a public house in uniform, playing 15 games of billiards and consuming numerous gins and peppermint'. Not unreasonably, Standish hoped that 'vigilance' of this kind was not much in vogue in the force. O'Donnell should be reprimanded for 'a clear error in sanctioning such proceedings without duly reporting the matter to his superintendent'. A repetition of such an irregularity would result in a reduction in rank. O'Donnell's disciplinary record was spotless until this incident, and he took the stern reprimand to heart.

Standish instructed Mason to caution Anthony for being in a billiard room all night and to reprimand him for using insulting language. Anthony had escaped a fine or demotion, but he was no doubt upset to be pinged for using insulting language to Cook given the insults Cook had heaped on him, including threatening to assault him, an officer of the law.

Due to the bad blood between the policeman and the publican, Standish decided to relocate Anthony as soon as a replacement could be identified. He did not want the feud to escalate. Anthony was incensed. He had backing in the town. Nine residents – a justice of the peace, another hotel owner, the postmaster, four storekeepers, a quartz crusher, and one of his billiards partners, the slaughterman William Crichton – wrote to Mason with 'deep regret that a complaint has been laid against Mounted Constable Strahan'. They commended him as 'an active, zealous and intelligent officer of steady habits and excellent moral character' and noted that 'during his residence amongst us he has gained the goodwill of the great mass of our population'. The 'well-disposed portion' of the community would regret Anthony's removal, while 'those whose evil practices he has done much to control or punish' would be satisfied. They beseeched Mason to heed their 'unimpaired' confidence in Anthony. While this recommendation was sincere, Anthony may have asked them to intercede on his behalf.

But Mason would not second-guess his boss. He informed Standish on 18 December that the cautions and reprimands for O'Donnell and Strahan had been recorded. Constable McInnerney had arrived from Melbourne to replace Anthony, who would leave Bealiba forthwith.

Cook doubtless felt vindicated – Constable Strahan was gone from Bealiba. But he had little time to savour his victory. Calamity struck less than two weeks later.

At midnight on New Year's Day 1867, Cook closed his pub. The International Hotel was large: eleven rooms, including a bar, a dining room, a billiard room and a parlour. Sometimes guests stayed in the hotel, but there were none on this night. His servant, Louisa Stevenson, had already retired to her bed in a partitioned part of the dining room. The only others in the building were two of the Cooks' four children.

Margaret was in Maryborough with the two other children. It seems odd that Margaret was so far from home at seven months pregnant, especially when she had lost three infants. Travelling to Maryborough would have meant an arduous journey by coach or cart. Was she visiting relatives? Had she gone on a shopping expedition, purchasing items that couldn't be secured in Bealiba? Or were the Cooks estranged in early 1867?

Before retiring to bed, Cook fed his horse in the stable and toured the hotel with a candle, entering every room, except two which were unused, checking that all was in order. He extinguished the lamps and locked the front and back doors. He then slumped gratefully into bed in a room behind the parlour, which he was sharing with the children. It was after 12.30am before he settled.

Soon after he lay down, one of the children became restless. He got up and slapped the child, grabbing a blanket from his bed to sleep on the sofa in the parlour.

Ten or fifteen minutes later, he heard a dog barking in the yard and footsteps passing outside the pub, crunching on the gravel. He thought nothing of it, turning over and falling asleep. Not long afterwards, the dog's bark woke him with a start, and he heard what sounded like something falling in the bar. He got up and saw, to his horror, the reflection of fire in the dining room and the bar.

Built before 1861, the International Hotel was made of pine and corrugated iron, aside from the chimneys, which were brick or stone. The walls and ceilings were lined with calico and paper. Cook tried to make his way through to the servant's bedroom, but burning calico came cascading down from the ceiling and stopped him. He called out loudly and Louisa awoke to find the ceiling entirely on fire. She jumped out of bed and fled through the dining room into the yard. Cook ran back to the parlour and grabbed his children, one under each arm, and dashed out into the street.

Richard Davis, who was up watching over a quartz crushing machine, heard Cook's cry of 'Fire!' and turned around to see flames crowning the hotel's roof. He dashed across to meet Cook emerging from the burning building in his nightshirt, saying, 'For Christ's sake, take the children.' The publican rushed back into the building, risking his life, in a bid to save what property he could. He emerged with two boxes and two sets of drawers, wrenched from their frames. He tried to plunge back into the inferno to salvage a rifle, a revolver and money, but Davis restrained him as the flames consumed the building. Leaving Cook with his children, Davis circled the yard to lead Louisa to safety.

The hotel was reduced to ashes in half an hour. The *Dunolly Express* reported that it was fortunate 'there was not the slightest breath of wind at the time, or the consequence must have been far worse, as there are three or four stacks of hay in close proximity to the buildings'. At one point the house next door seemed like it too would be consumed by the flames, but a few buckets of water thrown over the gable end saved it. The fence between the two properties was razed.

Although he and his children had escaped unharmed, Cook's financial losses were hefty. He had insured his building, the furniture and the billiard table with the Victorian Insurance Office for £600. But he reckoned the combined value of the building and these items came to around £1000. Much worse, the considerable commercial stock was uninsured. The fire destroyed a sizeable quantity of alcohol, stored in the bar and the cellar. Cases of brandy, kegs of ale and bottles of whisky, Old Tom gin, wine, sherry, port, champagne, bitters, sarsaparilla, lemonade and blackcurrant wine went up in smoke. Also lost: 1250 cigars, 30 pounds of tobacco, 1100 weight of butter, a chest of tea, a barrel of herrings, sugar, vegetables and bacon. Cook estimated that this stock was worth another £300, bringing his total losses to £1300, a large sum in 1867.

What caused the fire? Some suspected arson. As I read the newspaper reports, I wondered, with a sense of dread and something like disgust, if my great-great-grandfather could have been responsible. He had a motive – Cook had bested him. He had not wanted to leave Bealiba but had been ordered to vacate. Life in a frontier town was harsh, and often one had to find justice outside the courts. Had he decided to wreak his revenge by creeping back into Bealiba at night, when most were asleep, to set fire to the hotel?

I knew it unlikely, though, that a police officer would put lives at risk, including children. Anthony had a temper, unquestionably, and could be stubborn and abrasive, but there is no evidence that he was cold-blooded. On the contrary – his superiors attested he was a conscientious and ambitious policeman. That's not to say he wouldn't have continued to pursue Cook through the local courts for minor offences, motivated both by a desire to enforce the law and by spite. Yet it's hard to believe he would have been willing to put his career at risk by committing arson.

The verdict of an inquest in Dunolly on 3 January, before a jury of twelve (including one who had written in support of Anthony's continued tenure), was equivocal enough to leave open the possibility that the fire was deliberately lit. Only three people addressed the inquest: Cook; his servant, Louisa Stevenson; and the miner Richard Davis. It is striking that no one in an official position, including anyone from the Bealiba police, testified. The publican's testimony accounted for the bulk of the evidence. He mentioned the footsteps he had heard before falling asleep. He was anxious to rebut any suggestion that he had caused the fire, insisting he had been sober and had made sure all lamps and candles were extinguished and all doors locked. He never stored rubbish under the house and only kept a modest amount of kerosene under a seat at the bar. No fires had been lit in the fireplaces for months, aside from in the detached kitchen. He said he had no idea how the fire had started. Louisa claimed that she had doused her candle when she turned in. She confessed that she had been too frightened to notice much about the fire and hadn't heard the dog barking. Davis could add little. Unsurprisingly, the jury concluded that there was insufficient evidence to determine how the fire began, though they believed it most likely to be an accident. And fires were hardly uncommon, especially during dry periods.[6]

The surviving record doesn't reveal how Anthony reacted when he heard about Cook's misfortune. Did he feel sympathy? Or did he feel Cook had it coming?

The publican set about building a new hotel, this time constructed of brick, on the same spot. While the pub was being built, the Cooks moved to a goldfield near town. If Cook and his wife were estranged, the rift apparently healed. Margaret gave birth to her eighth child, Ellen, in March 1867. Unlike most birth certificates, Ellen's had an odd annotation: 'After declaration made as by law required.' Was her paternity at issue?

Whoever her father – and one has to assume in the absence of anything concrete to the contrary that it was Cook – Ellen died at three months old, of mesenteric disease. The Cooks had lost four children in two years. Although he detested the Bealiba pub-owner, perhaps flinty-hearted Anthony Strahan might have been moved by the hardships that pelted down on the Cooks. Even in a time when so many children perished, four infant deaths in such quick succession must have caused intense grief.

Cook became ill around the time of Ellen's birth and declined over the next eighteen months, succumbing in 1868 at the age of forty-nine. He died before the new hotel was completed. Margaret, left to fend for herself and the four surviving children, married her husband's mate, Hamilton Todd, in 1869. Margaret ran the new pub with Hamilton until her death in 1883. As far as we know, she never met Anthony again.

4

TRAGEDY AND VICE

Anthony's work as a country copper in his new posting at Avoca, about forty minutes south of Bealiba, concerned mainly familiar problems – residents drinking too much and getting rowdy. But he soon faced unfamiliar situations.

Like other Victorian towns in the goldfields, Avoca had a significant Chinese community. Many of these residents, almost all men from China's southern provinces, had joined the goldrushes in the 1850s and early 1860s. Most worked the alluvial diggings, but some took up other professions. They frequently encountered discrimination, prejudice and violence, with European miners resenting what they saw as unfair competition.

Commonly held convictions about how the Chinese lived and behaved often stood in stark contrast to reality. Europeans routinely condemned the Chinese for being dirty and unhealthy, and spreading filth and diseases, yet a visiting government health inspector found the colony's Chinese camps in 1857 to be 'patterns of order and cleanliness', far cleaner and more ordered than nearby European settlements. The fierce anti-Chinese sentiment, which had seen white miners attack Chinese miners at places such as Buckland in northeast Victoria in 1857, had abated somewhat by the latter 1860s. But exclusion and prejudice ran deep. Although an earlier legal requirement to live in separate camps had lapsed, the Chinese continued to reside in their own distinct communities, partly by choice and partly due to ongoing discrimination and seclusion. The press typically reported on crime in colourful terms, but its coverage of Chinese suspects was lurid, portraying them as alien figures with bizarre habits and dark intentions. Crime rates were lower among the Chinese than the general population, but this didn't stop disproportionate and damning attention on incidents involving Chinese offenders. Aspects of Chinese life exacerbated this tendency to see all Chinese in a derogatory fashion, for some set up opium dens and engaged in gambling. Given they were almost all male, the Chinese in Australia were often accused of indulging in sodomy.

Anthony's upbringing in Kildare had not given him any reference points to come to grips with such a significant cross-cultural encounter. What he knew about the Chinese population of the colony he had picked up on the job over the last four years, almost certainly imbibing many of the prevailing prejudices. He had arrested Chinese individuals before arriving in Avoca, such as an Ah Sing in Bealiba in 1866, for selling spurious gold. But it was the Chinese passion for gambling that drew him into a much more dramatic incident. Illegal under the colony's law, gambling was seen as a 'Chinese vice', the root of other evils, from opium-smoking and licentiousness to general dishonesty and thievery. And the Chinese were heathens to boot, even gambling on Sundays. Such perceptions were shot through with condescension and hypocrisy, for Europeans were quite happy to lay a wager at the horse races, in a card game or around a billiard table, but there's little doubt many Chinese gambled with gusto.

Having received information about what the *Talbot Leader* called 'a notorious gambling house on the Deep Lead', a police contingent from Avoca proceeded to the spot in question on the night of 15 February 1867 under the command of Sergeant Mathew Conniff, a twelve-year veteran of the RIC. Thirty-seven and just under six feet tall, he was at the peak of his powers – he had been promoted just two weeks earlier – and was determined to make a mark. He took three other policemen with him: Senior Constable Thomas Shanklin, Constable Robert Young and Anthony.

The police approached the den around 11pm, rushing the front entrance in the dark undetected by two men keeping watch. 'Immediately after the police got into the building,' *The Leader* reported, 'the Chinese, numbering fully 100 men, rushed in all directions in order to effect their escape.' Conniff and his constables secured the gambling instruments and silver coin amounting to 30 shillings. Having scrambled out of the den, the gamblers did not flee into the night, however; they fought back, tearing weatherboards from the building and pelting the police with planks and stones. 'In this perfect shower of missiles Conniff and Shanklin were hit, the former on the [face], which was completely laid open from the nose to the lip, and one of his teeth shattered; and the latter on the left eye, producing a frightful wound,' the newspaper noted. Anthony found himself amid a riot.

Things were becoming hairy, as the Chinese fought back against this embodiment of colonial power with everything they had. Stones rained down. Punches were thrown. With the police heavily outnumbered, less experienced officers might have panicked. Luckily, quick-thinking Shanklin fired two rounds from his revolver into the ground. The sound of these shots was enough to bring everyone to a halt. *The Leader* employed its best racialist language to describe what happened next: 'Aware now that the police were armed, the Mongolian courage oozed out and they betook themselves for safety to flight. After a most desperate and determined resistance by two of the Chinese, who struggled, kicked, and fought until there was scarcely a shred of clothing on their backs, they were at length secured.'

The police arrived back in Avoca at 10am the next morning 'covered with blood, dust, and dirt', and the two prisoners were placed in the lock-up. Further arrests were expected, as many of the gamblers were known to the police. The paper praised the four policemen, declaring they deserved the highest praise for demonstrating courage, determination and coolness when they could have fired on the mob to save themselves.

The incident at the Deep Lead was carried in newspapers across the colonies under the headline 'Desperate Affray'.[1] It gripped the minds of Europeans because it seemed to confirm their long-held beliefs and fears: the Chinese could not be trusted; they were always up to no good, engaging in all manner of illicit activities; they were prone to unruliness and violence; they were strange outsiders who did not, in short, belong in the colonies.

Only two months later, two European men entered the Avoca station mid-afternoon on 11 May and informed Anthony that an Aboriginal woman, Chemimi, had died near Lamplough, a small town a few kilometres south. Anthony set off south to retrieve the body.

The scene of a hectic short-lived alluvial goldrush in 1859–60, Lamplough by 1867 had only seventy miners working the diggings and a small surviving Indigenous population. When he arrived, Anthony spoke to Chemimi's distraught husband, Moses, and examined the body. There was no obvious cause of death.

The next day, the coroner, a lawyer named Leonard Worsley, convened an inquest into Chemimi's death. Moses testified first: his wife had been ill for a long time, he said. She had not seen a doctor or taken any medicine. She had eaten only oatmeal gruel with sugar during her final two days. After his wife's death, Moses had walked into town to tell the owner of the Clare Castle Hotel, George Cartwright. Moses made his mark, an 'x', on the witness statement.

Cartwright next confirmed that Moses had come into his pub to say 'his lubra' had died at daybreak. Cartwright reassured him that he would send word to the police in Avoca. Moses 'was not able to walk there himself from weakness'. Cartwright had asked a Mr Sweet and a Mr Fish to carry news of Chemimi's death to Avoca.

Anthony testified that he had been notified by the two men on 11 May that 'there was a dead black woman at Lamplough'. He had gone into the bush near the town with Moses to examine the body and had removed it to 'where it now lies' in the town.

Local doctor John McMahon's post-mortem examination revealed that Chemimi had been 'very much emaciated' at the time of death. Finding no signs of violence, he had opened up the body, finding a healthy heart and healthy lungs but 'a very much enlarged liver', perhaps twice the normal size. Upon opening the liver, he had discovered many cysts, including one the size of an infant's head, and a large quantity of whitish matter. His conclusion was factual but heartbreaking: 'The cause of death was disease of the liver. The deceased I should say was about 25 years of age.'

Colonisation had triggered an appalling collapse in Victoria's Aboriginal population. Although natural causes played a part, many deaths were the product of other, pernicious factors: settler violence; diseases introduced by the colonisers; a new and often poor diet; and alcoholism. The wholesale destruction of many aspects of Indigenous life, including access to traditional lands and food sources, resulted in more than deep psychosocial and emotional trauma. In his history of Aboriginal Victorians, historian Richard Broome writes that Victoria had around 10,000 Aboriginal inhabitants at the time of first contact with Europeans. By 1860, only twenty-five years after Melbourne was established, this number had plummeted to just 1800, a minuscule 0.3 per cent of the population.[2] Exacerbating this precipitous drop, Aboriginal men had come to outnumber Aboriginal women considerably, meaning the Indigenous birth rate was extremely low and still falling.

Chemimi's people, the Djadjawurrung, who had lived for generations in the watersheds of what became known as the Avoca and Loddon rivers, suffered an alarming rate of death. In 1836, they had numbered between 900 and 1900; four years later, only 282.[3] The goldrushes increased the pressure on Indigenous society and culture, curtailing even more drastically access to traditional lands and food sources and desecrating sacred sites. The number of Djadjawurrung shrank further, as many perished prematurely or left the area. Some who stayed were employed by Europeans as shepherds, stockriders, station hands and domestic servants; others did not fare as well, barely subsisting on the margins of white society, often resorting to begging or prostitution to survive. Chemimi and her husband were caught in this trap. She was young but horribly unwell. Bush pubs and grog shanties were common, and alcohol plentiful, possibly explaining the dreadful state of Chemimi's liver. The death of a young woman of childbearing age was a tragedy for the local Indigenous population. Victoria's Aboriginal community could not afford to lose women such as Chemimi. Moses's frailty also suggested that he too might have been nearing death.

For reasons unclear, on 17 May the Secretary of the Law Department in Melbourne wrote to Leonard Worsley asking him to explain why he had decided that an inquest was necessary. Worsley replied to the Minister for Justice, setting out a combination of factors. His first reason was incontestable: Chemimi had not been treated by a doctor and the cause of her death was unknown. His other reasons revealed much about the colony's social dynamics and the prevailing perceptions of Indigenous people. He contended that 'the circumstances of a moral character and social position affording reasonable guarantees against the commission of a crime were totally wanting'. The deceased had 'belonged to a very unhappy class of women', and men of 'not the most respectable character' lived in the area where she had died. Worsley's language was moralistic, even accusatory, yet evasive. He implied that Chemimi was a prostitute but neglected to mention that she was Aboriginal. If Indigenous men were often rendered anonymous, almost invisible, in colonial Victoria, this was even more the case for Indigenous women.

Worsley also revealed a personal reason for convening the inquest. The deceased had come to his residence a few days before her death and she had been seen wandering around Lamplough for some days. Did he feel guilty, perhaps conceding that he should have assisted a woman who was clearly ill?

The Law Department wrote back on 22 May to say Worsley's explanation had been satisfactory, without elucidating.[4]

The transcript of the inquest did not record Anthony's reaction to the untimely death. Like all Victorian policemen of the period, he had received no formal training in how to interact with Indigenous Australians. It is likely that he had come to accept the largely negative opinions of his contemporaries. Most Europeans in the 1850s and 1860s saw Aboriginal peoples as savages, members of a primitive race destined to die out. William Westgarth, a merchant, expressed an entirely common view in his 1854 book *The Colony of Victoria*: 'It could almost seem an immutable law of nature that such inferior dark races should disappear – people hardly see how – before the white colonist.'[5] Few white residents departed from this damning assessment. Richard Broome contends that the racial divide had become more pronounced in colonial Victoria: 'There was less intimacy in the 1850s between Aboriginal people and settlers compared to the early Port Phillip days.'⁶

By the time Anthony walked into the bush outside Lamplough to view Chemimi's depleted body, many Europeans had little or nothing to do with the colony's embattled and marginalised Indigenous inhabitants. As a policeman, he had a duty of care towards Aboriginal peoples in his district – but if he saw them as inferior, strange and unsettling, like so many of his contemporaries, he would have felt little guilt over a death like Chemimi's. And yet the colony's community policing body did bear some collective responsibility for the fact that yet another young Indigenous woman had died painfully, well before her time. Her death was one more statistic tracing the bloody impact of while colonisation.

More tragedy was to come. In October 1867, Anthony confronted another daunting aspect of his job as a policeman in a newly settled colony: nine-year-old Augustus Schmidt had disappeared into the bush.

Anthony grew up in Ireland's Midland counties, where the land had been cultivated, fenced and built on for generations. The west and northwest of Ireland were more rugged and less populated, and even some parts of western Wicklow, to the east of Kildare, were comparatively wild and uninhabited. By contrast, you rarely had to travel far in Kildare before you encountered other people; the Strahan farm near Timolin was surrounded by other properties, laneways, villages and towns, frequently dating back to the Middle Ages. Anthony was raised in a familiar, non-threatening landscape. It is likely he was never really lost, and if he ever did lose his way he would have quickly encountered others to point him in the right direction. Anthony's homeland was also compact. In his history of Ireland, John Gibney reminds us that 'only 486 kilometres separate [Ireland's] northernmost and southernmost points, and 274 kilometres separate the furthest points on the eastern and western coasts'.⁷

The landmass of Victoria, in contrast, is more than three times the size of Ireland. Running east to west, the state stretches to more than 1500 kilometres; its northernmost and southernmost points are more than 530 kilometres apart. Back then, large tracts were still covered by rugged bush. Even the more settled areas retained swathes of mostly uninhabited bush and rolling farmland. And beyond Victoria lay the vast expanse of the continent.

Although much larger than Ireland, Victoria had a smaller and more dispersed population. In the late 1860s, the population of Ireland was still over five million, despite the ravages of the Famine and the waves of mass emigration. By contrast, in 1871, less than thirty years after the foundation of Melbourne, Victoria's population was just over 730,000. Victorian towns were also widely scattered. The distance between one settlement and another was frequently considerable, with little human presence in between. As a mounted policeman, Anthony had ridden across a good portion of the colony around Avoca, so he had become more accustomed to long distances, lonely roads and the strange bush flora and fauna. But the landscape was still foreign and could seem untamed and eerie, so silent, even savage, by contrast with Kildare. If it was difficult to get lost for long in Ireland's hedge-lined lanes and roads, the bush could swallow people up.

Augustus Schmidt, the son of a German selector, had been doing nothing unusual on the morning of Sunday 13 October 1867. His mother, Agnes, had watched him playing quietly not more than 100 yards from the family hut near Amphitheatre, a small town southwest of Avoca. But she had turned around some time later to find that her son had disappeared. Amphitheatre had seen its own goldrush in 1853, but by the 1860s it was a small farming and timber community. It was surrounded by gullies and ranges, mostly covered in thick scrub. *The Avoca Mail and Pyrenees District Advertiser* remarked in 1867 that the ferns and wattle were so dense that 'horses are hidden from sight at a few paces distant'.

A search by Augustus's father, Charles, and other farmers failed to find the boy. The next day, with the distraught parents waiting at the family hut, hoping their son would emerge from the bush safe and sound, the Schmidts' neighbours scoured the local area again, to no avail. Although spring had arrived, the nights were still bitterly cold. It was time for the Victoria Police to become involved. The constable stationed at Glenlogie, Seymour Larkan, led a third search on 15 October. Larkan, a few months younger than Anthony, had proved a capable officer. He felt the disappearance of Augustus keenly, for he and his wife, Ellen, had just had their fourth child. Despite his best efforts, the search on 15 October proved fruitless.

Anthony joined the rescue effort on 16 October. He led one search party and Larkan another. Both groups went out early in the morning and searched until dark, dragging every likely hole and exploring all the creeks, but found nothing. By this time, Augustus had been missing for four days in inhospitable terrain. Anthony perhaps lost heart, returning to Avoca. Maybe he was just more realistic than others about the prospects of finding the boy alive. *The Avoca Mail and Pyrenees District Advertiser* agreed, lamenting on 17 October that 'another has been added to that sad list of Australia's saddest calamity – a child lost in the bush'. It concluded that Augustus, 'the poor little fellow', had found his grave among the wattles and ferns, possibly only a short distance from his home.

Larkan did not give up and organised a fifth search on 20 October with Senior Constable Thomas Shanklin, this time marshalling seventy helpers. When this extensive search failed, Larkan finally admitted defeat, telling Superintendent Mason that every searcher was 'completely knocked up'.[8] Augustus had disappeared without trace.

Fourteen months later, a bullock driver stumbled across a boy's skeleton in a paddock on the Amphitheatre station. Larkan was the informant at the inquest. Charles and Agnes buried their son in the grounds of their own property.[9]

Anthony was no doubt unnerved, perhaps even haunted, by a landscape that could seem hostile, almost predatory, taking a young life. He did not yet have children of his own – but that would soon change.

At some point in 1867, after he returned from the search for Augustus, Anthony met a young woman in Avoca. Catherine Tannim, who had recently arrived from County Westmeath in Ireland, was twenty years old. The relationship moved quickly and, as was often the case in an era before the widespread use of contraceptives, Catherine became pregnant, in December 1867.

This development caused tensions. Relations between the two seemed to sour shortly after she told him the news. She left Avoca. In January 1868, Anthony asked Mason for two months leave from 20 February to 20 April to attend to 'personal affairs', which he did not spell out, at least in writing. Mason informed Chief Commissioner Standish that Anthony was 'deserving of this indulgence'. He was 'a well-conducted man, active in the discharge of his duties', and had only taken ten days leave in the five years and four months since joining the force. Anthony's impressive work ethic is yet more evidence that he was conscientious, not to say driven. Standish readily accepted Mason's recommendation, noting it made sense to transfer Anthony to the depot in Melbourne, allowing him to take leave from there, with another mounted constable filling his spot in Avoca.

It seems striking, even a little odd, that Anthony would request two months leave when he had only previously taken ten days off in five and a half years. But he needed so much time because he was making the long journey to New Zealand. The surviving record does not disclose why he needed to travel across the Tasman or where he went. Reading between the lines, it is probable that Catherine had travelled to New Zealand, perhaps to join family, and Anthony had followed to sort things out between them. He turned twenty-seven in New Zealand, an age many would have thought to marry and settle down.

If it was in search of Catherine that Anthony went to New Zealand, he must have persuaded her to return to Victoria, for she gave birth to their daughter, Nina, on 13 August 1868 in a house on Cardigan Street in Carlton. Anthony was also back in Melbourne, working at the police depot – he had been fined 5 shillings three months earlier, on 17 May 1868, for over-riding his troop horse when returning from despatch duty (regulations stipulated that officers could not ride their horses faster than 5 miles per hour). On the birth certificate, Catherine claimed she and

Anthony had married in Avoca in 1867, but no evidence of such a marriage has come to light. It is likely Catherine claimed she was married to hide the fact that Nina was illegitimate, for being born out of wedlock came with great shame and disapproval. One Strahan family history speculates that Catherine was already married to another man. It is not known if the young couple lived together in Melbourne, though Catherine was most likely residing in Carlton, not far from where Anthony was working at the police depot on Swanston Street.[10]

Shortly after he became a father, Anthony received bad news from Ireland about his own. Those who migrated to the colonies usually paid an unavoidable price: unless they could afford the long journey back to their homeland, they never saw their family again. News to the colonies was conveyed by ship, and as the voyage took many weeks, residents found out about events at home some time after they had occurred. This is what happened to Anthony when he found out in mid-1868 that Anthony Strahan senior had died in Timolin on 22 December 1867, at the age of sixty-eight. Anthony senior had been buried with his own father, Edward, in the cemetery beside Baltinglass Abbey in Wicklow, not far from the family farm.

Anthony had not seen his father for seven years. As part of a close-knit family, he must have felt conflicted, even a little guilty, about being so far away when his father died, though he had migrated with his father's blessing. He might have taken heart from the fact that his mother, Anne, would not be destitute, for his father left his estate, close to £800, to his wife. Nor would Anne be abandoned. She would reside in Baltinglass, with five of her twelve children living nearby, in Kildare, Wicklow and Carlow.

Anthony was under strain. In contrast to his comparatively carefree days as a constable learning the ropes in central Victoria, life had become complicated. He was entangled in an ambivalent relationship in Melbourne. Providing for Catherine and their infant daughter on a small salary must have been taxing at times, emotionally and financially. His nerves were also frayed by being stationed in Melbourne; he preferred the work of a rural policeman. Perhaps these factors contributed to a disciplinary infraction in October, when his temper got the better of him again. He was charged with insulting a constable and using abusive language in the depot's barracks. Although he pled not guilty, four other constables gave evidence against him, and the verdict was swift. He was fined 4 shillings.

Who could Anthony turn to at this challenging time? Could he rely on his family in Victoria? The Strahan clan in the colony had expanded again. Anthony and his siblings Edward, Mary and Deborah had been joined in Melbourne by two other brothers, Richard and Simon. Three years younger than Anthony, Richard had landed in June 1865 as an unassisted immigrant. A clerk, he had passed the civil service examination in December 1866 and followed Edward into teaching. Simon, eight years younger than Anthony and a farrier by trade, had arrived in November 1868, the last member of the family to leave Ireland.

Edward was teaching at the state school attached to St Peter's Eastern Hill in central Melbourne. He was living in the school residence with his wife, Sarah Ann; their four children (they had lost their first three as infants); and his unmarried sister, Deborah. Edward had become increasingly strict in his Presbyterian faith, even objecting to singing in his house. Anthony did not share his oldest brother's stern faith. They could both be determined, but this determination expressed itself differently. Edward was controlled; Anthony was fiery. The pious older man found much to disapprove of in his younger brother: Anthony had conducted an immoral relationship with Catherine, he had fathered an illegitimate child and he was prone to invective. It is unlikely that Anthony would have turned for support to Edward or to Deborah, who were closely aligned, even if they were willing to give it.

By the early 1870s Richard had settled in Wallan Wallan and Beveridge, just north of Melbourne, and was teaching in the local schools. He had a strong bond with Edward, likely due to their shared profession and religious outlook. Edward would be one of the witnesses when Richard married Margaret Jane Low Tait in 1875 at Emerald Hill, and later that decade, Richard and Margaret would baptise their children at St Peter's.

Mary was living with her husband, William Young, and their daughter, Martha, in central Melbourne. Perhaps she and Anthony were friendly, though she may not have had a relationship with any of her siblings. When she remarried in 1878, none of them acted as a witness.

It was with Simon, the youngest brother, that Anthony had the closest bond. Soon after arriving in Melbourne, Simon joined the Victoria Police, becoming a mounted constable at the age of twenty-one. The two sets of brothers had chosen different professions. Did Edward frown on a career in the police? Perhaps not, but he no doubt saw teaching, especially at a denominational school, as more respectable. If Anthony had offended his older brother by fathering a child outside of marriage, Simon soon found his own way of invoking censure. He married a Catholic, Jane Dooley, in 1870 at St Patrick's Cathedral in Melbourne, right opposite St Peter's Eastern Hill. Jane was born in Athy in Kildare, so it's possible she and Simon met before they left Ireland. Simon was the only Strahan to marry a Papist, likely putting him and his wife on the outer of the wider Strahan family. Edward was no doubt unimpressed.

Whether Anthony confided in Simon or any of his siblings, physical distance soon exacerbated any emotional, temperamental or social distance. In February 1869, Anthony was transferred to Belvoir (later renamed Wodonga), more than 320 kilometres northeast of Melbourne, on the Murray River. He wanted to get back to what he saw as the real work of a police officer in the colony's towns and countryside. Perhaps he was only too happy to escape his complicated private affairs in Melbourne. Catherine did not accompany Anthony to Belvoir.

Anthony got himself into trouble only a few months into his new posting. In May 1869 he left the district without permission, securing a reprimand. It is possible he returned to Melbourne for a quick visit to resolve things with Catherine. Later that same month, an anonymous complainant wrote to Superintendent Bowes Wilson in Beechworth claiming he had seen Anthony playing cards all Saturday night and being drunk on the Albury racecourse. Was Anthony enjoying his newfound bachelorhood? While he wasn't typically a big drinker, this wouldn't have been the first time that he had stayed in a hotel all night gambling. Luckily for Anthony, Wilson concluded the complainant was a member of the criminal class who would go to any lengths to get his revenge on a policeman and dropped the matter.[11]

Anthony was transferred again, taking up duty 40 kilometres to the south, in Beechworth. There is no evidence Anthony was pushing for a return to Melbourne. Perhaps he had no choice in his postings, but he seemed happy in the bush.

He continued to incur disciplinary infractions. He was cautioned on 22 August by Sergeant Thomas Baber for being absent from his barracks without leave. Nina would have turned one on 13 August. Had Anthony travelled to Melbourne to attend her birthday? If so, it seems this was the last time that he saw Nina or Catherine. His disciplinary record contains no further infractions for being absent without leave, suggesting he made no more dashes to Melbourne. Catherine likely gave up on him. If she had family in New Zealand, she could have returned there, putting herself and Nina beyond easy reach. Whatever had made it impossible for him to reconcile with Catherine, Anthony had lost a daughter.

5

THE CONVICT STAIN

In Beechworth Anthony was alone again, by choice or not, settling into his new assignment. By late 1868 he was an experienced and well-regarded policeman. Despite a persistent tendency to use abusive language when annoyed or crossed, he was rated highly by his superior in December 1868. Anthony had cut his teeth in the goldmining towns of central Victoria, learning almost entirely on the job. Beechworth presented a different challenge.

Perched 550 metres above sea level on a wooded granite plateau, Beechworth would remain the most important town in the Ovens district until 1880. In his history of the town, Tom Griffiths captures Beechworth's character well: 'The town had all the atmosphere of being in the hills. Visitors often commented on the "wild" and "rocky" terrain; they called the scenery "grand" and "romantic". The granite plateau, although not very high, rose sharply from the valley and was thus precisely defined in its difference.'[1] Although the local goldrush had peaked in 1857, the population had stabilised at around 3000 in the 1860s. Goldmining continued in the area, with several surges, including in the 1870s. The Shire of Beechworth, which stretched across 482 square kilometres and encompassed Beechworth itself, as well as smaller settlements such as Stanley, Wooragee, Eldorado, Nine Mile Creek, Woolshed, Sebastopol, Reid's Creek and Everton, boasted a population of more than 9000.

When Anthony took up duty, Beechworth was well-established and prosperous, with a post office, several churches, a gaol, a powder magazine, a general hospital and a mental hospital, a benevolent asylum, two foundries, a sawmill and a tannery, several banks and theatres, two breweries and a cordial manufactory. A range of shops stocked smart clothes, fine watches and other goods. A row of pale golden government buildings – a court, a sub-treasury, a warden's office and a police station – ran along one end of Ford Street. *The Ovens and Murray Advertiser* had published its first edition in 1855 and was building up a healthy circulation that ran south to Benalla and Mansfield and north up to the towns along the Murray River. Hotels competed for customers, including the Commercial Hotel on Ford Street, which was remodelled by Thomas Tanswell in 1873, and the stone-and-brick London Tavern on Camp Street.[2] In an echo of the Strahan family's deep connections with the Ovens district, in 1970 my parents and eight other couples purchased the London Tavern, long neglected and dilapidated, to save it from likely destruction.

Superintendent Hugh Ross Barclay oversaw the Ovens district, which covered a large area, with fifteen stations. Anthony had already worked under him when they had both been stationed in central Victoria several years before. Barclay was a seasoned officer of twenty years standing, having joined the force as a cadet in October 1852 and served in locations around the colony, including Benalla, Avoca and Portland. Promoted to superintendent in 1862, he took charge of the Ovens district in 1868, arriving in Beechworth with his second wife, Harriett, and their seven children. Two decades in the force had taken a toll, and it would become apparent in a few years that Barclay was unwell. The older policeman was also an able prosecutor, and he played a significant role in my great-great-grandfather's career.

Anthony was now nearly thirty. The disciplinary infractions had stopped, suggesting he had a better hold on his temper, at least for the time being. He already knew that the tasks of a policeman in colonial Victoria extended beyond typical police work, and he got a good taste of this in Beechworth. Members of the force were often instructed to undertake other duties for the government – something many believed was an unreasonable hindrance to carrying out proper policing functions. Performed for little or no additional pay, these duties spanned activities from collecting agricultural statistics and enforcing compulsory vaccinations against smallpox to handling mental health cases and following up instances of truancy.[3] In December 1869, Anthony was appointed an inspector of Beechworth's slaughter yards, and a year later as a bailiff. These duties meant he was even more involved in the town's daily life, perhaps enhancing his local standing. But some tasks could cause tensions with locals. Several policemen began competing with selectors for land. 'As these police were also sometimes Crown Lands Bailiffs or inspected selections for bailiffs,' writes Carole Woods in her history of Beechworth, 'an appalling conflict of interest existed.'[4] Anthony was not interested in acquiring land, but he would be later in his career.

The Beechworth area could be rowdy and violent. Much of the population was transient, with many men drifting in and out of the district. On the night of 7 December 1869, the three Crawford sisters were alone in the family home at Two Mile Creek, their parents away harvesting. A stranger, James Martin, came to the hut and asked the eldest child, fourteen-year-old Victoria, for a glass of water. After drinking the water, he left but soon came back, pounding on the door and demanding to be let in. Victoria at first refused, but relented when Martin said he would break down the door with an axe and tomahawk her sisters. Telling Victoria that he would cut her throat if she screamed, Martin dragged her off into the ranges behind the school. There, concealed in the dark, Martin held her for some hours, violating her several times through her weeping. After he eventually abandoned her, Victoria ran home and later raised the alarm in Beechworth at 2am on 8 December.

Armed with a description of Martin, Anthony was despatched a day later, on 9 December, to a farm near Myrtleford, 25 kilometres to the south, where the alleged culprit was working. On the way to the farm, Anthony encountered a man driving along a track with a dray with a team of bullocks. He quickly realised it was the wanted man.

In a fateful error, Anthony allowed Martin to drive the dray back to the homestead. On entering the barn, purportedly to tie up the bullocks, Martin cast aside his bullock whip and made his escape: he lifted a trapdoor over a race used to turn a wheel for chaff-cutting and disappeared into the rushes and underwood. Anthony called for backup. Then, he waited with dogged determination for eight hours until a tall figure moved stealthily into the open in the moon's uncertain light.

Anthony rushed at Martin, who fled, again disappearing into the vegetation. The police officer searched through the scrub until he found Martin, who lunged at him, grabbing him by the throat. A struggle ensued.

Under the headline 'A Dastardly Outrage', *The Advertiser* described Anthony's struggle with the miscreant: 'Several times they were both down, and as the prisoner is a very powerful fellow, fighting perhaps for his neck, it was no child's play.' The press had in the past carried occasional factual accounts of Anthony's arrests, but this was the first time he was portrayed as a hero, in a valiant battle to apprehend a dangerous miscreant.

In the nick of time a second constable appeared, and Martin was subdued and taken to the Beechworth lock-up. On 11 December, Victoria picked him out at a line-up as the man who had carried her into the bush. Martin had form. He was 'one of the most prominent of the Eldorado rioters' and had been imprisoned previously for obtaining goods under false pretences. Revealing some easy intercolonial rivalry, *The Advertiser* noted that Martin was 'a native of Sydney'.[5]

Martin's committal hearing on a charge of rape took place before the Beechworth police court on 20 December. After hearing the evidence, *The Advertiser* thought the case against the defendant was clear and grave, noting that Victoria Crawford had 'entered into details quite unfit for publication, but which went to show that a capital offence had been committed on three different occasions'. The Police Magistrates committed Martin to stand trial before the circuit court.

When Martin was brought before Justice Sir William Stawell in Beechworth on 20 April 1870, the prosecution's case unravelled in ways that said much about the mores of the day. Sexual exploitation of children and young women was rife, but offenders often escaped punishment. Although her testimony was supported by several witnesses, including her eight-year-old sister Margaret, Victoria Crawford rather than James Martin effectively ended up in the dock. The age of consent for girls in

Victoria was remarkably low, varying between ten or twelve years in 1860s. From the modern perspective, this seems extraordinarily young, but it was supposed to afford girls some protection – there was no age of consent for boys.[6] The defendant's barrister, John Bowman, painted her as a licentious girl who had consorted with a number of men, including, he insinuated damningly, Chinese. A doctor, John Dempster, said he had found no marks of violence on Victoria when he examined her, adding that she had 'already been tampered with'. *The Advertiser* changed its tune: 'The evidence of the prosecutrix revealed the existence of the most repulsive and degraded aspect of immorality amongst females of tender age. The fact of a child allowing herself to be forcibly carried away from her home in the arms of a casual male visitor at between ten and eleven o'clock of the night, and subsequently tacitly permitting her person to be violated at three different times, is sufficient to startle the circumspection of the severest morality.'[7]

Anthony's own evidence concentrated on proving the arrest and was uncontroversial, but Victoria testified that he had threatened to bring her into the lock-up if she did not give up the prisoner's name, despite her initial reluctance. Even given the era's harsh attitudes, this looked heartless. Anthony's characteristic determination to bring a culprit to justice had got the better of him. He seemed unaware of the trauma that could be caused by threatening a young girl who had so recently suffered such a heinous crime. And if he had some inkling of what he was doing, inflicting further pain on Victoria was less important than putting Martin away.

If he hoped that forcing Victoria to divulge her attacker's identity would secure a conviction, Anthony was disappointed. After consulting for two hours, the jury found Martin not guilty. At least the relatively lengthy deliberation – many jury cases of the day were decided quite quickly – suggested that at least some of the jurymen believed Martin was a bad type and had done wrong.

Other crimes were less confronting, the routine stuff of a policeman's life in a busy district. Theft, from nicking personal items through to cattle duffing and horse stealing, was a common occurrence. So was drunkenness, with many men seeing heavy drinking as an expression of masculinity and the bottle as a source of solace. In January 1870 two brothers, the former convicts Thomas and Michael Lavelle, stole a keg from Beechworth Brewery, taking their bounty back to their farm on the Ovens River. When Anthony rode out to the farm, he found the thieves slumped in separate beds, blind drunk, with an empty keg. The Lavelle brothers were given a fourteen-day prison sentence by the Beechworth police court. Though they escaped hard labour, their harsh sentence might have been influenced by the fact they were hardly conventional – they shared the same woman, another ex-convict, Bridget Halloran, as their wife.

Anthony's work also took him deep into the countryside. As a mounted constable, he patrolled a large area. On 1 May, he left Beechworth in search of a man who had stuck up a William Moore in Bowmans Forest, riding around the area and then across to the small town of Tarrawingee, 65 kilometres in all. The next day his search took him to Eldorado, back through Bowman's Forest and on to Whorouly – another 80 kilometres of riding. He found the culprit, William Shuttle, living near Tarrawingee. He had ridden more than 200 kilometres in three days to find Shuttle, such was his determination. His troop horse was exhausted and he hired a private horse to secure the arrest warrant.[8]

The Chinese population in the Ovens district was large – more than 3000 in 1870. A good number lived in Beechworth itself, on Spring Creek, with smaller groups in the settlements scattered around the local goldfields, including Buckland, Woolshed, Two Mile Creek and Yackandandah. In 1868, 1000 Chinese in the area were storekeepers, market gardeners or hawkers, while some had gone into rearing sheep and harvesting.[9] Europeans were employing Chinese to work their claims on the goldfields. Fifteen opium dens were operating in the district, and gambling remained prolific in the Chinese camps.[10]

Anthony inevitably became involved in patrolling the Chinese camps in and around Beechworth. On 17 March 1870, he arrested Ah Gow, alias Ah Sam, for stealing grapes from a vineyard. The defence said Ah Gow had 'sung out' to the vineyard's owner, offering to pay for the grapes. The police court was unimpressed, noting that the vineyard was surrounded by a six-foot fence, and sentenced the defendant to one month in prison. This seems a severe sentence, not least because the grapes were only worth 2 shillings. *The Advertiser* claimed Ah Gow had made a masonic sign to the Chinese interpreter with his pigtail during the trial,[11] apparently confirming for Anthony and the other Europeans present that the Chinese were a strange race given to mysterious rituals. Even Ah Gow's full name remained a mystery, 'Ah' being a common colloquial Cantonese honorific placed in front of a person's given name, creating an everyday name. Chinese defendants were likely happy enough not to provide their actual names, maintaining a certain anonymity.[12]

If Anthony's working days were busy and varied, his private life during this time remains shadowy. He left no letters or a diary, but it is possible to catch glimmers of what occupied him when he wasn't in the station or in the saddle. On 24 March 1870, he placed a personal item in *The Advertiser* for a missing friend, Murthay O'Donnell, who had last been heard of two years before, working with a survey party in the Beechworth area. Anthony appealed for any information concerning O'Donnell's whereabouts, adding that he had a letter of some importance for him. Did O'Donnell ever reappear? The record is silent.

Within a year, Anthony was transferred to Eldorado, 22 kilometres west of Beechworth. The town lies at the foot of the Woolshed Valley, where the hilly country meets the plains running southeast to Wangaratta. A naval captain and drover, William Baker, had established a run in the area in 1840, naming it Eldorado, though his choice of name had nothing to do with gold. Rather, he believed the country around his run was ideal for grazing sheep and would allow him to make a fortune. Eldorado remained a sleepy place until gold was discovered in the mid-1850s. By the time Anthony arrived in 1871, it was booming on the back of another goldrush. The population had swelled to more than 1500 and the town boasted several churches, a court, a school, three newspapers and, as was customary, numerous hotels. Several thousand miners, including many Cornishmen who had come to Victoria from South Australia, worked the diggings near the town, bringing the population to around 4000. Although the Eldorado goldrushes were to prove temporary, in 1871 the future seemed glittering; even floods a year earlier had not dampened enthusiasm. Such a rapid population surge unavoidably strained law and order. The police station in Eldorado opened in 1857, closed in 1859 and reopened in 1866.[13]

In 1871, the Eldorado police contingent was three strong: Sergeant William Chadwick; Samuel Wellwood, a foot constable; and Anthony, a mounted constable. It was here that Anthony formed strong personal bonds. The three officers had much in common, for they were all Irish Protestants. Chadwick, born in 1829, had worked on the railways in Ireland before migrating to Victoria and joining the police in 1853. An Anglican, he married Fanny Bruen, a nineteen-year-old English–Welsh immigrant, in 1865. Consistently rated as steady and efficient by his superiors, Chadwick was promoted to sergeant in April 1866. Born in 1843, Wellwood was a labourer and farmer from County Monaghan in Ulster, Northern Ireland. He was Presbyterian and had served with the RIC for a few months before migrating to Victoria in 1863. He joined the force in 1864 and married Margaret Farrigan eighteen months later.

The three policemen had a big job. They were responsible for policing a booming mining town – the miners often rowdy and given to hard drinking as they looked for a lucky break – and the surrounding region, which included sizeable agricultural holdings.[14] It was a tough task for any officer, even one as dedicated as Anthony.

Soon after he arrived in Eldorado, Anthony's personal life began to bloom. He started stepping out with 21-year-old Marion Evans.

When she formed a relationship with Anthony in 1869 or 1870, Marion was working as a housekeeper at Reidsdale, the home of the Reid family, just down the road from Tarrawingee. She was employed by one of the region's leading families, and it brought Anthony into their orbit. Yet despite these connections, Marion wasn't the most typical companion for a policeman. The youngest of three daughters, she came from a closely knit but colourful family. In fact, her background was downright disreputable, for she was the daughter of convicts.

Edward, my maternal third-great-grandfather, was born in Holywell, on the estuary of the River Dee in Flintshire, northern Wales, in 1819. Edward came from a humble family and was something of a rough. He was only five-foot two but made up for his diminutive stature with a gutsy temperament. Like many other illiterate working men, he boasted two tattoos, likely drawn with gunpowder or charcoal – an E on the inside of his right arm and a half-moon between the finger and thumb on his left hand.

Holywell in the early nineteenth century was a sizeable market town. Much of the population worked in its cotton mills, copper smelteries and factories, or in nearby lead mines. A labourer who probably moved through unskilled jobs, Edward was impoverished and had limited prospects, and soon became a petty thief. In a study of Tasmania's convicts, Alison Alexander rightly argues that 'large sections of the working class accepted theft as a reasonable way to eke out scanty earnings in tough times'.[15] Industrialisation had destroyed many traditional jobs, forcing thousands of people into the burgeoning towns and cities in search of work. Living conditions in working-class localities were tough, and violence and drunkenness were common.

A habitual thief, Edward was imprisoned in the 1830s, first for a short time for minor stealing offences, then with a longer sentence for filching eight silver spoons and forks, and finally for nine months for lifting a writing desk and box. He was acquitted in 1835 of stealing a handkerchief. His prison record rated him a bad character with bad connections. His luck ran out in April 1837 when a Liverpool court convicted him, at the age of seventeen, of breaking into a dwelling to steal plates. This time the punishment was severe: a fourteen-year prison sentence and transportation to Van Diemen's Land.

After spending time incarcerated in a bleak hulk subsisting on a meagre diet of skilly (porridge), salt meat, bread and biscuits, Edward was despatched to the penal colony on the *Recovery* in June 1837 with 279 other male convicts, including 113 serving life sentences. Britain did not create a fleet of purpose-built prison ships to transport its convicts, relying instead on merchant vessels refitted with cells and bunks. Launched in Batavia in 1799, the *Recovery* had already made three convict voyages to New South Wales; this would be its last journey to the Australian colonies. Although they were crammed below deck for most of the time in fetid conditions, the convicts were allowed out on deck for exercise and fresh air. The *Recovery* arrived in Hobart on 8 October 1837 after a direct voyage lasting 129 days. Five perished en route, but Edward was young and hardy.

Like many other convicts, Edward was often unruly. The penal colony punished less serious offences in three ways: the lash, hard labour in irons and the treadwheel. Edward would experience all three during his first two years in Van Diemen's Land. He received thirty-five lashes in November 1838 for neglecting his duty, and served three days on the treadwheel in July 1839 for absenting himself without leave and a full two weeks in September for idleness and insolence. The treadwheel, or everlasting staircase, encapsulated the cruel utilitarian logic that drove the convict system, for it both inflicted a painful punishment and generated economic benefit. Convicts, up to forty at a time, were placed in a revolving wooden cylinder and forced to keep stepping on rotating planks, hour after hour, grinding corn or pumping water.

But the lash and the ever-lasting staircase didn't tame Edward. On 7 October 1839, almost exactly two years after he had made landfall in the penal colony, Edward was sentenced to six months hard labour for being in possession of rum and absent from work. Drunkenness would be an ongoing problem for the young Welshman.

Edward did his hard labour south of Launceston, first in Cleveland, then Campbell Town and finally near Avoca. In the early 1840s, he met another convict, Eliza Redman, and they sought permission to marry in March 1843. While this request ground its way through the colony's bureaucracy, Edward started his climb out of servitude. He received his ticket of leave on 24 November 1843, six years after arriving in Van Diemen's Land. This meant he was essentially independent, although technically still under sentence. He resided for a time in Swansea, on the east coast, but soon moved inland to Campbell Town, where he married Eliza in January 1844 at St Luke's Anglican Church.

Eliza Redman was born in 1823 on St John Street in London's East End, the daughter of Mary Ann and John Bird, a bricklayer. In the mid-1820s, the family lived on White Horse Alley, one of the city's narrow laneways that dated back to the early seventeenth century. Some in the extended Redman family network believed Eliza's stories that she was part Jewish. However, Eliza was hardly a paragon of honesty, telling plenty of fibs and using various surnames to cover her tracks, though she most often went by Redman, her mother's maiden name. She may have lied about being partly Jewish to create a little more mystique. Eliza was baptised on 11 May 1823 at the Church of St Sepulchre in Holborn, where her parents had married the year before. St Sepulchre was appropriately located, it would turn out, almost directly opposite the Central Criminal Court, commonly known as the Old Bailey.

Like her future husband, Eliza was poor. Unlike Edward, she could read and write. My third-great-grandmother deployed her literacy skills as a thief and was something of a skilled professional. By her teenage years she had become adept at conning the owners of draperies or watch shops in the city's better suburbs, posing as a domestic servant of a trusted customer in need of a new dress or a watch. She cased the shops she was intending to rob carefully. Well-spoken and confident, she cajoled the shop assistants and sometimes even the half-wary owners into handing over goods and then scarpered. She quickly pawned her loot, using pawnbrokers in different localities. As Janet McCalman has observed, London was the capital for fencing valuable stolen goods and crimes of deception and imposition.[16] Eliza was very much at home there, but she became too bold, pulling off too many jobs too quickly, drawing attention. The Metropolitan Police arrested her and her mother, Mary Ann, on 5 December 1840, placing them in Newgate Gaol, virtually next door to the Old Bailey.

The two women were brought before Mr Maltby at the Old Bailey on 14 December. Eliza faced three charges of stealing 90 yards of mousseline de laine, several gold watches and two shawls. Eliza's mother was charged with feloniously receiving the goods, knowing them to be stolen. Eliza tried to shift the blame from her mother, saying Mary Ann believed the fabric and shawls had been purchased. Mary Ann claimed her daughter was an actress and had used her income to buy the goods. These attempts to fend off the charges fell flat. Maltby found Eliza guilty of larceny, ruling that she should be transported for fourteen years; she was just sixteen. Mary Ann was found guilty of receiving stolen goods and sentenced to be transported for seven years.

Eliza's trial attracted much attention, both because she had seemed so reputable and because her crimes proved she was undeniably clever. *The Morning Post* declared her 'of respectable appearance' and noted, almost with admiration, that she had succeeded in defrauding tradesmen of their property in an 'ingenious manner'.

Mary Ann was not transported, perhaps because she had seven other children, the youngest only a year old – though the authorities often ignored the personal circumstances of prisoners in determining their fate. Whatever the reason, she was returned to Newgate to serve her sentence. In April 1841, Eliza left London on the *Rajah* with 189 other female convicts, two serving life sentences. According to the penal records, she was a needle-woman and a nurse. She was a shade under five foot, with a fair complexion, light brown hair and brown eyes. During the 105-day voyage, Eliza joined other convicts in making a beautiful quilt, using materials supplied by a philanthropic body and demonstrating fine needlework skills. The Rajah Quilt is now housed in the National Gallery of Australia in Canberra.

Ten convicts perished during the voyage, but Eliza arrived in Hobart in July 1841 fit and well. On 31 December, she entered the service of a Mr Hartnett as a domestic servant in Longford, a town south of Launceston.

Eliza remained strong-willed and defiant. Soon after commencing work for Hartnett, she was charged with 'uselessness' and returned to the gaol in Launceston to reconsider her ways. She returned to Hartnett's service but got into more serious trouble in 1842. The police court in Longford found her guilty of misconduct and pilfering some of Hartnett's property and sentenced her to six months' hard labour in the Launceston Female

Factory. The colony's four female factories were bleak places; six months at the wash tubs was tough.

When she married Edward Evans in 1844, Eliza was nineteen. It was appropriate, if ironic, that the marriage certificate gave 'dressmaker' as her occupation. Due to the enormous sex imbalance, Eliza had plenty of potential partners to choose from. 'Perhaps as many as three quarters of the males who arrived in the early colonial era would never marry,' writes Frank Bongiorno, 'and most of those who missed out were convicts and emancipists.'[17] Edward must have had something going for him to win the affections of such a tough, self-possessed woman. But Eliza had much to gain from the marriage as well. 'In a patriarchal society, women needed both a male protector and a male breadwinner,' writes Janet McCalman, 'and those who failed to secure such protection were the most vulnerable members of society, apart from Aboriginal Tasmanians.'[18]

The authorities generally approved of marriages between convicts, believing they made the men behave better.[19] However, marriage failed to quieten Eliza's rowdy husband. Less than three months after the wedding, Edward, then twenty-five, was charged with assault, though he was discharged. In November 1844, with Eliza pregnant, he was convicted of misconduct and using profane language and sentenced to one month's hard labour on the Town Surveyors Gang in Launceston. Two months later, he was admonished for being drunk and disorderly. He evaded yet another misconduct charge in February 1845.

Old habits die hard, and Eliza too continued to get into trouble. She was doing another stint for misbehaving, this time at the Cascades Female Factory in Hobart, when she gave birth to their first child, Winifred Eliza, on 10 April 1845. Giving birth in prison seemed to provide Eliza enough reason to re-evaluate her life, for this was the last time she would run afoul of the colony's penal laws. She was smart enough to know that constantly getting into trouble was likely to end badly.

But Edward hadn't yet learnt the same lesson. Four weeks after Winifred's birth, he was charged with being in a pub after hours and sentenced to two months' hard labour on the road gang. Granted his ticket of leave in November 1845, Edward still found it hard to stay on the right side of the law. On 18 January 1847, he was fined 10 shillings, money the young couple could ill afford, for being drunk. Never one to keep quiet if she was roused, Eliza likely let her husband know in good strong East End language that she wasn't impressed.

It seems the fine convinced the turbulent Welshman to calm down, for he stayed out of trouble for the rest of his time in Van Diemen's Land. He also had a growing family to provide for. Having likely lost an infant son in 1846, Eliza gave birth to two more healthy daughters, Margaret in May 1847 in Hobart and Marion, Anthony's future sweetheart, in 1848 at Gravelly Beach on the Tamar River, near Launceston. Edward was given a conditional pardon in July 1850, allowing him to move around but not leave Australia. The family's fortunes were improving. Issued with a certificate of freedom in June 1851, Edward followed the path of around 30,000 freed Vandemonian convicts, who headed to Victoria.[20] He left Launceston on 29 December on the *City of Melbourne*, scouting the way to a new life. Eight months later, Eliza followed, boarding the *Yarra Yarra* on 20 August 1852 as a steerage passenger with the three girls: Winifred, aged seven; Margaret, five; and Marion, four.[21]

Alison Alexander observes that most convicts in Van Diemen's Land had a relatively benign experience, unless they committed serious additional offences and were sucked into the penal stations, where conditions were harsher. Life was tough, but it was also tough back in Britain. Convicts had lower death rates than soldiers housed in barracks. 'On average their diet was better, with more calories per day, than the working class in Britain; they had more medical care; the government provided better shelter,' she writes.[22] All the available information suggests that Eliza and Edward did not suffer unduly during their convict years. But the impact of their convict experience did not end when they arrived in Victoria. The past could not be left behind. The convict stain was marked across the Australian colonies by the 1850s. No matter how trivial the original offence or whether an individual had reformed, freed convicts were mistrusted. Many free settlers saw them as irretrievably immoral and criminally minded. The taint was even more pernicious for women. 'Almost all commentators at the time,' writes Alexander, 'saw female convicts as dreadful, worse behaved than men: rowdy, rebellious, disobedient, drunken, and far too free with their sexual favours.'[23] Yet Victoria's goldfields, with a highly transient population, provided the best setting to start afresh. No one knew Edward and Eliza. Like other freed convicts, they took steps to conceal their past, though they generally used their own names.

It seems Eliza gave birth to a fifth child, Edward, in the Ovens district in late 1852. By 1853, with the goldrush in full swing, the Evans family was living in Beechworth. Edward had learnt a few things from his wife because he opened a drapery. Some or all of the family likely worked in the store. Winifred, the eldest daughter, became a bonnet-maker. Business must have been brisk as Beechworth's population exploded.

Eliza began an affair in 1856 or 1857 with John Ferguson, a labourer and wood-splitter from Carrickfergus, a seaside town in northern Ireland. This was scandalous – it is estimated only 3 to 5 per cent of married women had relations outside marriage in the 1870s, though the true number was likely somewhat higher.[24] But Eliza was a strong personality who had already proved that she was willing to resist the prevailing social and moral conventions. It seems she was seeing John for some time while still living with Edward. Perhaps Edward was drinking heavily, straining the marriage.

Life became more complicated. Eliza gave birth to another son, William, by Edward in 1857, but fell pregnant to John some months later. Although Eliza eventually moved in with John and took on the name Ferguson, the two didn't marry. They lived for a time near Carisbrook in central Victoria, John likely working on a station. Had they cleared out of the Beechworth area to avoid an aggrieved, irate Edward Evans?

Eliza gave birth to John's daughter at Charlotte Plains in 1858. They took steps to disguise Eliza's convict past when Jane was born, claiming on the birth certificate that they had married in Adelaide in 1848. This was smart; South Australia had not been a penal colony. As a professional thief, Eliza had used aliases in London and she did so again, using 'Howard' as her unmarried family name on the birth certificate.

A few months after Jane's birth, Eliza and John were in Eldorado, John working on the gold diggings. It is likely Eliza decided to return to the Beechworth district because Winifred had fallen pregnant at only fourteen to a man twice her age, George Morgan. Winifred and George married in Wangaratta's Trinity Church in June 1859. Eliza and John Ferguson were the witnesses. Winifred gave birth to a son in Eldorado in early 1860.

It is possible Eliza and John returned because Edward Evans had departed. He disappears from Beechworth by 1859. He could have died, though no death record has come to light. Or he could have decamped. An Edward Evans escaped from police custody in Lancefield in November 1863 after stealing leather from a tannery; the *Kyneton Observer* described him as 'an old hand from the other side' (Tasmania). Two months later, likely the same Edward Evans was charged with robbery and shooting with intent to kill following a raid on the Tooborac Hotel. A court was unforgiving, sentencing the accused, who admitted to leading a gang of bushrangers, to twenty-four years in prison. Released from Sandhurst Gaol thirteen years later, this man quickly got into trouble again. Arrested at 3am on 31 July at a railway crossing in the Melbourne suburb of Richmond carrying what looked like house-breaking tools, he was given a two-year sentence for being a rogue and a vagabond. Prison records indicated that he had come to Victoria from Tasmania. He walked out of Pentridge Prison in February 1879, aged sixty. These biographical details tally up, but several men called Edward Evans with similar birth dates were transported to Van Diemen's Land, leaving our Edward's fate shrouded in doubt.

Meanwhile, a case before the Beechworth police court on 3 February 1860 demonstrated that Eliza remained hot-tempered. She and another woman from Eldorado, Ann Neill, became embroiled in a public verbal stoush that escalated into a fist fight involving their menfolk. Both women lodged summonses against each other, though the court concluded that Neill's 'impetuous temper and unbridled tongue' had been the cause of the affray and found against her and her husband, imposing a £1 fine and instructing them to pay £10 in damages and the court costs. One newspaper noted that the language used in the row was 'utterly unfit for publication'.

Six months later, Eliza gave birth to a son in Eldorado, at the age of thirty-seven. Winifred was the only person to attend the birth, even though she was only fifteen and herself a young mother. Eliza and John again claimed on the birth certificate that they had married in Adelaide, though this time they said the union had taken place in 1854. Eliza once more gave Howard as her unmarried surname. Eliza had a third and final illegitimate child in 1862, Winifred again by her side. By then Eliza's second daughter, Margaret, had married Henry Nielson, a blacksmith from Denmark. Margaret was seventeen. She signed the marriage certificate with an X, indicating that she was illiterate, like Winifred. Eliza had been unable to pass on her literacy to her two oldest children.

Margaret and Henry left Eldorado in 1866 to take up a farm on the banks of the Mitta Mitta River, near the small goldmining town of Snowy Creek in the Great Dividing Range. Their union would be the most enduring in the family, resulting in eight children. When Anthony met Marion, he was not to know that Margaret and Henry would come to play an important part in his life.

By the late 1860s, brothers Robert and Curtis Reid were leading figures in the political, economic, religious and cultural affairs of northeast Victoria. Robert was a magistrate, vice-president of the Wangaratta hospital committee and an organiser of social events for the district, including racing meets at Wangaratta. He lived on his station, Clear Water, near Eldorado. Curtis, Marion's future employer, resided at the old family homestead, Reidsdale, near the Ovens River. He was known for his talents as a cricketer, an amateur singer, a pigeon shooter and a breeder of Leicester sheep. Presiding over the opening of the new Anglican church in Tarrawingee in 1866, he took up important positions in the district, becoming a judge for the Murray Agricultural and Horticultural Association, President of the Wangaratta Jockey Club and the Local Guardian of Aborigines in 1871. Robert and Curtis were both elected to the North Ovens Shire Council.

Curtis and his wife Sophie advertised for a general servant in August 1868, and Marion, then twenty, might have secured the position. But in late 1868, Curtis decided to quit the northeast and relocate to Melbourne to become a partner in a business. He apparently intended the move to be permanent, selling virtually all his property, including farm animals. The change turned out to be temporary; Curtis returned to the Ovens district only a year later. Marion was certainly part of the household when he and Sophie reached their property, Reidsdale, in December 1870 or January 1871. She was already in a relationship with Anthony at that time.

How did they meet? Probably in town, perhaps when Marion was shopping for the Reid household. Or did Anthony have some reason to call on Reidsdale? Whatever the circumstances, Marion clearly caught the eye of the Eldorado constable.

The young Marion was a strong woman, though she lacked her mother's confrontational temperament. Marion was known to be kind and a stickler for cleanliness and orderliness, a trait no doubt honed by working for the Reids. Soon after Curtis and Sophie returned to Reidsdale, she fell pregnant to Anthony. Curtis did not dismiss her even though she was pregnant and unwed; pregnancies outside marriage were common at the time.

Marion gave birth at Reidsdale to a son, Anthony Oliver, at 11pm on 11 December 1871. Eliza and Winifred were in attendance. Anthony was absent. That wasn't unusual for the time, but the birth certificate indicated that everything may not have been right with their relationship. Although Anthony Oliver was clearly named after his father, the deputy registrar had written in and then crossed out Strahan as his family name, and the birth certificate did not include the name of the father. Was Anthony about to repeat what he had done three years earlier in Melbourne, when he had parted ways with Catherine Tannim after she gave birth?

Anthony's personal affairs in late 1871 were again complicated. If he had not yet severed all links with Catherine, he would have been juggling two relationships with women at opposite ends of the colony. He was now father to two children born out of wedlock. In contrast to Catherine, who appeared to be alone in Melbourne, Marion was surrounded by family.

Eliza was living in Eldorado with her de facto husband and their children. Winifred was residing in the town with her second husband (her first had died in 1866), James McEvoy, a figure of some standing who co-owned a gold and tin mine near Eldorado. Anthony would have been under no illusion that he would have to reckon with Marion's family if he deserted her. He was also aware that the Reid brothers were among the district's leading figures. If a report in *The Advertiser* on 31 October 1871 can be believed, Curtis had become even richer, making £5000 'by a lucky purchase of some buildings in Melbourne'. Robert, the magistrate, presided over both civil and criminal cases. Anthony could not afford to get offside with two men who wielded considerable local power.

Marion was the daughter of convicts, and her mother had been living with a man outside wedlock, with three illegitimate children. There can be little doubt that Anthony's devout brother Edward would not have approved of the relationship. But Anthony did seem to care for Marion. He was soon confronted by the town's snobbery when he, but not Marion, was invited to a ball at the Athenaeum Hall in Beechworth. It was predictable that as a man in possession of a temper, Anthony refused to take this insult meekly. Before the ball, he went to the hall and dusted the floor with black pepper, ensuring that later in the evening the ladies sullied their dresses as they danced. He no doubt took great pleasure when the soiled dresses caused much distress. Clouds of pepper swirled into the air, causing mayhem, and the dance was called off. This act of revenge was hardly befitting of a policeman, but it said something about the Irishman's determination to stand up for himself and the mother of his child.

It seems unlikely Marion would have stayed at Reidsdale after Anthony Oliver's birth. Caring for her son would have interfered with her work. She probably left Reidsdale and moved to Eldorado to stay with her mother, bringing her closer to Anthony, who was living near the police station. Perhaps this brought them closer together in more ways than one, for their relationship was to continue for the rest of Anthony's life.

6

SAUCY JACK

Around the time of his son's birth, Anthony's policing career was taking off. He was in the right place at the right time, for that archetypal outlaw of the Australian colonies, the bushranger, was taking centre stage.

The first bushrangers were convict bolters – men running from captivity, often desperate, operating in a land that was strange and rough. By the 1860s, the local press was covering the exploits of a new breed of bushrangers, and the police efforts to catch them, in great, often colourful, detail. Peter Smith writes that this new breed of outlaw 'were mostly free men, native-born, bush-bred, skilled horsemen who identified with the country and were proud and untamed rather than desperate and downtrodden'.[1] Four men fitted this bill. Ben Hall carried out scores of robberies with various sidekicks across New South Wales between 1863 and 1865, although he didn't kill anyone. Known for his 'flashy' ways and charm, Hall dressed nattily, treated women with courtesy and engaged in daring deeds. He was in many ways a forerunner to Ned Kelly. Daniel 'Mad Dog' Morgan was a more fearsome character, killing a New South Wales police sergeant in 1864. The Clarke brothers, Thomas and John, were perhaps even more brutal, committing more than seventy robberies and a string of murders and prompting the New South Wales government to pass the *Felons Apprehension Act* in 1865, which introduced the concept of outlawry and placed wanted bushrangers beyond the protection of the law, allowing citizens to shoot them on sight.[2] All four men were shot by police or executed between 1865 and 1867.

Contemporary opinion about bushrangers was polarised. Depending on one's standpoint, bushrangers were either daring, even romantic, battling the colony's rich and powerful, or violent criminals preying upon rich and poor alike for personal gain. This dichotomy painted a morality play, with either the bushrangers or the police appearing as heroes. The polarisation has carried across the generations, with some writers and historians taking up stark positions, casting bushrangers such as the Kellys as social bandits and devil-may-care outlaws or as depraved thugs and ne'er-do-wells. The full picture is more complicated than these stereotypes allow. Much of the population at the time, whether they saw bushrangers as social bandits or crude hoodlums, avidly followed their exploits through the press with a mixture of excitement, macabre fascination and fear.

One bushranger, Harry Power, a former convict born in Ireland, became closely associated with northeast Victoria. He developed a flamboyant and, for some, swashbuckling reputation. Power received a thirteen-year prison sentence in 1855 for wounding a police officer near Maryborough but escaped from the Pentridge Stockade in 1862. Holed up in the bush, he was assisted by Irish Catholic farmers, including the Quinns and the Kellys. In February 1864, he was arrested and sentenced to seven years' imprisonment for horse-stealing. After again escaping from Pentridge in 1869, he committed a spree of robberies across Victoria, until he was arrested by superintendents Charles Nicolson and Francis Hare in 1870 near the Quinn property on the King River. He was brought before the court in Beechworth, where he received a fifteen-year prison sentence with hard labour for bushranging.[3] Anthony Strahan was stationed in Beechworth at the time, but he does not appear to have played a part in Power's apprehension. But Power nonetheless had an ominous impact on Anthony's career: he had helped to mould the criminal ways of a young Ned Kelly.

As a policeman, Anthony knew where he stood. He had no truck with romantic notions about folk heroes – bushrangers were lawbreakers and they had to be apprehended. He had his first encounter with two in early 1872. On 13 February, a hawker from Melbourne, John Higgins, was sleeping in his wagon at Tarrawingee, near the Red Lion Hotel and

John Connors's store. In the early hours of the morning, John Trembath and Charles Watson galloped out of the darkness, one on a bay mare and the other a grey horse, and bailed up Higgins, threatening to blow out his brains if he didn't hand over his money. They were undeterred by the proximity of the Tarrawingee police station, suggesting they were either brazen or daft. But they chose the wrong victim. Higgins calmly tied up his tilt and cocked his revolver. Circling the wagon, Watson whipped out a gun and pulled the trigger. The snap of the cap was unmistakable, but the gun didn't fire. Higgins ran across to Connors's store, crying for help, as his assailants galloped off towards Eldorado.

James Connors, the five-year-old son of the store owner, found a hat on the road to Eldorado early on 14 February. It was handed in to Constable Edward Shoebridge at the Tarrawingee station. The hat had bullet holes near the crown. Shoebridge rode to Eldorado to inform Sergeant Chadwick that two bushrangers had attempted to rob a hawker, bringing the hat with him. Anthony realised that he had seen the hat when Trembath had been held in the Eldorado lock-up for a trivial offence a short time ago. He had interrogated Trembath about the holes.

Chadwick sent Anthony to Tarrawingee to find out if anyone had seen Trembath. Several locals said they had noticed Trembath and another man on horseback the night before. Armed with this apparent confirmation, Anthony rode out with Chadwick and Shoebridge to a hut in the ranges where the two men were staying, only a kilometre from Tarrawingee.

Trembath and Watson gave a clipped and unconvincing account of their whereabouts on the previous night. They insisted they had nothing to do with an attempted stick-up and had not ridden for months. Anthony searched the hut and found a revolver and an unloaded shotgun. The latter had a cap on, but the cap had been exploded. Grey hairs were on the gun's muzzle, suggesting it had been carried on a grey horse. He also found a saddle with sweat on the lining, indicating it had been used recently.

The police officers returned to Tarrawingee to verify the account the two men had given of their movements. Anthony quickly established that they were lying. He and Chadwick rode back to the hut, where they arrested the would-be bushrangers without a struggle. The police had nabbed the culprits within twelve hours of the botched robbery, leading *The Ovens and Murray Advertiser* (known commonly as *The Advertiser*) to claim: 'We must, not for the first time, congratulate the district on the efficiency of its police force.'[4]

John Trembath and Charles Watson appeared before Justice Redmond Barry at the circuit court in Beechworth on 16 April, charged with attempted highway robbery under arms. Barry had been on the bench of the Victorian Supreme Court for just over twenty years by that time. An Irish Anglican by birth and the son of a major-general in the British Army, he was a man of wide-ranging social, cultural and philanthropic interests, supporting various causes and organisations. But he had developed a reputation as a harsh judge in criminal matters. Peter Ryan rightly observes that Barry 'valued the purely retributive elements of the [criminal] law', though he notes that the judge reflected the hard standards of a frontier society.[5]

Both men pleaded not guilty. But both also had a criminal record. A miner born in Cornwall, 41-year-old Trembath had been convicted of at least two offences, one for robbery in company in Ballarat in 1856 and a second offence in 1861 under the alias John Slater. Partly bald, he was of medium height, around five-foot seven. A bush carpenter born in Tasmania and small of stature, no more than five-foot three, Watson was younger than Trembath (his birth date is unclear, though he was likely twenty-six in 1872), but he had a more extensive criminal record. Under the alias James Wheeler, he and two other men had broken into a house in Melbourne before daybreak in 1865 and stolen a fancy chimney timepiece. As the youngest of the three thieves, Watson was given a one-year prison sentence while his accomplices were given three-year sentences. Watson was a habitual thief, for he was convicted of larceny in 1870 and again in January 1872, serving one month in Beechworth Gaol. He was released on 3 February, less than two weeks before the bungled highway robbery at Tarrawingee. The attempt to stick up Higgins represented an escalation in Watson's behaviour, for it seems he had not previously used a firearm in any of his crimes. He and Trembath were looking at serious prison time if they were convicted.

The Crown prosecutor who mounted the case against the two men, Charles Smyth, was experienced and well-connected. Born in Ireland and educated in England, the 44-year-old was a good friend of Chief Commissioner Standish and sometimes served as a judge. Some thought his long nose and sharp style gave him a hawk-like appearance. But he was an able prosecutor: he usually spoke without notes.

This was the biggest case in Anthony's near decade-long career. It was the first time he had captured armed robbers. Higgins, the hawker, was the first prosecution witness to take the stand, and he recounted the events of 13 February in unvarnished language. He identified Trembath, adding that he had been wearing a hat, and said that Watson was the other assailant to the best of his belief. He insisted it was the man riding the bay horse – Watson – who had fired a single-barrelled gun. Following Smyth's examination, Trembath questioned Higgins, though *The Advertiser* observed that the prisoner pursued 'a most purposeless examination', eliciting replies almost more damaging to the defence than the prosecution. Watson questioned the hawker in an equally fruitless manner.

Several other witnesses filled in what Trembath and Watson had done in the hours before the attempted robbery. Francis Martell, a publican in Eldorado, said the two had drunk a glass of ale in his place about 9:30pm. Margaret Robert, wife of the landlord of the All Nations Hotel in Eldorado, recalled that the two men had come into her place between 9 and 10pm. In each pub, the men had arrived and departed together. They had clearly been fortifying themselves for the coming deed. Salvatori Caradoni, an Italian carter residing in Eldorado, testified that Trembath had been cutting firewood for him on 10 February. He had next seen him at close to midnight on 13 February. Caradoni had been in bed when Trembath had come to his house asking for a saddle and a gun. He had given Trembath a saddle, but he told his late-night visitor that his gun, a single-barrelled rifle, was next door at the Parrs'. Anne Parr testified that she had heard Caradoni and Trembath having a loud conversation around midnight. Shortly afterwards, Trembath had appeared at her place, asking for the gun. Parr said she had passed the gun to him through a window.

Trembath had asked if it was loaded, and Parr had replied that it was not. He had declared that he was going to his camp. Parr added she had seen Trembath earlier in the day wearing a hat exactly like that produced in the court, but when questioned by Watson, she admitted she had not seen anyone with Trembath that night.

What had the bushrangers done after the robbery had gone awry? Mary Anne Cawse lived on the other side of Reedy Creek, not in Eldorado itself. She knew Trembath well, though she told the court he was generally called Saucy Jack; it seems Trembath was something of a ladies' man. Cawse said barking dogs awoke her early in the morning of 14 February. After a knock at the door, she looked out the window to find Trembath with a gun, holding a grey horse by the bridle. Watson had been with him, leading a bay horse with no saddle. Trembath asked her to tell his wife that he had received a letter and had to travel 50 miles away. He had been across the creek to get the two horses for the trip, he said, and asked Cawse if she would let his wife stay with her. Cawse refused. Watson told Trembath to ask Cawse for her husband's saddle. She again refused. The two men left, with Watson declaring, 'If she's so bloody particular, let's get on.' Cawse's testimony made it clear Trembath had been intending to flee Eldorado, abandoning his wife – hardly the conduct of an innocent man.

When Trembath got his chance to question Cawse, he seemed intent on casting aspersions on her character. He appeared to imply that he had encountered her in Gippsland as a prostitute. Then he suggested that Anthony had schooled her on her testimony. Cawse denied this. She agreed with Trembath's contention that he was drunk on 14 February but disagreed that he was too drunk to ride. Watson, meanwhile, suggested that it was too dark to recognise him. Cawse disagreed, stating it was light enough to see him because he had been standing close to the window.

The prosecution case was looking strong. The three policemen involved in the arrests, Sergeant Chadwick and Constables Shoebridge and Strahan, corroborated the evidence given by the other witnesses. The accused had claimed they had been at Martell's pub in Eldorado until midnight on

13 February. Anthony had established this was untrue by questioning several people in Eldorado, including Mary Cawse. Anthony told the court that he had found an unloaded gun and a saddle when he searched the hut.

Trembath addressed the jury, *The Advertiser* reported, 'very much in the style of an itinerant ranting preacher, with plenty of energy, but very little substance in his argument, his remarks tending neither to prove nor refute anything in particular, being mainly confined, indeed, to abuse of the witnesses, and assertions to the effect that he was on the whole rather an injured individual, and that all witnesses for the prosecution, Sergeant Chadwick particularly, were perjured villains of the deepest dye'. Trembath called a character witness, Richard Jones, but this gambit failed as well. Jones said he had known Trembath a little for about nine months, and only because the accused had called at his pub in Myrtleford.

The jury readily found the prisoners guilty. Barry sentenced Trembath to five years' imprisonment and Watson to five and a half years, in each case with the first year to be served in irons. The would-be bushrangers were despatched to Pentridge Prison. In one sense they were damn lucky. If the gun had not misfired, they might have faced a more serious charge, even murder, which would have led them to the gallows. Trembath had apparently stayed out of trouble for over a decade. Perhaps he had been convicted of other offences under aliases, or avoided detection. Or had young Watson led him back to a life of crime?

Anthony was satisfied that he had helped to put the men away for good stretches. Trembath was reunited with his wife when he was released in June 1876. He and Anthony were not done with each other, however, and would cross paths again in 1880. It is unknown what happened to Watson after he walked out of Pentridge in 1876.

Superintendent Barclay was pleased with the convictions and wrote to Chief Commissioner Standish: 'The promptitude and acumen displayed by the Eldorado police is deserving of great praise, resulting as it did in the committal of these offenders within 24 hours of the time of the offence notwithstanding that their description was very meagrely and somewhat erroneously given by Higgins, and that they were unknown to the police as Criminals.' Barclay recommended that Chadwick and Anthony receive £5 rewards, affirming that both officers had made unremitting exertions, as much of the evidence, especially against Watson, had been circumstantial. Standish concurred.

Anthony had won the confidence of another superintendent. Much as he had been supported by Superintendent Mason in Avoca, Anthony would come to enjoy Barclay's backing over the next few years.

After that, the high-profile cases came thick and fast. Anthony and Chadwick became a tight team. Across early 1872, someone was stealing horses in the Eldorado area. The police suspected William Campbell, a known offender. When Anthony questioned him on a road outside the town on the afternoon of 21 April, Campbell realised the game was up. Late that night, he fled into the bush with his wife and a stolen horse and buggy. Anthony and Chadwick set out in pursuit, following the buggy's tracks north. Campbell was wily. The buggy's tracks left the road at one point, running off into the bush, where they seemed to disappear suddenly at a brush fence. All seemed lost until Chadwick noticed that the fence had been carefully reassembled, hiding the buggy's tracks. The two policemen gave chase and eventually found Campbell on 22 April camped atop a range in the heart of dense scrub, within a few kilometres of the border with New South Wales.

Campbell was brought before the Beechworth general sessions on 5 August, with a large crowd watching. After a brief discussion, the jury found him guilty, and he was sentenced to five years' imprisonment with hard labour. His sentence was as harsh as those imposed on Trembath and Watson, even though the latter had been convicted of attempted armed highway robbery. Horses were a critical part of the colonial economy, both as working animals on farms and a means of transport, particularly because Victoria's rail system was still limited. They were valuable property, and horse-stealing was punished severely.

Barclay was again impressed by his officers in Eldorado and wrote to Standish on 20 August recommending that Sergeant Chadwick and Constable Strahan receive £3 rewards for their 'highly creditable conduct':

'This arrest gave very great satisfaction as Campbell had been following his nefarious career for some time.' Standish approved the rewards, stating that the case 'reflects great credit on the police'.[6] A decade into his career, Anthony's reputation as an efficient and capable police officer was becoming entrenched, and the rewards supplemented his modest income.

At the very time Campbell was stealing horses, another crook was committing a string of well-planned burglaries, breaking into miners' huts. He had evaded detection for some months. With characteristically patient detective work, Anthony donned plain clothes to watch Ah Wah as he moved around Eldorado and surrounds. The robberies generally took place during the day, when miners were at their diggings. Anthony and Chadwick traced Ah Wah to Sebastopol, a busy settlement in the Woolshed Valley. There Anthony searched him and found a key, trying the doors of several huts with it until one opened. Inside he found the loot, all humble items: a possum-skin rug, blankets, clothing and bags of sugar. He might have been, as *The Advertiser* claimed, 'a big hulking Chinaman', but Ah Wah went quietly when Anthony slapped on the Darby handcuffs. Chadwick informed Superintendent Barclay that Ah Wah was 'an adept at crime', hiding the proceeds of his robberies in a hut some distance from where he resided. Ah Wah had 'carried on his nefarious game in so systematic a manner it made it much more difficult to capture him'.

Ah Wah was arraigned before Justice Barry at the circuit court in Beechworth on 17 October on charges of housebreaking and receiving stolen property. He was undefended and pleaded not guilty. After hearing damning evidence from several witnesses, the jury reached a guilty verdict on all counts without retiring from the courtroom. The prosecutor noted that the accused had previous convictions, the last one receiving three years at Beechworth in 1869. Ah Wah at first denied having ever been in Beechworth Gaol, but upon a long roll of convictions being read out, he admitted to having been sentenced to three years for stealing securities at Yackandandah.

Even by his own unforgiving standards, Barry gave Ah Wah a harsh sentence – eight years' imprisonment with hard labour. Ah Wah was a habitual criminal and this was his fifth conviction, but Barry had given Trembath and Watson, European defendants, less severe sentences even though they had committed a more serious offence. Ah Wah had stolen trivial items and he hadn't threatened anyone with a gun, let alone pulled the trigger. Was Barry influenced by the fact that Ah Wah was Chinese and spoke broken English? It is also troubling that Ah Wah was not represented by a lawyer. Barry was deficient, if not downright wrong, in not ensuring that Ah Wah was properly defended.[7]

Anthony likely saw nothing wrong with severe sentences. Arresting Ah Wah had added to his reputation, with Barclay recommending another £2 reward for his indefatigable efforts.

When he left the courtroom in Beechworth on 17 October, Anthony was not to know that he was about to walk into the biggest case of his policing career. And this time, he wouldn't be dealing with wily thieves and half-cocked attempts at highway robbery. Instead, he would be confronted by the most violent act of bushranging in Victoria since Mad Dog Morgan had prompted so much fear in the 1860s.

PART II
THE OUTRAGE
AND THE JUNCTION

 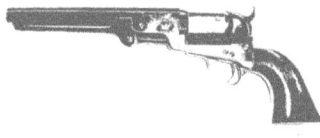

THE JUNCTION

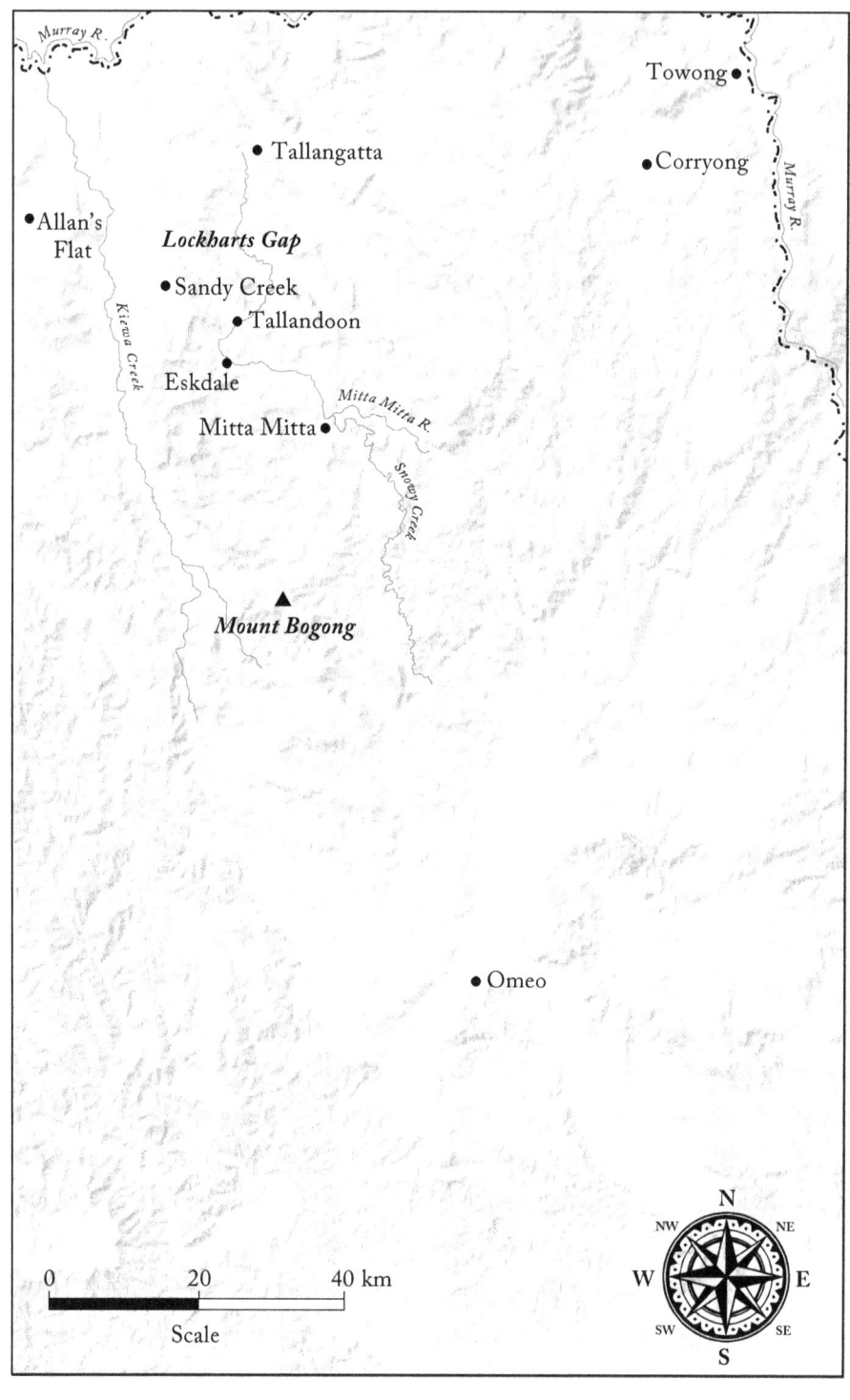

7

SOMETHING WICKED THIS WAY COMES

In late 1872, three young men were working as wood-splitters in the thick box and iron-bark forests that ran through Watchbox Swamp and the Pilot Ranges between Eldorado, Beechworth and Wooragee. The woodcutters were a storybook trio – one decidedly tall, the second of medium height and the third reasonably short. Felling trees was hard and thankless work that didn't pay well, and the three woodcutters decided there was an easier way to get some money. On 15 October, they rode out of their camp in the Pilot Ranges after sundown intent on committing robbery.

They chose their target carefully. A township had sprung up on an old squatter's run known as Woorajay during the goldrushes, but by 1872 most of the gold had been dug up and the population had shrunk considerably. Wooragee was merely a small mining and agricultural town on the road between Beechworth and Albury. It suited the three men's purposes. It was comparatively isolated and it was close, but not too close, to their campsite in the ranges. It had a good sprinkling of dwellings and a few businesses that could be plundered. There was a small school with a dusty earthen floor and a Wesleyan church that had just been completed. A coach conveyed passengers along the road from Beechworth through Wooragee to Albury, but did not run at night, which meant there were few passers-by in the evening. And perhaps most importantly, unlike Beechworth, Eldorado and Yackandandah, it had no permanent police presence. At the peak of the goldrush, a police station and a court of petty sessions had operated nearby at Woolshed, but both had closed in 1869, with the Beechworth station assuming responsibility for maintaining order in Wooragee and the Woolshed.

The men's clothes revealed their hard luck: they wore moleskins patched on the knee and dirty wide-awake hats. The medium-sized man was in a tattered pilot-cloth coat with raised seams, torn at the back, near the collar. The short man was carrying what looked like a double-barrelled pistol. Leaving their taller companion with the horses, they approached a hut on the edge of the town owned by Peter Mitchell. Pietro had migrated from Turin in Italy some years before, anglicising his name and settling in Wooragee. He had married Catherine McLeod, a native of Skye in Scotland and a domestic servant in Beechworth, in 1864. Eight years later, Peter, thirty-three, and Catherine, twenty-six, were making a humble living as gardeners to support themselves and their three young children, including an infant.

It was a gloomy night, bursts of rain falling as the two men walked towards the Mitchells' place. The short man wore a brown veil over his face as a disguise; his companion used the puggaree (a scarf that could act as a sun shield) from his hat to hide his identity, doubled over his face and tucked under his chin. Both makeshift masks had holes cut out for the eyes. When the bushrangers approached the door of the hut at 7.30pm, Catherine was home, the children asleep in the back room. Peter was in the cow shed, around eight yards from the kitchen. The medium-sized man knocked and demanded entry.

'Where's your money?' he yelled.

Catherine told him that she had none.

The would-be thief's eyes settled on a shotgun hanging on the wall. Made in Germany, it was single-barrelled and large-bore, with a stock mended with a cord. He claimed the gun and demanded ammunition and saddles. Catherine said she had neither. She was petrified, fearing the intruders intended to harm, even kill, her. Frustrated, the two men went to look for her husband. As they were returning with him five minutes later, the taller man glanced down the hill and asked who lived in two nearby huts. Peter replied that one hut was occupied by a woman and her children, the other by an old miner. He thought neither would have guns and ammunition.

Back inside his own hut, Peter handed over a canister containing shot and a flask filled with powder, but he couldn't find any caps (that is, bullets). As Peter searched fruitlessly, the man of middling height became impatient, snapping aggressively, 'Look sharp, look sharp.' Peter asked if his unwelcome visitors would be kind enough to leave the gun behind, as he had much want of it. The robbers refused. They left the hut, instructing Peter to stay inside, warning that they would shoot him if they saw him outside.

Moving along the road into town, the men, both now armed, approached Wooragee's post office. Henry Gale, a baker by trade and a Londoner by birth, had been appointed postmaster only a few months earlier. He ran both the post office, which doubled as his home, and a nearby bakehouse with his wife, Margaret, an Irish Catholic. As the would-be bushrangers stormed towards the post office, Henry was down the track at his bakehouse, leaving Margaret behind the counter. Margaret was talking to a customer, William Jarvis, a young bullock-driver who lived in the town. Jarvis had finished a long day carting props for Chinese miners. The bushrangers knocked vigorously on the door. When Jarvis answered, the two ruffians were standing on either side of the door, their weapons levelled.

'Come outside, you bugger, or I'll blow your brains out,' snapped the taller man. His voice was gruff, portending violence. There was no doubt that he meant business.

The son of a convict transported to New South Wales, Jarvis was not going to take any reckless risks. He was only twenty-four, with a young wife and an infant daughter. He came out on to the verandah with his hands up, making sure the two intruders could see he was not going to do anything stupid. Margaret followed.

'There's £50 inside in that bloody house. I'll have it. Go in and get it or I'll shoot you,' said the taller man. He rudely ushered Margaret back inside to find the money, instructing his mate to watch Jarvis.

Once at the till, Margaret denied she had any money to hand over.

'That be buggered – there is £50,' the thug shouted, promising to blow Margaret's brains out if he had to ask her again.

'I haven't got £50,' Margaret repeated. She said she had already banked her takings in Beechworth.

Jarvis realised this angry young man was close to exploding. 'If you have got any money, you had better give it to him.' Margaret relented, taking a lamp to the back to fetch a tin box that contained a few shillings. Her captor found a second flask of gunpowder and a box of caps. Margaret also handed over a bag of shot. The intruder shook the bag derisively, declaring he didn't want any bloody rubbish. He asked for a saddle. Margaret showed him one, but he cast it aside, unimpressed by its quality.

Revealing that the night's events were beginning to take a toll, the ruffian asked for a drink: brandy, rum, whiskey, gin, 'it didn't matter a bugger which'. But Margaret didn't have any spirits, saying he could take the lamp and search the premises if he liked. As the men were leaving the store, frustrated by the lack of goods to pillage, they warned Margaret Gale and William Jarvis to remain inside or they would be shot, claiming that another two men were down the road keeping watch.

The bushrangers headed into town, where they encountered Margaret's husband, Henry Gale, who was walking home from the bakehouse. The shorter bushranger accosted Gale, pointing his pistol at his head. 'Stand, you bugger, or I'll shoot you.'

A cloud came across the moon, making the gloom under the trees even darker.

Gale thought his assailant was joking and told him to lower the pistol.

'If I put a ball in your head that will not be a joke,' the young man replied. 'Turn out that bloody money.' Gale said he had no money, turning out his empty pockets.

The taller robber searched the storekeeper, finding nothing. But the two men insisted that Gale was concealing £50, calling him a bloody liar and telling him to walk into the bush. Knowing he would place himself in even more danger if he complied, Gale kept his cool, saying, 'What is the use of taking me into the bush? Aren't you satisfied that I haven't got any money?' He said what little money he had was already banked.

The two ruffians finally gave up. 'Go to your store and don't come out tonight – there are men up the road and down the road … if you come out, I'll shoot you,' the younger man warned. Gale watched the two men walk further into town, past the chapel, heading towards the school.

Within sixty minutes, the two woodcutters-cum-bushrangers had threatened to kill five of Wooragee's residents, and had stolen a shotgun, some powder, shot and caps and a small quantity of money. Their rampage was about to escalate.

They reached the Wooragee Hotel at about 9pm to find the building locked. The front doors had no external handles – they could only be opened from the inside. A bracket lamp lit up the front bar, revealing it was empty. The detached kitchen, connected to the front of the building by a short verandah, was illuminated by a second lamp. The publican, John Watt, and three customers, Hugh Pierce, John Kennedy and Thomas Frazer, were sitting around the kitchen table chatting at the end of a long day. A pound-keeper from Albury, Kennedy was the son of an Irish convict transported to Sydney. He had had his own brush with the law in 1863 when a court had issued a warrant for his arrest for fraudulent insolvency. He had stayed clear of the law since then and had much to lose in 1872, for he had a wife and nine children, the youngest not yet a year old, back in Albury. Just shy of six feet tall, he was athletic and could vault straight into his saddle with a short running jump.

Watt's wife, Ellen, who had been popping in and out of the kitchen during the evening, was outside attending to farmyard tasks. John Watt and Ellen Anderson were Scottish immigrants, having arrived in Sydney in the late 1850s and marrying in Woolloomooloo in 1859, when they were twenty-four. They had soon left Sydney and John had secured a position with a cousin, Alexander Black, an assistant surveyor in the Victorian government. Black and Watt carried out a geodetic survey in the northeast of the colony to determine the boundary between Victoria and New South Wales. Watt then turned to farming near Beechworth before taking on the Wooragee Hotel in early 1870. By October 1872, John had decided to give up the pub by the end of the year and return to farming close to Yackandandah. Had the weather not been so wet over recent days, he would have been away from Wooragee on the evening of 15 October, at Yackandandah, finalising the arrangements to acquire a farm.[1] But the heavy rain kept him at the pub, with terrible consequences.

As she was giving milk to a foal in the stable, Ellen saw two men go past the blacksmith's store and the hotel's front gate, one walking three paces in front of the other. The clouds had cleared and the moonlight was bright, giving Ellen a view of the men, who were carrying something, though she could not tell what. A short time afterwards, Ellen was back inside when she heard a knock on the front door and asked her husband to answer it. John walked up the passage connecting the kitchen to the bar and opened the door, to be confronted by two menacing men. 'Stand out here or I'll blow out your brains,' the taller robber yelled.

John kept a gun in the bar, but he had no time to grab it. Instead of stepping out on to the verandah as Jarvis had at the store, John made a fateful decision. He turned and fled back towards the kitchen. One of the assailants fired, spraying shot down the passage, hitting John Watt in the left side as he turned back towards the front door. Some of the pellets struck Kennedy in the left arm. The house was full of gun smoke. The attempt to rob the hotel had gone horribly wrong. The loud crack of the shot was heard by the Gales and the Mitchells, on the other side of Wooragee. Despite their swaggering and thuggish threats, the bushrangers had likely not intended to shoot anyone, and they bolted in panic, first on foot and then on horseback after they had met up with their mate who was looking after their mounts. They rode off into the night towards the ranges.

John staggered into the kitchen, blood running down the left side of his body. His coat, waistcoat and shirt were shot through. He sat down but soon tried to stand up, pressing his hand on the table before collapsing. Kennedy propped him up against the wall, tending his wound. When Frazer got up to see what the matter was, John warned: 'Don't go outside – I felt the shots flying about my head.'

Ellen rushed into the kitchen, but Pierce had secured the door. When the young man realised it was Mrs Watt outside, not one of the attackers, he opened the door. Ellen found her husband lying on the floor, bleeding profusely. She could see that the shot had pockmarked the walls of the passage and the kitchen. John said he wasn't going to make it. Ellen placed a pillow under his head. Frazer dashed out to secure assistance but found none that could help in such a dire situation. Wooragee didn't have its own doctor.

Kennedy rode off to Beechworth to get help. His wound was relatively minor. Beechworth was 16 kilometres to the southwest and Kennedy knew he had to hurry, for the publican was badly wounded.

A few hours later, Dr William Walsh reached the hotel to find John Watt in a parlous condition, lying on the floor in front of the fire. He had already lost a great deal of blood and felt very cold. The exit wound on his back, below his shoulder blade, was the size of a man's fist. Walsh was astounded that Watt was still alive, but feared his patient would not last much longer. Meanwhile, back in Beechworth, Dr Henry Fox dug a slug out of Kennedy's arm.[2]

Elsewhere in Beechworth, Superintendent Barclay feared he might have a gang of bushrangers loose in the region. Anxious that more shootings might take place, he sent a midnight telegram to Chief Commissioner Standish summarising what had happened in Wooragee a few hours earlier. Drawing on what the ailing Watt had said, he provided a general description of the offenders: 'First man five feet nine, medium build, 30 years, light complexion, hair straight, red spot on face, wore dark coat buttoned at neck, moleskin trousers, light low crowned hat – second man five feet six, dark coat, monkey jacket, moleskin trousers.' Barclay said his officers were in pursuit of the full particulars.[3]

On 16 October, a magistrate from Beechworth, George Graham, came to the hotel to take down Watt's statement about the events of the night before. Graham was a prominent local farmer and corn merchant, with land holdings in the Wooragee Valley. Watt, who believed he had 'no hope of recovery', made a dying declaration. He affirmed that 'the one that fired was a medium size man, ill-looking and thin; he had a cap on; I don't think he had very many whiskers, which were dark; he spoke with a gruff voice; he was a youngish man. I don't think I could recognise him.' Barclay fired off another telegram to Standish, advising that Watt was dying. Noting the offenders had fled in the confusion after the raid, he recommended that Standish approve the immediate offer of a £100 reward.

The Advertiser reported on 17 October that John Watt had rallied – 'it is not impossible that he may recover, but in such case it will be a literal snatching from the jaws of death'. Worryingly for the police, who were trying to reassure a frightened district, the paper noted that no information had yet come to light about the assailants.

A day later, Barclay informed Standish that all available officers in the district, including Detective John Christie, who was attending a circuit court session in Beechworth, were searching for the culprits, though he was conscious of not leaving other localities unprotected. He said a telegram had been despatched to stations along the border with New South Wales to intercept the offenders should they try to cross the Murray: 'The river is so high that crossing it at any other place than the bridges or punts is impracticable.' Despite taking these steps, Barclay regretted to say there was 'no clue' who the perpetrators were. He supposed they were strangers to the district and were 'still hiding in the ranges within a few miles of where the outrage was committed'. He admitted the scrub was so dense in some places it was scarcely passable. The offenders would 'have to come out to purchase or obtain provisions and I feel that they cannot long elude the vigilance of the police'. He ventured it was 'probable that the offenders may be sheltered and secured by some of the shanty keepers in the locality'.

The police had concluded they were dealing with what they called 'the criminal class'. Many criminals in the colony were repeat offenders, and if they were impoverished it was unsurprising that others who were also struggling came to identify with them and assist them. But it seems odd that Barclay thought shanty-keepers in the district would aid strangers, people with whom they had no bond; and the perpetrators of the crimes in Wooragee had attacked humble folk, not the rich. The post office store and the hotel were not grand establishments. Barclay reiterated to Standish that the offer of a £100 reward would 'procur[e] such information for us as will speedily lead to their apprehension'.

The police were under pressure to apprehend the offenders. They initially suspected two men: Frederick Melthorpe, who had been acquitted of cattlestealing in Beechworth in August 1872, and Frederick Harper, who had been convicted on two counts of larceny, the second in Beechworth just four months before. But both men were soon discounted.

The police thought they had cracked the case on 18 October when they took two other men into custody. John Hartley and Edward Sams had the right form. On 13 October 1862, almost ten years earlier to the day, they had raided a farm on the Indigo Creek at Albury Gap. Their physiques fitted the descriptions of the two men who had committed what was already being called the Wooragee Outrage: Sams was relatively tall, just under five-foot nine, and Hartley quite short. A shoemaker and stone-cutter by trade born in 1833 in Cork, Sams was about the right age. Their modus operandi in 1862 resembled that used in Wooragee on 15 October 1872. Armed with a doubled-barrelled pistol, Sams had fired two shots at a man working for the farmer, one taking the hat clean off his head without drawing blood. Hartley had turned the farmer's own gun on him, only being disarmed after a scuffle. Sams and Hartley had threatened to 'blow out the brains' of the farmer and his employee, the very same threat that had been used in Wooragee. In the end, they had fled without any loot. In a striking coincidence, two constables had arrested them on the Beechworth road near the Rising Sun Hotel in, of all places, Wooragee.[4] Both men had been convicted of highway robbery under arms in October 1862, Sams receiving a ten-year prison sentence and Hartley a seven-year sentence. The latter had left prison in August 1867, but Sams was discharged from Pentridge in mid-May 1872, only five months before the attack on Wooragee.

It is easy to see why the police thought they had their men. The fit was uncanny. But it soon became apparent that nothing tied Sams and Hartley to the Wooragee Outrage and they were released. It was now four days since the bushrangers had rampaged through Wooragee and the police were no closer to pinning them down. This lack of progress sent ripples of unease through the state. Where and who were the assailants, and what were they going to do next? Newspapers across the colonies were following the Wooragee Outrage and some police stations seemed as worried as the public. The officer in charge of the station in Sale sent a telegram to Standish, asking for descriptions of the two wanted men and 'information reporting probabilities of [them] making this way'.[5]

With anxiety mounting, it was Constable Anthony Strahan in Eldorado who made the much-needed breakthrough on Saturday 19 October. Policemen were often on necessarily close, even intimate, terms with the shady and sometimes outright criminal members of society. With so much discussion in the district about what had happened in Wooragee, Anthony suddenly remembered that Peter Brady, a farmer from Chiltern, had told him on the very day of the Wooragee Outrage that one of his sons, Thomas, and several other men, including his son's workmate James Smith, had been intending to stick up the coach carrying gold from Eldorado, shooting the accompanying constable in an ambush. As the constable who normally acted as the escort for the Eldorado coach, Anthony noted Peter Brady's claim, though he first dismissed it as hot air. He was distracted over the next few days by other matters, including his appearance at the circuit court in Beechworth on 17 October in the Ah Wah case. However, with the general description of the assailants in the Wooragee incident in wide circulation, he decided that perhaps Smith and Brady had been deadly serious about committing a robbery, one way or another.

Anthony walked into Sergeant Chadwick's office at the Eldorado station and told him about his suspicions. Chadwick agreed that the threat to hold up the escort suggested that Smith and Brady could be the perpetrators of the Wooragee Outrage. Why was Peter Brady dobbing in one of his sons? Anthony knew the Brady and Smith families. He and Chadwick rode out to the Brady farm at Skelton Creek near Chiltern, aware the two young men sometimes stayed there. The policemen questioned Peter Brady about Thomas, getting evasive and contradictory answers. Asked whether his son was at home, Peter replied no. Asked when his son had last been at home, Peter said Tom had left the house on Monday 14 October and returned early on Wednesday 16 October. Anthony searched the place and found a locked box. He asked for the key, threatening otherwise to break the box open. Peter confessed his son would return in the afternoon to split a log and asked the policemen to come back then. Sensing they might be on to something, Chadwick sent Anthony to Chiltern to fetch another constable while he kept watch on old man Brady.

When Anthony and Constable John Nixon returned to the farm, Thomas Brady had indeed appeared. Anthony realised that Tom was wearing a net on his hat similar to that the residents of Wooragee had said one of the assailants had been using to disguise himself. After removing the net from Tom's hat, he searched the younger Brady's bedroom, finding a box of shots and caps and a green veil. Astoundingly, Thomas hadn't removed these incriminating items, perhaps wrongly believing the law would not catch up with him. Anthony noticed two horses, one brown and the other black, in the paddock beside the house – they fitted the descriptions of the horses used in the raid. Anthony knew the horses belonged to Thomas and James Smith, having often seen the young men riding them. He also suspected that they had been stolen in New South Wales.

Armed with this evidence, Anthony, Sergeant Chadwick and Constable Nixon rode across to the woodcutters' campsite at Watchbox Swamp, taking Thomas Brady with them. The three policemen had good reason to be toey. Brady and Smith had likely committed a violent attack, grievously wounding a man. Smith was apparently armed and dangerous, and he had been accompanied by a third as-yet-unknown man. Anthony and his colleagues did not know what to expect. Would Smith resist arrest, forcing the police to draw their revolvers? Would more blood be spilt? Most officers rarely if ever used their firearms in the course of discharging their duties, and nothing on the record indicates that Anthony had yet fired his revolver while on duty, let alone in a gunfight. As a policeman, he understood it was vital to know as much as he could about what he was up against, assessing character, motive and risk, but the information at hand was often incomplete, sketchy or contradictory, leaving him to deal with unpredictable situations. Everything we know about Anthony's character, with its pugnacious streak, suggests he would have responded vigorously if he was confronted by a violent or armed offender.

The policemen soon realised they had no cause for concern. They found Brady and Smith at Watchbox Swamp at the woodcutters' mia mia, a temporary shelter made of branches, bark and leaves, with William Happenstein. Anthony interrogated the three men separately. By this time, the young woodcutters were far from belligerent. Were they stunned by what they had done and horrified that they had been tracked down so quickly? Anthony told Smith that he fitted the description of the man who had fired at John Watt in Wooragee with intent to kill on Tuesday 15 October. He asked him where he had slept on Monday and Tuesday nights. Smith said he had spent Monday night at old man Brady's house and Tuesday night at Deep Creek with Tom Brady and William Happenstein. Anthony questioned Happenstein next, who claimed that he had spent both nights at the Brady house in the company of Tom Brady and James Smith. Brady gave the same account as Smith. Anthony knew they were lying. Not only were the three accounts inconsistent, but Peter Brady had already told Anthony and Chadwick only hours ago that Tom and his friends had not slept at the house near Skeleton Creek on Monday night.

Chadwick told the three men they would be charged with attempted highway robbery and they were placed in the Chiltern lock-up. On Sunday 20 October, they were moved to the Beechworth lock-up. The case against them was mounting: a young Wooragee girl, Alice Morgan, had just handed in a crucial piece of evidence, a canister containing mixed shot, which she found under a wattle tree near her aunt's house, not far from the hotel. Worse, old man Brady and his other son, Peter junior, had confirmed the brown and the black horses did indeed belong to Tom and James.

8

CHAIN REACTION

The police believed Thomas Brady and James Smith were related, the sons of former convicts. They learnt that Smith had recently returned to the Ovens district after serving time in New South Wales for armed robbery. They were right: the two men were cousins, and Smith was a convicted felon. But unlike most bushrangers, they were not from convict stock.

Peter Brady and Hugh Smith arrived in Sydney in January 1840 on the *Crusader* from Dublin with another 190 government-assisted migrants. Smith was an illiterate Catholic farm worker from County Cavan in Ireland, and he disembarked in Sydney alone. Peter Brady was a Catholic carpenter from Cavan. He came ashore with his wife, Catherine, and their six children. Thomas had been born on board shortly before the ship docked in Sydney.

Peter and Hugh both settled close to Goulburn in southern New South Wales. Each farmed the land but found the going hard. Supporting a large family, Peter Brady was the first to quit, moving south in 1853 during the goldrush in the Ovens district. He put down roots at Skeleton Creek, a name to send shivers down the spine. Perhaps this was an omen, for life continued to be tough. Peter set up a farm, what the police later described as 'a small piece of ground', and worked the local diggings. However, like so many others, his mining efforts proved fruitless. He was declared insolvent in 1867, with debts of £91 but assets of only £3, suggesting his family was living in penury. By this time, Thomas would have been twenty-seven, and it must have been hard to see his father fall so low. Not surprisingly, the Brady marriage was disintegrating under the strain. Peter took action against his wife in the Chiltern police court, applying for Catherine to be bound over to keep the peace – that is, agree not to trouble her husband.

Peter felt he was at the bottom of the social ladder. His measly farm would never lift his family out of poverty and mining had only led to ruination. A brief stint driving carts also turned out to be unprofitable. No matter what he did, he seemed doomed to fail. He must have felt a corrosive mixture of despair and anger.

The year 1872 proved to be the family's annus horribilis. Suffering from heart disease, Catherine collapsed and died on the Beechworth road outside Chiltern on 30 January. Peter was now seventy-three, widowed and impoverished. His two youngest sons, Thomas and Peter, were still living with him, though the former intermittently. Peter junior went broke in July, adding to the family's woes.[1]

Confronted with the grinding challenge of earning an honest quid by farming a marginal plot, Peter junior had been dabbling in illegal activities for some time. Back in 1864, police officers had suspected that Peter junior and Thomas had stuck up a Chinese miner, Ah How, but lacked the evidence to press a charge. The police had concluded that the Bradys were 'men of very questionable character'. The two apparently stayed clear of the law over the next eight years, whether by sticking to non-criminal means of making a living or sheer good luck. However, by late 1872 Thomas was in a downward spiral. He was thirty-two, unmarried and going nowhere. On 21 August, he appeared before the Beechworth police court on a charge of drunkenness. Having spent the night in the lock-up, he was discharged without further penalty. But his drinking continued. He appeared before the police court for a second time on 11 September on another drunkenness charge. This time he had been in the lock-up for an entire day, but the magistrate still imposed an additional sentence, a fine of 5 shillings or another twelve hours in the lock-up. Did Thomas decide to join his cousin in raiding Wooragee because he felt like life's loser? Or was he simply reverting to bad habits?

Hugh Smith was also caught in a cycle of hardship and failure. Several McCabes were on board *The Crusader*. Smith married one of the McCabe women, Anne, an illiterate laundry maid, in Campbelltown in June 1846, linking together three Irish Catholic families. By 1856, he and Anne were providing for five children. Perhaps influenced by Peter, Hugh moved to Victoria as well, stopping at Black Dog Creek, not far from Skeleton Creek. He soon gave up fossicking for gold, working instead as a carter, driving a wagon over Mount Pilot to the Ovens goldfields. The Smith family moved from place to place, finally settling at Eldorado, where Hugh ran a small farm. Anne gave birth to their eighth child in 1863. The Smiths were holding things together, just, but calamity struck in February 1864. With her husband at work and the older children at school, Anne was at home with her two youngest. Somehow a fire started and got out of control. Anne saved her children, but she was terribly burned. She fought hard to live but tetanus set in, and she died eleven days later, at the age of thirty-eight.

Anne's death hit the family hard, but none more so than her eldest son, James, then fourteen. Within three years, James Smith was working for Thomas Gidley, a local squatter, former publican and butcher. Gidley would come to play a decisive role in the young man's life, helping to put him on the track towards a life of crime.

Even if he came by most of his money by honest means, Gidley, born in County Cork in 1829, was a tough operator and seemingly willing to cross the line, purloining a few cattle and sheep here and there to increase his own holdings and at times not paying his employees. Despite the best efforts of the prosecutor, Charles Smyth, two juries acquitted Gidley of cattle stealing in 1863. Smyth and Gidley would become bitter enemies, clashing in the courts over the next decade. The police and many squatters and farmers in the Ovens district nursed a grudge, believing Gidley had evaded justice. Five-foot five, he was pugnacious, prone to heavy drinking and given to abusive language. He didn't back away from a fight, literally; his nose was broken at some point in one. Many wanted to see him behind bars.

In 1866, Gidley made the most audacious move of his life by acquiring the Eldorado West run. He now counted among the biggest landowners in the district. James was doing odd jobs around the run and saw a few things. On 27 January 1867, Gidley was brought before the Chiltern police court on five counts of cattle-stealing. Denied bail, he was placed in Beechworth Gaol. Revealing his substantial means, he hired Richard Ireland QC, a former attorney-general of Victoria (and a well-known bon vivant), as his barrister on a retainer of 150 guineas. The trial on the first count took place at the circuit court in Beechworth before Justice Barry, with the same prosecutor, Charles Smyth, this time determined to get his man. The prosecution's star witness was none other than James Smith.

After a hearing lasting five hours, the jury took another hour to acquit Gidley. *The Advertiser* was unsurprised: 'Even where his testimony appeared credible, [Smith] had come so freshly – in fact, straight into the witness box – from the hands of the police, he had apparently been so well schooled, and seemed so manifestly to be seeking a conviction at all hazards that the jury would have none of him ... no sensible and unprejudiced person who heard his evidence would hang a dog upon it.'

Smyth was appalled by the verdict and asked for the remaining cases to be moved to Melbourne. James Smith, only seventeen, was again critical to the prosecution's prospects of nailing Gidley. However, Smith failed to show, perhaps because he had been brought before the circuit court in Beechworth on 13 April on a charge of obtaining goods under false pretences. An agitated Smyth asked for the trial to be delayed for several weeks until his witness could be located. However, it soon became clear that Smith had absconded to New South Wales, leaving the prosecution's case to collapse. Gidley walked free again, and Smyth was furious. In a blazing editorial on 11 June, *The Advertiser* was indignant. It was 'notorious that a very strong feeling as to Gidley's guilt prevails, and that his continued escapes from the hands of justice are openly deplored'. Yet these escapes were due to 'the manner in which the cases have been brought up – recklessly, regardless of expense, with a foregone conclusion, and with unreliable, tutored and almost vindictive evidence'.

The paper saw a broader point: 'If crime is to be arrested in an English community it will not be by persecution.' As an Irishman, Gidley no doubt felt persecution was an English specialty inflicted more often on him and his countrymen. Gidley had escaped the wrath of the law, but his young offsider was now on the run.

James Smith had inadvertently become the reason for the failure to convict a squatter widely thought to be guilty. But he had good reason to be concerned about the effort to prosecute Thomas Gidley: he had likely played a role in his employer's cattle duffing and could have ended up in prison himself. And becoming a police stooge to stay out of prison was an unwelcome alternative.

Smith headed into southern New South Wales in May or June 1867. He was drawn to the area around Goulburn, where many of his mother's family, the McCabes, lived. Two uncles, two aunts and around twenty cousins were settled in the region, mostly farming. He could have retreated into this safe family network, making a fresh start. Instead, he quickly hooked in with two others who were only going to get him into even more trouble: John Irvine Scott, alias Jack the Devil, and John Lewis, commonly known as Black Jack because he was either part Aboriginal or part Pacific Islander.

Within a short time of meeting, the three decided to team up. Scott was the ringleader. He had been a member of the Bluecap Gang that had been marauding across the Levels and the Lower Murrumbidgee for some time. In July 1867, Robert Cottrell, alias Captain Blue Cap, Scott and another gang member had robbed a pub and store on the Levels, taking money, silver and various goods, including grog, powder and caps, guns, clothing and a saddle. A heavy bout of celebratory drinking at a pastoral run had ended acrimoniously and Scott had left the gang.

On 27 August, Smith and his new friends robbed a hawker on a road near Bagdad Station, making off with two watches, a piece of calico, one shirt and eight pounds of tobacco. A day later, they raided a grazier's store at Combaning. Lewis added insult to injury by helping himself to the man's horse. With their loot, they took shelter in a hut on Bagdad Station. On

30 August, the men rode across to Junee and ransacked Henry Williams's hotel, taking £3 and a sizeable quantity of rum, ginger wine and champagne. They returned to their hut for a night of carousing. They had big plans for further raids. Smith didn't know it then, but he was engaging in a dry run for the attack on Wooragee five years later.

The crime spree came to an end the very next day. Senior Constable Ussher and two other Cootamundra policemen happened to be riding through the area on 30 August when they located the bushrangers at the hut near Bagdad. After nightfall, when all was quiet, they crept cautiously up to the hut and waited for morning. At daybreak, they fired two shots into the hut's walls.

Scott surrendered. Smith and Lewis were not willing to give up so easily and absconded into the bush. A chase ensued. Ussher got close and fired his rifle at the young men. Smith stopped and turned around, clutching a revolver, perhaps ready to fight back. However, after some hesitation, he too gave up, throwing his revolver on the ground.

Ussher called on Lewis repeatedly to surrender. But the bushranger raised his arm and levelled a revolver. Ussher yelled out, 'You black dog, are you going to shoot me?' He took aim at Lewis and fired, but missed. Lewis realised the game was up and surrendered.

The policemen searched the hut, finding an impressive array of loot and weapons, including a sixteen-shooter rifle and over 100 rounds. It took two constables to lift the haul onto a horse. The presence of so many weapons suggested the bushrangers had been preparing for a shootout. They were lucky common sense or fear prevailed and they opted not to shoot at the police, or none of them may have seen their next birthday.

On 21 September, the Burrangong police court committed the bushrangers to stand trial on three charges of robbery under arms. Lewis was also charged with stealing a horse, quipping, 'I had a good day's ride out of him.' *The Wagga Wagga Express* was derisive in its assessment of the defendants: 'They were a miserable set of dirty, half-starved looking striplings, and about as great a contrast to the popular ideal of bold dashing highwaymen as could well have been conceived.' Lewis was subjected to an additional level of scorn. In the many reports about the trio's escapades, the newspapers referred to the two white offenders by their names, although they could not resist occasionally calling Scott 'Jack the Devil'. By contrast, they called Lewis 'Black Jack' without fail, not once using his actual name. They routinely employed contemptuous, dehumanising terms, calling him 'a darkie', 'a half caste' or, a little more politely, 'the black fellow'.

The trial in Wagga Wagga on 21 October 1867 before the New South Wales Chief Justice, Sir Alfred Stephen, was brief. The three prisoners pleaded guilty to all charges. Stephen said he trusted none of the accused had been induced to plead guilty in the hope they would receive a lighter sentence. If they had, he intoned, they had indulged in vain expectations. The chief justice had become known for meting out severe sentences. He asked how old the young men were, perhaps considering how likely their prospects of rehabilitation. Scott thought he was seventeen or eighteen. He said he had been born in Tarcutta, adding that his parents were dead. Smith said he would be eighteen next month – even though he had already turned eighteen several weeks before. Lewis didn't know how old he was, but the court assumed he was eighteen. He was more likely only sixteen or seventeen. *The Wagga Wagga Express* was impressed by Scott, describing him as 'a shrewd, intelligent looking fellow' who gave 'quick and ready answers, with pointed sensible replies to all questions'. It was less enthralled by the other two, describing Smith as 'a heavy round-featured lad' and Lewis as 'a stolid looking half-caste'.

Stephen was as unsparing as he had promised. He declared that bushranging had become 'a chronic evil in the land' that had to be quelled with the strong arm of the law. It was a crime in which no courage or gallantry was shown, because the perpetrators took their victims unarmed and at a disadvantage. If resistance was encountered, bloodshed and murder were the likely results. The prisoners had plundered rich and poor alike. What had they ultimately gained? 'They had endured hardships, suffered exposure, been in continual dread of their apprehension, had led a hard, laborious and risky life, and had never been successful after all.' Captain

Thunderbolt was the only bushranger to have escaped justice for any length of time; all others had been either shot, hanged or were undergoing long terms of imprisonment. 'Bushranging is not a profitable trade,' Stephen avowed, 'and this is a fact which cannot be too generally impressed upon the colonial youth.' By confessing their misdeeds, Scott and Smith had made some steps towards reformation. Stephen believed they had told the truth, and he hoped their repentance was sincere. They had pled guilty to crimes that rendered them liable to sixty years' imprisonment. Although it was painful to pass heavy sentences, Stephen declared, he could not do less than sentence them to ten years' imprisonment, with hard labour, for each offence. Yet the sentences would be concurrent; ten years would be 'the extreme limit of their punishment'. The government might decide to mitigate their sentences, and if it did, he would not report unfavourably. It is telling that the chief justice left Lewis to last and said little about his charges, simply applying the same sentence.

James Smith and his collaborators were taken to Goulburn Gaol, before being transferred to Parramatta Gaol in August 1868. As Stephen had anticipated, the government showed leniency and released Smith and Lewis in June 1872. The two each served less than five years, though Scott spent somewhat longer inside, no doubt as he was seen as the ringleader.

Five years in prison would have been hard, and they apparently did nothing to reform Smith's character. Shortly after he was discharged from Parramatta, he robbed a store and stole a horse, heading south across the Murray to his family in northeast Victoria. When he turned up some weeks later, his father, Hugh, was still working as a carter and trying to make a go of his farm. Although the two older daughters had married and moved out, the other five children, aged between nine and nineteen, were living with their father.

James Smith had a family network to fall back on again and could have opted to go straight, but he was illiterate and had a chequered employment history, along with a criminal record. The die was cast. In the weeks before descending on Wooragee on 15 October, he roped in his cousin, Thomas Brady, and possibly other members of the Brady family into committing a series of crimes. The two young men were united by a burning, belligerent sense that fate was against them. They had both seen their fathers struggle, turning their hands to different trades in a grim, desperate bid to get ahead, but fail time after time. In September and October 1872, they stole several horses around the Ovens district, sending them into New South Wales, and robbed a Chinese miner, taking food and other goods from his hut (Anthony Strahan found some of these items when he searched the Brady hut on 19 October). These offences did not involve firearms; the raid on Wooragee represented a serious escalation.

Even though he was nine years younger than Thomas Brady, Smith took the lead in these crimes, using the tactics he had learnt five years earlier with John Scott and John Lewis. If anything, he had returned to Victoria a more violent man. Outside the hut on the Bagdad Station, he had thought about shooting Senior Constable Ussher, but had wisely backed down. Perhaps he drew the wrong lesson from the encounter. He had hesitated to shoot then, but he certainly didn't waver when it came to pulling the trigger when John Watt was fleeing down the hallway of the Wooragee Hotel. This was to be his downfall.

The *Advertiser* had stated that Watt appeared to be rallying. Dr Walsh knew better. He attended Watt regularly, sometimes visiting him twice a day, and twice spending the night beside his patient's bed. Walsh would have cleaned out and perhaps cauterised Watt's wound before binding his torso tightly in bandages. Decades before the discovery of penicillin, infection was the biggest danger. His family and friends likely prayed for his recovery, but Watt showed little sign of responding to treatment. Ellen was distraught.

The Victoria Police had arrested the perpetrators of the attack on Wooragee, but they lacked enough direct evidence, including the murder weapon, to make charges stick. On 21 October, Superintendent Barclay held an identification parade in the yard of the Beechworth police station, mixing in the three arrested men with several townsfolk. William Jarvis, the bullock-driver who had been in the Wooragee post office when it had been robbed, picked out Smith's voice as the same as that of the man who threatened him, but was unwilling to positively identify Smith. Still, it was enough. Smith, Brady and Happenstein, all dressed as bushmen, appeared in the Beechworth police court. A large crowd gathered to catch a glimpse of the suspects. With four justices of the peace presiding, including landowner George Graham, and Dr Henry Fox, who had removed the slug from John Kennedy's left arm, the police charged the three men with robbery under arms and attempted murder.

According to *The Advertiser*, Smith, with 'an overhanging forehead and a rather determined-looking mouth', regarded proceedings with 'an air of apparent unconcern' while Brady, a short, stout man, was 'almost expressionless'. Smith's apparent indifference was surely feigned and Brady's perhaps suggested shock rather than a lack of feeling. Or maybe they thought a display of indifference would indicate their innocence. The third accused didn't hide his apprehension: a 'tall dark man, with almost forbidding cast of countenance', William Happenstein 'seemed very nervous, his eyes shifting from place to place, and having that peculiar startled gaze resembling in some degree that of a wild beast anxious to escape from its pursuers'. To *The Advertiser*, his 'wild restless glances' were due to the fact he was a bushman 'unused to the busy haunts of man'. This conclusion oddly missed the obvious point: Happenstein knew he was in deep trouble. The three men were remanded in custody to appear before the court again on 28 October.[2]

Barclay was worried that the identification parade had proved inconclusive and informed the detective branch in Melbourne that his officers were looking for corroborative evidence. He remained convinced that the offer of a £100 reward would help to crack the case and asked Chief Commissioner Standish in two urgent telegrams on 22 October if the Chief Secretary had approved the reward. Ellen Watt had engaged William Zincke, the Beechworth solicitor who had represented the obstreperous and wily squatter Thomas Gidley in 1867, to represent her husband. Barclay noted that Zincke strongly concurred with this course of action and said 'other persons were likely to be implicated' in what had transpired in Wooragee.

Meanwhile, Constable Anthony Strahan had discovered that John Lewis, alias Black Jack, had come south with his old mate James Smith after they had been released from Parramatta Gaol. He traced Lewis to the Phillips brickyard at One Mile Creek near Wangaratta on the evening of 22 October and arrested him on suspicion of being involved in the Wooragee Outrage, incarcerating him in the Wangaratta lock-up. *The Advertiser* reported that Lewis was a wood splitter by trade, adding that he and Smith had been 'companions of the chain in the sister colony'. Although it used his actual name in its reports, unlike the newspapers in New South Wales five years earlier, *The Advertiser* described Lewis in similarly lurid terms, as 'a dark, swarthy, villainous-looking fellow'. A day after the arrest, Barclay informed Standish by telegram that the new prisoner, 'a darkie [from the] isles of France', would be placed in another identification parade to see if someone from Wooragee could confirm that he had been involved in the Outrage.

It is unsurprising that Barclay employed derogatory language in such an unreflective way. Such terminology was embedded in the mental furniture of most of the population; it was rarely questioned. Barclay's message confirmed one thing: Lewis was not Aboriginal. At least one of his parents was almost certainly a labourer taken from either New Caledonia or the New Hebrides (now Vanuatu) during the infamous 'blackbirding' trade. Without disclosing where it was getting its information from, *The Advertiser* claimed that Watt had described the man who shot him as 'dark … in appearance almost like a half-caste'. Such a man had been working for Watt some time ago, *The Advertiser* alleged, and the publican had initially thought it was his former employee on the verandah when he had opened the hotel's front door, exclaiming, 'Hullo George.'[3]

In his update for Standish on 23 October, Barclay emphasised that the stakes had been raised – John Watt was 'sinking fast'. It was now clear that he would not survive. *The Advertiser* got wind of Watt's imminent demise too, reporting that 'no hopes were entertained of his recovery'. This meant the accused were about to face a murder charge.

Barclay decided to take the four prisoners to Wooragee on 23 October, accompanied by several constables, to place them before the publican to see if he could identify the man who had shot him. Watt was lying in his bed at the Wooragee Hotel, horribly weak and barely able to speak. With two senior members of the local community – George Graham and Reverend William Howard, the minister of Beechworth's Anglican Christ Church – looking on as witnesses, the police brought Brady into the bedroom first. Watt said he did not think this was the man who had shot him. When Happenstein was ushered into the room, Watt was certain, stating, 'That is not the man at all. He is much taller than the man who fired the gun.' By the time Smith was brought into the room, Watt had become even more feeble, speaking in a faint voice, partially, it seemed, to himself. Graham lifted the curtain to let more light into the room and Watt turned his head, looked at Smith and mumbled a few unintelligible words. Howard bent down, close to the pillow, and heard Watt say, 'That is very much like the man who shot me.'[4] The police had what they needed.

John Watt died shortly after 4am on 25 October. He was thirty-nine and had been married for thirteen years. He had no children, leaving Ellen alone. *The Advertiser* noted that his death had 'caused a thrill of horror and indignation throughout the district' – the wretches who had killed him were regarded with 'the utmost detestation'.[5]

Only hours after Watt had died, James Alley, the police magistrate and warden of the local goldfields, convened a coronial inquest in Wooragee before a jury of twelve local men, including William Jarvis. The inclusion of Jarvis underscored the tightly knit nature of the local community, but it was odd, even improper, given he could be a witness in any future proceedings. The four accused were present, standing awkwardly to one side. Barclay declared that he had brought the prisoners to the inquest because the evidence might affect them and they should therefore be given a chance to question the witnesses if they chose to do so. But was this proper or fair? Smith, Brady, Happenstein and Lewis were being placed in plain view of the very people who would be testifying in a trial. Simply their presence suggested that the four men were the right suspects, even that they were guilty. Surely this undercut the presumption of innocence.

After explaining that no one could be charged before a coroner's jury, Alley called Ellen Watt as the first witness. She testified that the night of 15 October had been light and she had been able to discern the forms, though not the exact features, of the two men who had walked past the front gate before the knock on the hotel's front door. She stated that she had seen 'people here today who might represent them'. Standing up, she regarded the four prisoners steadily. 'I believe that the first man [James Smith] was the man who passed first, carrying the gun, and the third man [Thomas Brady] was the one who followed.' Ellen admitted, though, that she could not swear that Smith and Brady were the two men; they 'only resemble them'. This was a pretty shaky identification. Ellen said the first man had been carrying something, but she was unable to tell if it was a gun. Her husband had told her that the first man had a gun. Kennedy and Frazer recalled that they had heard a gunshot before Watt staggered into the kitchen bleeding profusely, but both admitted they had not seen who was at the door.

Dr Walsh told the inquest that he had had 'very little hope from the first' that Watt would survive. Indeed, on the first night he had thought the publican would surely faint and pass into unconsciousness had he tried to sit up in bed. He had told Watt that he was in danger of immediate death and the publican had made his will and two dying declarations. Unable to write because he was so weak, Watt had instead made his mark on the three documents. Walsh testified that the gunshot had fractured Watt's eighth and ninth ribs and caused a heavy loss of blood. Noting that he and a second doctor, William Dobbyn, had extracted pieces of slug or shot from between Watt's skin and ribs, he said he had no doubt that the wound had caused Watt's death.

In summing up, Alley said it was reasonable to conclude that the deceased had died from a gunshot wound, but that it was not yet possible to determine who had inflicted the wound. After a short consultation, the jury found that 'John Watt came by his death at Wooragee, in the colony of Victoria, on the 25th day of October from a gunshot wound inflicted by some party or parties unknown'.[6] He was buried in Beechworth Cemetery on 27 October, with a Presbyterian minister conducting the rites.

With the prisoners back in the Beechworth lock-up, Barclay informed Standish that the inquest had delivered an open verdict. He noted that only two of the witnesses he would call during a trial had so far been prepared to state that they could identify Smith or Brady. Several others were fairly satisfied that Smith and Brady were the culprits but would not yet swear to it. Revealing that he was becoming increasingly nervous about the lack of conclusive evidence and the possibility that any prosecution might fail, Barclay broached offering a pardon to one of the men in custody if they would testify. He said he would ask for yet another remand in the Beechworth police court later that day. He urged Standish to send the bills up to Beechworth by 31 October so he could place advertisements in local newspapers and get his officers to put up posters around the district.

Barclay was not the only one becoming agitated. Other people in the town were getting het up, and Barclay sent a follow-up telegram to Standish, shorter but sharper in tone, stating that the press and the public were 'anxious' to know about the proposed reward.[7]

Standish was stung into action. Writing to the Chief Secretary, James Francis, he affirmed that the police likely had the men responsible for the Wooragee Outrage in custody 'but there is some doubt entertainable as to the completeness of identification of one of the men' and recommended 'the immediate offer of a government reward of £100 for such information as will lead to the conviction of the offenders'. Standish gave extensive descriptions of the two offenders, no doubt to reassure Francis that the police were not acting on a whim. The reward was approved without hesitation. Two hundred posters were despatched to Beechworth on the 6am train on 29 October.[8]

With the reward posters up around the northeast, Smith, Brady, Happenstein and Lewis were brought before the Beechworth police court on 31 October in a committal hearing. The proceedings would take up the best part of two days. Watt's death had created a sensation around the case and the courthouse was packed. *The Advertiser* was somewhat scandalised: 'Amongst those present were persons from all parts of the district, not forgetting a fair sprinkling of females, and a considerable infusion of the juvenile element – some of the parents of Beechworth evidently being of opinion ... that a trial for murder is calculated to have a beneficial effect on the minds of the rising generation'. The bench was unusually full, with six justices of the peace joining the police magistrate 'giving the dais a somewhat animated appearance'.

Barclay stepped forward as the police prosecutor. He immediately asked for the fourth accused, John Lewis, to be discharged on the basis that the police had established that he had not been involved in any way in the Wooragee Outrage. Lewis left the dock with some relief, but he was promptly re-arrested outside the courthouse for stealing a pony from Mary Johnson at her hotel in Junee, southern New South Wales, on 24 September. He had already provided useful information about the accused, and Barclay was hopeful of obtaining more.

With Lewis under arrest for a less serious offence, Barclay charged Smith, Brady and Happenstein with robbing Henry Gale under arms. He amended the second charge – shooting John Watt with intent to kill – to wilful murder. If found guilty, the three men would hang.

Over the next two days, a series of witnesses, including Anthony Strahan, set out the evidence against the accused. Peter and Catherine Mitchell testified that two men had stolen a shotgun from their hut and that Smith and Brady resembled those men. Henry Gale recounted how the same men had threatened to shoot him on the Wooragee road. Although he admitted that the faces of his assailants were 'disfigured' by their disguises, the gloomy night and the trees, he said, 'I have an idea that Thomas Brady was the man who stood in front of me with the pistol ... there is some resemblance in the stature of the man'. Ellen Watt said her husband had given her a good description of the two men who had attacked him: the taller man had high cheekbones and light-coloured hair on his chin; the shorter man had a sandy complexion. Smith and Brady fitted these descriptions. She noted that the clothes produced in court were those worn by her husband when he had been shot, though she had washed them before giving them to the police. Thomas Frazer and John Kennedy described the attack, Kennedy saying he had been shot in the left arm when one of the men had blasted Watt.

The younger Peter Brady tried to shift the blame away from his brother, even if that meant implicating his cousin. He testified that Smith and Happenstein had told him they were considering stealing horses from the other side of the river, asking him if he would move the horses on. Thomas had not been present during this conversation. More damningly, he claimed Smith had once remarked to him that he was 'not particular as to whether he stuck up anybody or not', though he had not mentioned holding up the Eldorado gold escort. Peter said he had informed Constable Strahan about this comment before the Wooragee Outrage. He also recalled that he had ridden out to the campsite at Watchbox Swamp on 10 October with rations for his brother and his workmates, but Happenstein had told him 'they had enough to do them for a while'. Peter had sat down and had a cup of tea, asking where the tea had come from. Happenstein had revealed that he, Thomas and James Smith had gone to the campsite of a Chinese man, taking what provisions they needed. Peter testified that Ah Hing had later approached him stating that he had been robbed. This last story implicated all three accused, but the balance of Peter's testimony painted Happenstein and Smith as the real miscreants.

William Jarvis had no doubts about who had accosted him when he opened the door of the post office. He was adamant it had been Smith who had called him a wretch and threatened to blow out his brains. He declared that he had picked out Smith in the line-up at the Beechworth police station without hesitation. Smith had carried the gun the whole time he was in the Gales' store, Jarvis continued, before heading off with Brady down the road. Asked how he could recognise Smith, Jarvis said he had made out his whiskers and hair through the handkerchief he had been using to disguise himself. He testified that he had followed the trail of two unshod horses with Sergeant Thomas Baber and Constable Patrick

Mullane on 17 October – he had grown up in the bush and knew how to track horses. The tracks had gone into Rat's Castle, a flat at the back of the Lady Franklin Ranges, turning off at a sawpit in the direction of the Pilot Ranges. 'After that we lost the trail. The trail did not seem to be more than two days old … No rain had fallen since the tracks had been made.' Jarvis had gone into the Pilot Ranges for a second time with Detective Joseph Brown on 29 October, he said. They had found abandoned coats and other clothing.[9]

The first day of the committal hearing came to a close and Smith, Brady and Happenstein were returned to Beechworth Gaol. The proceedings had not gone well for the accused, but it was generally agreed that the case against Happenstein was the weakest. Perhaps to cover their bases, the police charged Happenstein and his wife, Peter Brady senior and Peter Brady junior with larceny from a dwelling. When the hearing reopened on the morning of 1 November, the police decided it was time to rattle the accused, breaking through their apparent insouciance. Before the three men were brought into the courtroom, a police officer placed the canister of shot that had been used in the Wooragee raid on the barristers' table. As he commenced the proceedings, Barclay picked up the canister, almost inadvertently, and shook it in full view of the accused. The effect of this theatrical gesture was 'electrical', according to *The Advertiser*: 'Smith's jaw dropped, as if unable to breathe, his chest rising and falling so strongly as to be perceptible to the eye at a considerable distance. After an apparently violent struggle, he succeeded in regaining his composure.' Brady and Happenstein were also 'visibly affected by the sight of the canister'.

After this contrived but effective opening gambit, Barclay called Sergeant Baber to the stand. The 41-year-old Baber was something of a rarity in the force, for he was born in England. He had been working as a policeman in Victoria for nearly twenty years, winning high praise from his superiors. Baber told the court that he and Jarvis had followed the tracks of the two unshod horses descending from the Old Sydney Road, through the ranges around Rat's Castle, past a deserted hut and sawpit, to the Watchbox Swamp. Arthur Jessop, a local boy, had been sitting on the verandah of his home near Chiltern early on 16 October when he had seen two men galloping towards Chiltern at about 6am. He testified that he had later gone to the Brady paddock with Superintendent Barclay, Constable Strahan and Detective Christie to help pick out the horses the two men had been riding.

If Peter Brady junior tried to shift the blame away from his brother, Peter senior boosted the prosecution's case, shifting the blame back on to Tom. It was almost as if he was trying to dob in his son. He stated that Tom and his mates had not slept at his house on the nights of 14 and 15 October. Rather, they had all returned on the morning of 16 October. The horses in question belonged to Tom and James.

Anthony Strahan was the last witness. He stated that he knew the three accused: 'I received information of the Wooragee Outrage and went in search of the offenders.' He replayed the conversations he had had with the accused at the campsite, when they had given evasive and contradictory accounts of their movements over 14 and 15 October. He testified that he had found a brown net, a green veil and a box of shot and caps at the home of Peter Brady senior. Finally, he recalled that he had identified the two horses used by Thomas Brady and James Smith in an adjacent paddock. With Anthony's testimony, Barclay brought the prosecution's case to a close. The accused were asked if they wanted to question the witnesses, but they remained silent. The bench swiftly committed them to face trial before the circuit court for wilful murder and robbery under arms.[10]

Barclay wrote, with no small amount of satisfaction and relief, to Standish on 1 November, affirming that they had the right men in custody: 'Everything points towards the men having commenced a life of depredation and serious crime in this colony, which has happily been checked this early.' He praised the zeal and efficiency of his officers, whose indefatigable efforts, including many arduous rides, had traced the offenders and secured valuable corroborative information, establishing 'a satisfactory chain of circumstantial evidence'. He underlined the excellent service of Sergeant Chadwick and Constable Strahan, who had apprehended the offenders. The accused had not robbed the rich; he pointed out that the witnesses from Wooragee were all poor and he had had to convey them to Beechworth for the hearing by coach. He was quick to reassure Standish that the expense had been necessary.

Standish replied quickly: 'It affords me great gratification to see that the members of the Force engaged in the case have displayed so much zeal and intelligence in tracking the perpetrators of this most grave offence – and that too in the face of great difficulty.' The Ovens police had always had a reputation for efficiency and the Wooragee Outrage had confirmed that standing. He asked Barclay to convey 'his hearty recognition of their meritorious conduct' and extended his special thanks to Barclay himself for everything he had done, including in the police court. Last, he stressed that he was sure all due regard had been paid in expending funds during the investigation, adding that 'the gravity of the crime and the anxiety felt by the public would have justified almost any expense'.[11]

Standish was right to hold off on any premature celebrations. Although the evidence against the accused looked damning, the prosecution case still had serious, possibly fatal, holes, especially the absence of the murder weapon. On 2 November, Anthony Strahan rode out of Eldorado in search of the shotgun that had been used to shoot Watt. Oddly, Peter Brady junior accompanied him. The two men rode across a good portion of the district in search of the weapon. What was Peter up to? He had tried to shift the blame from his brother during the committal hearing, and now he was out riding with a constable trying to locate the crucial piece of evidence.

Anthony rode nearly 100 kilometres on 5 November and another 145 kilometres on 6 November, to no avail. The gun remained elusive. His troop horse was exhausted and he hired a private horse to continue the quest on 7 November, but his efforts again came to nil.

Back in Eldorado, he received a bill from Peter Brady, asking for £1 for every day that he had been in the saddle ostensibly aiding the search for the gun. So Peter's motive for accompanying Anthony was at least partly pecuniary. The Brady family was struggling, and it is unsurprising that Peter had tried to make a quid or two out of the job. Another thought about Peter's motives springs to mind. Given the search had failed, had he been leading Anthony on a wild goose chase, guiding him to the wrong areas?

Anthony's persistence nonetheless paid off on 9 November. Sergeant Chadwick and Anthony led a search party on Robert Reid's Wooragee run, around a kilometre from the clearing where the three accused had camped at Watchbox Swamp. After scouring through a large area, Reid's overseer, Michael Canny, found the gun and a powder flask hidden in a hollow log. The gun was loaded with a charge of mixed shot. It matched the description of that stolen from Mitchell's hut, having a broken stock tied up with cord. Just as importantly, the shot in the gun closely resembled that which had been both extracted from Watt and found in a canister recovered from Wooragee. *The Advertiser* was triumphant, proclaiming that another link had been made in 'the almost complete chain of circumstantial evidence in the Wooragee murder case'.[12]

Police across the district were finally able to catch their breath for the first time after three frenetic weeks. Barclay, no doubt keen to show his appreciation for Anthony and Sergeant Chadwick but aware it was too early to recommend rewards for his officers over this case when the trial was still months off, wrote to Standish on 14 November to recommend both men receive £2 rewards for their efforts in apprehending the thief Ah Wah back in August. But this recommendation didn't mean Barclay was going to give Anthony a free pass. Barclay had always paid due regard to economy. He asked Anthony why he had not been riding his troop horse on 7 November, incurring the cost of hiring a private horse. Anthony explained that his troop horse was simply incapable of continuing the search and Barclay relented, reimbursing him.[13]

Anthony had spent weeks pursuing Watt's killers, first arresting the suspects and then riding long distances to find crucial evidence, leaving little time for anything else. At the end of November, he was gratified when he was informed that Standish had approved the £2 rewards for himself and Chadwick. Though given everything that had happened since, the Ah Wah case must have seemed like small beer.

Anthony finally had a chance to pause and take stock of his life. His son, Anthony Oliver, turned one on 11 December and he knew that he had to sort out his relationship with Marion Evans. Finally, two years after they had met, Anthony and Marion married on 30 December in the Congregational Parsonage in Eldorado. He was thirty-two and she twenty-two. Although Marion's family, many of whom lived in and around Eldorado, would have been present, it is unknown if any of Anthony's siblings attended. If so, they didn't act as witnesses. Perhaps Eldorado was too far away from Melbourne. Or did some of Anthony's brothers and sisters object to him marrying a woman of convict stock?

Lucy Marshall, one of Marion's friends, and Samuel Wellwood, Anthony's young colleague at the Eldorado station, witnessed the marriage. Wellwood attended the ceremony with his second wife, Elizabeth Gladstone. Samuel would have been a reaffirming friend, for he was another Irish Protestant and only three years younger than Anthony. Strengthening the bond between the Strahans and Wellwoods, Marion and Elizabeth had both given birth in Eldorado in 1871 to their first children. On the marriage certificate, Marion gave Melbourne, not Gravelly Beach in Tasmania, as her birthplace, almost certainly to conceal her parents' convict origins. Melbourne was only fitting for the wife of a colonial policeman.

9

JUDGEMENT DAY

Watt's murder trial commenced before the Beechworth circuit court on 18 April 1873, almost five months after Anthony Strahan had arrested the suspects. In the balance were the lives of the accused, who had been depicted in the press as fearsome bushrangers and brutal killers. The community followed the proceedings with keen interest.

Sixty-year-old Justice Edward Eyre Williams was presiding. Born in Somerset in 1813, Williams migrated to Victoria in 1842, gaining admittance to the colonial bar. After stints as the chief commissioner of insolvent estates and as solicitor-general, he became the second puisne judge of the Supreme Court on 21 July 1852, appointed to address a rising workload. Williams was seen as a capable judge, with *The Argus* opining that he was patient and assiduous. 'Much of his time was spent on circuit,' writes Robert Miller in the *Australian Dictionary of Biography*, 'and he gained a reputation for disposing of his work speedily to maintain a tight schedule of travel, sometimes keeping the court sitting until 2am.'[1] It was fitting that he had presided over the circuit court's first session in Beechworth sixteen years before.

The Advertiser thought both prisoners had 'improved in appearance during their long incarceration awaiting trial' and noted that they delivered their pleas of not guilty in firm voices. Neither could take the stand because Victorian law mandated that an accused could not give sworn evidence on his or her own behalf.

Charles Smyth was the prosecutor once more. He opened by observing that 'a great deal of excitement had been caused by the murder for which the prisoners at the bar were arraigned'. He had been present in the district when the deed was committed and was aware that it had been spoken and written about at great length. He asked the jury to put aside any opinions they might have formed, urging them to adjudge the evidence carefully. The police had shown an 'almost unerring instinct' for following up 'the slight traces' of evidence in connection with a crime that 'at first appeared to be involved in hopeless mystery'. The prosecution's case faced one obvious problem: on the night of the attack, Watt had apparently identified Brady as the man who had fired the shotgun, but several days before his death, he had said it had been Smith who shot him. Smyth dismissed this discrepancy. 'If several men went together to commit a crime, those who aided and abetted were equally guilty in the eye of the law with the actual perpetrator of the deed.'

Smyth called the principal witnesses who had testified at the committal hearing. Although Catherine and Peter Mitchell could not swear that Brady and Smith were the men who had stolen their shotgun, William Jarvis and Margaret Gale were adamant that Smith was one of the two assailants who had robbed the post office. 'I had good opportunities of seeing his face,' Jarvis testified. 'It appeared to be covered with a very thin puggaree. I took particular note of his height, build and everything; I have no doubt that he is the man.' Gale was equally emphatic: 'I do not hesitate for a moment in saying that Smith is the man who came into the store with a gun.' Although he could not see the features of the man who had stuck him on the road, Henry Gale said he knew Brady's voice well, having been acquainted with him for over two and a half of years, supplying him at times with goods.

Brady and Smith's whereabouts on the night of 14 October, the day before the attack on Wooragee, had been something of a mystery. Two new witnesses clarified. Margaret Slocomb, a barmaid at the Telegraph Hotel in Chiltern, said the two men had come in for a drink at about 10pm, staying for about ten minutes. Brady had asked Slocomb if she recognised his companion. She had replied that she had never seen him before. She recalled that Smith had been wearing a drab hat with a black band. Jane Peck, a Scottish immigrant who had come out to Victoria in 1854, had been widowed only three months before the Wooragee Outrage. Her husband's death had left her in a vulnerable position: she was thirty-six and had eight children. She told the court that Brady and another man she did not know had come to her house at 7.30pm, staying for an hour and a half. She was quick to affirm that her house was 'not a public house'. Had Brady called in to see a friend? Was he offering solace? Or had Jane been forced to turn to prostitution to support herself and her children? It was not uncommon for women in difficult circumstances to combine part-time prostitution with other occupations to get by.[2]

Next, Smyth called his star witness: William Happenstein, who had turned against his co-accused and become an informant for the Crown. Barclay's strategy of offering one of the accused a pardon if he turned on his mates had borne fruit. Happenstein testified that Brady had told him and Smith at their campsite on 15 October that they should stick up a store in Wooragee that had £50, claiming the money could be got by prizing a slab off one of the walls. At sundown, Brady and Smith had ridden off through the Pilot Ranges towards Wooragee, but they had soon returned to the camp, saying they wanted Happenstein to look after their horses while they robbed the store. Happenstein attested that the two men had left Watchbox Swamp with a small American axe. This implement would later be mistaken by several people, including Henry Gale, for a pistol. 'When we got near Wooragee,' Happenstein continued, 'the prisoners left me in the scrub, with the horses, and went somewhere'. They had had no firearms at that point. They had come back more than half an hour later, Smith with the axe and Brady with a gun. Happenstein said Brady and Smith had left him in the bush with the horses for a second time, returning forty-five minutes later. It was during this interval that the two had robbed Gale's store.

Happenstein testified that he and his workmates had ridden down a lane towards the Wesleyan chapel before proceeding on foot towards the Wooragee Hotel. Brady had told Happenstein to wait in a paddock behind a fence around 60 yards from the hotel, instructing him to 'slip up and whistle' if he heard horsemen approaching. '[Brady and Smith] went across the road to the hotel; Brady still had the gun; Smith had a dirty white handkerchief across his face … [Brady] had something over his face; I think it was the crepe off his hat.' Happenstein claimed he had heard a gunshot shortly after the two men approached the hotel. Brady and Smith had rushed back to the paddock. Happenstein had asked them if they had shot anyone. 'No,' both men had replied. Brady had taken more ammunition from his breast pocket, reloading the gun. The three fled: 'Smith led the mare I was on as I had bad eyesight.'

Happenstein affirmed that he had decided to 'unbosom' himself in January 1873 when he had spoken to a clergyman in Beechworth Gaol. He had told Superintendent Barclay that he wanted to clear his conscience, asking for nothing in return. The police had made him no promises, he insisted. But he had never been to prison before and did not wish to change that.

The case against Brady and Smith was compelling, though Happenstein's evidence had introduced uncertainty about who had shot Watt. Anthony took the stand next, stating that he had been present when Michael Canny had found the gun, a powder flask and some shot in a hollow log on the Wooragee run. He confirmed that he had found a small box of shot and a green veil in Tom Brady's room at the Brady house.

Dr Walsh added to the damning testimony, stating that the gun must have been pointed directly at John Watt when he was shot.

In addressing the jury, Smyth was concise. He noted that some testimony had been excluded from the trial owing to the unexpected absence of Peter Brady junior. Smyth had intended to call Bradys senior and junior but both had absconded, not wanting to be inveigled into giving more damning evidence against Thomas. This was immaterial, Smyth declared, because there was sufficient evidence to convict Brady and Smith without this testimony.

The court had appointed Frederick Brown to appear for the defence. At fifty-four, Brown had been a leading figure in Beechworth for many years. Arriving in the district in 1853, he worked as an auctioneer, then ran a goldmining agency and became a local magistrate before completing a law degree in London. He opened his practice in Beechworth in 1864 and had served several stints as the mayor. Underlining the interconnected nature of the local elite, he married Louise Docker, the daughter of Reverend Joseph Docker, the owner of the prosperous Bontharambo run. Brown was an experienced criminal lawyer, having represented either the defence or the prosecution in various cases before the police and circuit courts in Beechworth over the previous eight years. While the accused had no say in selecting Brown, they took heart from this.

In closing, Brown spoke for much longer – he was arguing for the lives of two men. He stressed that the evidence was circumstantial and had discrepancies. The witnesses had given 'weak and shadowy descriptions'. He dismissed Jarvis's testimony: 'The voice of a man once heard, a man's face hidden by a veil, the build and general appearance of a man, five hundred of whom could easily be picked out, were not sufficient evidences to enable the witness to speak positively as to the identity of Smith.' He was even more damning about Happenstein: 'Once a liar always a liar, at least in such matters as these. If he had told the truth to the apprehending constable [Anthony Strahan], his statement in the witness box was a lie.' Brown alleged that 'another marauding expedition' might have committed the murder at Wooragee, as men might hide in the dense scrub around the area for weeks. This was a far reach because there had never been any suggestion that another band of outlaws was afoot in October 1872. Brown noted that Watt had identified Smith several days after he had been injured, when he had been weakened by the loss of blood, seeing 'his weeping wife by his bedside', knowing there was no hope of recovery: 'Taking these circumstances into account, might it not be considered that Mr Watt's recollection was affected?' Last, Brown challenged the medical evidence, less than convincingly, alleging that the shot would have scattered from the shotgun in a downward direction. He called on the jury to acquit the prisoners.

In summing up, Justice Williams was blunt. He said Smyth had been 'quite right in telling the jury that where several men were in company together for an unlawful purpose, one of whom committed a crime, the others were equally guilty as having been present aiding and abetting'. As for the key figure in the trial, Happenstein: 'there was always something suspicious about the evidence of a man who goes with others to commit a crime and then turns round to sheet it home to his former companions'. The 'after life' of an informer must be 'very uncomfortable'. But Happenstein's testimony strengthened the prosecution's case if the jury chose to believe it, reaffirming the circumstantial evidence, which 'dovetailed together, beyond the possibility of a mistake'. If the jury believed Happenstein, the crime was 'brought home to the prisoners at the bar'. He concluded that the case was 'a very serious one, serious for the prisoners and serious for society'.

The jury retired at 7pm. It took them only an hour to find Brady and Smith guilty of wilful murder. Williams asked the two if they wanted to say why a sentence of death should not be pronounced. Smith said nothing, but Brady 'made an indistinct murmur, which was understood by some of those nearest the dock', *The Advertiser* reported, 'to be "yes", but he said nothing further'.[3]

After a lengthy pause, Williams pronounced that the death sentence was inevitable – no other verdict could be returned:

> In times past, when men were determined on obtaining gold at any cost, murders like that committed at Wooragee had occurred. These times had happily gone, but the prisoners had resuscitated this class of crime, and had murdered Mr Watt in the most cold-blooded manner. The man was doing no harm, was interfering in no way with the prisoners, yet he had been shot down by them at the door of his own house. The prisoners seemed to have issued from their lair in the recesses of Mount Pilot, like wild beasts of prey, bent on bloodshed.[4]

The judge ordered that the prisoners be taken to the place from whence they came and there be hanged by the neck until dead, on such day as be appointed by the governor-in-council. He beseeched Brady and Smith, 'not as a judge to the criminal, but as one man to another, to see their clergyman, think seriously of the awful position in which they were placed, and make fitting preparation for their approaching doom'.

The Advertiser observed that Williams seemed greatly affected by the sentence he had inflicted, his voice softening as he delivered it. But this was a misapprehension, for Williams had been in poor health for some years, rendering his voice weak.[5]

However, the sentence had a devastating effect on the accused. Smith leaned against the wall, staring fixedly into space. Brady's lips quivered as though he intended to speak, but he remained silent. The two stood reluctantly in the dock until they were handed over to Charles Thompson, Governor of Beechworth Gaol. Smith whispered something to Brady as he passed him, perhaps a word of solace or support.

The Advertiser declared that the jury had reached a righteous decision. The convicted men had attacked 'a lonely wayside public house' after dark, killing 'an inoffensive and much respected resident'. Two ruthless predators preying on an honest husband and working man. 'Fortunately for the peace and mind and security of lonely dwellers in the bush, and perhaps also for those who may be inclined to enter into a criminal career, justice has been vindicated by the charge having been brought home to the guilty parties.' It was 'lamentable to see two healthy men have their career cut short by an ignominious death', but Smith had 'commenced his criminal career with the too common and much too-lightly esteemed offence of cattle stealing, and ended it as a murderer's doom'. Happenstein had been no more than an accessory after the fact, a 'waiting man' taking care of the horses and keeping watch. While 'as a rule, we have a strong dislike' of the evidence of informers, in Happenstein's case 'there are several circumstances that lift the testimony out of the usual category'.

The paper heaped praise on Anthony and his colleagues, stating they should receive the highest credit, having shown 'great sagacity and skill by the way in which they added link after link until they made the chain of evidence complete'. The final lines of the article had the ring of a homily: 'Once a criminal career is commenced it is hard to tell where it will end. In a country like this, where honest labour is well rewarded, crimes of every description are as unprofitable as they are wicked.'[6]

The Advertiser's report was reproduced in newspapers across the colonies. The Watt murder had become a larger story, reaching well beyond the Ovens district, and Anthony Strahan was at the centre of it all.

Beechworth lacked an executioner. On 2 May 1873, the Governor of Victoria, Sir George Ferguson Bowen, approved the warrant to execute James Smith and Thomas Brady. The same day, the Sheriff's office informed the Attorney-General, George Kerford, that the man who usually carried out executions in the colony was available. This man had normally been so employed when a prisoner, and he was escorted to execution sites by a warden or other official. It was advised that he was usually paid £5, though it was not indicated if this was per execution or per assignment, plus travelling expenses. The office added that good use could be made of the executioner because another prisoner was due to be executed in Castlemaine. Kerferd approved the despatch, mandating that the hangman be accompanied by a warden, even though he had just been released from gaol.[7]

The man in question was William Bamford, often known simply as 'the Bamford', who had been the colony's principal flagellator and hangman for sixteen years. By the time he arrived in Beechworth in May 1873, the 64-year-old had become a legendary, even notorious, figure across the Australian colonies, the subject of many colourful press reports. Born in Burnley, England, in 1808, he started life as a woolcomber before joining the British Army in search of excitement. He proved an unruly soldier. After receiving 300 lashes for an offence committed while his regiment was stationed in Hampshire, Bamford was transported to Van Diemen's Land in 1841 for deserting (he had been absent for a mere twelve days). The record from his transportation described him as 'well behaved and anxious to be useful'. Obtaining his free certificate in 1848, he moved to Victoria during the goldrushes. His gruesome break came in 1857 when he was serving a short sentence in Melbourne Gaol. The colony's hangman, old Jack Harris, and his assistant both disappeared, leaving no one to carry out a death sentence against a murderer. Bamford had come across a way of being useful: he stepped forward to pull the bolt and became the colony's official executioner.

Over the next sixteen years, Bamford carried out seventy-one hangings in Victoria. His unruly ways continued. Unmarried and unencumbered by responsibilities, he squatted in the scrub in unoccupied land around

Melbourne. He drank frequently and hard, often brawling. He was regularly imprisoned for minor offences, usually vagrancy or drunken and disorderly conduct. 'Any money he received from the Government [for carrying out a hanging or a flogging] was soon squandered,' *The Argus* observed in 1870, 'in the company of a degraded lot of both sexes, who used to look out for him when he was expected to leave gaol with money in his pocket, and join him in his drunken orgies.'

One escapade in August 1870 was typical. After executing a man called Cusack, Bamford engaged in what *The Argus* described as a lawn party with 'fellow outcasts who also inhabit the wilds between the Yarra and the Observatory'. After 'a noisy orgy', Bamford abused the schoolmaster at the Immigrants House 'in disgusting terms' and was given a two-month sentence. These prison sentences became part of his work regime, for he would place himself in gaol for several days before he was due to carry out a hanging to sober up and come to the task clean and solemn. He famously kept count of his executions, once looking down the drop with satisfaction and commenting, 'The best job in the country – that makes forty-seven.' *The Argus* said Bamford could be relied upon, for he went about his work quietly and efficiently.[8]

Today, the authorities in some countries that retain the death penalty go to lengths to ensure that no one involved in an execution knows with certainty that they were responsible for the condemned individual's death. In the United States, prisoners on death row are usually executed by lethal injection, with two wardens pushing a switch, only one of which delivers the fatal dose. In Indonesia, not every soldier in a firing squad is given live ammunition, so each man can walk away thinking he might have shot a blank. Hangings back then included no such niceties. Bamford knew he was responsible for the demise of men, and he enjoyed the task.

Bamford was sent to prison again in early 1873. He had recently taken up quarters 'in the cheerful neighbourhood of the morgue', making his toilet in front of the windows of the stationmaster's house, offending the family. He was sentenced to two months' imprisonment for vagrancy.[9] So he was conveniently ensconced in Melbourne Gaol five weeks later when two fellow inmates were convicted of engaging in 'an unnatural offense'. The men were given a harsh sentence – another two years' imprisonment with hard labour and twenty lashes. Bamford administered the flogging.

Released in April, Bamford was soon relieved of the office of the colony's flogger when an asthmatic fit meant he was barely able to administer the requisite number of lashes on another unfortunate fellow. But he was still deemed fit enough to carry out executions.[10]

By the time he arrived in Beechworth on 12 May to hang Smith and Brady, Bamford had become a ghoulish figure, the stuff of nightmares, his threatening visage made more unnerving by the missing eye he had lost in a fight in Melbourne fifteen years earlier. Around sixty people gathered in the gaol to watch the executions. Some were compelled to be present by duty. It seems highly likely that Anthony and the other police involved in the case would have attended. Others were representatives of the press. But most were there, *The Advertiser* observed, 'simply avid of strong excitement'. For these spectators, *The Advertiser* had only mild judgement: 'They were present to gratify a morbid taste, and they gratified it; c'est tout! If they enjoyed it, no one will grudge them their enjoyment; if they did not enjoy it, it may perhaps be hoped that they learned a useful lesson.'

The prison guards struck off the irons at 7am and the two condemned men were handed over to the sheriff. Smith was the first to be brought out of the holding cell, which was only eight feet from the gallows. With Bamford pinioning his arms behind his back, he 'trembled in every limb', wrote *The Ovens Spectator*, 'and we question whether his countenance was more livid after death than at this moment'. Smith's physical appearance had fallen away during the weeks leading up to the executions.

Bamford did not waste any time in placing the rope around Smith's neck, the knot high up under the left ear in the English style. The young man, not yet twenty-four, seemed on the verge of saying something, but choked on his words, his lips quivering. At length, having composed himself somewhat, he asked the sheriff if he could speak. *The Ovens Spectator* opined that Smith clearly feared 'he would be "turned off" before he had the opportunity of saying what he desired'. Surveying the crowd below nervously, he declared in a quiet, low voice, 'All that I have to say is that I have given a statement to the Governor of the gaol of what we have to say in our defence.' Bamford drew the cap over Smith's face swiftly. The sounds around Smith then became muffled and strangely distant. He surely knew now there was no way back.

Time became both frighteningly fast and horribly slow. Bamford returned to the holding cell to bring Brady forth. Brady was visibly shaking. While Reverend Dean Tierney recited prayers at the foot of the scaffold, Bamford quickly placed the rope around Brady's neck, covering his face with a white cap. Smith repeated Tierney's prayers, and without pause, almost before Brady would have realised what was happening, Bamford pulled the lever and the condemned men plunged down. Brady died almost instantly, but Smith struggled violently for two or three minutes and died very hard. 'The bodies were left hanging the usual time prescribed by law,' *The Ovens Spectator* concluded. *The Argus* noted that Smith's body was 'terribly livid', though Brady's appeared 'comparatively natural'. They were both wearing the same clothes they had worn during the trial.

Twelve jurymen certified that Smith and Brady were 'hanged by the neck until their bodies were dead'. Dr Walsh examined the bodies and confirmed this.[11] It is likely that few members of the jury harboured doubts about what they had been asked to witness; the overwhelming majority of the Victorian population in the late nineteenth century supported the death penalty. But they were not made of stone. Hangings were messy and confronting. Both men had lost control of their bowels on the gallows.

The Advertiser was sombre: 'Yesterday was enacted in the Beechworth Gaol, one of these tragedies which are the necessity, as they are the curse, of civilised communities.' Yet if it felt no delight in the executions, it was unrepentant in believing Smith and Brady deserved their fate for 'one of the most causeless and brutal murders in the colony'.[12] The country cop who had apprehended them, Anthony Strahan, agreed wholeheartedly.

10

LOOSE ENDS

The Advertiser's owner, Richard Warren, felt that the public should be given the chance to read James Smith and Thomas Brady's statement. This was the last declaration of two young criminals whose lives had been taken; *The Advertiser*'s readers, who had followed the case so intimately, deserved to know if Smith and Brady had repented or proclaimed their innocence.

The paper asked the Sheriff for a copy on the very day of the executions. The Sheriff replied that he was unable to comply, encouraging Warren to write to the Chief Secretary, James Francis. Warren was incensed by the refusal to offer up the statement, accusing the Sheriff of being 'afraid to do his duty to the public, and afraid, it seems, of doing anything'. But Francis also refused to release it to the press.

Three weeks later, the Speaker rose in the Legislative Assembly in Melbourne to insist that the statement had been suppressed because it had not contained any denial of guilt, casting instead 'charges and accusations all round upon persons whom there was no reason to suspect of any complicity in crime'. The government had rightly declined to publish it 'in common justice and honesty'.[1]

As I read the official documents and newspaper reports about the Wooragee Outrage, I too found it troubling that the voices of the condemned had remained silent during their trial, aside from a few fragmentary remarks reported by others. This left a gaping hole at the heart of what had happened in Wooragee on 15 October 1872.

I combed through file after file in the Public Record Office Victoria in a bid to locate the elusive statement. Just when I was about to give up, deciding the authorities had destroyed it, I found it in the last file on my long list, a bundle of papers from Beechworth Gaol. It had stayed concealed and apparently lost for so long, it was likely that few, if anyone, had read it in the intervening 145 years.

Reading the last statement of two condemned men was chilling and moving. The men had had several weeks after the trial to think about what they wanted to say. Thomas Brady, the literate one of the pair, wrote on behalf of himself and his cousin. He completed the statement on 7 May and handed it to the Governor of Beechworth Gaol on 11 May, the day before the executions, asking that it be given to the Sheriff after he and Smith were dead. Over fourteen packed pages, the handwriting mostly neat, the syntax and spelling sometimes poor, Brady set out the other side of the story. At the outset, he affirmed that he and his cousin would 'adhere to the Strict Truth … endeavour to show our case as it realy is and hold up the evidence to the light of truth'.

Across the first four pages, Brady and Smith concentrated on what had always been one of the prosecution's weak points, the shaky identification of the alleged offenders by key witnesses. If the men could be believed, the identifications that had been made in the first ten days after the raid on Wooragee were more problematic than Barclay had admitted to Chief Commissioner Standish. At the identification parade at the Beechworth police station, four people walked into the yard one by one, Brady wrote, passing first in front of and then behind the line of men. Catherine Mitchell was the first witness brought into the yard. Asked by the police if she recognised anyone, she 'said yes and went and placed her hand on Happenstein's chest'. Her husband, Peter, said 'Smith looked something like one of the men', but William Jarvis, the bullock wagon driver, said he could not recognise anyone. The police pointed out Smith, but Jarvis 'answered that he could not swear to him'. Margaret Gale was asked the same question. She walked across, took a man by the hand and appeared to examine it. The man was middle-aged with fair hair and a sandy beard, about five-foot five inches in height. 'She left him and then took Smith by the hand and examined his hand also. She left him and passed in the rear of where we were standing. We did not hear her make any remark.' This part of Brady and Smith's account accorded with Barclay's version of events to Standish. But Brady added a crucial element. He wrote that after the identification parade, he and Smith were taken separately into an office in the station where the four witnesses were waiting. The police asked each of them several questions 'so that those persons could hear us speaking'. Brady suggested that the police had fitted them up, making sure the witnesses had ample opportunity to identify them as the culprits.

At the Wooragee Hotel on 23 October, Brady wrote, Sergeant Baber 'kept his hand placed upon [my] shoulder' but Watt 'said that is not one of the men quite distinctly'. Baber next took Smith into the bedroom. Smith stood on the left side of the bed, George Graham and the Reverend William Howard on the right side, at the bedhead, and Barclay at the foot. 'Mr Watt muttered some words which was not intilagable.' Brady contended that Barclay came to the head of the bed, bending down and placing his ear to Watt's mouth. Watt moved his hand backwards and forwards, indicating that Smith was not one of the men. Brady asked why Barclay was not called to the witness stand and questioned about this hand gesture.

At the inquest into Watt's death, '… there was four of us under arrest present, the fourth man being a half caste named John Lewis'. The police had made them stand in a single line in plain view of the coroner and jury. Henry Gale, the postmaster and storekeeper, heard Brady speaking at the inquest but later falsely stated in court that he had never heard him speak until the trial. There, Gale had testified that he would not swear to Brady's voice 'as the voice of the man that stuck him up [though] it was something like it'. Brady contended that Gale had been 'acuated by feelings of strong animosity against me'. He and his brother, Peter, had purchased goods from Gale's store under Peter's name some time ago. The three had become embroiled in a disagreement about the account balance; Gale had summonsed Peter to court and secured a verdict against him. Peter had later become insolvent, and Gale had never been paid. Brady insisted that

Gale had refused to extend credit to other customers, saying he had been 'swindled by the Bradys'. Among 'other strong expressions', the storekeeper had said 'if they ever came in his way he would have satisfaction'.

Brady next asserted that the lawyer William Zincke, who had been present at the inquest, had had a grudge of his own against Smith. Wrongly noting that Zincke was 'in the employ of the Police' (he had been engaged by Ellen Watt), Brady insisted that the lawyer had spent some time at the inquest conversing with a witness, William Jarvis, with both men pointing several times at the accused. Zincke had 'entertained anything but friendly feelings' towards Smith due to a case that had been heard at the Chiltern police court. Here Brady brought up Smith's entanglement with Thomas Gidley, the controversial squatter who had fended off cattle-stealing charges in 1867. Zincke had represented Gidley on these charges. Brady gave Smith's account of what had happened, expressing his cousin's claims in the first person: 'I was a witness in the case for the Crown against Gidley. Inspector Langley asked me if Mr Zincke told me to swear I stole the cattle and not Mr Gidley. I answered yes he did tell me to swear that I took the cattle in question and stick to it like hell. As soon as I answered Mr Langleys question Mr Zincke took up his hat and left the court vowing vengance against me.'

Here Smith shed light on the machinations behind his decision to abscond to New South Wales rather than testify against Gidley in Melbourne. It would seem the young man had been pressured by both sides in Gidley's 1867 cattle-stealing cases.

After disputing various other parts of the prosecution's evidence, Brady said he could 'most solemnly and impaticly deny' that he had been in Wooragee on 15 October, claiming he could prove that he had instead been at a Mrs Clarke's place, where he had borrowed an axe, and later at Mr Dry's farm, about a half a mile from his father's property. A third person, Mr Bullock, who lived in Chiltern, could corroborate his whereabouts because he had been collecting wood near his father's farm. Brady seemed to be clutching at straws. None of these people had come forward at any point during the six months between Brady's arrest and the day he was executed.

It was not until the tenth page that the two turned their sights on the man who had proved so decisive in the trial, their one-time workmate William Happenstein. 'Our solicitor told us on the first day the court opened that Heppenstenn was going to give evidence for the Crown against us but that he did not know what he was going to say.' Brady's tone, which had been mostly measured, became fierce: 'Is it not monsterous that we were not allowed an opportunity to call witnesses to contradict his evidence which would have proved him to be the vile perjurer he is.' In his eagerness to expose holes in Happenstein's evidence, Brady made a telling inadvertent admission:

> He pretends to say he saw what he describes and he cannot say which of us shot the man. Can anyone believe him. Let them place themselves in the same position. Do you not think that any person that saw so distinctly as he describes he did could not also have told who fired the shot … Can anyone believe that men would be so insane as to bring a third person with them to witness the crime he says we committed. There is several discripencies in his evidence we have not touched on, we leave the Public to deal with them, Heppenstenn at the time of his arrest began by telling lies and ended up swearing lies.

Brady and Smith's fury at their co-accused's betrayal was scorching. Their former workmate had 'recklessly sacrificed' their lives, and if his conscience had been troubling him before, 'the crime he has now committed ought to drive him mad, the vilest and most unheard of perjury concievable'. Brady claimed that Detective Christie had offered him both a reward and a pardon if he revealed who shot Watt, but he had refused to do so. He alleged that the police had repeated this offer several times while he was in gaol awaiting trial, including via his brother Peter; the police had even proposed what evidence he should give. Other than Christie, he did not name the officers who had allegedly tried to rig the evidence. If he can be believed, the police were trying to get Brady to turn on his cousin and dob him in, seeing Smith as the ringleader. Brady contended that the police had also tried to convince Lewis to turn informant, but he too had refused to betray his old mates.

Brady wanted to rebut another claim levelled at him and his cousin: that they had intended to 'commence a career of crime' by sticking up the Eldorado escort and shooting the accompanying police officer, who was usually, as we know, Constable Anthony Strahan. Brady maintained that he and Smith had not planned to rob the escort. Justice Williams had dismissed their lawyer's suggestion at the trial that others had been responsible for what had happened at Wooragee, but Brady claimed that two men, Billy Oatman and a friend, had been splitting wood in Wooragee at the time. Based on their previous behaviour, they were 'not above suspicion'. Oatman had been 'tried at Wagga Wagga about five and half years ago' for 'shooting a Chinaman'. He was acquitted but later boasted publicly that he did it. Brady claimed this man resembled Smith in height and stature and had a similarly fair complexion, with light blue eyes. Brady alleged that a third man, Tolesberry, was living near Sebastopol. He was a friend of Happenstein and had been working in the Pilot Range. Any of these men could have looked like him and Smith had they been disguised in the right way, he asserted.

Brady also took issue with the quality of the legal representation the men had received. He claimed that the Governor of the Gaol and the Chief Warden had come to his cell and said he could choose between two lawyers who worked regularly at the Beechworth court, Frederick Brown and Denis O'Leary, to represent him at trial. Brady said he had chosen O'Leary. He wrote he had been surprised when he had found out he would be represented by Brown instead. 'I said nothing at the time because I thought Mr O'Leary had been asked to defend me and refused.' Brown had told him that he had been given insufficient time to prepare a defence. Brady noted, 'the Police had six months to get up the case against us and the solicitor that was appointed to get up our defence had only about forty-eight hours'.

Brady concluded by stating that he and Smith would 'leave it in the hands of the public to do justice to our memory and clear our character of the foul stain that has been placed upon it'. He stressed that it 'is our dying request that this statement will be made public'.[2]

What should one make of these last words of two men on the eve of their execution? Much of the statement reads like the pleas of schoolboys. It is unconvincing when it tries to shift the blame for the raid on Wooragee onto shadowy, unknown figures. The police investigation had considered other suspects, who were ruled out quickly, but never anyone called Oatman or Tolesberry. If they existed, the police found no good reason to track them down and question them.

Tellingly, in questioning Happenstein's inability to identify which of them had fired the shot that killed Watt, Brady and Smith admitted that one of them had done so. How could their claims elsewhere be believed? The two were clearly guilty. But they did raise some valid questions about the process that had led them to the gallows. The identifications of the suspects had always been shaky. If Brady and Smith can be believed, the police had led, even coached, some witnesses. It is easy to see why the government withheld the statement from the public, for the two accused Superintendent Barclay and Sergeant Baber of acting improperly.

It is notable that Brady and Smith did not mention Anthony Strahan, even though he had been the one to lead the investigation in their direction after a tip-off and to arrest them. He had also found key pieces of evidence at Peter Brady's place and had testified in the committal hearing and the trial. They seemed to have no issue with his conduct. Perhaps this reflected his reputation for being fair and diligent in his police work. Nor did Brady and Smith have a bone to pick with Sergeant Chadwick. They did, however, make allegations about several leading members of the Beechworth community, including the magistrate George Graham and the lawyer William Zincke.

James Smith and Thomas Brady felt they owed the world nothing. Life often did bad things to the poor. Levels of casual violence were high in the late nineteenth century; heavy drinking was widespread; work in country areas was limited. Colonial Victoria had treated Smith and Brady harshly and they had lashed out. Were they the victims of bad luck and ill fate, given the poverty that kept their families down? It is a tempting conclusion.

And yet many facing similarly hard circumstances did not turn to crime. Confronted with adversity, they worked hard and made the best of a bad lot, sometimes succeeding, sometimes going under. Smith's own father, Hugh, was one such man. Ultimately, Smith and Brady made their own choices, no matter how tough their circumstances. They had been seduced by the lure of easy money, and their choices ended up costing them their lives. They were not monsters, but they had a mean streak, especially Smith. In arresting the two young men, Anthony Strahan set in motion a sequence of events that led to their death; but he did the right thing by bringing two criminals to justice. Had they not been nabbed, Smith and Brady could well have gone on to act even more recklessly and violently. The Wooragee Outrage already marked an escalation in their behaviour. Anthony may have prevented further bloodshed. Even though I don't support capital punishment, I felt some pride. My great-great-grandfather had done what needed to be done.

Shortly after they were executed, Brady and Smith were buried in the grounds of the Beechworth Gaol. Father Tierney and the Governor of the Gaol, Charles Thompson, witnessed the burial. No family members were present.

Happenstein was released from gaol two days later. Even if most in the area believed he had done the right thing, he would have been loathed by the Brady and Smith families, and other local criminal elements, for turning informer. He and his wife likely left town as soon as they could. Happenstein had spent some time in Tasmania earlier in his life and he may have returned – some records indicate that a William Heppenstein died at Table Cape in 1918.

After he was discharged from the committal hearing over Watt's death and re-arrested outside the courtroom for stealing a horse, John Lewis was placed in Beechworth Gaol to await trial. Following a series of remands, the police were ready to proceed. Lewis, who had been languishing in gaol for two months, was brought before the police court on Christmas Eve 1872. The prosecutor only called one witness, Constable Anthony Strahan, who confirmed that he had seen the prisoner riding the horse in the Eldorado–Chiltern area on several occasions in September and October. Lewis had told him that 'Jemmy' – James Smith – had given the horse to him. As the horse had been stolen in New South Wales, the bench acceded to the police request to remand the case to Wagga Wagga: the very same town where Lewis had been convicted of committing highway robbery five and a half years earlier. He was escorted across the Murray and into an Albury lock-up.

Lewis was brought to trial before Acting Judge D G Forbes in Wagga Wagga on 3 February 1873 on two charges: stealing a horse, the property of Mary Johnson, and receiving the same, knowing it to be stolen. Johnson testified that she had seen 'a coloured man about Junee' around the time the horse had vanished. She said 'the man was very much like the prisoner', noting that he had come into her store for some goods. A local newspaper reported that the prisoner, John Lewis, alias Black Jack, 'a well-built, determined-looking half caste', pleaded not guilty.

Anthony was the main witness. He had ridden north from Eldorado to Wagga Wagga to attend the trial. He told the court that he had arrested Lewis twice, first on 22 October for highway robbery, of which he had been discharged, and again on 31 October, on the two charges before the court. He stated that he had first seen Lewis on the horse on 29 September. Questioned by the accused, Anthony declared that he had seen him riding on the horse again on 12 October on the road between Chiltern and Eldorado. He had said nothing more than 'Good day, mate' as the two passed, but he had taken note of the horse's brands. He attested that he had later found the horse in Peter Brady's paddock; Lewis had told him he had acquired the horse from Jemmy Smith, who was now under committal for a capital offence in Victoria. *The Wagga Wagga Advertiser* observed: 'The prisoner, who evinced greater intelligence than is generally found in his class, made a long but rambling statement to the effect that he was at work upon the two days on which the constable had stated that he had seen him riding the horse.' The jury swiftly returned a guilty verdict. The police underlined Lewis's previous convictions, and Forbes sentenced him to three years' imprisonment with hard labour in Darlinghurst.[3]

Lewis knew his fate before his mates in Beechworth knew theirs; they were still more than two months away from their own trial.

Peter Brady senior fled to central Victoria, taking on a job as a farm labourer near the small town of Buangor. No doubt he felt Buangor was sufficiently far away from the courtroom that would soon decide his son's fate. The farmer John McCormick, realising his new worker was frail, put Brady on a threshing machine because this was not too taxing. The harvesting was being done at – of all places – Mount Mistake. As he stood beside the thresher, did Peter wonder about the irony of the name? Did he dwell on the mistakes his son had made? That he had made as a father?

On the evening of 15 March, as the workers were relaxing at their campsite after dinner, Peter was smoking a pipe, keeping to himself, his back turned to the other labourers, when he had a fit. He died within minutes. Two of his workmates, relative strangers until moments ago, held him, one by the hand and the other by the head, as his heart gave out. It was a sad and lonely death. He died about a month before Justice Williams handed down a death sentence on Thomas.

The younger Peter Brady stayed in northeast Victoria for some years after his brother's execution, as far as can be determined. He put the modest family farm at Skeleton Creek up for sale in August 1876. James Smith's father, Hugh, also remained in the area. He was not called as a witness during the trial, suggesting he was not involved in his son's illegal activities. Had he given up on James, deciding he was beyond redemption? Or had he stoically witnessed the prosecution of his son? He died in the Melbourne suburb of Richmond in April 1893 at age seventy-four, having outlived his eldest son by almost twenty years.

The Wooragee Outrage inevitably affected the residents of the town. Margaret Gale was deeply shaken. She had believed that Smith was going to kill her that night, and she had been compelled to relive the harrowing events repeatedly by giving evidence at the identification parade, the committal hearing and the trial. Her health declined rapidly, and Dr Walsh, who had tried to save John Watt's life, travelled out to Wooragee to treat her. He found there was little he could do, and Margaret died of apoplexy and severe exhaustion at age thirty-four on 7 July 1873, less than two months after Smith and Brady had been hanged. Reverend Tierney, the Catholic priest who had administered the last rites to the two condemned men, had married Margaret and Henry in Beechworth in 1869 and now presided over her burial at Beechworth Cemetery. Many criminals and police in late-nineteenth-century Victoria were of Irish origin, but Margaret was a reminder that many of the victims of crime came from Irish stock as well.

Henry Gale moved on, marrying Margaret's younger sister, Sarah, in 1874. He remained the postmaster and baker in Wooragee for many years, and he and Sarah had two children. Henry and Sarah died in Wooragee in 1913, only months apart.

The Wooragee Outrage was a significant event in the careers of the officials involved. Anthony Strahan and the other policemen in the case became public figures, heroes who had brought two murderers to justice. Their efforts were highlighted by those campaigning for better conditions for the police. On 23 April 1873, *The Advertiser* declared that successive ministries had promised to assist the police, but had lamentably failed: '[T]he inducements held out to them to enter the force have been violated; promotion, the only fitting reward for efficiency and intelligent zeal, has been for years at a standstill; their pay has been again and again reduced in carrying out a penny-wise system of economy; and the fund that they themselves have contributed has been misappropriated and frittered away.' Despite this ill-treatment, the officers of the force had 'always been ready to put their lives in their hands, and go forth on the most dangerous enterprises in the detection of crime'. Constable Strahan and Sergeant Chadwick in particular should be recognised because they had followed up what had at first seemed 'the slenderest of clues until they succeeded in fixing the guilt on the criminals in a manner that left no room for doubt'. They had brought the perpetrators of villainy to justice and restored the confidence of 'the dwellers in sequestered localities'.

Superintendent Barclay was intent on ensuring that his officers were rewarded for cracking the case. On 26 April, he wrote to Standish that Sergeant Chadwick and Constable Strahan had performed particularly meritorious service, recommending each receive a £25 reward and be promoted one step in their respective grades. Standish queried if any other officers should receive a portion of the reward as well. Barclay responded that many officers, including Sergeant Baber and Detective Christie, had performed well, but he thought only two, Chadwick and Strahan, should be singled out for a reward. Standish accepted Barclay's assessment and Chadwick and Anthony received their £25 in early June.[4] Given Anthony's low income, this would have helped the family budget considerably.

Standish was keen to recognise Hugh Barclay. On 9 May 1873, he said he was aware the Wooragee Outrage had cost Barclay 'much trouble and anxiety and it must be very pleasing to him to see it brought to so successful an end'. Barclay was promoted a year later to Superintendent (First Class). But he was not to enjoy this new position for long; he fell critically ill in June 1876. He died weeks later, at age fifty. The press praised Barclay as an old colonist who had joined the force in the rough early days. *The Argus* spoke for many when it said Barclay was 'highly esteemed by his brother officers and his death will be regretted by all who knew him'.[5]

If policemen such as Barclay were remembered well in the northeast, the Wooragee murderers, James Smith and Thomas Brady, secured a dark place in the region's folklore. On a Sunday afternoon in July 1873, only two months after the bushrangers had been executed, a reporter from *The Advertiser* visited Beechworth Gaol. Charles Thompson, its Governor, was waiting at the front gate. He was proud of his prison, and he conducted a tour. The reporter was impressed by the gaol's 'good management, order and strict discipline', concluding that there was no more cleanly kept and better ordered prison in the colony. He was intrigued by the radiating yard, which had a sentry box at the centre of a wheel with seven walled compartments fanning out. It was here that prisoners condemned to death were allowed some solitary exercise before their execution, reminding them that 'there is but a step between them and the grave'. It was in these 'dread man's yards' that some of the executed men were buried, even though the bedrock was only three feet below the surface in many places. As he walked around the yards, the journalist noticed a series of initials and numbers inscribed on the walls, the latter indicating how many feet the men had been buried from the walls. In one yard, he found the only tombstone for Smith and Brady: 'J S and T B, five feet.' Thompson explained that 'these murderers were buried in coffins filled with quick-lime … the probabilities were that very little of them now remains, although so recently buried'.

Another journalist from *The Advertiser* returned the following year for a tour. The gaol was only housing eighteen inmates and five men awaiting trial, including a schoolmaster charged with indecent assault, because most of the long-term prisoners had been moved to Pentridge. Everything again seemed in good order, but the reporter hadn't come to check on this. He was drawn to the storeroom, which contained plenty of items to indulge the curiosity of 'the lover of the sensational': the rope used to hang Smith, Brady and 'such like murderous celebrities'; the manacles that had restrained the notorious criminals; and 'the cat, a cruel looking weapon'.[6]

In May 1873, Anthony was reassigned to Snowy Creek. *The Advertiser* said Constable Strahan was 'a highly deserving officer' and hoped the reassignment was 'a step towards permanent promotion'.[7]

The Wooragee Outrage was the biggest case Anthony Strahan had pursued. It must have been a heady experience to be a central figure in bringing two high-profile criminals to justice. But he was not to know that even more dramatic events lay ahead.

11

A MASTER OF HIS OWN DOMAIN

In May 1873, Anthony and Marion left Eldorado with their eighteen-month-old son, Anthony Oliver, on the long road to Snowy Creek, a small town at the junction of the Mitta Mitta River and Snowy Creek in the Great Dividing Range. Four major river systems – the Ovens, the Broken, the Kiewa and the Mitta Mitta – flow through northeast Victoria into the Murray. Anthony and Marion were accustomed to the Ovens, which travels sedately through the plains to the west of the Great Dividing Range. The Mitta Mitta was different. Taking snow melt in spring off Mount Bogong, Victoria's highest peak, it cuts along a lengthy, narrow valley, through gorges, hills and dense forests, meeting the Murray east of Albury. While the Ovens district was reasonably well settled by Europeans in the 1870s, with a network of towns, encampments and farms, the Mitta Valley was only lightly occupied by Europeans, with large swathes of wild terrain.

Traversed by Hamilton Hume and William Hovell in 1824, the Mitta Valley was first settled by Europeans in the mid-1830s. Two brothers, James and William Wyse, took up a station at the head of the valley in 1837, and a few other farmers followed. The European population remained scant until the discovery of gold in 1852, and a township, variously called Snowy Creek or the Junction, sprang up on the Wyse station as miners came into the diggings. More gold was discovered at nearby Thunder and Lightning Creek (so named because it was prone, one journal noted in 1858, to 'fearful thunderstorms') and further up the Mitta Mitta at Granite Flat, the Wombat and Dark River. At the height of the goldrush, the largely itinerant population reached 1000, including many Chinese, with the main settlements at Snowy Creek and Granite Flat, 7 kilometres to the south. Snowy Creek had a police station by 1859 and a post office by 1870. By the time Anthony was posted to replace Constable Redmond Carroll as the town's sole police officer, Snowy Creek had several stores and pubs, including the Laurel, and a rough and ready school. *The Ovens and Murray Advertiser* noted in November 1873, with some consternation, that it had 'no public library' or any institution with 'a religious tendency'. Although the main rushes had finished by 1873, alluvial goldmining continued along the creeks for some years. Many found nothing but hard luck, a failure captured by place names such as Mount Misery and Disappointment Track. As mining shrank, more men went into farming, taking up land along the Mitta Mitta. Some ran cattle or sheep; others planted wheat, oats, maize and potatoes. Although the first attempts to cultivate tobacco in 1874 did not fare well when slugs ate the plants, tobacco production took off on some selections. The European and Chinese population fell to between 400 and 500 in the 1870s. No more than forty-five Aboriginal people were likely living in the area by 1863, and the Indigenous population had all but vanished a decade later, when Anthony arrived.

At first blush, being assigned to Snowy Creek might have seemed a backward step for a constable who had played a crucial part in a major case that had gripped the colony's imagination for months. Compared with Eldorado, Snowy Creek was isolated, connected to the rest of the colony by limited and often uncertain transport and communication links. Beechworth, the township's administrative centre for all manner of official functions from law and order to mining, lay 100 kilometres to the west. A Crawford and Connolly coach connected Snowy Creek to Tallangatta, 60 kilometres to the north, which provided many services. Omeo was far to the south, in Gippsland. But Snowy Creek made sense for several reasons. Anthony would oversee his own station. Perhaps equally importantly, he had family there. Although the force normally moved its officers without taking their wishes into account, Anthony may have asked to be transferred to Snowy Creek, for one of his wife's older sisters, Margaret, lived on a farm on the banks of the Mitta Mitta, not far from the town, with her Danish-born husband, Henry Neilson. The Neilsons had three children, providing a supportive family environment for Anthony, Marion and their own child.

The 130-kilometre journey from Eldorado was arduous. The road, no more than a dirt track, was often turned to mud by rain. With their modest household effects loaded onto a cart, Anthony and Marion rode east through Yackandandah, past Allans Flat and Staghorn Flat, and across the Kiewa River. After Kiewa, they turned south past Sandy Creek and on through the Lockhart Gap, which afforded fine views across the landscape. From the Gap, they descended into the Mitta Valley itself. The final stretch of the journey followed the Mitta Mitta for 28 kilometres, passing by two small communities, Tallandoon and Eskdale, first settled in the 1840s. Luckily the Strahans were not travelling in the winter or spring, when floods often made the road impassable. A lone rider unencumbered by a cart could ride from Snowy Creek to Beechworth in just over twenty-four hours if he went full tilt. The Strahans' journey would have taken at least two days. Although well-defined, the road to Snowy Creek was notoriously difficult for strangers to navigate and often in poor repair. On several occasions travellers had to ford the river. These crossing spots were not always easy to locate, even with apparently good directions, as the police magistrate, Robert Pitcairn, found in 1875 when he rode into the river and plunged into a water hole 20 feet deep. Luckily his horse was at home in the water and Pitcairn floated downstream to the ford and emerged from the river unscathed. Help was not close by if you did run into serious trouble.

When Anthony and Marion pulled up in Snowy Creek, they found the police station located in an odd and inconvenient spot, on the point of a spur at the junction of the Mitta Mitta and Snowy Creek. Although on the road running north to Tallangatta, it was separated from the township by the creek. One could reach the station across a narrow footbridge, but those on horseback could only wade through the creek. If the water was high, horses were compelled to swim. Making this even trickier, the creek's banks were steep. When I visited the site in 2018 with my wife, Lily, and my daughter, Katya, Mount Misery loomed over us, and it was easy to see how the elements could cause trouble, quickly and dramatically.

Once they had crossed the creek – Marion on foot with Anthony Oliver in her arms, Anthony wading through the water with his horse – the Strahans saw that the police compound, which included the station and their living quarters, was far from impressive. It was nothing like the solid stone or brick buildings in Eldorado. The living quarters did not even have a closet. Anthony immediately wrote to his superintendent in Beechworth, Hugh Barclay, asking for permission to put up a closet 'as it is very unpleasing to be at this station without one'. Barclay agreed, writing to Chief Commissioner Standish on 9 June 1873 seeking approval for 'this trifling expenditure' and noting that Anthony would carry the cost if necessary until he could be reimbursed. Proving again that he was closely involved in even the force's most mundane matters, Standish instructed that the work be done at once.[1]

Inadequate toilet facilities were far from the most serious defect. Not long after their arrival, Inspector Alexander Brooke Smith visited to conduct a regular inspection. His report was damning. The chimneys of the dwelling and the cook house were in such poor repair that there was a serious risk of a fire breaking out in either building. The backs of the fireplaces were open in places. The bark and shingle forage storage was 'in such a tumble down as to be positively dangerous during a high wind'. He recommended that the kitchen and the store be replaced immediately. A few weeks later, Anthony wrote to Barclay to report that he was afraid to light a fire in the kitchen and the sleeping quarters because the chimneys were so dilapidated. Other minor repairs, such as re-papering and re-lining the walls, were also urgent.

Improving the police compound had become even more important for the Strahans because their family had recently expanded. Marion gave birth to a second child, Alicia Maria, on 26 November 1873, in the quarters attached to the station. She was assisted by a local midwife, Lucy Greaves. Twenty years older than Marion, Lucy was a vital part of the community, living with her husband and daughter on a farm not far from the township. Midwives such as Greaves performed a crucial role in small country towns, especially those like Snowy Creek, which lacked a local doctor. The well-being of mothers and newborns rested very much in the hands of wise women who had accumulated a fund of practical and often lifesaving knowledge over the years.

With a new baby and a toddler, Anthony and Marion were underwhelmed by their ramshackle living quarters. In April 1874, Anthony pointed out to his superiors that the shabby state of the compound also affected the station's official operations. Visiting constables had to sleep in the decrepit kitchen; a skillion would provide better sleeping arrangements for visitors, he said. Anthony's predecessors at the station had also amassed a quantity of useless items – old blankets, pillowcases and rugs; an iron pot and a frying pan; brooms and tools; a bucket and a boiler. Anthony was given permission to destroy them.[2]

Anthony's discontent was significantly assuaged when he received news on 24 May 1874 that Standish had decided to fill a vacancy by promoting him to the rank of senior constable. In a letter confirming the promotion, Standish told Superintendent Barclay he was pleased to recognise Constable Strahan's 'zeal and aptitude in the late Wooragee murder case' and 'his excellent conduct generally'. *The Advertiser* was vindicated, writing that the long-delayed promotion was just reward for cracking the Watt case: 'It may not be generally known that Smith and Brady had, at the time of the murder, formed a plan for the sticking up of the Yackandandah or Eldorado escort and for the shooting of Constable Strahan … and it was timely warning from a friend, who was somehow in the secret, to Strahan which put him on the right track and led to the arrest of the murderers.'[3] The 'friend', of course, was Brady's own father.

Even so, Anthony had to wait many months before Standish finally approved the £81, 10 shillings and 6 sixpence to erect a new kitchen and repair the forage store. This delay forced the family to endure wholly inadequate facilities through a long and turbulent winter. Although the township of Snowy Creek was only 254 metres above sea level, the surrounding mountains reached well above 1000 metres. On 29 August, *The Advertiser* reported that 'an unusual amount of snow has fallen during the winter and is still lying to a considerable depth below the ordinary snow line, causing travelling to be slow and somewhat difficult'. Ominously, the heavy snow portended floods in the spring, with *The Advertiser* advising 'settlers on the low-lying lands [to take] every precaution for the safety of their stock and other movable property'. Floods arrived in October. But it was not only the farmers along the Mitta Mitta who were caught out. Flanked by the river and Snowy Creek, the police compound was partially flooded, damaging the footings and flooring of already shaky buildings.

Anthony's efforts to address these problems underscored Snowy Creek's isolation. In Eldorado and Beechworth, he had worked in well-established, bustling communities, which were connected both to other towns in the region and to Melbourne by regular coach and mail services. On the edge of the northeast, deep in mountainous terrain, Snowy Creek was out of sight and often out of mind. While this had its advantages, allowing for greater autonomy, it meant that Anthony could no longer simply talk to his superiors to resolve issues; he now had to communicate everything by letter. The postal service between Snowy Creek and the rest of the state was terrible. One irate letter to the Melbourne *Leader* under the pseudonym 'Mitta Mitta' on 18 October 1873 voiced a complaint keenly felt by the area's residents: 'The Snowy Creek and Mitta Mitta mail reaches Kiewa on Fridays at 1pm, and takes from that time until 11pm on Sundays to travel 35 miles (Kiewa to Mitta Mitta), an average speed of about a mile per hour.' Residents then had the indignity of only having a short window of reply, for the post closed on Mondays at 10am and 'crawled away to arrive at Kiewa at 2pm the following day, thus attaining the extra speed of about one and a quarter mile per hour'. Did the mail travel at the same rate, he asked, in any other part of her Majesty's dominions? Even *The Advertiser*, the region's principal newspaper, took some days to reach the town, so news about all manner of things, from political developments to local tenders for roadworks, reached the Mitta Valley later than other localities.

The town's residents relied on the Ovens District Hospital in Beechworth, more than 100 kilometres away. In such a small community, every death was felt keenly, especially that of a child. Soon after Anthony and Marion settled into the town, Frances McCann, the daughter of Torrens and Annie McCann, died at the age of five after a lingering illness.[4] Although it was hardly uncommon for children to die young in the nineteenth century, that did not mean parents were not devastated by the loss of a daughter or a son. Torrens and Annie, Irish immigrants who had come to the diggings in the Mitta Valley in 1862 before taking up a selection, had already suffered grievous loss, for diphtheria had come to Snowy Creek in 1866 and taken their two other children, Hugh, eight, and Mary, only three and a half. They were observant Catholics and had played a leading part in building a church in Granite Flat, the first permanent Catholic place of worship in the alpine region, but their faith was tested by losing three children in seven years. Annie, pregnant with a fourth, was deeply shaken.

It was not only illness that claimed lives prematurely. As Anthony had found years before in Bealiba and Avoca, the bush was full of danger. Two weeks after Frances McCann died, a farmer rushed into the police compound to report that an eight-year-old boy, Archie Drummond, had been playing in the bush with his older brother when a snake had bitten him on the leg. By the time Anthony reached the Drummonds' shanty, Archibald was already dead. Henry Bowler, the owner of Mitta Mitta Station who performed some official functions in the area, decided that a coronial inquest was not required, and Anthony informed William and Annie Drummond, humble Scottish immigrant farmers, that they could bury their boy.[5] When Anthony had joined the search for Augustus Schmidt outside Amphitheatre in central Victoria in 1867, he had no children of his own. Now that he was a father, he gained a sharp new understanding of the grief that any parent felt when a child was lost.

Sometimes living in such a rugged location, struggling to make a living, became too much, and desperation, even madness, set in. The bush enveloping the Mitta Valley could intensify a sense of hopelessness. On 7 July 1874, a Mr Duncan rushed into the police station to inform Anthony that William Cardwell, an Irish immigrant who had taken up a farm on the banks of the Mitta Mitta, had gone missing. Anthony rode down to the Cardwell property to find William's deeply worried wife, Mary. Pregnant with their eighth child, fear painfully evident in her voice, she told him her husband had been 'strange in his manners for three or four days' and revealed that he had spent three years in a mental asylum in America. He had got up that morning early as usual, she continued, but had sat for a time in the kitchen brooding. Mary had sensed that all was not well. When he had walked out of the house at 7am, she had instructed their eldest child, thirteen-year-old Thomas, to follow his father. William had left the house in his usual garb: moleskin trousers, a light shirt and a brown hat. The fog was thick and Thomas lost sight of his father near the river.

Walking down towards the Mitta Mitta, Anthony could see that William's tracks went to the very bank of the river and no further. He organised a search party, which looked hopefully for tracks on the other side of the river, but found none. Anthony and a search party scoured a wider area around the Cardwell farm but found no trace of the missing man.[6]

Although he was six foot, William was slight: not more than 10 stone, the weight of a man who fretted. He was known for his temperate habits, so drink was not the cause of his discontents. William had disappeared in the past, but he had always been found. Anthony continued the search over the next few days, dragging the river downstream, but discovered nothing. Hope faded.

On 18 July, noting that William 'had for some time been liable to occasional fits of despondency, amounting at times almost to insanity', *The Argus* concluded 'there cannot be a doubt that the unfortunate man entered the turgid stream and was carried away by its waters'. Standish asked for an update on Cardwell's fate. Anthony replied on 2 August to say no new information had come to light despite a diligent search. By the middle of August, William's wife, Mary, had come to the awful conclusion that her husband was dead. Had he decided his family was better off without him?

Two months after the disappearance, on 7 September, John Read entered the station to inform Anthony that a body had been found downriver.

Anthony rode along the Mitta Mitta to find Cardwell's badly decomposed corpse wedged between boulders. It was his grim duty to haul it out of the river, onto a horse and into town. Deciding there was no suspicion about what had happened, he released the body to Mary. This was an act of kindness, for convening an inquest would have led to a delay in burying William, prolonging his family's anguish, and resulted in a formal finding of suicide. The stigma surrounding suicide was intense. Everyone in Snowy Creek knew what had transpired, but Anthony saw no reason to have this recorded. Police work meant knowing where to strike the balance between bureaucracy and empathy. In another act of solicitude, the registrar in Snowy Creek stated on the death certificate that William was 'supposed to have been accidentally drowned'. Mary Cardwell was a woman who deserved a break: when she buried William on 8 September, she was seven months pregnant.

Mary gave birth to her eighth child on 12 December 1874, at the age of forty-two. Lucy Greaves was by her side. The bereaved widow now faced the prospect of bringing up eight children alone in a remote locality. This daunting task was made yet more challenging by the fact that William had died intestate. It took Mary months to get his estate, valued at £329, signed over to her. She was able to fall back on William's brothers for help. Robert Cardwell was already living in Snowy Creek, running several stores. A second brother, Alexander, took up a selection along the Mitta Mitta in 1875, perhaps in part to be close to his bereaved sister-in-law.

As the only policeman in the Mitta Valley, Anthony had quickly discovered that being part of this community meant being there in times of tragedy. But his new assignment was less stressful in other ways. Whereas the Ovens district had a large population, which generated a considerable volume and variety of crimes, the much smaller community in Snowy Creek and the surrounding area presented fewer law-and-order challenges. Most of Anthony's cases ended up before the police courts in Yackandandah, Wodonga and Omeo, requiring him to ride back and forth either along the difficult road running north through the Lockhart Gap or south through even more challenging terrain. A sample of the matters he brought before the courts between 1873 and 1875 reveals what kept him busy: a diminutive but feisty local, Bob 'the Mailman' Connolly, who was nabbed for stealing horses; a lunatic who was despatched to the Kew Asylum in Melbourne; a labourer who was fined for deserting his wife and two sons because he was 'addicted to drink'; a miner who was incarcerated for fourteen days for stealing a saddle from outside the Harp of Erin Hotel in Granite Flat; and a Chinese man, Lee Sin, who was given a harsher sentence – one month's imprisonment with hard labour – for stealing a saucepan and some hinges and bolts from a butcher at Lightning Creek.[7] Anthony had more time on his hands than he had in the past to perform the other duties that routinely accrued to the local policeman. He became the inspector of local slaughterhouses and the keeper of the gaol, a log cabin with one cell.

Life for the Strahan family had settled into a manageable rhythm. Anthony continued to work his customary long hours, seven days a week, but he was the master of his own time. On 11 March 1875, Marion had a third child, appropriately named Marion. Lucy Greaves again assisted the birth. Marion arrived safe and sound – but the wider Strahan–Neilson clan realised less than three weeks later just how chancy life could be in an isolated location far from medical help.

Marion's older sister, Margaret, was four months pregnant when she left her house beside the river at 10am on 31 March to pick pumpkins and melons. Entering a nearby paddock, she trod on a large red-bellied black snake, which twined itself around her right leg and bit her on the calf. The snake seemed ready to attack again, and Margaret fought it off. Her husband, Henry, was driving a team of bullocks 3 kilometres away. With great presence of mind and no small amount of courage, Margaret cut through her stocking with a knife, slicing out a piece of her calf where she had been bitten. On getting home, she found a second bite near her ankle, which she cut out too, with a steady nerve. She called out to her neighbour, a Chinese tobacco farmer, for help. The neighbour despatched messengers to Henry and the police, and tied a ligature tight above the wounds.

A horrified Anthony galloped downriver with a bottle of ammonia in his saddle bag, reaching the Neilson homestead two hours after Margaret had been bitten. By this time, she was raving and unable to recognise anyone. With what one local described as 'great coolness and skill', Anthony gave Margaret some brandy and then poured ammonia over the site of her injuries to neutralise any remaining venom. Ten minutes later, Margaret was recovering. At 11pm, she was overcome by convulsions – but these subsided and she rallied. Anthony had saved his sister-in-law. A week later, Margaret was fully recovered and seemed 'only to suffer from the rather severe gashes she inflicted on herself when cutting out the poison from the flesh'. Oddly, she had told her neighbours a day or two before she was bitten that she had dreamed about a snake pursuing her.[8]

Snowy Creek was a small community and Anthony, as the sole full-time representative of the colonial government, was drawn more deeply into its affairs. Under the *Education Act of 1872*, all children had to attend classes from age six until adolescence, unless they lived 2 miles or more from the local school.[9] Anthony was required to enforce the *Act*, keeping an eye on the locality's children. Riding around the area, he soon noticed that some parents were not sending their children to school because they relied on their labour. Children on rural properties routinely performed helpful chores, with boys cutting wood or rounding up stock and girls looking after their siblings or picking vegetables. Some knew nothing but a life of work. Knowing many families faced tough circumstances, Anthony didn't enforce the *Act* inflexibly. A small-town policeman sometimes had to turn a blind eye.

Churches played an important role in nineteenth-century Victoria, undertaking many of the services today provided by the welfare state, as Geoffrey Blainey observes: 'The priests and parsons were the busiest social workers; they visited the sick and the lonely, and soothed the dying. Many churches provided relief to the poor.'[10] Snowy Creek was not well served in this respect. It had no resident clergyman, Protestant or Catholic. The Wesleyans were the most active denomination on the goldfields, and a Wesleyan minister based in Yackandandah visited the Mitta Valley when he could. He found the inhabitants of Snowy Creek a cheerfully irreverent bunch. At the end of one sermon, he wound up by saying, 'Well my friends, I don't know what more I shall say to you.' Quick as a flash, one old man quipped, 'Sir, just say amen, for I want a drink.'

Other ministers found the residents of Snowy Creek hardy and wary. 'Occasionally strange visitors find their way to this remote part of the world,' noted *The Murray and Hume Times* in June 1875, 'and show a zeal for our spiritual welfare which would be quite refreshing, were it not that, in return, they expect us to take a still warmer regard in their temporal interests.' On this occasion, 'a stranger of a grave and reserved demeanour' had arrived unannounced in the town and conducted several services. Always grateful to receive visitors in their remote location, residents put up the preacher in comfortable circumstances, and a sizeable congregation turned out to hear him speak in the evening. 'At the close of his address, the reverend gentleman stated that it was usual to make a collection, and signified that his hearers would be wanting in their duty, if they did not show a practical faith in the doctrine of St Paul that "the labourer is worthy of his hire".' As most of the audience shuffled uncomfortably, one forthright man made clear that he was unimpressed by this nakedly self-interested pitch, and 'a wordy warfare' ensued. The disgruntled Creekite persuaded the preacher to return the following morning for a second sermon. The next morning, unwilling to acknowledge the reverend as 'a chosen vessel', he staked out the sermon with a placard, questioning the preacher's motives. Few other locals bothered to attend the sermon and the preacher left Snowy Creek grumbling about the dirty trick that had been played on him.

It was not only the local people who could be hostile. One of the valley's apparently all too abundant snakes decided to disrupt a divine service being conducted by another visiting bush missionary on 5 December 1875. As the missionary was holding forth, a black snake, measuring a good six feet, slithered among the congregation, creating an understandable commotion – not quite a re-enactment, perhaps, of the story of Adam and Eve.[11]

Marion and Anthony attended Protestant services when they took place, not least because many townsfolk, especially those who regarded themselves as the respectable backbone of the community, expected to see their policeman in attendance. Although he was no teetotaller, Anthony knew well that excessive drinking could lead to trouble, which would often wind up at his door. He was likely happy that some Wesleyan meetings took the form of temperance gatherings. Anthony was not sectarian, having worked agreeably with fellow officers who were Catholics. This was a boon because the Mitta Valley had a sizeable Catholic contingent. This community embraced many of the valley's poorest residents, as in other parts of the colony. It was important to Anthony to strike up a rapport with the owner of Mitta Mitta Station, Henry Bowler, not only one of the region's biggest landowners but also its leading Catholic layman.

The consecration of a new Catholic church was an important event in a community that so often felt cut off and ignored. On 1 December 1876, the first Catholic Bishop of Sandhurst, Dr Martin Crane, came to Granite Flat to open the new Catholic church, St Mary's. Crane had been taken aback when he had arrived in Sandhurst in early 1875 to find that his diocese in Victoria contained forty churches, many of them in poor repair, and a paltry seven resident priests. He went on an energetic drive over the next seven years to build more churches, and so he was gratified to be consecrating a new place of worship in one of the more isolated corners of his diocese. Underscoring support for the Church in the valley, Crane stayed at Mitta Mitta Station the night before the ceremony, which attracted Catholics from outlying areas, who came into Granite Flat on horseback.[12]

Well might the inhabitants of the Mitta Valley heed the Lord's word, for nature continued to present daunting challenges. Even in a region often hit by adverse weather, 1875 was a year of extremes. Bushfires ripped through the Upper Murray and the Mitta Valley in January: 'Unfortunately, although rain clouds from time to time make their appearance, they disperse without discharging their contents, and there is as little appearance of the drought coming to an end,' *The Ovens and Murray Advertiser* lamented.[13] Many farmers were already in 'great straits for feed and water for their stock'. Anthony and Marion had become accustomed to bushfires as an unavoidable fact of life, but such conflagrations were still disconcerting. When the rain finally arrived, it came in a deluge. The flood in 1874 had been bad, but the one that descended on the Valley during the winter of 1875 was worse. An occasional correspondent in *The Ovens and Murray Advertiser*, writing under the delicious pen name Wandering Willie, described a scene of chaos and destruction. The water rose rapidly late at night on 31 August, leaving little time for preparations. Within four hours, the flood was fearsome:

> The height to which it attained on the flats was far beyond that witnessed by the oldest settlers in the locality. The destruction caused to selectors' fences and cultivation is unprecedented; indeed there is not, for a distance of thirty miles, a paddock left secure, the whole of the fencing, in some cases, having been carried away, and a large amount of debris left instead by the raging waters. In some instances life was in danger, and much loss has been sustained both by squatters and selectors.[14]

The body of one man, who had tried to cross the river on his horse, was found several weeks later.

The floodwaters surged into the police compound in Snowy Creek, damaging the buildings that had been painstakingly repaired and frightening Anthony and Marion, who had three children under the age of four. Two weeks after the flood had receded, the buildings were still wet and covered in mud. Marion's already taxing daily workload, looking after a house, a husband working long hours and three young children, had become more onerous. Wandering Willie spoke for everyone when he declared at the end of September: 'It is to be hoped that neither the squatters nor selectors of the Mitta Valley will experience the like again.'

The impact of the flood was all too evident when R.C. Flockhart, a Wesleyan parson based in Beechworth, and a friend came through the Mitta Valley in February 1876 to deliver lectures on the virtues of education. Flockhart's companion observed that the flood had washed away the bridge across Snowy Creek: 'Although part of the township is on either side nothing has been done towards rebuilding the bridge, and now the only communication is by a punt provided by the people themselves.'

Little mining was going on, though one group had 'a sluicing claim of great proportions' that was paying well. Its banks in parts were nearly 100 feet high.[15]

Anthony repaired the flood damage at the station, and Marion gave birth to a fourth child, Thomas, in June 1876. The town meanwhile continued to acquire a more permanent feel, as a Mechanics Institute opened, providing a meeting place for the townsfolk. One administrative change occurred that year: the town was officially renamed Mitta Mitta, though many people continued to refer to it as Snowy Creek. Old names died hard in such a remote locale.

Three and a half years into his assignment in Mitta Mitta, Anthony had become a part of the local community. He had good reason to be satisfied. Crime in the area remained low, due in part to his good efforts. He was on amicable terms with the vast bulk of the residents, meaning they kept him informed and relied on him.

But it wasn't all plain sailing. In 1875, Anthony became embroiled in a protracted feud with James Aitken, an obstreperous store owner in Mitta Mitta. They traded accusations and insults for months. The stoush escalated when Aitken wrote to Inspector Alexander Brooke Smith in Beechworth on 14 October 1876, accusing Anthony of feeding his own fowl with government stores, placing his private horse in the police stable and poisoning a dog: 'When feeding his fowls, he gave vent to some loud yells in a manner to create grave doubts of his sanity.' Aitken alleged that Anthony had walked into his store in uniform 'in a very excited manner with clenched fists and pale face', yelling that 'he would not allow me to be "peeping and pimping" after him'. Aitken wrote to Brooke Smith again a week later, charging that Anthony had exhibited his 'petty spleen' by poking out his tongue as he had ridden down the street past his store.

A cautious, at times lazy and often ineffective policeman, Brooke Smith knew he had to do something to ascertain if Aitken's allegations had substance. He asked his subordinate for an explanation. A furious Anthony denied the accusations, writing a six-page rebuttal, the longest document he would pen in his entire career. He rejected any suggestion that he had misused the station's stores or stable. He insisted that the storekeeper bore 'a very bad character in this quarter for dog poisonings and for many other bad actions'. As for the recent altercation on the street, he claimed Aitken had called him 'a liar, a thief and more a lunatic than a constable'.

What to make of this acrimonious exchange? Some of Aitken's allegations hit the mark. We know Anthony had a hot temper. It seems plausible that he would have stormed into Aitken's store, almost on the verge of violence, when he found out that the shopkeeper was spying on him and going around the town making allegations of misconduct. The contention that Anthony had poked out his tongue is silly enough to have the ring of truth about it. But Aitken was a bully and not popular around the town.

The whole matter could have ended here. But the two antagonists were stubborn. Anthony enlisted a powerful supporter: landowner Henry Bowler, who had served on the Towong Shire Council and as a magistrate at the Tallangatta police court. He liked Anthony and had crossed swords himself with Aitken three years earlier. Putting pen to paper on 27 October, he told Brooke Smith that he had 'never known a more meddlesome person [than Aitken] or one who appeared to take such delight in making mischief'. Noting his considerable dealings with policemen in the area over the years, he certified that Anthony was 'the best and most efficient man we have had here'. He argued that a policeman in the execution of his duty must give slight offence: 'With Mr Aitken this is a matter very easily accomplished and once done in ever so trivial a matter makes the fellow an everlasting and unscrupulous enemy.'

Bowler gave his own example of Aitken's vengefulness. When he had defeated a candidate nominated by Aitken at a school board meeting, the storekeeper had accused Bowler of improper land dealings, organising 'the most vexatious persecution by beating up all sorts of imaginary evidence', including a petition with fictitious signatures. Aitken had insisted that Bowler had to disprove the charges, reversing the burden of proof. Anthony was being treated in the same pernicious way. Aitken had been frequently heard to say he would not rest until Anthony had been removed from the district. Bowler trusted that would not happen.

On 2 November, Brooke Smith sent a report to Commissioner Standish, rejecting Aitken's allegations as vindictive and attesting to Anthony's efficiency as a senior constable. Standish saw no need for a formal inquiry and agreed that Aitken should summons Anthony to the police court if he felt he had a case to make. Bowler's intervention had been influential. The owner of fine racehorses that competed in the Melbourne Cup, he was respected and well-liked across the colony and his word carried weight.

Aitken, however, refused to accept this rebuff. He enlisted his own powerful supporter, the member of the Legislative Assembly for Murray, William Witt. A druggist by trade born in England in 1833, Witt was a leading figure in the northeast. On 23 November, he wrote to Standish from his Queen Street offices in Melbourne: Aitken, a friend and a constituent, would like to see the Chief Commissioner on a matter relating to the police at Snowy Creek. 'You will oblige me by granting an interview and showing your best consideration to the complaint.' But Standish had had enough of Aitken and did not grant the interview.

The feud did end up in the police court in Tallangatta in December 1876 for one final round, with Anthony summonsing Aitken to face a charge of using abusive language. But the case was dismissed, much to Anthony's chagrin.[16] Although he was disappointed, Anthony was quick in his report back to Brooke Smith to point out that Aitken had summonsed him before the Tallangatta police court a year earlier for using obscene language. On that occasion, the magistrate had dismissed the summons, saying he did not 'believe one word of what [Aitken] had said in court'.

The legal squabble between Anthony Strahan and James Aitken ended in a draw. Neither had managed to secure a conviction against the other. But Anthony had come out with the better outcome. Unlike what had happened in Bealiba a decade before, he was not removed from the district. The two men must have continued to rankle each other month after month, and perhaps this lit a fuse in Anthony that he took with him into his next posting.

A MASTER OF HIS OWN DOMAIN

Anthony might have been the master of his own domain for most of the year, but the long arm of the police administration in Melbourne still reached out to even remote sub-districts. In July 1877, Inspecting Superintendent Charles Hope Nicolson visited Mitta Mitta. Nicolson was an ambitious, hard-working officer who had been in the force since the mid-1850s, running the detective branch for fourteen tough years. Back in May 1870, when he had overseen the Kyneton district, Nicolson had tried unsuccessfully to persuade the young Ned Kelly to reject a life of crime and make a fresh start. Only weeks later, flanked by Superintendent Francis Hare and Sergeant William Montfort, he had tracked down Ned's bushranging mentor, Harry Power, arresting him near James Quinn's property on the King River.

Born in Dundee in Scotland, Nicolson was a stern, hard-working and rather cerebral Presbyterian with exacting standards and a receding hairline. In his book on the Kelly hunt written in the 1950s, the journalist Frank Clune noted that Nicolson 'was a strict disciplinarian, insisting on spick and span uniforms, rigid routine and military methods, including much drill and saluting of him by the lower ranks'.[17] Nicolson had been shot in the face by a bushranger as a young constable, leaving him with a scar and chronic pain. Perhaps in part because of this pain, he could be ill-tempered and sometimes heavy-handed.[18] As the inspecting superintendent, he was the second-ranked officer in the force.

When Nicolson rode into Mitta Mitta, the sub-district's population was no more than 540, around 400 Europeans and 140 Chinese. While some were still engaged in mining, most residents were farmers. Nicolson pulled up at the police camp on 29 July, catching Anthony off guard, likely deliberately. True to form in his report, he recorded Anthony's appearance as 'slovenly', though he conceded that he had arrived around evening stables, when a constable was likely to be dishevelled. Although he was unimpressed by Anthony's physical appearance, Nicolson found him to be 'self-possessed and intelligent', noting he had a reputation in the Ovens district for being 'a very efficient Constable'. In a notation on Nicolson's report, Anthony's commander, Brooke Smith, agreed, contending that

'Strahan is not at any time as smart looking in appearance as he is in his duties'.

Nicolson observed that the level of crime in the area was low. Over the past year, Anthony had prosecuted one case of larceny by a husband and wife, arrested one man for drunken and disorderly conduct and followed up two cases of horse stealing, though on each occasion the horse had merely strayed before being recovered. Anthony had been otherwise conducting regular police patrols, observing passing strangers and stock, and discharging his responsibilities as the Crown Lands Bailiff. Nicolson concluded that the station's financial arrangements were in order and rated Anthony's general conduct and discipline as good. Anthony's troop horse, a five-year-old bay mare, was sound and of 'a good stamp', even though it was 'rather heavy looking and coarse bred for hill work'.

Nicolson's report made it apparent that Anthony was not overly stretched in the conduct of his duties in the Mitta Valley. Indeed, by 1877 life for Senior Constable Strahan and his family had taken up an agreeable pattern. Even though he was keen to claim the next promotion to the rank of sergeant, Anthony could well have decided that he was happy to stay in Mitta Mitta, at least for another year or two. Or perhaps, after almost six relatively uneventful years, he was ready for a challenge. Whether or not he wanted to leave Mitta Mitta, events in Greta, a small town to the west on the edge of the Oxley Flats, were about to change his life dramatically.

PART III
THE KELLY OUTBREAK

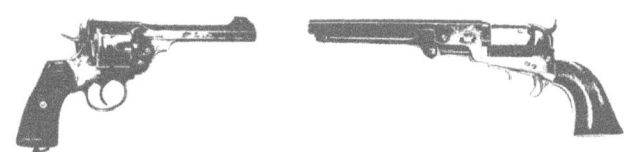

KELLY COUNTRY

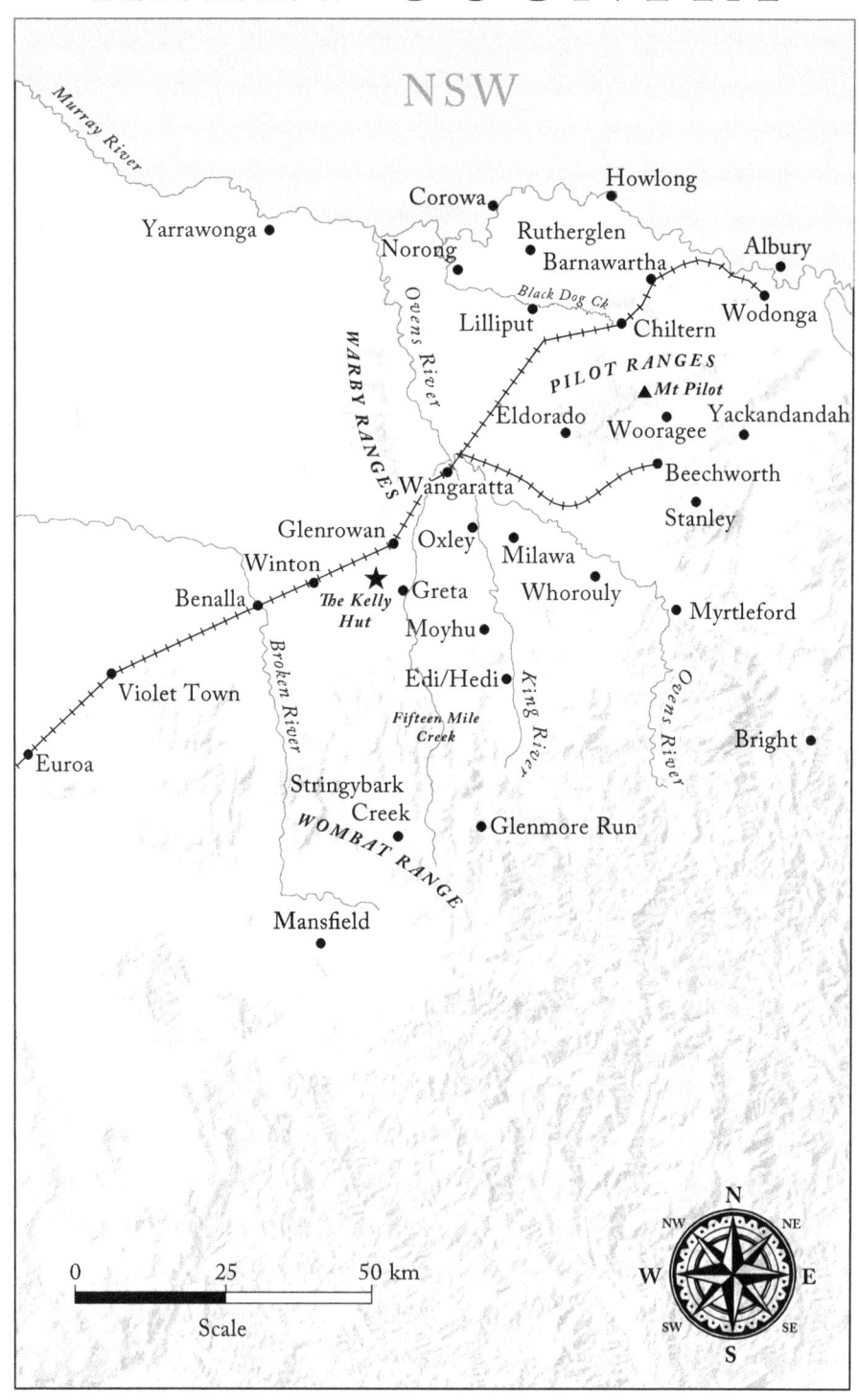

12

THE GRETA MOB

Anthony was not a man built to coast through life. He was ambitious and driven, at times even restless. He stared down a challenge. When he was told that he was being reassigned to Greta, he knew, like the rest of the Victoria Police, of the town's reputation. In 1877, in the months leading up to his relocation, *The Ovens and Murray Advertiser* covered the criminal activities of two brothers, Edward and Daniel Kelly. Yet these occasional reports gave him little sense of just how much trouble lay ahead. The next two years would test him in many ways. His workload would mount, his powers of physical and mental endurance would be pushed to the limit, his family would be placed in danger and his health would take a hit. Over the hard times ahead, he might have even wished that he was back at the junction of the Mitta Mitta River and Snowy Creek, enjoying a quieter and more uneventful life.

At first glance, Greta seems like an improbable place for one of Australia's most significant national stories to begin. Mitta Mitta's population was about the same size as Greta's, but petty criminals like Bob 'the Mailman' Connolly were small fry compared to the Kelly brothers and their gang.

Situated on the Oxley Plains in northeast Victoria, the area around what became known as Greta was first settled by European farmers in the early 1840s. From its inception, the small settlement derived some importance from its location on the original main road between Sydney and Melbourne, with coaches and wagons stopping to rest and change horses. It was surveyed as a town in 1852, with the land being carved out of the Green Vale run, and a township developed among the red gums along the banks of Fifteen Mile Creek. It expanded during the goldrushes as people travelled north to the diggings around Beechworth, and land surrounding the town was surveyed for selection between 1860 and 1866, boosting the number of farmers.[1] Greta seemed well-located, almost equidistant between Benalla to the west, Wangaratta to the north, Beechworth to the northeast and Bright to the east. But the township's fortunes flagged, first as the Beechworth goldrushes waned and then in the early 1870s, when the Victorian government sensibly decided to extend the main rail line north from Benalla through Glenrowan to Wangaratta, bypassing Greta and Eldorado entirely.

In the late 1870s, Greta was a small community, with a scattering of dwellings, a post office, a general store, a school, a blacksmith and a shoemaker, a stone-and-brick Primitivist Methodist church and a smaller wooden Catholic chapel, and the police station, which had first opened in 1852, closed and then reopened in 1870. Bridget O'Brien, an Irish immigrant, had been running the town's one hotel, the Victoria, since her husband's death in a horse-riding accident in 1874. The local population was roughly two-thirds Protestant and one-third Catholic. Interdenominational relations were mostly amicable, though the members of each faith tended to take up land close to one another. Although Greta remained modest in size – no more than a few hundred people – the surrounding farms, some quite large, gave the area some economic importance. The local economy was based on a mixture of cultivation, especially of wheat and oats, and grazing, of both sheep and cattle. The road on the town's northern edge split in three directions: one fork turning left around the Fifteen Mile Swamp towards Wangaratta, 33 kilometres to the north; a second heading across the King and Ovens rivers towards Beechworth; and a third bending to the right towards Moyhu and the Upper King Valley. Glenrowan lay 20 kilometres to the north, on the rail line.

Greta would have remained largely unnoteworthy were it not for the rise of the Greta mob, a group of wild young men, mostly the Victorian-born sons of selectors, who became known for their horsemanship, tough talk, rowdy drinking and criminal ways. The unruly Greta boys tucked the chinstraps of their hats under their noses distinctively. Similar mobs of young larrikins whipped up a storm in Wangaratta, Oxley, Mansfield and Wodonga, but it was the Greta mob and its four most well-known members – Ned and Dan Kelly, Steve Hart and Joe Byrne – who were destined to become legends. As early as 1870, Chief Commissioner Standish insisted that Greta was 'a very hotbed of criminals'.[2] And this is where happenstance intervened, propelling Anthony Strahan inexorably towards his fateful conversation with Ned Kelly's uncle, Pat Quinn, and those hot purported words that would ricochet down the decades.

The Kelly, Quinn and Lloyd families were at the heart of the Greta mob. This family network was bound together by the four daughters of James and Mary Quinn, Irish Catholics who came to Australia as free settlers. Ellen married John 'Red' Kelly, who was transported as a convict; Jane and Kate married the Lloyd brothers, Tom and Jack; and Margaret married another, unrelated, Quinn, Patrick. From its beginnings, the Greta mob had a strong Irish-Australian character. The Kelly, Quinn and Lloyd boys were all the sons of Irish immigrants, convict or free, as were other mob members such as the McAuliffes and the Delaneys.

Red and Ellen lived first at Beveridge, on the edge of Melbourne, before moving during the summer of 1863–64 to Avenel, another 60 kilometres north. Following Red's death in 1866, largely due to alcoholism, Ellen and her seven children – sons Ned, Jim and Dan and daughters Annie, Maggie, Kate and Grace – moved to Greta, in Victoria's northeast. The location was no accident. Ellen's father had purchased the 25,000-acre Glenmore run between Greta and Mansfield at the head of the King River in 1864, settling there with Mary and his sons, John (Jack) and James (Jim). The run was situated to the southwest of Greta and close to a route for funnelling stolen stock into New South Wales.

Ellen lived at first in a derelict hotel with her sisters Jane and Kate and their children. Her sisters' husbands, Tom and Jack Lloyd, were serving sentences in Beechworth for cattle-stealing. The three women barely got by. But life got tougher in 1868, when a drunken Jim Kelly, Ned's uncle and a cattle duffer, argued with Ellen and set fire to the hotel. Six months later, Ellen paid the deposit for an 88-acre selection on Eleven Mile Creek in the Warby Ranges on Robert McBean's Kilfera run, 7 kilometres to the west of Greta, towards Glenrowan. Little was done over the years to farm the selection, which was held back by poor soil and irregular rainfall. Instead, Ellen set up a sly grog shop in her shanty, which became notorious in the district as a venue for gambling and licentious behaviour. Her customers were a mixed bunch: locals, passing travellers and more than a few shady characters.

The historian John McQuilton argues that northeast Victoria's reputation as a haven for the colony's habitual criminals is inaccurate, observing that its crime rate mostly matched its proportion of the overall population, aside from a few wilder years. But it is well to remember that the overall level of crime was high across Victoria. Stock theft in the northeast was three times higher than elsewhere in the state, and the Kellys, Quinns and Lloyds were at the heart of this thriving racket, moving their booty into and out of New South Wales, especially when the Murray was low, via a network of helpers and receivers. The mob stole horses, Doug Morrissey writes, from as far away as Gippsland and the western district.[3] Kelly, Quinn and Lloyd men were arrested for different offences in the 1860s and 1870s, sometimes being discharged and sometimes being convicted, receiving prison sentences of a few months through to several years. McQuilton notes many stock theft charges failed, ascribing this to police incompetence or worse. Although police missteps did play a part, stock theft was hard to prove. Cattle and horses were often stolen at night from unfenced and unmonitored paddocks, and these thieves were expert at altering brands. Some clan members, including Jack Lloyd senior, avoided getting caught despite the police and stockowners knowing they were guilty. By 1874, Ned Kelly had served two prison sentences even though he was only nineteen: three months in 1870 for assault and sending an indecent letter (mailing a parcel containing calf testicles and a crude note to a childless couple), and three years between 1871 and 1874 for receiving a stolen horse.

Many people in the colony felt the Greta mob was out of control. Unfortunately Constable Hugh Thom was in command of the Greta station, and he wasn't one of the force's finest. In April 1877, not long before he rode into Mitta Mitta to assess Anthony Strahan's station, Inspecting Superintendent Charles Nicolson had visited Greta on a similar unannounced inspection. Greta was a two-man station at that time, with Thom commanding a younger constable, J.J. Hayes. A Glaswegian by birth, Thom had joined the force at the age of twenty-three in 1869, on the same day that Anthony's younger brother, Simon, had been taken on. He had spent his career in the northeast, serving in Stanley (a goldmining town near Beechworth), Bright and then Greta from around September 1876. In Greta, Thom faced the usual load of a policeman at a small country station, juggling his police work with other tasks, becoming the inspector of nuisances.

When Nicolson arrived in 1877, Thom had been in Greta for nine months. In his report, Nicolson said Thom was an intelligent officer and noted that the station's arms were clean and serviceable, but he was otherwise unimpressed. Thom was dressed in 'a soiled dirty jumper, dirty breeches, and a crushed uniform hat, beard untrimmed'. Nicolson recorded that James Hayes was 'intelligent and promising looking, but not so smart as when he first arrived from the depot; the example of his superior officer, Constable Thom, in that respect has evidently not been improving of him'. Nicolson could be nit-picking, even priggish, but he had a point. Thom's shambolic appearance wasn't representing the force in the right manner in a restless locality, generating a picture of laxity, unprofessionalism and ineffectiveness.

More damningly, Nicolson concluded that the commanding constable in a town infamous for its mob was doing little to stop the crime wave sweeping the area. Thom had been conducting few patrols, allowing his horse to become fat through inactivity. Nicolson decided that Thom was not capable of coping with the Greta gang. Sergeant Arthur Steele, the energetic and pugnacious officer who ran the station in Wangaratta, took an equally dim view, later telling the Royal Commission into the Kelly Outbreak that Thom was intemperate: 'I cannot say exactly that I have seen him absolutely drunk, but he used to come in a muddled state; he seemed to remain in a sort of stupid state for some time.' Thom appeared to be on intimate terms with the Kellys' friends, conversing carelessly with them for hours in the pub while 'at the same time, perhaps, their comrades were about the district on horseback'. At the royal commission, Steele insisted much trouble would have been avoided if Thom had 'made proper endeavours' and captured the Kellys early on. He said he had advised his superiors that Thom should be removed from Greta because he was 'almost useless'. Superintendent Francis Hare concurred, describing Thom as 'unsteady'. Many locals wanted the lackadaisical policeman gone.

Following his inspection, Nicolson told Standish the arrangement in Greta had to change. Steele was keeping offenders in the area under 'as good surveillance as the distance and means at his disposal will permit', but this wasn't enough. Thom had to go. 'Until the Gang ... is rooted out of the neighbourhood one of the most experienced and successful mounted constables in the district will be required in charge of Greta.' Standish agreed, and selected the replacement personally. It proved difficult to find a suitable substitute, especially because the force was stretched even more thinly in 1877 following another budget squeeze that saw positions cut. Nicolson was sore about the cuts, which he opposed, the more so because Standish implemented them without consulting him.[4]

Standish settled on Anthony Strahan as the replacement. This choice made sense. Anthony had come through this recent inspection in better shape than Thom. Nicolson might have found his dress slovenly, but he had rated Anthony's professional skills highly. Anthony had apprehended two sets of would-be bushrangers in the early 1870s, first Trembath and Watson and then Smith and Brady, attesting to his ability to handle difficult cases. On each occasion, he had made the arrests quickly and secured convictions. Nicolson had seen during his inspection that this capable officer wasn't taxed in Mitta Mitta, with its low level of inoffensive crime. It made no sense to leave a tenacious and effective officer in a backwater.

Standish's decision created lasting bad blood between Thom and Anthony, affecting their ability to work together in the future. Ironically, Thom was moved to Eldorado, where Anthony had made a mark for himself. He had a lot to live up to.

As a married man with children, Anthony couldn't move to Greta straight away. During Nicolson's inspection in 1877, Marion was four months pregnant; she gave birth to Jessie on 30 October. It was clear neither she nor the baby would be ready for the arduous journey to Greta for some weeks.

By the beginning of 1878, Marion and Jessie were both doing well and Anthony decided it was time to leave Mitta Mitta. But nature intervened. Victoria had been gripped by an intense drought since 1876, and savage heat arrived in the northeast on 7 January. The desiccated countryside erupted into fire. 'One of our reporters, who chanced to be in that part of the country,' wrote *The Ovens and Murray Advertiser*, 'met some men riding hard for help, but owing to the harvesting, and other causes, help was not forthcoming, or it was too late.' Fires were 'raging in almost every direction', including around Beechworth and Yackandandah, choking the sky with smoke. The road from Mitta Mitta to Greta passed through this very countryside and the Strahans had to wait.

Rain brought relief. On 12 February, *The Advertiser* declared that drought had lifted. So, after organising their affairs in Mitta Mitta, Anthony and Marion departed for Greta. This was a more taxing journey than the one they had made to Snowy Creek five years earlier. In 1873 they had travelled the 130 kilometres from Eldorado in late autumn with one child. Now they were making a longer journey – close to 200 kilometres – in the heat of summer with five children. Jessie was just three months old when they piled their modest possessions on a wagon and travelled down the road that went through the Lockhart Gap and across the Kiewa Valley to Beechworth. It was still hot. The route took the Strahans through terrain where fire had consumed crops, grazing land and fences. At least the final leg from Beechworth to Greta saw countryside unaffected by fire. The harvest was good despite the drought, with farms on the Oxley Plains threshing heavy yields.

When they pulled up in Greta on 15 February, Anthony and Marion confronted a familiar problem: a ramshackle station. The police had long known about the parlous state of the station and its living quarters. Ernest

Flood, who had been posted in Greta in the early 1870s, told the Kelly royal commission that 'the house was so unhealthy my family could not live in it'.[5] Bridget O'Brien, the proprietor of the Victoria Hotel, owned the cottage. She was a tough landlord. On 17 October 1877, she wrote to Inspector Brooke Smith offering to make repairs, but only on hard terms:

> I will cause such repairs to be effected to the foundations of the cottage occupied by the Police at Greta, as will prevent the damp from rising. I will cause the damp bricks in the walls to be removed and replaced by dry bricks on the following conditions. First the Police Department will take a lease of the premises for a period of five years. Second a rental of £52 per year will be paid as at present. If the Department prefers purchasing I will sell the premises for the sum of £300.

Under the tight fiscal circumstances, purchasing the property was impossible. But neither was Standish inclined to rent the cottage for another five years given the rising damp. He asked Brooke Smith to find alternative accommodation. But Brooke Smith reported that there was 'not a building in the little village except this to rent for police purposes. I do not think anyone in the neighbourhood would undertake to build a station for the purposes of rental.' He was sure the station could be made healthy if O'Brien made considerable repairs. Standish accepted this, stating on 8 November: 'As the warmer weather is coming on which will do away with the inconvenience till the next winter, this matter can stand over for say four months during which time the police may look out for better quarters and also submit any offer they may obtain to erect other premises for a station.'

And so Anthony and Marion moved into a health hazard. This was worrying for the parents of five children, including an infant. Hot weather mitigated the health threat for some weeks, keeping the rising damp at bay, but Anthony moved to remedy things as autumn approached. By March 1878, Brooke Smith had been transferred to Wangaratta, taking charge of the station there, a task that proved sadly beyond his abilities as the Kelly Outbreak escalated. His successor in Beechworth was Superintendent Hussey Chomley. An Irish Protestant born in Dublin in August 1832,

Chomley joined the Melbourne and County of Bourke Police as a cadet in 1852, just before the formation of the Victoria Police. He worked his way up through the ranks. Chomley was loyal, honest, disciplined, conservative and easy-going, but limited and prosaic.[6] He was hardly a star, but he was more effective than his predecessor.

On 26 March, Anthony underlined what his colleagues knew only too well: 'the buildings at this station are badly in want of repairs'. Aside from the cottage's rising damp, the store required 'repairing at once as every shower of rain that falls damages the forage'. The stable and the store needed new doors.[7] Despite these frustrations, the Greta posting was a feather in Anthony's cap, an indication he was seen by his superiors as an experienced and trusted officer, ready to take on challenges. Marion faced a tougher set of circumstances. While her husband was moving around the district doing exciting and possibly career-advancing work, she was home alone looking after five children. When she arrived in Greta, Marion was twenty-nine and had already lived in several towns across the northeast, meaning she was acquainted with the challenge of settling into a new community. Yet in Snowy Creek Marion had been part of a close family group, with her sister living nearby. She knew no one in Greta. Her mother and sister Winifred were living in Eldorado, but that was 50 kilometres away. As the wife of the town's only policeman, she was accepted, even respected, by some residents, but much of the population regarded her with reserve, suspicion or worse.

Marion's routine was gruelling. Aside from looking after five children, she had to do all the tasks that were part of keeping a household running in the 1870s. The wood-burning stove was the heart of the house, especially during winter, and Marion used it for heating, cooking, washing and ironing. Geoffrey Blainey observes that women in nineteenth-century Victoria had to make many of the daily items now produced in factories, such as jams, soap, soup, biscuits, candles, clothes and even bread. This was especially so in a small town like Greta, which had one general store. Hawkers met some household needs, but Marion likely often had to make do herself. She could rely on few mechanical aids to lighten the burden, aside perhaps from a wringer. She and Anthony might have had a wire-walled meat safe, but ice chests did not yet exist and stopping food from going off was a challenge. Like other women, Marion pickled meat, often rendering it sour. Wash day meant washing, boiling, rinsing, blueing, wringing, drying, starching, mangling and ironing the clothes of seven people. Once herself a domestic servant, Marion had no household staff of her own. The eldest child, Anthony Oliver, might have helped with a few things, such as fetching wood, but he would have started school at six, keeping him away from home during class.[8]

While he didn't confront this remorseless domestic grind, Anthony had a difficult job in his own right. The Greta mob and the Kellys seemed an ever-mounting problem. Although many in the northeast had no truck with the mob, seeing them as nothing but trouble, others sympathised with them, bearing a grudge against the district's squatters and the police. These local pressures reflected broader trends. Anthony had arrived in Greta at a time of significant discontent across Victoria. Several factors were at work. The drought had wrought significant damage, forcing farmers to drive their stock over long distances in search of water. Only three weeks before Anthony reached Greta, *The Advertiser* noted that the whole region was affected: 'This scarcity of grass and water is very general on the heads of the various tributary creeks running to both the Ovens and King Rivers.' The recent bushfires had only added to the drought's toll, consuming grass and fencing. Desperate farmers even resorted to cutting down saplings and feeding them to their stock.[9] Exacerbating the horrible impact of drought and fire, grain prices were falling, and the revenue generated by goldmining continued to decline, putting more pressure on the colonial government's budget. Selectors had mixed fortunes. Some were building up their holdings, paying their rent on time and avoiding indebtedness. But others were struggling, working allotments that were too small or poor in quality. They had often started out with insufficient capital to make a go of farming, and some lacked the necessary skills. Debt levels rose and hostility to the banks climbed. *The Advertiser* took the higher number of criminal cases coming before the courts as 'substantial proof' of the drought's evil effects: 'Every form of business or trade has experienced a certain amount of stagnation, and business people, having found it impossible to collect their outstanding accounts, have been compelled to press their debtors.'[10]

Reflecting these tensions, Victoria experienced a protracted political crisis between 1877 and 1881 as the parliament became a battleground between liberals and conservatives, small farmers and squatters. The liberal Chief Secretary, Graham Berry, and the firebrands in his cabinet such as Peter Lalor (of Eureka fame) and Francis Longmore clashed with the Legislative Council, which was dominated by conservative landed interests. 'The struggle erupted in December 1877,' writes the political scientist Paul Strangio, 'when the council deferred Supply ostensibly because it refused to be coerced into sanctioning an expenditure item for the payment of members of parliament that was appended to the Appropriation Bill.' Just as drought and bushfires were ravaging the northeast, Berry and his allies made an abrupt move on 9 January, dismissing 300 civil servants, including several heads of departments; judges from the county, mines and insolvency courts; police magistrates; and wardens of the goldfields, prosecutors and coroners. These sackings became known as Black Wednesday. Much of the colony was shocked. *The Ovens and Murray Advertiser* noted on 12 January that there was 'much talk as to the effect of the "mowing down" – for it cannot be called "weeding" – in the Civil Service.' By 24 January, another 100 civil servants were removed, bringing the total to 400. This upheaval reached into the northeast. The Berry government justified the sackings as a matter of financial exigency, but it was motivated, notes Strangio, 'by a desire to reform an intransigent public service blighted by a culture of patronage'.[11] Although many civil servants were eventually reinstated, what *The Advertiser* called 'the present deplorable state of things' inevitably created a sense of tumult.

The police were spared during Black Wednesday, but big changes would soon envelop the force, generating additional strain and making it more difficult to curb the Kelly Outbreak. Some changes in police deployment in the northeast over the previous few years had already made Anthony's job in Greta more challenging. When the rail link from Benalla to Wangaratta was completed in 1873, Superintendent Hugh Barclay told Standish that 'the necessity for police protection at Glenmore no longer exists'. He recommended closing the station.[12] Superintendent Nicolson demurred and Standish kept the station open, for good reason: *The Advertiser* noted that Harry Power, the bushranger, had 'long obtained shelter … in the fastnesses of Glenmore'.[13] But after the Quinns took land further north towards Greta and sold the Glenmore run in 1875, the Glenmore police station closed. This would prove to be a poor decision because it made the police deployment in the critical triangle between Mansfield, Benalla and Beechworth much thinner.

Bigger towns such as Benalla, Wangaratta and Beechworth served broader policing functions and hosted large police stations. By contrast, smaller towns were still staffed by solitary officers. This had not proven a problem for Anthony in Mitta Mitta, where the population had been small and the level of crime low, though even there the residents lobbied Standish to station two men in the valley.[14] But Greta in 1878 presented a different picture. As the sole policeman in the town, Anthony faced the real possibility that he might be intimidated or harmed by the Greta mob and its supporters. Steele later insisted at the Kelly royal commission that posting one officer in a place like Greta was almost useless. He admitted that Anthony had been placed in an invidious, almost impossible, situation: 'I did not think it was safe for him to go out. If I were there myself alone at Greta I would not feel disposed to knock about amongst those people.' Steele thought the Greta station should have had at least two men. So staffed, he ventured, it would have been able to contain the area's 'bare-faced' horse stealing, the murders that would later shake the colony would not have occurred and the Kellys would have been in gaol instead of at large.[15] Posted alone in a restless area at a turbulent time, Anthony was placed in a dangerous position.

Making matters worse, morale among frontline policemen was poor in some areas, in part because the force was so stretched. Low morale led to internal backbiting. Although they were both Protestants, Anthony

Strahan and Hugh Thom were almost destined to clash. It probably did not help matters that Anthony was Irish and Thom, Scottish. The police included few Scots, and they may have sometimes seen themselves as a cut above their Irish colleagues. Did Thom look down on Anthony? Anthony was unimpressed by Thom, sharing Steele's opinion that he was intemperate. And Thom returned fire, describing Anthony as 'blathering' – a view apparently shared, McQuilton contends, by other constables, though he provides no details about who these officers might have been.[16] It is true that Anthony was rarely short of a word, offering his sharp opinions freely, ready for a verbal stoush if need be. And it was hardly surprising that Thom was truculent, for he had been relieved, after all, of his position in Greta, and Anthony was his replacement. This must have stung, and a man like Anthony was unlikely to have gone out of his way to spare his colleague's hurt feelings.

13

OVER THE EDGE

Sergeant Arthur Steele's assessment of the volatile state of play in and around Greta was entirely accurate. Anthony likely hoped he could settle into his Greta assignment gradually, finding his bearings and getting to know some of the locals. But this was not to be. He was thrown right into the thick of it little more than a month after arriving in Greta.

On 15 March 1878, three days after Anthony turned thirty-eight, Charles Darvall JP, a businessman who had lived in the northeast since the mid-1860s after migrating from Southampton, issued a warrant in the Chiltern police court to arrest Ned Kelly for stealing eleven horses in August 1877. And so, still a virtual stranger in the locality, Anthony found himself at the pointy end of the task of trying to apprehend one of the district's most troublesome ruffians.

Darvall's warrant was no small deal; the horses were worth £170, a handsome sum. The four complainants on the warrant – John Cavanagh Farrell, James Whitty and his nephew James Albert Whitty, and Robert Jeffrey – were all Irish immigrants. Born in Wexford in 1812, James Whitty was the eldest and most prominent. He had arrived in the Port Phillip district in 1840 as an illiterate and penniless assisted migrant. A number of siblings and cousins had followed him, creating an extensive family network in Victoria. He had built up substantial land holdings over the years by dint of hard work and canny purchases, often transacted in conjunction with his relatives and a friend, Andrew Byrne. Although they didn't have the same sway as the district's wealthy English Protestant families, the Whittys had achieved some social, economic and even political standing in the district by the 1870s. Family members served on the Wangaratta and Oxley councils, owned hotels and played a leading role in local horse racing. Two younger Whittys, Thomas and Charles, became policemen. Keen to protect what he had built up, James Whitty joined the North Eastern Stock Protection League, which gave rewards to policemen who recovered stolen stock, reinforcing the links between the police and landowners, both squatters and selectors. Dispelling the notion that he was some kind of antipodean Robin Hood, stealing from the rich and giving to the poor, Ned had lifted horses from several Greta and Moyhu selectors around the time that he robbed Whitty.

Anthony knew some of the Stock Protection League members well, including the Docker brothers, the owners of the sprawling Bontharambo run. He would have likely met the Whittys soon after arriving in Greta. He shared the League's view that the Kellys were inveterate thieves and troublemakers. In early April 1878, a few weeks after the warrant had been issued in Chiltern, Anthony and Sergeant Steele led two police parties in a bid to arrest Ned. They scoured the region, first around the Kelly farm on Eleven Mile Creek and then up into the hills, but without success. Ned knew the northeast well and avoided apprehension, perhaps skipping across the Murray. Some thought he might be working as a log splitter in southern New South Wales after selling a herd of stolen horses.

Events moved fast. On 8 April the Chiltern bench issued additional warrants to arrest Dan Kelly, Ned's younger brother, and one of the Kellys' cousins, John 'Jack' Lloyd junior, over the horse theft. Dan and Jack had just been released from Beechworth Gaol after serving four months for causing wilful damage to the home of a hawker and storekeeper in Winton, David Goodman, a Jewish immigrant, on the night of 27 September 1877. They had appeared at the Goodman house with another member of the clan, Tom Lloyd junior, when David was away on business, leaving his wife, Amelia, and children home alone. The three young men, who had been drunk, had gone on a rampage, smashing doors and windows. Tom did not walk free with his cousins in early April; he was serving an additional four-month sentence for assaulting Amelia. He was perhaps lucky: not only had he sidestepped a more serious charge of indecent assault, but being incarcerated meant he was not subject to Darvall's warrants like his cousins. He would not leave Beechworth Gaol until July, by which time much had happened.

The police were under intense pressure to deal with the Greta mob. Inspector Brooke Smith granted Anthony six days' leave from Greta station to undertake a patrol into New South Wales to follow up another lead on the whereabouts of the Kellys.[1] Sensibly deciding he could not leave the Greta station unattended, Brooke Smith despatched a telegram on 12 April to Sergeant James Whelan in Benalla, instructing him to send Constable Alexander Fitzpatrick to Greta. Whelan ordered Fitzpatrick to ride to Greta and remain at the station with Marion and the children until Anthony returned. This would be a fateful decision, setting off a chain of events that would escalate the confrontation between the police and the Kellys.

Many contemporaries and most historians have judged Fitzpatrick harshly. Only twenty-one in 1878, Fitzpatrick was an inexperienced policeman who had managed to join the force largely because the Crown prosecutor, Charles Smyth, had lobbied Standish on his behalf. Peter FitzSimons takes a dim view of Fitzpatrick: 'Since joining the force in April of the previous year, his police record has been a litany of louche laxity, ill-disciplined drinking, slovenliness and being placed on official reports.' But not everyone has accepted this portrait. Leo Kennedy – the great-grandson of Sergeant Michael Kennedy, who would come to play such a tragic part in the Kelly saga – paints a different picture, claiming Fitzpatrick has been the victim of a long Kelly-inspired smear campaign. Underscoring the complex relations that often link coppers and criminals, Doug Morrissey points out that Ned and Constable Fitzpatrick were occasional drinking buddies.[2]

It took Fitzpatrick a good two days to return to Benalla from a stint of duty in Cashel. He finally departed for Greta on 15 April. This delay left the Greta station unattended and Anthony's family alone for several days.

Fitzpatrick would never reach Greta. On his way, he stopped off in Winton to down at least one brandy and lemonade. Suitably fortified, he decided to go alone to Ellen Kelly's hut. He had two motivations for doing so: he wanted to make a name for himself by arresting Dan and he was sweet on young Kate. It was nonetheless foolhardy to appear at the Kelly household alone. Some months earlier, Superintendent Nicolson had warned his officers not to approach the Kelly hut solo: 'If there are two constables together bad characters are always afraid to proceed with extremities with them because one constable is a witness and support to the other.'[3]

What happened in the Kelly hut on 15 April remains unclear. Even though he sides with the Kellys, John McQuilton concedes that it was 'a confused event, none of the principals telling the truth'. Suffice to say, Fitzpatrick claimed when he returned to Benalla in the early hours of 16 April that he had been shot in the left arm by Ned and hit on the head with a shovel by Ellen. Given the conflicting and shifting accounts offered by different participants in the argument inside the Kelly hut, it is impossible to know if Ned was present, and some evidence suggests the wound on Fitzpatrick's arm was not caused by a gun shot. Many saw him as a perjurer. The Kellys and their friends charged that Fitzpatrick had trespassed on Ellen's land without a warrant and behaved badly. They made a damaging allegation that would haunt the constable and later the whole Kelly story: they claimed he had tried to molest Kate during his tumultuous visit.

Anthony returned to Greta on 15 April, the very day Fitzpatrick was supposed to arrive. It is not hard to imagine how he would have reacted. He had been away in New South Wales searching for Ned only to soon discover that his quarry was apparently back at the Kelly hut, less than 7 kilometres from Greta. Anthony could not be blamed if he was unimpressed that the police had left his wife and children in Greta unprotected for several days. He was likely more than unimpressed by Fitzpatrick's tardiness, and wouldn't have been backward in castigating his colleague when they crossed paths over the coming weeks.

The brawl in the hut on 15 April took the Kellys' conflict with the police to a new level. It now seemed they were ready to shoot policemen. Anthony had already had a brush with such violence, for the two men behind the Wooragee Outrage, Smith and Brady, had apparently intended to shoot him in 1872.

Even though he had given his account of the confrontation with the Kellys in a semi-inebriated state, Fitzpatrick's claims were readily accepted by his colleagues. On 16 April, the Benalla bench issued warrants to arrest Ned for attempted murder and Dan, Ellen and two family friends, William 'Brickey' Williamson and William Skillion (the latter had married Maggie Kelly) for aiding and abetting. Williamson had form, for he was part of Ned's horse-stealing ring. The Benalla police sent a telegram to stations across the colony at 9am: 'Constable Fitzpatrick in attempting to arrest Dan Kelly at Greta yesterday for horse stealing was shot in the wrist by Ned Kelly when warding off a blow of a shovel made by Mrs Kelly, other suspected offenders were there also armed.'[4]

Anthony was about to have a busy day. First, he tied up a loose end. He knew Ned and Dan's cousin, Jack Lloyd, the third man listed in the horse-stealing warrants, had not fled the area. He arrested Jack at his father's farm and incarcerated him in the Greta lock-up at 11am. At the time of his arrest, Jack had only one shilling in his pocket. Unlike his cousins, he was illiterate.

Sergeant Arthur Steele and Detective Joseph Brown arrived later in the day. Anthony rode out to the Kelly hut with them in the afternoon to execute the arrest warrants issued that morning in Benalla. After watching from a nearby hill into the evening, waiting to see if the Kelly boys would turn up, the three policemen entered the hut to find Ellen alone with her daughters Kate and three-day-old Alice. Little Alice's father, George King, a flashy young Californian who in early 1874 had married Ellen Kelly, nearly twenty years his senior, was nowhere to be seen. A leader of the horse-stealing ring along with his stepson Ned, King had vanished in late 1877 after the Whitty raid, abandoning his wife and children. His fate is unknown to this day.

In his report, Anthony described his encounter with the Kelly matriarch:

> Asked her if she was present when her son Ned Kelly shot at Constable Fitzpatrick and wounded him in the arm. She said it would be hard for me to see him when he was not at my place. I said to her do you

mean to tell me that Constable Fitzpatrick was not at your place on the night of the 15th April. She said I have not seen Constable Fitzpatrick since you and him were at my place, and that is over a month. And as for my son Ned, I have not seen him for months.

Kate gave the same story as her mother. They were lying. Anthony questioned Ellen's son-in-law, William Skillion, at his selection. He too fibbed, insisting he had not been at the Kelly hut the evening before. But he made a key admission: 'I seen Constable Fitzpatrick pass my place about 5 o'clock in the evening going in the direction of the Kelly place and that was the last I saw of him.'[5] At this point, Steele opted not to arrest Ellen or Skillion, riding instead with Brown and Anthony across to Williamson's place to apprehend him.

After incarcerating Williamson in the Greta lock-up alongside Jack Lloyd, the three policemen returned to Eleven Mile Creek in the early hours of 17 April, arresting first Skillion and then Ellen. Ned would later claim Anthony and his colleagues burst into the Kelly hut with revolvers drawn and threatened to blow his mother's brains out if she moved. In his account of the Kelly Outbreak, Grantlee Kieza notes that Steele gave a much more restrained account of the arrest, as one might expect: Ellen was allowed to say goodbye to her older children and her notoriously wild brother, 'Mad' Jimmy Quinn.[6] The three policemen took Skillion and Ellen, who was holding little Alice in her arms, into Greta on horseback.

Anthony had four high-profile prisoners in his lock-up. Later in the day, Jack Lloyd was transferred to Benalla to face a committal hearing on the horse-stealing charge. Ellen, Skillion and Williamson were only held in Greta for a day as well. Anthony's humble log lock-up was unsuited to holding multiple prisoners for anything but a short period.

Many years later, Marion told one of her grandchildren that she had looked after Ellen and her daughter during that cold night in the lock-up. While she made Ellen as comfortable as possible in the cell, ensuring she was warm and had proper food, she took Alice into the Strahan home itself. Ever since, the wider Strahan clan has believed that these acts of kindness earnt some gratitude from Ned and his brother.[7]

On 18 April, as the police were transferring Ellen, Skillion and Williamson to Benalla on a dray to await a committal hearing, Ned and Dan were spotted by passers-by shoeing their horses in a gully in the Warby Ranges near Glenrowan. Ned had a revolver strapped at his side. He was furious that his mother had been imprisoned, believing her arrest to be another example of police persecution. 'For a boy who'd been the man about the house,' writes Clare Wright, 'the failure to protect his mum from harm was crushing.'[8]

The arrest of Ellen for aiding and abetting the attempted murder of Fitzgerald drew Anthony into the heart of the drama surrounding the Kellys. But this didn't mean the other pressures in his life vanished. He had a family to protect. Marion was glad her husband was home again. She was hardy but being left alone at such a time had not been easy. Her grinding routine was made more difficult by the continuing ramshackle state of the station. The cottage's problems, especially the rising damp, were getting worse as the weather became colder and wetter. Realising she had to compromise, Bridget O'Brien agreed in late April to fix the cottage, meeting the force's requirements without increasing the rent or altering the lease.[9] It was important for the police to maintain good relations with O'Brien, for she was a significant figure in Greta. The Victoria Hotel was a meeting place for locals, including the Greta mob. O'Brien's brother-in-law, Daniel Kennedy, a former teacher, helped out in the pub and was to become one of the most productive police informants, providing a stream of information under the name the Diseased Stock Agent (the diseased stock in question being the Kelly Gang itself).

Anthony continued to look for the Kellys, now working with Detective Michael Ward. Irish by birth, the 32-year-old Ward had been a detective since 1876. A dapper fellow with rimless spectacles, an elaborate waxed moustache and a neat chin beard,[10] he knew the northeast well, having been in the district in the early 1870s. Destined to become a controversial figure in the Kelly saga, he was despatched from Melbourne by the head of the detective branch, Inspector Frederick Secretan, to join the search for Ned. He was convinced the upcoming court hearing for Ellen would prompt Ned and Dan to visit their sisters, Maggie and Kate. He arrived in Benalla on 25 April and got to work straight away, setting off with Anthony and two constables around 7pm to stake out the Kelly hut. It was a bleak autumn night, 'raining heavens and very dark', according to Ward. Six kilometres from the Kelly hut, Ward and Anthony found a dray abandoned on the Greta road without a horse. The dray was carrying two bags of flour and other articles. Ward and Anthony searched the area around the dray, soon finding Maggie and Kate, sitting bedraggled on a log. Dressed in light clothing and sodden, they said they had become confused in the dark and could not find their way home. They provided no explanation for the absent horse. Ward gave Kate a flask of whisky and she took a swig. He later told the royal commission it was clear that Anthony knew the Kelly girls 'very well'. While the two constables took the girls home to Maggie's place, Ward and Anthony watched over Ellen's hut for several hours, but no one appeared.[11]

Rumours swirled around the district as to the whereabouts of the Kellys. The police were dependent on tip-offs to track down suspects. Anthony had received several crucial tip-offs in the past, such as when Thomas Brady's father provided vital information that helped to identify the perpetrators of the Wooragee Outrage. However, relying on verbal information was problematic. Many tip-offs proved false – sometimes deliberately so, but often people were simply mistaken, passing on sketchy information they believed to be true. In an era before modern communications, tip-offs often reached the police, especially in areas where the population was dispersed, days late, often too late to act. It was critical to act swiftly when credible information came to hand, a challenge that dogged the Kelly hunt. It was equally important for policemen to build relationships based on trust with people in their communities, enhancing the prospect of coming across timely and accurate information. The Kellys, meanwhile, were acting on their own tip-offs conveyed by 'telegraphs', sympathisers who passed on information about the movements of the police. These telegraphs sometimes passed on dud information, but they often helped the Kellys elude arrest.

While the Kellys were absconding, the Greta mob continued to run riot. On 26 April they descended on Benalla, where Ellen Kelly was in the watch house with Skillion and Williamson. 'Drinking, swearing and fighting was the order of the night,' reported *The Benalla Standard* on 30 April, 'and they indulged in it at the top of their bent. Stripped to the waist in the middle of the footpath, challenging all and sundry to fight, was the chief pastime. Nobody seemed inclined to take up the challenge – no, even the police! Where are they? May very well be asked, but we can only answer: in the usual place – absent.' Noting that shopkeepers were compelled to close their shutters, *The Standard* lamented what it insisted was the regular absence of the police. 'If there are not enough men here, we should have more; but, if those already here are afraid to do their duty, they should be removed at once. We would not write thus strongly were it not for the fact that life and property are in jeopardy at the present moment owing to the neglect of the police district.' When Nicolson asked Sergeant Whelan to explain why the police had done nothing to control the riot, he explained indignantly that he had been keeping watch over Ellen and her fellow prisoners as well as a lunatic patient.[12]

Meanwhile, the horse-stealing case against Jack Lloyd came unstuck. Lloyd was brought before Charles Darvall in the Chiltern police court on 25 April on the charge of helping to steal the eleven horses in 1877. Anthony, as the arresting officer, testified on behalf of the Victoria Police. However, none of the four accusers was able to identify Lloyd, and Darvall discharged him.[13] This outcome was unsurprising. The four accusers had not been present when the horses had been lifted, so they were unable to testify that Jack Lloyd had been one of the culprits. Lloyd's discharge was testament to the courts' ability to deliver verdicts in favour of the Greta mob even after the incident at the Kelly hut had raised the temperature considerably.

A more important case concerning the mob's horse-stealing racket came before Chief Justice Sir William Stawell on 2 May at the Court of Assize in

Beechworth. Two German brothers, William and Gustav Baumgarten, as well as Samuel Kennedy, William Cooke and John Studders, were charged with being part of the horse-stealing ring. The charges in part covered the horses stolen from James Whitty. The proceedings took up most of the day, and the jury returned a mixed verdict: it found Cooke guilty but Gustav Baumgarten and Studders not guilty. Despite deliberating for some time, it could not agree on the charges against William Baumgarten and Kennedy, and Chief Justice Stawell remanded both men to face trial again before the same court at a later date. A defiant Cooke insisted he was innocent. But Stawell said he was sure Cooke was one of the leaders of the horse-stealing gang and gave him an eight-year prison sentence with hard labour.[14]

With the effort to shut down the horse-rustling racket delivering patchy results, the police were under mounting pressure to apprehend the Kellys. Several officers were placed on special duty in late April to concentrate on the search. Anthony and Detective Ward were joined by three constables. Ernest Flood and James Hayes both knew Greta from previous postings. The third was Charles Whitty, one of James Whitty's nephews. After joining the force as a mounted constable in 1877 at twenty-one, Charles was posted to Shepparton and Murchison before being deployed to Benalla to assist the Kelly hunt. Was Charles chosen to join the hunt because his uncle was one of the four complainants on the horse-stealing warrants? He had a keener and perhaps vested interest in apprehending the culprits than other officers engaged in the search. In April 1878, he had been in the force for just one year.

On 7 May, Ward received information that suggested the Kellys were hiding at Ryan's Creek, around 10 kilometres from Stringybark Creek, in the Wombat Ranges. He set off into the hills, taking Anthony, Whitty, Hayes and a fourth constable, Mooney, with him. The police contingent searched for three days but yet again found no trace of the Kellys, who were hiding higher up in the ranges.[15] A frustrated Ward returned to Melbourne.

A week after the abortive search through the Wombat Ranges, Ellen Kelly, Skillion and Williamson appeared before the police court in Benalla in a committal hearing. They were represented by William Zincke, the experienced Beechworth lawyer, while Superintendent Hussey Chomley acted for the Crown. Following Fitzpatrick's testimony, the bench committed the defendants to stand trial before the Court of Assize in October. Bail was set for Ellen at a hefty sum, two sureties of £50 each, far beyond her means.

Ellen and her co-accused were moved to Beechworth to await trial. By this time, discontent about the Greta mob was even more intense. On 28 May, *The Advertiser* declared:

> Some people pooh pooh the idea, but the fact remains that in and around the pleasant little farming area of Greta there is about as nice a nest of thieves and dangerous vagabonds as can be found in any part of the colony, and although from time to time some efforts have been made to root them out, they continue to commit their depredations. The recent horse-stealing cases which occupied so much attention [in] Beechworth pointed directly to the existence of an organised gang of horse stealers … Edward Kelly, with his brother Daniel, is still at large, and though a price has been put upon his head, and for weeks past the police have been busily engaged looking for them, hitherto all their efforts have been fruitless. We know Ned Kelly to be a lawless desperado, who, if driven into a corner, would stop at nothing, and who, now that he is wanted, must sooner or later do something serious, and therefore in the interests of public safety, it is incumbent upon the Government to do everything in their power to effect his capture.

While the search for her sons continued, Ellen endured two uncomfortable weeks in Beechworth Gaol with her infant daughter as winter descended. According to a short unpublished Strahan family history, Marion Strahan and Ellen became close during this time. Marion took clothing and food to Ellen while she was locked up in a cold, hard cell.[16] This story seems improbable. Marion had five children to look after and Beechworth was far away from Greta, a day's journey by cart or wagon. In any case, two Greta farmers each paid £50 to meet Ellen's bail in June and she returned to her hut until her trial.[17] Perhaps Marion assisted Ellen after her release.

By this time, Ned and Dan had become as elusive as ghosts, with sightings occurring across northeast Victoria and southern New South Wales. Anthony followed up one lead on 28 May, calling on Robert Mason at his property, Fairfield Park, south of Greta. Mason came from a complicated family that walked both sides of the law. His father, Robert senior, an ex-convict transported to New South Wales in 1827, had purchased the Fifteen Mile Creek run at Hanson South near Greta in the mid-1850s. Over the years, Robert the elder combined honest farming – growing potatoes, tending livestock, milking cows, making cheese and butchering meat – with criminal side ventures, mostly stealing cattle, sheep and horses, to boost his income. The police suspected that the former convict sometimes helped the Greta mob to move stolen animals north across the Murray, keeping him under surveillance. The younger Robert Mason was, by contrast, an upright man who expanded his landholdings by dint of hard work and astute purchases, though he didn't sever his links with his dubious father. A noted horse-breeder and a fine buckjump rider, he married Ellen Whitty, a niece of James Whitty, in 1873, thereby creating a kinship link with one of the district's largest honest landowners. By 1878, his holdings had grown to 2000 acres.

When Anthony pulled up at Fairfield Park, Robert senior, at seventy-seven, had withdrawn from active farming. His links with the Greta mob had waned. Proving that loyalties between criminals are shifting and expedient, Ned had tried to steal one of his horses in 1876 or 1877. Mason junior certainly had nothing to hide. Having married into the Whitty family, he had no reason to protect Ned and Dan. He told Anthony a stranger had stayed overnight at Fairfield Park on 19 May looking for work as a horse-breaker. Mason said he had seen a revolver on his visitor, though he had taken no notice, thinking he was a copper. Mason thought the stranger had been about Fifteen Mile Creek for ten days but couldn't provide a name.

On his way back to Greta, Anthony was informed that the same man was at Tom Lloyd senior's farm. Anthony gave his horse a spell, leaving Greta after midnight. He watched Lloyd's place on Eleven Mile Creek all night, but he saw nothing untoward.

Returning to Greta early on 29 May, Anthony was told the stranger was at Hart's farm on Fifteen Mile Creek. Richard Hart, an Irish immigrant, was working two selections, one south of Wangaratta and another at the foot of the Warby Ranges. Two of Hart's sons, Dick and Steve, were members of the Greta mob. By this time, Anthony's troop horse was exhausted and he hired a private horse to ride down to Fifteen Mile Creek, where he found the stranger with Jack Lloyd, breaking in a colt. The man gave his name as James McCoy, saying he had been staying around Wangaratta for the last two years. Anthony searched his swag but found no revolver. He later informed Inspector Brooke Smith that McCoy, if that was his real name, didn't fit the description of anyone in the Police Gazette. He noted that McCoy was now breaking in a horse for John Kelly, one of Ned's uncles, at Fifteen Mile Creek.[18] 'McCoy' could have been an alias, though a shepherd called James McCoy was discharged in 1872 as an accomplice in the unsolved Selby and Bennett murder case dating back to 1863 (a hawker and his assistant were found tied to a tree near Stawell, their heads bashed in with a hammer).

Anthony's patrol on 28 and 29 May highlighted both his tenacity and the taxing task facing the police in chasing multiple Kelly leads. What would he have done had McCoy turned out to be Ned or another gang member? He was riding alone.

Not long after he tracked down McCoy, Anthony received a visitor in Greta: Sergeant Michael Kennedy from Mansfield. Anthony and his guest shared much. They were both Irish. Kennedy was born in Westmeath in 1842, just two years after Anthony was born in Kildare. They were married, each with five children. Their wives, Marion and Bridget, were almost the same age. True, Kennedy was a Catholic, but both men had demonstrated they could work with Catholics and Protestants alike. Both had served with the Irish police before migrating, Anthony with the Royal Irish Constabulary and Kennedy with the Dublin Metropolitan Police. Kennedy had landed in Melbourne with his parents in 1864, joining the Victoria Police as a foot constable. Like Anthony, he transferred to the mounted division.[19] When he pulled up in Greta with Constable Thomas

McIntyre, Kennedy was a respected policeman, a good bushman and a fine horse rider. He was liked by his superiors and subordinates.

The Mansfield police officers stayed overnight. Anthony and his visitors discussed the job's frustrations. Kennedy said he and McIntyre had just ridden north from Mansfield in search of the Kellys, passing through the Wombat Ranges and zigzagging up towards the head of the King River. They had called in at the station in Hedi, another one-man post, and come close to Harry Power's hideout.[20] Mansfield and Greta were not connected by a road and the going had been rugged. Kennedy admitted that his enquiries had come to nothing, though he was sure the Kellys were holed up in the wild countryside between Greta and Mansfield. Anthony confessed his own efforts to locate the Kellys had failed. Happy to have a sympathetic ear, he underlined the difficulties of managing the station in Greta alone. Even as he was looking for the Kellys, other tasks continued to intrude on his police work. In May 1878 the Oxley council appointed him as the local inspector for slaughterhouses.[21]

Around this time, the Victoria Police made one sensible decision, ditching the uniform that had been in place for some years. Out went the accoutrements that seemed to owe more to the traditions of a bygone era than practicality: the military-style sashes and the black cylindrical shako hats. Instead, the officers of the force donned a new kit modelled on the British Metropolitan Police, with navy blue trousers, capes and leather bobby helmets.[22]

This change was welcome, but the work of the Victoria Police was complicated by a political decision made in Melbourne in June. The government reorganised the police force, creating considerable additional strains for officers across the colony. Victoria's population had reached 879,000, suggesting the force should have been expanded, including at senior levels, to maintain law and order across a bigger population. Instead, the shake-up, which was driven by budget cuts, reduced the number of police districts from thirteen to eight. Five superintendents – including Joseph Mason, Anthony's old commander in Avoca – were pensioned off, with no replacements appointed. The reorganisation hit hardest in the northeast.

The northeast district, with its headquarters in Beechworth, was combined with the Upper Goulburn district, with its headquarters in Mansfield, and part of the Kilmore district. The new district was vast: more than 17,700 square kilometres, stretching from Yarrawonga and Corryong on the Murray to Woods Point on the Goulburn River and across to Rushworth. Half of this area was covered by mountainous terrain. The district embraced forty-nine stations manned by only 100 officers. Beechworth became a second-rank station; the new district headquarters was located in Benalla, though some thought it should have been situated in Wangaratta. *The Advertiser* was unimpressed: 'We consider that the district is too large for any one man to manage, and that experience will prove it to be unworkable.'[23]

The next two years would prove *The Advertiser* sadly right. John Sadleir, who had joined the force as a cadet in 1852 and been promoted to superintendent in 1874, was placed in charge of the district, moving from Mansfield to Benalla. Born in Tipperary in Ireland, he was a methodical, fair, hard-working and professional policeman. He knew he had been given a difficult, if not impossible, job. He later told the Kelly royal commission that the northeast district was 'so large as to be quite beyond control'. On taking charge, he pointed this out to Standish, who agreed, but could do nothing because the government insisted on the new arrangements in light of the parlous budgetary situation.

Anthony was now reporting to a superintendent with too much to do. At least the force recognised the escalating situation in and around Greta, posting a second officer, Constable Cornelius Ryan, on temporary duty to the station there in mid-1878. Ryan had not been a policeman for long, having joined up in 1875, but he was familiar with the northeast: he had served in Yarrawonga on the Murray River before moving to Greta. In late July, Anthony and Ryan were on patrol when they saw two horsemen on Bald Hill. Suspecting the riders were the Kellys, they rode up as quietly as they could to capture them. However, when they reached the hill, the men had disappeared. Yet again Anthony felt he had come close.

The Kellys had now been on the run for three months. Shortly after what could have been a near miss, Sadleir visited Greta for the first time on

30 July. Anthony was frustrated, telling Sadleir that he and Ryan couldn't do much to arrest Ned or even disturb him from the neighbourhood. During his visit, Sadleir spoke to a farmer on King River who said 'in a somewhat mysterious way' that 'the Kellys were in the neighbourhood of Connolly's or towards the Wombat or Holland Creek'.

Back in Benalla, Sadleir considered what he had been told by Anthony and the farmer. On 10 August, he wrote to his old colleague in Mansfield, Sergeant Kennedy, saying it seemed Ned was located somewhere between Greta and the Wombat Ranges. He set out a plan: 'It has been proposed to collect, for the purposes of a thorough search, what constables are in the district who know Kelly personally, sending say two of them to Mansfield to act with [you] from that end, and the others to act with the Greta Police, and to search simultaneously up and down the King River and neighbouring places.'

Kennedy wrote back on 16 August. He agreed Kelly had 'secreted himself in some isolated part of that country lying between the Wombat and King River, in a similar way to which Power did'. Given the distances involved and the impenetrable countryside, he said the Mansfield party would need to establish a camp some distance beyond the Wombat, perhaps at Stringybark Creek. From this base, the Mansfield men could 'keep up a continuous search' between there and the King River, Fifteen Mile Creek and Hollands Creek, while the Greta party could operate on the flat country along the rivers and creeks.[24]

This plan was not implemented for some weeks, mostly because the police were preoccupied with tying up other Kelly matters. The Court of Assize convened in Beechworth in October before Justice Barry. The Kellys and their associates featured heavily. On 9 October, the first day of the session, Ellen Kelly, Williamson and Skillion stood trial for aiding and abetting the attempt to murder Constable Fitzpatrick on 15 April. Superintendent Chomley was the prosecutor, while John Bowman, a well-regarded barrister and a former Beechworth mayor, represented the accused. William Zincke was back as the defence's instructing solicitor. Fitzpatrick took centre stage, repeating his account of what had happened in the Kelly hut. On the surface, it was convincing. But John Nicholson, a Benalla doctor, testified that one of the wounds on Fitzpatrick's left wrist might not have been caused by a bullet, casting doubt on the constable's story. Chomley accused two farmers who tried to give Skillion an alibi of perjury. After deliberating for two hours, the jury found the defendants guilty.

It was perhaps appropriate that William Baumgarten and Samuel Kennedy appeared before Barry the next day to face the unresolved horse-stealing charge. Underlining just how divided opinion was across the district, it took nearly an hour to empanel the jury, with forty-two candidates being challenged, roughly in even numbers by the prosecution and the defence. The prosecution called a string of witnesses, including James Whitty and several other farmers, to build its case. Although the defence did its best to pick holes in this testimony, the prosecution's case was strong and the jury found both accused guilty.

On 12 October, Barry sentenced Williamson and Skillion to six years' imprisonment for aiding and abetting the attempt to murder Fitzpatrick, and Ellen Kelly to three. Presumably Ned's mother was given a lighter sentence, even though she had whacked Fitzpatrick over the head with a shovel, because she was a woman and a mother. Sometimes the patriarchal norms of the day favoured women, but not often. Barry hoped these sentences would 'lead to the disbanding of the gang of lawless persons, who have for years banded themselves together in the neighbourhood against the police'. He told Ellen that he would have sent her son Ned away for twenty-one years had he appeared alongside her in the dock.[25]

If you believed Fitzpatrick's account, these sentences were just. If, by contrast, you thought the constable was a liar, they were plain wrong. Ellen's sentence enraged her sons, who became even more convinced the family was being persecuted by the police and the courts. A portion of the community sympathised with the Kellys; others thought they were getting what they deserved.

Turning to the horse-stealing case, Barry sentenced Kennedy to six years' imprisonment and Baumgarten to four. *The Advertiser* was implacable: 'A gang of horsestealers has long ... flourished in the North-Eastern district, they have pursued their nefarious avocations with wonderful cleverness and systematic shrewdness, they have been materially assisted by a nest of receivers.'[26] The paper said that Ned had undoubtedly participated in the ring's operations, using the alias Thompson. It regretted that he was still at large.

14

A FEW WORDS

On 22 or 23 October 1878, with emotions running high across the district in the wake of Ellen Kelly's conviction, Anthony rode out to a farm in the hills near Greta. He was attempting to determine the whereabouts of Ned and Dan, following up on a hunch he had. Anthony was again riding alone, suggesting he didn't expect to encounter the Kelly boys themselves at the farm. He knew they were hiding elsewhere, deep in the ranges. But he suspected the wily farmer was assisting them, providing information and provisions.

That farmer was a man named Patrick Quinn. Married to Margaret, Ellen Kelly's sister, he was Ned and Dan's uncle. The young outlaws were close to Quinn, as they were with many in their extended family, and may even have picked up a trick or two from him. For Pat Quinn had his own chequered history with the law. Police had long suspected that he was up to no good. And he could be violent. In August 1870 he had bashed Senior Constable Edward Hall outside the Greta police station in an altercation involving his brother-in-law, Jimmy Quinn, who was being arrested for assault and using threatening and abusive language. As Hall knelt to handcuff Jimmy, Pat swung a stirrup-iron on the end of its leather like a skull-cracker, smashing Hall on the head twice, inflicting a severe laceration across the scalp. As he did, Jimmy yelled, 'Stave his head in.' Pat was found guilty of inflicting bodily harm and sentenced to four years in prison.[1] His loyalty to the family was clear.

There was no love lost between Anthony and Quinn. Like most police, Anthony would have reserved a special dislike for anyone convicted of assaulting a police officer, and he was aware of Quinn's reputation for duplicity, sometimes helping out the police with information and sometimes misleading them. He would have hardly relished seeking him out. But the protracted search for the Kellys was frustrating for the Victoria Police, and Anthony felt that Quinn could hold a key. So he rode the 11 kilometres south-east from the Greta station to Pat Quinn's farm at Hanson South.

When Anthony arrived at the property and dismounted, he encountered Pat on the grounds. What happened next is notoriously unclear, but the conversation started abruptly and ended acrimoniously, according to the two existing reports of the encounter, both authored by those in the Kelly camp. While what was actually said by each man remains shrouded in uncertainty, Ned had little doubt about what had transpired. Some months later, after so much that was ugly and violent had happened, Ned gave his account of the conversation between his uncle and Anthony in his famous Jerilderie Letter. Partway through the letter, Ned declared that 'Strachan' had said 'he would not ask me to stand he would shoot me first like a dog'.[2]

These menacing words occupy a prominent place in most of the books that have been written over the decades about the Kelly Outbreak. Some writers have taken Anthony's purported threat as clear evidence that the police never intended to apprehend the Kellys and were always determined to kill them. The journalist and author Frank Clune set the pattern in his 1954 book about Ned Kelly, reprinted many times over the years under different titles. He didn't quote the Jerilderie Letter word for word, instead saying that Senior Constable Strahan had boasted he would 'shoot Ned like a dog'. He didn't say where and when Anthony had allegedly uttered these words. He gives Anthony two other fleeting mentions, leaving him a thin, anonymous character in his drama, stripping him of his first name.[3]

Writing in 1979, John McQuilton repeated what was becoming the standard narrative, affirming that Ned believed the police would shoot his party 'like dogs': 'The very expression used was taken from one of Strahan's threats made to Kelly relatives as to the fate of the brothers if they fell into his hands, a threat later judged to be a primary cause of the mischief.'

McQuilton took the threat directly from the Jerilderie Letter, providing no other source and taking it as incontrovertible fact. Nor did he provide any earlier example of Anthony's supposed bullying. He attributed the claim that Anthony's threat was a primary cause of 'the mischief' to a letter another police officer had written to Sadleir in 1898, twenty years after the Outbreak.[4] In line with his tendency to depersonalise both the squatters in the northeast and some of the victims of the crimes of the Kelly–Quinn–Lloyd clan, McQuilton always referred to Anthony simply as 'Strahan', never providing his first name. In the index he listed him incorrectly as 'H Strahan'.

The few points that McQuilton included about Anthony's career were also incorrect. He asserted that Anthony replaced Constable Flood at Greta (Anthony replaced Thom – Flood had left the station in 1874) and went on sick leave in April 1878 when Fitzpatrick was despatched to replace him (Anthony was granted leave to conduct a patrol into New South Wales to look for the Kellys). After repeating Thom's damning 'blathering' epithet without explaining why the two policemen had clashed, McQuilton had nothing good to say about Anthony Strahan. He contended that Anthony was one of the many policemen who used the controversial offence of 'having meat (or a hide) in his/her possession for which he/she could not satisfactorily account' to prosecute poor selectors. He asserted likewise that Anthony was incapable of listening to and working with locals like the Kellys. Again, this damning contention is unsupported by evidence.[5]

McQuilton's negative portrait of Anthony reflected a stinging assessment of the police in general. His critique contained valid points about the force's weaknesses, notably its poor or non-existent training regime, most grievously concerning bushcraft and weapons. He argued cogently that the police shake-up in 1877–78, which closed stations such as Glenmore and reduced other posts to one officer, compromised the force's ability to curb the northeast's escalating stock theft. And he was right that the Kelly royal commission uncovered shortcomings in the police's efforts to apprehend the Kellys. But McQuilton took his criticism too far, presenting most policemen in rural areas as buffoons and thugs:

City men who knew nothing of the bush were posted to rural stations while experienced bushmen patrolled Bourke Street. Easily lost in and fearful of the bush, the city men kept to the main roads, refusing to follow even bridle tracks, useless tactics in discouraging stock theft from bush paddocks ... For the ambitious constable, rural districts were to be avoided. Chances of promotion were better in Melbourne or the country towns ... By the late 1870s the police were the feared, and sometimes hated, intermediaries between selectors and the squatter-authority forces.[6]

While he exempted a few individuals, such as Sadleir and William Monfort, from this sweeping critique, McQuilton tarred the majority of the force with the same brush. Yet he seemed to have spent little time finding out who these officers were and what they did during their careers. To be sure, some officers fitted the pattern he sketched, but many did not. Anthony was an experienced bushman by 1878, having spent almost fourteen continuous years in rural areas, including at small, isolated stations like Snowy Creek. He had opted to remain in the countryside, shunning a posting in Melbourne. He had no desire to work on Bourke Street. Many other officers stationed in the northeast in the late 1870s had similarly spent years in the colony's rural districts. Some, like Charles Whitty, were born in the bush, growing up and working in rural precincts before becoming policemen. Later, when the Kelly Outbreak escalated dramatically after the Stringybark Creek killings, more urban police were deployed in the northeast in the bid to capture the Kellys. Some of these officers were out of their depth. But the force had little choice. It was already thinly stretched and needed to maintain law and order across the colony. It could not strip other districts of experienced country officers, for fear of leaving those areas vulnerable. McQuilton was almost trapped by the exigencies of his own argument: by contending that Kelly was a social bandit revolting against an unjust order, he needed to establish that most policemen underpinning that order were inherently wrongheaded, incompetent, biased, ill-intentioned and corrupt.

John Molony, head of the History Department at the Australian National University from 1982 to 1990, brought out his own book, *I Am Ned Kelly*, only months after *The Kelly Outbreak* was released. He reiterated the same narrative, but with two important twists. He cheekily reworked Anthony's purported threat, departing from the wording of the Jerilderie Letter by claiming that Senior Constable Strahan had declared: 'If I come across them [Ned and Dan] I'll shoot them like dogs.' More tellingly, he revealed that Anthony had uttered 'those ominous words' in a conversation with Pat Quinn several days before the gang's confrontation with the Victoria Police at Stringybark Creek. Molony contended that Anthony's threat shook 'Ned's confidence in immunity from being slaughtered by well-meaning policemen'. The stark brutality of the word 'slaughtered' jumped out at me when I tracked down a copy of Molony's book forty years later, in 2020. Surely a man was justified, Molony implied, in defending himself against such a horrible threat? Molony cited a different source for Anthony's threat: an affidavit by Quinn published in *The Argus* in November 1880, two years after the conversation in question apparently took place.[7]

Ian Jones, another influential member of the pro-Kelly camp, portrayed Anthony in a similar light in his biography of Ned, published in 1995. He too failed to provide Anthony's first name and said nothing about his life aside from a few cursory remarks along the lines set by McQuilton. He repeated the 'shoot me like a dog' threat, noting that it appeared in the Jerilderie Letter, but asserted that it was 'later confirmed by police sources'. Although he implied that *multiple* police sources *at the time* verified Anthony's threat, he was merely recalling, like McQuilton, the correspondence between Sadleir and one of his colleagues twenty years later. The letter in question revealed that some police officers came to believe that Anthony had made some kind of threat, but it contained no independent confirmation of the contents of the fateful conversation at Pat Quinn's farm. Jones went on to refer to 'the loudmouth Strahan', reinforcing Anthony's standing as one of the villains of the story.[8] Most tellingly, he failed to interrogate where, when and why Anthony might have made such a threat. He did not mention Pat Quinn, at least not at this point in his narrative. Anthony's voice was unheard aside from the purported threat.

In his biography of Ned released in 2013, Peter FitzSimons restated the heroic Kelly chronicle. Yet he at least made Anthony something more than a cardboard cut-out, using his first name and avoiding McQuilton's biographical errors. Importantly, he was the first writer to describe the conversation between Anthony and Pat Quinn on 22 or 23 October 1878 in detail. His account makes for a good read.

In his version, Anthony asked Quinn if he would lead the police to Ned. Quinn replied, 'If you get six men who are game, and will not shoot him, I will go with you at once. There are three men along with Kelly.'

Anthony noted that a £100 reward had been posted, but Quinn said he didn't want a reward and would let it go to the Wangaratta Hospital.

'All right, but I would like to keep some of it,' Anthony responded. 'I'll tell the Chief Commissioner of your offer. I am going to the Omeo after two horses. I'll come back in the course of three days.'

Quinn was uneasy about this and said, 'I will not show you where Kelly is if you are going to shoot him.'

Anthony replied in anger: 'I'll shoot him down like a dog. I'll carry two revolvers, and one I'll place by his side, and swear that he had it on him when I shot him.'

Quinn replied, 'Well, I won't show you then where to find him.'[9]

FitzSimons acknowledged that Anthony lost his temper according to 'Quinn's subsequent account'. But in fact every element of this exchange was drawn from this subsequent account. Quinn only made his account of his argument with Anthony known more than two years after the fact, when he gave an unsigned affidavit to the Victorian government on 9 November 1880, two days before Ned's execution in Melbourne. To state the obvious, we have Quinn's uncorroborated version of what happened. FitzSimons took Quinn's account at face value, failing to subject it to critical scrutiny. Yet Quinn was known to be ambivalent and unreliable. At various times he was a police informer, and his personal loyalties flip-flopped.[10] Even the Kellys didn't always trust their uncle.

In his unsigned affidavit, Quinn had a clear motive for spinning his conversation with Anthony: to portray Ned as the target of vicious police threats, thereby suggesting that his nephew had acted in self-defence in the killings at Stringybark Creek. He might have wanted to depict Anthony as conniving and greedy, sullying the reputation of the police. Pat Quinn was a man with complex and shifting interests, not a disinterested observer, so his claims about Anthony should be evaluated carefully.

The absence of Anthony's voice is compounded by the way the conversation is described. It was Anthony, not Quinn, who 'lost his temper' and became 'totally dismissive of any such bargaining'. The last sentence in FitzSimons's account says it all, painting Anthony as threatening and petulant, even childish: 'The miffed Strahan huffs off.' If he had just made a flaming threat, Anthony could have stormed off – but he could also have withdrawn in an icy fashion or, more likely, given he was rarely one to back down readily, held his ground until Quinn withdrew. We simply don't know because nothing in the surviving record reveals how Anthony behaved and felt on that fateful day. And it remains possible that Quinn verballed Anthony, wholly or in part, putting incendiary words in his mouth.

FitzSimons claims he is 'a devotee of the approach of the great nineteenth-century German historian Leopold von Ranke, whose view was that the best way to understand the past is to tell it "*wie es eigentlich gewesen ist*" – how it essentially was – understood on its own terms and relying heavily on primary documents, with the account unburdened by the historian giving his own analysis on the material presented.'[11] But he doesn't always follow this approach in *Ned Kelly*. He fills out parts of the Kelly story, drawing together a considerable body of material. However, he also adds plenty of colour and substantial invented dialogue. This approach engages readers, but it mixes elements drawn from actual sources with pure invention. History writing is always about the imaginative reconstruction of the past, and it inevitably involves conjecture; yet it's crucial to let your reader know when you are engaging in speculation. FitzSimons's biography is a frustrating read because it's often impossible to know what is pure guesswork.

Anthony appears again as a mostly spectral figure in three recent books in the Kelly canon, all published in 2021 or 2022. He's ill served for the most part. In *Nabbing Ned Kelly*, David Dufty presents Anthony in typically skimpy, vaguely pejorative and often inaccurate terms, leaving his first name out of the text, often getting his rank wrong and expunging him from some of the key parts of the Kelly Outbreak, including, ironically, the heated 'shoot him like a dog' threat. Dufty is very much in the anti-Kelly camp, describing Ned as 'a manipulative, violent psychopath' and praising the police. He moves other police officers to centre stage, especially Detective Michael Ward and Senior Constable Ernest Flood. All books, including this one, have to streamline the storyline and the complex cast of characters to some extent to avoid becoming interminably long and dense. Anthony falls by the wayside in *Nabbing Ned Kelly*.[12]

Coming from another corner in the Kelly history wars, Rebecca Wilson, one of the few women to write up the Kelly story, describes the police in *Kate Kelly* as 'a pack of wild dogs' who unashamedly abused their powers and came to devour Ned's mother, Ellen. True, she helpfully fills out Kate Kelly's story, mostly from the period after Ned's death, but she rearranges Anthony's argument with Pat Quinn to create an entirely false narrative. Wilson has Pat Quinn telling Kate, though it's quite unclear exactly when and where:

> Make sure you're letting Ned know that the scoundrel Constable Strachan were bragging about how Lonigan said he was gonna shoot first and ask questions later. Lassie, you make sure and tell him that, right. And let him know that Lonigan's plan were to lay a gun down beside Ned's dead body and say Ned tried ta shoot him. They had no intention of bringing him in alive. Strachan told me that himself. Bloody Lonigan even told Strachan that Ned deserved to die! For God's sake!

Wilson likely takes the misspelling of Anthony's name from the Jerilderie Letter. That's an inconsequential slip. More perniciously, there's nothing in the surviving record to indicate that such a conversation actually took place. And even then, rather than quoting from the words in Quinn's affidavit,

Wilson instead invents most of this purported conversation. From the affidavit, we know that Anthony didn't mention Lonigan once. That's hardly surprising. It's far from clear that Anthony even knew, before the events at Stringybark Creek had taken place, that Lonigan had joined the police search party in Mansfield. And it was Anthony of course, not Lonigan, who purportedly made the infamous threat to shoot Ned without asking him to surrender. It's hard not to conclude that Wilson puts these words into Lonigan's mouth to help justify what Ned did at Stringybark Creek.[13]

Grantlee Kieza presents Ned in a much more nuanced manner in *The Kelly Hunters*. While he provides a positive account of the police, he doesn't paint Ned in wholly dark terms, contending that he was capable of being heroic and hard-working *and* vain, violent and megalomaniacal. He portrays Anthony as a capable police force veteran, a Kelly hunter and one of Ned's sworn enemies. In doing so, he captures my great-great-grandfather's basic biographical details and avoids the errors that appear in other accounts. As for the infamous threat, he writes that Ned's 'spies' passed this 'boast' on to the gang, much as they transmitted other 'incorrect' pieces of information. Citing the Jerilderie Letter, not Quinn's affidavit, as the source for the threat, Kieza portrays Anthony in still thin but largely positive terms. But Anthony's own voice remains absent.[14]

All of the descriptions of Anthony's altercation with Pat Quinn suffer from a fundamental problem: whatever account Anthony might have made of this conversation has sadly not survived. Why? Throughout his career, Anthony was a diligent and frequent report writer. Documents go astray for all sorts of reasons, many entirely innocent, but it is more than passingly odd that most of the reports he would have written during his Greta assignment cannot be found. Neither can many pertinent documents about the Outbreak, including the gang's threatening letters to police and the land files for Ellen Kelly's selection, according to Ian MacFarlane, author of *The Kelly Gang Unmasked*. He contends that some pro-Kelly individuals could have 'disinfected' the gang's reputation by removing unflattering or incriminating documents from the public record.[15] This seems a stretch. Of course, another factor could have been at work. Did Anthony himself remove or destroy some of his own reports, perhaps because they contained things he was embarrassed about or wanted to hide? Did other policemen cull his reports for similar reasons? No evidence of this has come to light, but it wouldn't be the first (or last) time that police tampered with the official record.

It is probable that Anthony Strahan did issue some form of threat to Pat Quinn. As we know, he had a temper, a trait captured subtly in Thom's claim that his colleague was 'blathering' – that is, Senior Constable Strahan had a lip on him and didn't mind telling other people what he thought, often in strong terms. Anthony took offence relatively easily. But he had other reasons for talking to Quinn plainly. He regarded the extended Kelly–Quinn–Lloyd clan as malcontents and thieves. He mistrusted and likely feared them, for he was in a vulnerable position as the sole policeman in Greta. His sense of danger had been heightened by the apparent attempt to kill Fitzpatrick. And he felt keenly that the Kellys and their associates had never shown him the respect he was entitled to as a policeman, right from the time he had arrived in Greta – though he was hardly alone in this regard.

Historians less sympathetic to Ned Kelly present the altercation between Anthony and Quinn quite differently. Doug Morrissey captures best what likely happened, contending that Anthony's threat was made in the heat of a frustrating argument with Ned's notoriously flip-flopping uncle. 'It was never official or unofficial police policy [to shoot the Kellys], merely an argument clincher for Constable Strahan, who was being seriously messed around by Pat Quinn over the whereabouts of his two fugitive nephews.'[16] If he issued a threat in those hot terms, Anthony was also uttering a phrase used frequently in the nineteenth century, not least by the Kellys themselves. Ned often said he would shoot people who got in his way. Months before Anthony uttered his threat, Ned had made it plain that he would violently resist any attempt to apprehend him, telling none other than his uncle Pat Quinn in April 1878, 'if any man interferes with me I will shoot him'. In February 1879, he warned the people of Jerilderie that he would 'shoot them like dogs' if they tried to repair the telegraph line the Kelly Gang had cut. At the end of the Outbreak in June 1880, he threatened his hostages in Ann Jones's pub at Glenrowan in by-now characteristic terms: 'And if I ever hear any of you giving the police any information about us I will shoot you down like dogs.'[17]

Leo Kennedy is one writer who approaches the question of what Ned Kelly did and why from a personal angle. He is the great-grandson of Sergeant Michael Kennedy, the leader of the police contingent at Stringybark Creek. Pungently named *Black Snake*, Leo's 2018 book has a strong cathartic element, as he is adamant that his ancestor was murdered. He naturally focuses on his great-grandfather and comments sparingly on Anthony, leaving him once more as a largely anonymous figure in the Kelly story: he merely notes that Pat Quinn claimed in an unsigned affidavit just before Ned was executed that Anthony had threatened to shoot his nephew like a dog. Kennedy clearly finds Quinn's account mendacious. Far from celebrating Ned Kelly, Leo Kennedy says several generations of his family have suffered from intergenerational trauma as the killer of their ancestor has been converted into a national hero.[18]

This book, like Leo Kennedy's, is partly personal, but I grew up with a quite different family image of Ned Kelly. After my father died in 2003, I discovered a review copy of McQuilton's book on his shelves as I was sifting through his belongings with my brothers, Callum and Keir. Fifteen years later, as I turned to telling Anthony Strahan's life, I tracked down a copy of Dad's review in a special edition of the left-wing journal *Overland*, published in 1981 to mark the centenary of Ned Kelly's death. McQuilton was one of the other contributors. I had always known that Dad was a great fan of Ned Kelly, but I was still surprised by the fervour he brought to his review. Its title, 'The Iron Mask of Australia', was a sign of what was to come. 'Like many I have accepted Ned Kelly as a hero, a true spirit of my country, a telling champion in the battle of freedom against authority,' he wrote. Dad's ringing endorsement is a reminder that the Kelly story has always been in part about broader issues of ostensible national character. For my father, Ned was a symbol of Australian characteristics and values that were progressive and nationalist at the same time: egalitarianism, anti-authoritarianism, mateship, democracy and the rights of ordinary people.

Dad's piece wasn't just a book review. It was in part a memoir. He recalled searching in 1963 with Clem Christesen, the editor of the literary journal *Meanjin*, for two Kelly Gang hideouts in the Pilot Ranges, flanking the road between Beechworth and Chiltern. This was a secular pilgrimage for my father and his travelling companion. On the way, he and Clem visited the remains of the Kelly hut outside what is now called Greta West. He was, understandably, offended that parts of the decaying structure had been looted by renegade souvenir-hunters. He didn't approve of this breed of rebels. But enough of the building remained to fire his imagination: 'I have a souvenir, a photograph of Clem, posed in the sapling frame of the Kelly smithy, his foot on the bellows said to have been used to forge the gang's armour.' The then owner of the property, Charles Griffiths, told Dad he was sympathetic to the Kelly cause, but warned that he would set fire to his land if restoration of the home was allowed.

After visiting several pubs, Dad and Clem ventured into the Pilot Ranges. 'We found the two structures, dry-laid granite, fort-like walls, the view spanning the sweeping arc of country north of the Chiltern road. None but a fugitive or strange hermit ought to shelter there, so far above water and people,' he wrote, with an air of reverence. They went back to these rocky sites a few months later with their wives, Lynne (my mum) and Nina, and an archaeologist, Bill Culican:

> At the northern structure, Bill's precise trowelling revealed lines of nails, dropped to the ground from the burning of a wooden structure abutting granite. We repaired to Beechworth, to argue and sleep. Back in Melbourne, our investigations suspended, the headlines after a press conference read: 'Did Kelly Hide in these Forts? Kelly Hideaway Found? Did Kelly gang build these Forts?'

Dad and Clem returned to Melbourne with a plank they thought could have come from one of the Kelly hideouts. Dad held on to this secular relic for years.

Against this backdrop, it is not surprising that Dad praised McQuilton's book. He did take issue with aspects of its thesis, but for the most part Dad liked what he read: 'McQuilton has admirably demonstrated effects of dummying and political pressure by the squattocracy, forcing selectors into poor country; of harassment and persecution through a low calibre police force representing established interests; of the consequent reaction of the non-privileged leading to the Kelly Outbreak.'

When I was a child, Dad told me little about Anthony Strahan other than that he was a copper, he was called 'blathering Strahan' and he helped hunt 'our Ned'. I believed he was a bad sort. I was still a little taken aback, however, when Dad turned to Anthony at the end of his review. Like McQuilton himself, he doesn't give Anthony's first name, instead calling him 'Senior Constable blathering Strahan'. The pungent adjective had become, for my father, our ancestor's first name. He noted that McQuilton had cited Anthony 'as a major cause of the Outbreak for saying he would shoot the Kelly Gang down "like dogs"'. So there it is – that stark, brutal phrase that has become a feature of the Kelly story. Given his sympathies, it was perhaps inevitable that Dad was all too ready to condemn Anthony: 'He was my great-great-grandfather. Possibly he was illiterate – certainly misguided.'[19] Dad had become wedded to a negative account. John Molony, another writer who repeated Anthony's alleged 'ominous' threat without providing any critical analysis, thanks Dad in his book's acknowledgements. My father located himself firmly in one camp.

I have always shared Dad's social democratic and progressive nationalist outlook, and I grew up sharing, in a more diffuse way, his romantic view of Ned Kelly. But I have come to realise that virtually everything he knew about our ancestor, aside from the odd skerrick from family folklore, came from McQuilton's and Molony's books. This meant he accepted a slim and deeply biased view of his own forebear. No one should feel an automatic loyalty to their ancestors – we all should look back with a critical eye. But Dad had not, at least not in an informed way. It turned out he knew basically nothing about Anthony Strahan. He even got his own relationship with him wrong: Anthony was his great-grandfather, not his great-great-grandfather. Had Dad felt the unconscious need to push this bad seed, this sworn enemy of 'a telling champion in the battle of freedom against authority', further back in the family tree, distancing himself by another generation? He was also wrong about Anthony's literacy. Having read his police reports, rendered in his distinctive handwriting, I know that Anthony Strahan was literate. As for misguided – well, that depends on your point of view. But to reach a judgement about whether Anthony was misguided, one would need to know something about his life and career. Dad did not even know that Anthony's threat to 'shoot them like dogs' arose in a heated discussion with Ned Kelly's notoriously unreliable uncle.

My father was a talented, tenacious and creative archivist, committed to the preservation of Australia's past, yet he had not once visited the Public Record Office Victoria to see if he could find anything that might have revealed more about his forebear. He closed the door in part for ideological reasons, yet I knew he also had more personal reasons for accepting this dark view of his great-grandfather. Dad always told me that his own father – my grandfather, another Anthony Strahan – was 'a grade-A prick'. Dad and his siblings never forgave Tony, as he was known, for being a gambling womaniser who treated his family with a cavalier cruelty. His eldest child, my aunt Amy, once saw him in the local cinema in Albury in the late 1930s with his arm around the local brothel madam. Dad's mother, Laura, sent him off in the evenings to trail his father and ascertain who he was cavorting with. At the beginning of World War II, Tony went bankrupt because he had recklessly overextended his business. He sold off most of the family's possessions, leaving his wife and three children with little beyond a few plates and some cutlery, and joined the Australian Army at the age of forty without even bothering to tell his wife. He walked out on his family when Dad was not yet eleven, never to return.

Dad naturally sided with his Scottish-born mother, a Fleming. Even when he heard in 1962 that his father was dying, Dad refused to see him, foregoing the chance for a reconciliation. To the day he himself died in 2003, Dad hated his father. He carried a burning sense of abandonment and betrayal. This deep rupture with his father meant he rejected the Strahan side of his ancestry. He never spoke about his grandfather, another Frank, who toiled most of his life as a coalminer. This was particularly strange because Dad's historical speciality was mining history. Nor did he ever say that his great-grandmother, the policeman's wife, Marion, lived in Rutherglen until she died in 1939, when he was nine. A man whose professional life was devoted to preserving the traces of the past, he obliterated the Strahans from his own history. Had he looked, he would have discovered that the great-grandmother he never mentioned was the child of convicts. In Dad's radical nationalist cosmos, this heritage would have been something to be proud of. But he never knew because he never looked.

Dad's readiness to accept the dark view of his great-grandfather, I believe, had deep origins born in hurt and anger. In a sense, he conflated the two Anthonys, the allegedly illiterate and misguided copper and the cruel and selfish father, into one hateful figure. Born a generation later, I always accepted that my paternal grandfather was something of a bastard, but I never regarded him with animosity. I didn't need to – I never even met him. He died three years before I was born. This meant I have been able to approach Anthony Strahan the policeman dispassionately. Rather than blotting him out, I've wanted to recover and explore his story.

In retrieving that story, I've come to realise that other members of the wider Strahan family have preserved different memories of Senior Constable Anthony Strahan. According to the family anecdote that opens this book, Anthony and several other constables were crossing a bridge outside Wangaratta in mid-1878 when they were ambushed by the Kelly Gang. Ned let Anthony go unharmed because Marion Strahan had been kind to his mother when she was in gaol.[20] In this version of the past, Anthony was damn lucky, even blessed. In contrast, one of my second cousins, Melissa Traverso, recalls that her family has remembered Anthony differently. In her branch of the family, it was always said that he barricaded himself in his own police station, afraid to step out the front door, virtually held hostage by the Kellys.

I have found nothing in the surviving record to suggest that either event took place. Melissa's inherited family memory of Anthony lacks the biting personal dimension that underpinned Dad's scathing appraisal of our ancestor. She has a fond memory of her grandfather, Les, Tony's younger brother, and has no need to feel ambivalent or angry about the Strahan name. And the surviving record reveals that far from hiding in his police station, Anthony continued to go out on patrols, sometimes alone, for many months.

If Leo Kennedy is in part motivated by a burning sense that his ancestor, the murdered Sergeant Michael Kennedy, has been traduced over the years, my father was motivated by a quite different conviction that his great-grandfather was a bad egg. This sense of shame was compounded by his belief that another of the policemen who pursued Ned Kelly, Detective Michael Ward, was a similarly rotten character and one of our ancestors as well. Dad told me on several occasions that Ward, who was part of our family on the Strahan side – although he did not say exactly how – was a thug who persecuted Ned Kelly and molested young girls. Dad was ashamed that two of our ancestors had been men of such ill repute.

What little my father knew about Ward was also mainly derived from McQuilton's book. McQuilton said Ward was 'a deceitful man with an odious local reputation' who was 'openly accused of fathering several illegitimate children in the district'. He claimed Standish had been 'forced to call an official inquiry into allegations that Ward had sexually interfered with girl pupil-teachers at Beechworth State School'. Ward's bad behaviour did not stop there. McQuilton accused him of misleading his superiors, employing spies, conducting a vendetta against the Byrne family and using the hunt for Ned to channel contracts to provision the police search parties with food and other items to a mate in Beechworth.[21] Dad's easy acceptance of this account is problematic. Other historians have contested McQuilton's relentlessly negative portrait. Ian MacFarlane writes that Ward vigorously denied the allegations of misconduct against school-age girls: 'No prosecution of Ward ever eventuated, and it seems the charges were simply invented to discredit him.' Ward pressed one of his accusers at the royal commission, the schoolteacher James Wallace, a Kelly sympathiser, to verify the charges. Wallace couldn't. MacFarlane notes McQuilton's allegation concerning sexual misconduct relied on Wallace's inadequate testimony.[22] This is not to say Ward should not be held to account for his actions during the Kelly Outbreak, but he may also have been in part the victim of a smear campaign dating back to the 1880s. It is possible that Ward was not the unalloyed villain Dad thought he was.

My father was hazy about where Michael Ward fitted into our family tree. There was a good reason for this – Michael Ward wasn't related to us. It is true that Dad's grandfather, Frank, the youngest son of Anthony Strahan, married a Martha Ward in 1903 in Tongio West, a goldmining town in Gippsland. But she was unrelated to Michael Ward. The first person in the Ward side of our family to come to the Australian colonies was Martha's grandfather, William Dathe Ward. William was born in Suffolk in 1810, likely arriving in Sydney as a convict in 1839. Michael Ward was born in Ireland in 1845, the son of a John Ward. He married Ellen McDonald and later Margaret Aiken, women unconnected to the Strahans. By expecting the worst of his Strahan forebears and accepting McQuilton's scathing assessment of Michael Ward, Dad had found another, but quite false, reason to believe his family had been on the wrong side of history.

But Dad did lay claim to another Strahan who was active in Australia at the same time as Anthony, Sir George Strahan, the capable and well-liked governor of Tasmania between 1881 and 1886. Dad was proud that a town on the west coast of Tasmania was named after this ancestor. Sir George was in some ways an unlikely hero for my father because he was a pillar of the British establishment, having served in various colonial roles in Malta and Africa before arriving in Hobart. But perhaps Dad hankered for an honourable Strahan forebear. When I visited the fishing town of Strahan in 1987 with Lily, I too felt some ancestral pride.

The trouble is that years later, as I was writing this book, I discovered that Sir George was born in Scotland, and wasn't related to us at all. Our history is less adorned with bastards and eminent men than my father believed.

15

STRINGYBARK CREEK

Pat Quinn must have told his nephews, either directly or through another family member, that Anthony Strahan had threatened to shoot Ned like a dog. As Grantlee Kieza suggests, Ned likely heard about the threat soon after the conversation took place – although the Kellys were holed up in the Wombat Ranges, relatives, friends and sympathisers conveyed news and provisions to them quickly.

By this time, Joe Byrne and Steve Hart had joined the gang, though no one in the police yet knew they were hiding with the Kellys. Two days after Anthony's exchange with Pat Quinn, Superintendent Sadleir implemented the plan to catch the gang that he and Sergeant Kennedy had devised weeks earlier. On 25 October, he despatched two police parties to apprehend the Kellys in a pincer movement around the head of the King River, with one group leaving from Greta in the north and the other from Mansfield in the south. Sergeant Steele had been due to lead the Greta party but was forced to stand aside when he was required to testify before the Equity Court. Command of the Greta contingent was given instead to Anthony Strahan. Three other officers joined the Greta party: Senior Constable Edward Shoebridge from Bright and Constables Cornelius Ryan and Hugh Thom, the latter now stationed at Eldorado. Anthony had known Shoebridge for nearly a decade, having worked with him to catch the two would-be bushrangers Trembath and Watson in 1872. Shoebridge was familiar with Greta and its environs, having been stationed there for a year in 1875–76. Ryan and Anthony had been conducting patrols together for several months and were a good fit. Assigning Thom to the contingent was hardly wise, given he and Anthony had traded insults some months earlier. But constables were in short supply and Thom was available.

Sergeant Kennedy assumed command of the Mansfield party. He was joined by three constables: Michael Scanlan, Thomas McIntyre and Thomas Lonigan, then based at Violet Town. All four policeman had been born in Ireland. Kennedy and Scanlan were Catholics and firm friends. Both were married with children and regarded as skilled bushmen. Lonigan was added to the group because he knew Ned by sight, having famously grabbed him by the testicles during a scuffle in Benalla in 1877. The unmarried Lonigan had had a chequered career, getting into trouble for playing cards in a pub while in uniform and being fined for assaulting a drunken prisoner. McIntyre, another bachelor, was the last to join the group. By 1878, he had been in the force for nearly ten years and was a conscientious and generally well-regarded officer. Like Kennedy and Scanlan, he had never laid eyes on Ned or Dan.

Some writers have described the two police parties as de facto hit squads who rode into the Wombat Ranges with the express intention of killing the Kellys. There is no evidence for this suggestion. All the available information indicates that Kennedy and Anthony intended to apprehend the Kellys so the men could stand trial, but they were ready to use force if need be, either to defend themselves or to ensure the Kellys were arrested. At this time, the police knew that the Kelly boys could be violent, but they had no idea that they were capable of murder. It is quite possible, though, that Ned and Dan had come to the conclusion that the police parties descending on them were likely to shoot them. Anthony's alleged threat to Pat Quinn no doubt reinforced this fear. And Ned could have believed that a much larger contingent of police, as many as three parties with a total of thirteen officers, was coming for him and his gang.[1]

The police parties were not excessively armed. Each constable carried his standard-issue Webley revolver, an efficient weapon that was accurate over a fair distance. Both parties also brought along two rifles, including a Spencer rifle, the US-made weapon customarily assigned to officers accompanying gold escorts. The Spencer rifle was notoriously difficult to operate, especially by someone who had not used it before: the magazine was inserted into the butt of the rifle, the cartridges feeding into the breech through a lever on the trigger guard. Anthony was likely familiar with the Spencer from accompanying the Eldorado gold escort in the early 1870s. The second rifle carried by Kennedy's party was a light shotgun borrowed from a clergyman, in part to shoot game such as parrots to supplement food stocks. This quantity of weapons was appropriate, given that the eight constables were trying to apprehend two men who were known to be armed and violent and who had been on the run for more than six months.

Both parties rode in plain clothes, not uniforms. Some have taken this too as an indication that the police were travelling in a surreptitious manner with lethal intent. But mounted constables usually wore plain clothes when on patrol, especially extended forays into rugged country, to avoid damaging their uniforms. Crucially, they were required to pay for any repairs out of their own pocket.

The two police parties were intending to meet up near the head of the King River, close to Powers Lookout, overlooking the Quinns' old Glenmore run. They planned to scour an extensive area of rugged bush on the way. Mansfield had a good road to Benalla, while Greta had roads to both Benalla and Wangaratta, though the latter was in a deplorable state in 1878. But there was no road between Mansfield and Greta. In his account of the patrol, McIntyre described the country between the two towns as no-man's land: 'Full of inextricable hills and valleys with the multiplicity of the minor water courses making it difficult to know whether you were on the fall of the Broken or the Ovens Rivers; the whole formed a hiding place in which an army corps might have searched for the offenders and being within a short distance of them still fail to find them.'[2]

On 25 October, Anthony and his three constables left Greta at dawn and rode along Fifteen Mile Creek into the more remote country to the southeast. Sergeant Kennedy and his party also departed Mansfield before sunrise and rode around 32 kilometres northeast, travelling along the

Benalla Road, cutting across the Mount Battery run, fording the Broken River and passing Monk's Sawmill before reaching Stringybark Creek in the late afternoon. There they set up a base camp, as planned, near a derelict miners' hut.

Much that was to happen the next day might have been different had the two parties met up straightaway. Sadly, Anthony and his companions had no intention of making for Stringybark Creek. Instead, they set up their own, more temporary, camp around 10 kilometres from Stringybark Creek. Mounted constables could cover such a distance quickly, even though the terrain was difficult. But Anthony and his colleagues were following the agreed plan, making for Hedi, where they would join Kennedy's group to scour the area around the Glenmore run.

It seems McIntyre was the only person in the two groups who thought about linking up at an earlier point. Kennedy and his companions had paused for a rest on the way to Stringybark Creek at 2pm at Holland's Creek, a few kilometres to the west of the blazed boundary line that led to the head of the King. McIntyre asked Kennedy if they were going to join the Greta contingent. Kennedy replied in a jocular way, 'We don't want to meet them. If we do, we will find them out of tucker and they will eat us out.'

When he stopped at Stringybark Creek, Kennedy was not to know that he had set up camp less than 2 kilometres from the hut at Bullock Creek where the Kelly Gang was hiding. If the two parties had converged, it is doubtful that Ned and his gang would have been brazen or foolhardy enough to take on eight constables. They almost certainly would have fled instead.

Ned and his men likely came across the tracks of at least one of the police parties on 25 October, meaning they knew the hated traps were nearby. Ned could have opted to flee, avoiding a confrontation, but he decided instead on a bolder course. Late on the afternoon of 26 October, with Kennedy and Scanlan on patrol, McIntyre used the shotgun to shoot at parrots near the camp at Stringybark Creek, inadvertently alerting Ned's gang to their presence. Compounding matters, he lit a large fire. The location of the police camp was now unmistakable.

When the Kellys, Steve Hart and Joe Byrne crept up on the camp around 5pm, McIntyre was tending the fire and Lonigan was sitting on a log. Emerging from the spear grass, Ned strode into the camp, declaring, 'Bail up. Hold up your hands!'

McIntyre immediately surrendered.

What happened next is one of the most contested episodes in the Kelly history wars. Pro-Kelly writers contend that Lonigan crouched behind the log, drew his revolver and bobbed back up to fire, prompting Ned and his men to shoot. They assert that Ned and the other gang members were acting in self-defence when Lonigan was killed in a volley of shots.[3]

Although Anthony was not present at the camp, he nonetheless played an unwitting part in the horrible incident. Ned would later claim as part of his defence that he was convinced the trooper sitting on the log was Strahan, the policeman who had said he would 'shoot him like a dog'. He would also claim he was sure McIntyre was Ernest Flood, the trap who had allegedly ruined the life of his eldest sister, Annie, impregnating and abandoning her and sending her to an early grave. Ned's animosity towards Flood was in part self-serving. Doug Morrissey notes that the relationship between Flood and Annie was consensual and apparently met with no objection from the Kelly matriarch, Ellen. Ned had encountered Flood in a pub on several occasions before the Fitzpatrick affair and could have taken him to task about maltreating Annie, but he didn't.[4]

Taking Ned at his word, Ian Jones uses the names 'Strahan' and 'Flood', not 'Lonigan' and 'McIntyre', in his one-page description of this deadly encounter, which ends in the following contrived way:

> As Ned ran closer a strange thing happened. The helpless policeman with his hands raised had Flood's dark beard and Flood's large dark eyes, but he was taller. It was a stranger. And the dying man wasn't Strahan. Ned would find that it was Lonigan, who had 'black-balled' him in the bootmaker's shop brawl, who may have wrung from him that cry, 'If I ever kill a man, Lonigan, you'll be the first!'

Peter Carey uses the same narrative device in his novel *True History of the Kelly Gang*, calling Lonigan 'Strahan' for nearly two pages and repeating the sequence of actions described in Jones's book.[5] This version of what happened at Stringybark Creek has been taken up overseas. In his admiring comparison of the lives of Billy the Kid and Ned Kelly, the American historian Robert Utley paints a familiar picture: 'Ned planned Stringybark well. It went awry because the troopers failed to heed his commands. That forced him to shoot.'[6]

Other writers have held no truck with this scenario. Morrissey argues persuasively that Ned's claim made no sense: 'the Kelly brothers had watched the police camp from close quarters, probably for many hours prior to bailing them up. Strahan was the local Greta policeman, who had close contact with the Kelly family. So is it likely that Ned would have failed to recognise him?' And even if it had been Strahan, Morrissey continues, would this have excused cold-blooded murder? Ian MacFarlane agrees, contending that Ned was constructing 'a weird justification of self-defence'. Leo Kennedy does not even refer to the alleged identity confusion, refusing to engage with the story Ned would put about after the event. He suggests that Lonigan was shot as he was running towards the creek. 'Later claims by Ned that Lonigan took aim would be roundly refuted; Lonigan died empty-handed, his pistol holstered where he lay. He never stood a chance,' he writes.[7]

While impossible to know what Ned thought, it seems likely that he and the other gang members shot Lonigan quickly and that the constable was unable to wrench his revolver out of its notoriously cumbersome holster. It is fortunate for me that Anthony was not present because my great-grandfather, Frank, had not yet been conceived.

Ned harboured a bitter grudge against Anthony Strahan, as the Jerilderie Letter later revealed. With Lonigan's corpse lying nearby, Ned sat on a log beside the fire at the camp, talking to McIntyre as he waited for Kennedy and Scanlan to return. According to McIntyre, the bushranger made clear his deadly intentions as far as Anthony was concerned. 'There are four men in the Police,' Ned declared, 'and if ever I lay my hands upon them I will roast them alive: they are Flood, Steele, Strachan and Fitzpatrick.'

McIntyre was horrified: 'I felt more appalled at this threat than I did at any he had made previously, for the fire was a large one and presented the possibility of extreme torture.'[8]

Strange things have happened to this threat in recent Kelly literature. David Dufty removes three names from Ned's dreadful promise, leaving only Flood, presumably to keep the focus on him. This reductionism only serves to disguise the extent of Ned's murderous rage. Rebecca Wilson does the opposite, again resorting to embellishment. She retains the names of all four hated policeman but adds a fictitious final line, 'Strachan has been bragging that he would take me single-handed.'[9] I'm not discounting the possibility that my ancestor might have made such a boast at some time, but there's no record I have encountered of him ever actually doing so. It's certainly not in McIntyre's eyewitness account.

The terrified McIntyre realised Ned and his gang were fully capable of more murderous violence. When Kennedy and Scanlan returned to the camp, McIntyre told them to dismount and surrender, but both moved to resist. Within seconds, the gang shot Scanlan, who fell off his horse. While he was on all fours, bleeding profusely, Scanlan took another bullet under the right arm and collapsed dead. The fatal shot was fired by either Ned or Joe Byrne, depending on which historical account you read.[10] In the confusion, McIntyre fled on Kennedy's horse, which had run towards him after the sergeant had dismounted. Ned meanwhile pursued Kennedy into the dense bush, the two men ducking behind trees as they traded shots. Ned eventually ran down his quarry, shooting the sergeant in the chest at point-blank range when he was lying on the ground, already badly wounded. The outlaw interrogated his hapless victim, who was pleading for his life, for two hours before delivering the coup de grace.[11]

The two sides in the Kelly wars have offered sharply different interpretations of what happened at Stringybark Creek. McQuilton describes the events as 'a gun battle' in which three police 'died'; he claims that Dan was wounded. 'Stringybark Creek was tragic and deplorable,' he writes, 'but it was also the inevitable result of the heavy-handed police attention paid to the Kellys.' He contends that police persecution pushed the Kellys into fighting back: 'Stringybark Creek is the pivotal event in the Kelly Outbreak. The "murders" at Stringybark Creek became an article of faith for the police and some later writers.'[12] The inverted commas are telling. Kennedy and Morrissey reject this interpretation. For them, Stringybark Creek was an ambush and a massacre. Kennedy contends that the Kelly Gang approached the camp with many weapons, shot each policeman with a cold and calculated brutality, fired additional bullets into the corpses and made off with the dead officers' rings and watches. Morrissey writes that there was nothing spontaneous about the decision to attack the four police officers.[13]

In this fierce debate, I can't help feeling the truth lies somewhere in between. The gang behaved brutally, but they were also hyped up, enveloped by a red mist, adrenaline, fear, recrimination and anger pumping through their veins. This encounter, deep in the rugged bush, far from the outside world, in the fading light, was probably always going to end badly.

While the world was falling apart for Kennedy's party at Stringybark Creek, Anthony's party was continuing its patrol to the east. Anthony gave his team one wise instruction: no fires. This made their evening much colder in the wet spring weather but would not alert the Kellys to their whereabouts. He also instructed his party to stay together. At the Kelly royal commission in 1881, Sadleir admitted that he had not given the two parties instructions, either written or verbal, about avoiding fires or becoming separated: 'Of course every man concerned had his own life to look after, and if I had tied them down strictly to any particular line I might be responsible for the circumstances if anything happened to them in consequence.'[14] He was perhaps right to rely on the judgement of experienced policemen, and Kennedy's party was not to know that the Kellys were ensconced a short distance from Stringybark Creek. Anthony nonetheless gave sensible orders.

On 26 October, Anthony decided to head west towards the Glenmore station, located on a high range about 6 to 8 kilometres from the Wombat Ranges and not far from Powers Lookout. This path took the four policemen away from Stringybark Creek and, although they did not know it, the Kellys.

Unbeknown to either of the police parties, Detective Michael Ward had decided to ride off on his own patrol alone through the Wombat Ranges, armed with a small revolver. After coming within 6 kilometres of Stringybark Creek, he too headed towards Glenmore, crossing paths with Anthony on 26 October near Fifteen Mile Creek. Anthony and his companions were hungry, having had nothing to eat that day. This suggests the Greta party had set off with insufficient provisions, proving Kennedy right about protecting his party's tucker. Anthony told Ward he had seen nothing of Kennedy, adding that Ward was the first person he had come across since leaving Greta. Ward opted to ride with Anthony's party to Glenmore, where they rested overnight and reprovisioned.

On 27 October, as the Kelly Gang left the hideout at Bullock Creek, the Greta contingent and Ward parted ways. Ward rode off alone, heading towards Powers Lookout. Anthony told Ward he would ride across to Hedi and north on to Eldorado: 'I think I will get the two Kellys. I am certain they will be somewhere about Byrne's.'[15] Joe Byrne's family lived in the Woolshed Valley, not far from Eldorado, Anthony's old stomping ground.

That same day, McIntyre made it back to Mansfield after a terrifying ordeal, having crashed into branches during his wild ride and concealed himself in a wombat hole, to reveal what had happened at Stringybark Creek. Shock rippled across the colony. At this point, Kennedy's fate was unknown. A day later, news of the deaths of Lonigan and Scanlan reached Anthony, who sent a note to Ward via a young woman to let him know that the gang had killed two constables.[16]

After searching around Stringybark Creek, a contingent led by the commanding officer of the Mansfield station, Sub-Inspector Henry Pewtress – a diligent but overwhelmed policeman who had spent his career in Melbourne – found Kennedy's body in dense bush on 31 October, five days after he had been slain. They conveyed the body to a shaken Mansfield, along the way bumping into Anthony and his companions, who were themselves heading towards the town at the end of their patrol. Seeing the corpse of a well-respected policeman, marked by major wounds and already decomposing, must have been unnerving.

Although Sadleir shared Anthony's hunch that the Kellys had headed north, Superintendent Charles Nicolson, who had arrived in Benalla to direct the hunt, thought the Kellys were still in the Wombat Ranges. Anthony and his three companions were ordered to go back out to track down the gang. Anthony asked if he could have more constables and additional rifles; Pewtress gave him two of each.

Now six strong, Anthony's contingent rode out on 1 November to scour the rugged terrain between the west branch of the King River and Wombat Hill. Like his fellow officers, he was angry. Given his temperament and his past willingness to confront bushrangers, my great-great-grandfather was ready to use force if needed. An encounter with the gang would likely be bloody.

The patrol was arduous: as Anthony later told the press, 'the country traversed was something frightful, worse than the worst New Zealand country'. The weather was foul – rain, sleet and hail. It cleared on one day, allowing Anthony to get an extensive view of the King Valley from the high ground. He saw nothing of interest. The party came across horse tracks, but they were likely those of either another police party led by Sergeant Steele or horsemen working on the cattle stations beyond Mansfield. They stopped overnight at a rundown hut and later crossed the blazed track from Mansfield to Glenmore, though they opted not to descend to the Quinns' old property.

After being on patrol for four days, covering a considerable expanse, Anthony and his companions returned to Mansfield on the night of 4 November. Tom Lloyd junior and Jack Lloyd junior were swaggering about in town, perhaps to convince everyone they were not the two as-yet-unidentified men who had attacked the police at Stringybark Creek with the Kellys.[17] Anthony knew the Lloyd boys well, having arrested Jack for horse-stealing in April. At the time and later, many saw Tom as the fifth member of the gang, keeping watch and ferrying supplies.

Strahan's party had endured tough conditions, as *The Leader* noted: 'During that time they had to sleep in the open air in wet clothes, drinking cold water, and having little to eat. No one, they say, would believe what privations they had to undergo, nor could the state of the scrub and mountains be conceived without being seen.' Although tired, Anthony and his team were in good health and ready to go back out after they secured fresh provisions. *The Herald* declared:

> Both Strachan and Shewbridge are old and experienced bush men and they express themselves certain that the desperadoes are still in the district where the murders were committed. 'They say you can hear the tramp of horses about a quarter of a mile before you can see them, and a number of men could be concealed within a few yards of a passing patrol of police, and it would be impossible to detect them.[18]

This report suggests Anthony had changed his mind about the whereabouts of the Kellys. But Sadleir wisely refused to send a search party back into the Wombat, both because Anthony and his men were exhausted and because he was convinced the gang had fled from the area days ago, heading towards Greta. Sadleir ordered Anthony to return to Benalla.

Ironically, while her husband had been searching fruitlessly through the Wombat Ranges, Marion Strahan had been much closer to Ned.

16

THE ENDLESS CHASE

The Stringybark Creek killings raised the conflict between the Kellys and the police to a new level, suggesting each side would show the other no quarter. The violent death of three policemen shook the entire colony, and the Victoria Police, angry and fearful, often acted heavy-handedly over the coming months, ill-treating members of the Kelly family and the gang's sympathisers.

Standish rushed up to Benalla on the afternoon train on 6 November to confer with Nicolson and Sadleir about what to do next. They decided on a plan.

Anthony was now in a unique position, for he knew both the Greta and Wangaratta regions, where the Kelly, Lloyd and Hart families lived, and the area around Beechworth and the Woolshed, where the Byrne and Sherritt families resided. As a policeman in Beechworth and Eldorado in the late 1860s and early 1870s, he had come to know many of the families in the Woolshed, including the Sherritts. He was at the Beechworth police court on 1 March 1870 on a different matter (a drunk had assaulted him, damaging his uniform) when John Sherritt, a selector, was committed to trial for assaulting another farmer, James Kelty. Although the prosecution dropped the charge against John in February 1871,[1] Anthony would not forget that the Sherritt family sometimes got into strife. John's second-oldest son, Aaron, was a good friend of Joe Byrne. Cocky and young, Aaron was a member of the Greta mob and got into regular trouble with the law. He was fined in 1875 for unlawfully using a horse and imprisoned in 1876 for six months for being in the unlawful possession of the carcass of a cow, but in 1877 he evaded a charge of assaulting a Chinese man.

Early on 7 November, after a short rest, Anthony and Senior Constable Edward Shoebridge joined a large contingent of police, around twenty-three strong, in a raid on John Sherritt's hut in the Woolshed Valley. An old bark stripper had told Sadleir that the Kellys had been seen in the vicinity of the hut several days ago. The contingent was nominally under Standish's command, but it was the two superintendents, Sadleir and Nicolson, who led the raid. After a long and rather loud ride that would have eroded any element of surprise, two groups of police stormed the Sherritt hut at dawn from the front and back. Galloping in, they found no more than the sleepy Sherritts. Next they rode across to Aaron's selection, less than 2 kilometres away, on the edge of the tableland, but again found no trace of the Kellys.

With frustration growing, Sadleir and Nicolson led one last raid, this time on the dairy farm owned by Joe Byrne's mother, Margaret, near Sebastopol. This too produced no results, other than irritating the famously formidable Margaret Byrne. The whole operation proved to be an embarrassing fiasco, immortalised as the Charge of Sebastopol.

As the police officers took their breakfast near Margaret Byrne's hut, Aaron Sherritt approached their camp, an axe resting on one shoulder. He had been chopping wood nearby when the police had ridden in hard. Anthony introduced Sherritt to Sadleir and Nicolson: 'Here is a man who knows the Kellys well, and he will be of use to you; he knows all that is going on.' The two superintendents in turn brought the brash 23-year-old before Standish, initiating a relationship with the police that would cause much trouble. Sherritt agreed to supply the police with information so long as the life of his old friend, Joe Byrne, was spared.[2] It is still not known if Sherritt was a police spy or a double agent.

By mid-November, the Kelly hunt was the biggest story in the press by a long shot. Some coverage was overheated and inaccurate, at times comically so. *The Wangaratta Dispatch*'s critique of certain metropolitan papers was contemptuous:

Their ideas of the locality reminds us of the statements made at home [i.e. Britain] as to our Australian geography, which occasionally makes Sydney the capital of Victoria, or places Melbourne in the centre of Australia. Wooragee, the Buckland Gap, and Rats' Castle are spoken of as next to each other, and the whole topography of the district has been considerably mixed. As to the police movements, we are told, without the slightest reservation, that 'two bodies of troopers went out from Wangaratta today, well-armed, and in fine condition', and in the very next sentence the writer informs us 'their destination it is not advisable to mention, because every scrap of news reaches the outlaws sooner or later after publication'. Where is the reticence here which is so highly advisable?

The Dispatch noted that one paper had drawn an almost farcically erroneous comparison between the Kellys' crimes and the Wooragee Outrage. It took some pleasure in quoting the flawed metropolitan report word for word:

> The Rats' Castle lies between Barnawartha and Indigo Creek, about five miles from the former place. About five years ago it afforded temporary concealment to two Germans who murdered a publican at Wooragee, near Beechworth, but they were run down in three days by Sub-inspector Beaver. The Rats' Castle is scrubby, and caves are abundant, but the ranges are not lofty or of great extent, and would afford indifferent hiding for men on horseback.

The Dispatch pointed out that Rats Castle lay between Middle Creek and Indigo and was not scrubby at all, but on ground both open and high. 'If it possesses a cave, we have never found it when we wanted a friendly shelter.' The paper identified what many in the northeast knew only too well: a publican had indeed been murdered in Wooragee in 1872, but not by two Germans. The culprits, Smith and Brady, were Australians run down by Senior Constable Strahan, not Inspector Beaver. Although he was 'a good officer and a capital fellow to boot', Beaver had 'never run down anyone'. Lastly, *The Dispatch* noted that Anthony had arrested the offenders at 'the Pilot, miles from Rats' Castle, and on a totally different line of spurs'.[3] These reports, accurate and inaccurate, underscored two things: the Stringybark killings were the most infamous in the colony since the murder of John Watt in Wooragee; and Anthony Strahan was at the heart of both outrages.

With the abortive raids on the Sherritt and Byrne huts still fresh in his mind, Anthony took Superintendent Nicolson and Detective Ward to see an informant in Greta on 10 November. He was working his local contacts as hard as he could, but the Kellys remained elusive. On 15 November, the Victorian government decreed the four gang members outlaws, meaning they could be shot on sight. Towards the end of November, Anthony rode out again to Pat Quinn's property in the King Valley with Ward to ascertain if the wily farmer knew where his nephews were hiding.

Anthony's last conversation with Quinn had not gone well. This conversation too was difficult. Anthony was reputedly furious. He told Quinn that he had not been far away when Kennedy, Lonigan and Scanlan had been killed at Stringybark Creek. He stressed that he was now determined to bring the Kellys to justice.[4] After a protracted discussion, he and Ward persuaded Quinn to accompany them into Benalla to see Nicolson.

Quinn was in a talkative mood when he reached Benalla, admitting he had seen Steve Hart at a crossroad after Stringybark Creek and that Maggie Skillion, his niece, had come to his property looking for provisions for her brothers. He told Nicolson that the police faced a tough challenge: 'If you do not mind, those men [his nephews] will have a long reign because they are good bushmen and good horsemen and they do not care about grog, and it will be very hard to entrap them into any place.' He told Nicolson nonetheless that he would go with him and some troopers up the King Valley, around 40 kilometres past Glenmore, to a basin where the Kellys could be hiding. Nicolson readied a contingent to undertake the patrol, but the untrustworthy Quinn failed to return to Benalla.

An irate Nicolson sent Anthony back to Quinn's farm to find out why he had not shown up. Quinn told Anthony he was harvesting and could not leave his property. But he had also got cold feet, for he said he had become aware he might get himself shot if he was not careful. He failed to inform Anthony that a man called Tom Roach had just told him that he had seen Ned's gang not far away. Ned's uncle was still playing both ends of the stick. Ever keen to paint his own motives in the best light, Quinn would later tell the royal commission that Nicolson had offered to pay him, but he had refused. He alleged it was Nicolson who had failed to keep his end of the bargain, neglecting to come out to his farm as promised.[5]

After lying low for seven weeks following the Stringybark Creek killings, the Kelly Gang pulled off an audacious bank robbery in the central Victorian town of Euroa on 9–10 December. Setting a pattern that would be repeated in Jerilderie two months later, the gang held some hostages at the Faithful Creek homestead, which became their base of operations for the daring heist. While Joe Byrne watched the hostages, Ned, Dan and Steve Hart robbed the National Bank in Euroa, making off with £2260 in bank notes and gold in a sugar bag. The number of police in the northeast was increased to 214.[6]

A day later, Sadleir ordered Anthony to search the area around the Skillions' selection and then up into the ranges, looking for horse tracks or any other signs that the gang had headed in that direction. He told his subordinate that Ned would likely give a portion of the stolen money to his sister, Maggie. Sadleir instructed Anthony to start at the property of Jack McMonigle, an Irishman by birth and one of Ned's old friends, and to work his way across to William Tanner's place. Tanner was part of the Kelly–Quinn–Lloyd clan, for he had married one of Tom Lloyd's sisters, Mary. He was close to Ned. Acutely aware the Kellys were violent, Sadleir ordered Anthony to follow any tracks far enough to satisfy himself as to the direction the gang was travelling in and then to ride to the nearest police station to seek assistance. He did not want a repeat of Stringybark Creek.[7]

Anthony rode out to McMonigle's farm. Although he had once worked with Ned at a sawmill, McMonigle was disgusted by what the Kellys had done at Stringybark Creek, sending them a message saying he wanted nothing further to do with them. Given his change of heart, McMonigle was not in touch with the Kellys and could tell Anthony nothing.

Anthony next searched around the Skillions' place, but he found no horse tracks. Receiving a tip-off that Maggie had left a saddle at Francis Harty's farm near Winton, he rode there. Harty was a fervent Kelly sympathiser, once declaring, 'Ned Kelly is the best bloody man that has ever been in Benalla. I would fight up to my knees in blood for him.'[8] So he was unwilling to assist Anthony, denying any knowledge of the saddle.

Before returning to Greta, Anthony followed up one last lead. A farmer said he had seen the Thompson girl regularly walking past his place around 5pm, heading towards Glenrowan, returning about 10pm. But it turned out she had stopped this routine a week ago.

After his fruitless patrol, Anthony told Sadleir he had been unable to discover anything about the whereabouts of the Kellys. He said the Thompson girl was now staying at Pat Quinn's farm.[9]

Anthony seemed destined to cross paths with Pat Quinn time after time. He convinced Ned's feckless uncle in January 1879 to ride to Benalla again, this time to see Commissioner Standish. But Standish wasn't in Benalla and Quinn saw Superintendents Sadleir and Francis Hare instead. Sadleir asked Quinn if he was surprised that he hadn't been arrested as a Kelly sympathiser under the *Felons Apprehension Act 1878*. Quinn said he wasn't. Hare asked if Quinn would show the police a place at the head of the King River where the Kellys were possibly hiding. Quinn agreed and later accompanied a police contingent, which included Anthony, along the King, but claimed he couldn't identify the hiding place because bushfire had ravaged the area. This evasiveness angered Anthony, who reputedly told Quinn some time later, 'We'll never catch the Kellys until we arrest you.' Quinn was indignant: 'All you want is to get the reward raised and promotion, and to put the country to trouble and expense, all of which might have been saved but for your blundering and threatening to shoot the Kellys.'[10]

Anthony Strahan and Pat Quinn had developed a hearty mistrust of each other. My great-great-grandfather's relations with the family and friends of the Kellys had become irretrievably bitter.

The police decided to close the Greta station shortly after Anthony's third clash with Quinn. He was transferred on 21 January 1879 to the station at Wangaratta, moving in haste with Marion and their five children. Given that they were relocated suddenly, the Strahans were allocated an extra allowance to cover accommodation in Wangaratta.

It is unclear what prompted the police to act so quickly at just this point. Several factors were likely at play. From an operational standpoint, Anthony's movements were being observed by the Kelly Gang's family and friends, blunting his effectiveness. Sadleir said Anthony had quit the post to allow the search for the outlaws to be 'conducted with more secrecy'.[11] At the same time, as a single officer in the town at the heart of the Outbreak, Anthony was exposed. The gang and its sympathisers sent poison pen letters and caricatures to policemen, promising to harm them or ridiculing them. Ian Macfarlane notes that these threats were graphic, 'adorned with funeral crepe, pictures showing the gang shooting at police or sketches of coffins'.[12] Had Anthony received such threats? Quite possibly, because he had become notorious in Kelly circles as the policeman who had allegedly threatened to shoot Ned like a dog.

But even if he hadn't received threats, Anthony could have come to feel more anxious for other reasons. Marion was pregnant with their sixth child, Francis, my great-grandfather. Anthony could have decided it was time to leave Greta to ensure his wife – who had been under considerable stress over the previous year, often being left alone when he was on patrol – was not subjected to further worry.

During his posting in Greta, Anthony had been under the command of Sergeant Arthur Steele in Wangaratta. The two policemen had worked together for some time, arresting Ellen Kelly in April 1878. They were now located in the same station and would collaborate more closely over the coming months.

Just before his transfer, *The Advertiser* recognised that Anthony had played a central role in curbing the Greta mob along with Steele and Ernest Flood, who had just been promoted. It affirmed that 'the comparative recent immunity from wholesale horse and cattle stealing which has prevailed since the Baumgarten case was brought to light' was in large measure due to the efforts of these three officers: 'To them and a few others is also mainly due the bursting up of the gang, which for years had infested the country between the King and the Broken Rivers.'[13]

The horse-stealing ring might have been hit hard, with key members sent to prison, but Ned and his three sidekicks were still at large. In early February, Aaron Sherritt spoke to Superintendent Hare in Benalla. He claimed Joe Byrne had recently visited his selection in the Woolshed Valley, saying the Kellys intended to cross into New South Wales, perhaps to see a cousin in Goulburn. That very night the Victoria Police sprang into action, despatching officers to crossings along the Murray in the hope of intercepting the gang. Anthony led one party, keeping watch for several days.[14]

This was all to no avail. The patrols were concentrating on the wrong part of the border. The Kelly Gang carried out its second grand heist on 8 February when it rode into Jerilderie, a dusty town more than 400 kilometres to the west of Goulburn. Had Sherritt lied, deliberately sending the police in the wrong direction?

The four bushrangers occupied Jerilderie for three days, robbing a bank and holding hostages. It was here that Ned dictated to Joe Byrne what became known as the Jerilderie Letter, a rambling self-defence. In pithy but often blustering prose, he blamed others for what had happened, presenting himself as the victim of police persecution. Anthony appeared in the letter several times. First, Ned accused him of being one of the policemen who 'have got to hire cads [i.e., scoundrels]'. Next, he claimed Fitzpatrick had told Dan on 15 April 1878 to 'clear out that Sergeant Steele and Detective Brown and Strachan would be there before morning. Strachan had been over the Murray trying to get up a case against him'. The last reference would haunt Anthony: Ned said he took Constable Lonigan at Stringybark Creek 'to be Strachan', the man who 'said he would not ask me to stand, he would shoot me first like a dog'.[15]

Ned desperately wanted the colony's newspapers to publish his letter, but this was not to be. Summaries of parts of the letter were published not long after it was composed, but the entire text was not printed until 1930.

The police and government didn't want to release a full copy, fearing that would stir up even more trouble.

Although the public was left substantially in the dark, the letter was read by the colony's senior police officers. This meant Anthony's superiors were now aware that he had allegedly threatened to shoot Ned Kelly like a dog two days before Stringybark Creek. This is not to say they believed what Ned had written: in the wake of the cold-blooded killing of two or three of their comrades, the police were hardly inclined to take Ned at his word. On the contrary, Superintendent Hare spoke for his colleagues when he dismissed the letter as a pack of lies. Born in South Africa, the son of a British Army officer, and something of a giant of the day, measuring six-foot three and weighing 20 stone (127 kilograms), Hare was hardly one to be intimidated by Ned and his gang.

On 15 February, six days after the Kellys had emptied the bank in Jerilderie, Sherritt met Hare again, this time in Beechworth. He told the Superintendent that Dan Kelly would call on Joe Byrne's mother in the Woolshed the following night. Hare arranged to watch the house with both Sherritt and Detective Michael Ward. The next day, he rode across to Eldorado to secure reinforcements for the night's operation. Anthony was out of the town at the time, leading a police party looking for the gang, and Hare told one of his constables that Anthony's party should meet him in the evening at a certain place in the bush before proceeding to Mrs Byrne's house. But the message didn't get through, and Anthony's party did not arrive at the rendezvous point. Although he was outgunned without Anthony and his troopers, Hare decided nonetheless to ride to the Byrne hut with Ward and Sherritt. Again, it was to no avail. None of the gang materialised. Hare was 'very much put out'.[16] Such abortive operations sapped the confidence of the force and generated ever-mounting frustration.

The Jerilderie raid upped the ante in the Outbreak substantially. Ned and his three young associates had made off with £2141, augmenting their reputation as bold bushrangers. In response, towards the end of February the New South Wales and Victorian governments and several banks posted a massive £8000 reward, to be 'equitably apportioned between any persons giving information which shall lead to the apprehension of the offenders and any members of the police force or other persons who may actually effect such apprehension or assist thereat'. In time, this reward would itself become the centre of much recrimination, dragging in Anthony Strahan.

The very fact that the Jerilderie Letter was left unpublished only increased the sense of mystery surrounding the Kelly Gang. The summaries of parts of the letter that appeared in the press whetted the public's appetite. The hunt dominated newspapers across the colonies for months, so much so that readers could be forgiven for thinking the police did little else but search for Ned. Some histories of the Kelly Outbreak, especially those critical of the police, create a similar impression. The Kelly hunt was indeed the single biggest and most taxing undertaking confronting the police between 1878 and 1880, but members of the force still had to attend to myriad other matters. Often mundane issues required attention.

Anthony's precipitate departure from Greta left the now-vacant police station in disarray. On 3 March, six weeks after he left the town, he wrote to Sadleir in Benalla to report that Marion had been told by a local resident that the station's stable was falling to pieces, with marauding pigs destroying the forage. A considerable quantity of oats, bran and straw had been lost. Sadleir told Standish on 11 March that this loss was due to the insecurity of the buildings, adding that no one could be reasonably held responsible because Anthony had been instructed to quit the station so suddenly. Ever the stickler, Nicolson took umbrage at this state of affairs, writing on 25 March: 'I cannot but consider that this was very neglectful of Strahan who was aware of the condition of the store and absence of locks and should have reported the risk of damage if he was unable to remedy it.'

Sadleir was quick to defend Anthony, informing Standish on 27 March that Anthony had done all possible to secure the forage store. Standish agreed. Given the 'constant and sudden changes' in the deployment of the police in the district and the 'wretched tumbledown' state of the Greta store, he did not think Anthony could be charged over the loss, which had to be written off.[17] It's striking that Standish had enough time and powers of concentration to adjudicate in such trifling bureaucratic disputes at the height of the Kelly Outbreak. Perhaps he welcomed the retreat into more humdrum and controllable matters. This wasn't the first or the last time either that senior officers in the force crossed swords during the hunt for the Kellys.

While administrative matters took up time and energy, the police in the northeast still had to follow up other crimes. The Kelly Gang kept a low profile for an extended period after the Jerilderie raid, but Anthony was kept busy in Wangaratta. On 27 June 1879 he arrested Thomas Hopkins, 'a respectable looking man', according to *The Advertiser*, for stealing the purse of Catherine Kane, the wife of a constable. Catherine had dropped the purse while shopping; Hopkins had found it lying on the ground. Instead of handing it in, Hopkins had spent the contents on a haircut and a round of drinks at a pub. He came clean and pleaded guilty. Three months later, Anthony arrested David Fielding for stealing a coat and a Webley revolver from William Sayer, a bank clerk. Fielding, who had just arrived from New Zealand, admitted he had crept into Sayer's room at Murdoch's Hotel when the clerk was out, pilfering both items. He confessed to trying to sell the weapon to Walter West, the barber who had cut Hopkins's hair. He too pleaded guilty, receiving a four-month prison sentence.[18]

Even if the Kelly Gang had gone underground, horse-stealing remained a problem. Across June and July 1879, Peter McIntyre stole six horses in quick succession at Indigo Creek, Black Dog Creek, Chiltern and Gooramadda. Like many other criminals, McIntyre used several aliases, including Reid, Ring and Moran, to cover his tracks. But he was unwise enough to move on the horses locally, using a livery stable-keeper and an auctioneer in Wangaratta. Anthony saw McIntyre at the stables on 18 July and became suspicious, questioning him about two horses. McIntyre's answers were unconvincing, and Anthony carefully noted the animals' brands. He later recovered several horses, returning them to their owners. McIntyre was arrested some weeks later and charged. Faced with incontrovertible evidence, he pleaded guilty in October and was sentenced to five years' imprisonment with hard labour.[19] His conviction reinforced Anthony's reputation as a scourge of horse thieves.

Although he spent much time in Wangaratta pursuing other criminal cases, Anthony continued to be on special duty looking for the Kellys. This left Marion home alone. But she was resilient. Marion gave birth to her sixth child, my great-grandfather Francis, on 4 August 1879. It is not known whether Anthony was in town for the birth or out looking for the Kellys. A Strahan family history contends that Anthony sometimes went undercover on special duty and that the constables given this gruelling task 'were frequently mistaken as bushrangers themselves and were often fired upon'. It notes that Anthony would return home exhausted between forays across northeast Victoria and southern New South Wales.[20] Anthony did continue to chase leads concerning the Kellys, but I have been unable to verify these claims about daring undercover work. They could be another manifestation of the Kelly Outbreak's seemingly endless capacity to generate tall tales.

It was the McAuliffes who took Anthony back to Greta in September 1879. While attending the police court in Oxley on 17 September, Sergeant Steele heard about a shot being fired at the school in Greta and instructed Anthony to investigate. The school was situated near the farms of two selector families, the McAuliffes and the Nolans. The McAuliffes came from convict stock and were known Kelly sympathisers. Neighbour John Nolan was close to Bridget McAuliffe and her children, and he too became known as a Kelly supporter. In January 1879 he was arrested under the *Felons Apprehension Act* for aiding and abetting the Kellys but was discharged. The Nolans straddled the Kelly divide, sometimes awkwardly. At the very time that warrants were being issued in March 1878 to arrest the Kellys and Jack Lloyd for horse-stealing, a Constable Martin Nolan was transferred from Wodonga to Melbourne, where he would spend the next few years walking the beat in Collingwood. It is likely the police didn't want a member of the Nolan family stationed in the northeast when John was seen as a Kelly sympathiser.

Anthony knew the McAuliffes were part of the Greta mob. In line with standard policy, he did not ride to Greta on 18 September alone, taking Constable James Dixon with him. He spoke to the schoolteacher, Adelaide Henessey. She was diligent and well-liked, but she was in an uncomfortable position: her husband, Patrick, was a colourful character prone to drinking, brawling and using crude language in public. Some saw him as a Kelly sympathiser. Adelaide told Anthony she had informed the young McAuliffes five or six weeks earlier that they would be summonsed if they did not attend school more regularly. About three days later, a gunshot had been fired at the school at about 11pm. Adelaide was in bed and had been too afraid to look outside in case another shot was fired. She told Anthony she could not say conclusively who had fired the shot, but she believed the older McAuliffe boys, Denis and Patrick, had been responsible. Anthony examined the school door, finding forty grains of No. 2 shot. After returning to Wangaratta, he wrote up his report. He noted that Adelaide had admitted she had been too afraid to inform the police at the time of the incident because she lived and worked 'close to these people' and had small children of her own. With the teacher unable or unwilling to provide more information, Anthony concluded that nothing more could be done. He didn't question the McAuliffes, presumably because he didn't have enough to go on.[21] Taking place in the heart of Kelly country at the height of the Outbreak, this incident was a reminder that some Kelly supporters were quick to use violence to resolve matters big and small. Such casual thuggery created a climate of fear.

Just two weeks later, Anthony had another encounter with the Greta mob. On 2 October he saw Richard Hart, the older brother of Steve, and another man, John Meighan, talking animatedly outside the Wangaratta police court. The men were at loggerheads over the erection of a fence and a payment. Anthony heard Hart threatening Meighan. He informed Meighan that if he was afraid for his life, he should take out a summons to get Hart bound over to keep the peace.

Dick Hart was a hard man and a leading member of the Greta mob. It was widely thought he was in touch with the Kellys. Yet even though he knew Hart's younger brother was a gang member, Meighan filed a summons, and the matter came before the police magistrate, William Foster, a cousin of Governor La Trobe, on 16 October. Meighan testified that Hart had threatened to 'take it out of him', promising to throw him in the Ovens River. He insisted that he had been in fear for his life, afraid Hart would shoot him. But if it had come to blows, it wouldn't have been a fair fight: Meighan was seventy-four and Hart twenty-three. Anthony testified that he had heard Hart threatening Meighan. Foster found the case proven and bound over Hart to keep the peace for six months, ordering him to pay a surety of £25.[22] Anthony was likely satisfied by this outcome, but it was a piffling victory while the Kellys remained at large. He was dealing with the colony's most infamous criminals at one or two removes. The failure to catch the Kellys would have rankled.

17

ONE LAST STAND

Across early 1880 the Kellys stayed in hiding, their whereabouts the subject of fevered speculation. On 22 January, Melbourne's *The Herald* captured a mood that was at once agitated and exhausted:

> It is said that after the affair at Jerilderie the gang got over the Queensland border, and from that place made their exit from Australia. All sorts of rumors were circulated to prove this assertion … However, everybody did not give credence to those reports, and many knowing ones shook their heads and ventured to assert that they were still in the colony safe for a time in their old haunts. That the police believe the gang to be somewhere in the mountain ranges of the Ovens district is quite evident from their movements, which although conducted with the greatest secrecy, it is apparent tend towards one point, the discovery of a clue which might lead up to something tangible. Bands of troopers are constantly going and coming from the police stations, their destination being a mystery to all except themselves. As they generally return after a time, worn out and in rags, without having obtained a clue of any sort of the whereabouts of the gang, this sort of work begins to get monotonous after a time.

On 19 March 1880, Anthony was transferred from Wangaratta to take charge of the police station at Rutherglen. He had been relieved of the task of looking for the Kellys after so many hard months when he took on a station in a busy town. He was settling into his new post, attending to

Rutherglen's run-of-the-mill administrative and law-and-order matters, becoming the inspector of both slaughterhouses and nuisances, when the Kelly Gang's long lull ended in June 1880.

After hiding for so many months, his frustration mounting and his resources dwindling, Ned decided it was time to stage a much more daring operation. His plan was both straightforward and audacious: lure as many police officers as possible into the northeast on a special train sent to capture him; set a trap for the train to kill a large number of these constables, blunting the force's ability to strike back; and then raid a bank in Benalla or another town, making off with the loot. Ned knew that a train was the only way to move police across the country quickly and in numbers. Then and since, some have claimed Ned had wider political ambitions; Ian Jones claimed that Ned drew up a Declaration of the Republic of Northeastern Victoria and intended to fire off Chinese signal rockets to summon an army of sympathisers.[1] This claim seems misleading to me. Based on the available evidence, it seems clear Ned and his gang were planning another heist for quite ordinary criminal reasons: they had run out of money and needed more.

Ned's preparations were thorough, if unusual. First, in the months leading up to the operation, he fashioned the gang's iconic armour from plough mouldboards, stolen from farmers. It was this armour that my father, like so many other Australians, came to cherish as a symbol of a heroic rebel. Next, the gang had to commit a sufficiently bloody act to goad Commissioner Standish into despatching the special train. Ned settled on a target that would achieve two outcomes at once. At 6.30pm on Saturday 26 June, Joe Byrne approached the Woolshed Valley hut of his childhood friend, Aaron Sherritt, with Dan Kelly looking on. The gang had decided it was time to kill Sherritt because he had been lagging on them for many months. Three constables were stationed inside Sherritt's hut to protect him, but they would prove to be of no use. When Sherritt opened the back door, Byrne shot him through the throat and in the chest with a shotgun.

Meanwhile, Ned and Steve Hart put the next part of the gang's plan into effect, forcing some railway navvies to remove the tracks on a sharp bend on the rail line just past Glenrowan. Travelling north to find Sherritt's killers, the derailed train would plunge down the steep escapement, killing many on board. The gang would then gun down any survivors from above. Ned was planning to carry out a massacre.

The gang gathered at the Glenrowan Inn, run by Ann Jones, to await the arrival of the special train. Here they employed one of the tactics that had worked so well in Euroa and Jerilderie, holding sixty-odd people captive in the inn. The hostages were a mixed bunch, including fourteen children, a number of Kelly sympathisers and the local schoolteacher, Thomas Curnow.

Events didn't move as fast as the gang had anticipated. It took the Victoria Police some time to organise the special train, in part because a terrified Constable Harry Armstrong, who had been hiding in Sherritt's hut at the time of the murder, did not come forth to bring news of the terrible deed to Beechworth until 1.00pm on Sunday 27 June. While they waited for their trap to be sprung, the gang had a good time with the hostages in the inn, drinking, dancing and singing. Grantlee Kieza captures this surreal scene well. Ned even organised games behind the pub, winning 'the hop, step and jump, using a revolver in each hand as weights'.[2] He was relaxed enough at this point to let twenty-odd hostages go.

The special train finally departed Melbourne at 10.15pm on Sunday 27 June. A Queensland police officer, Sub-Inspector Stanhope O'Connor, was on board with his five Aboriginal trackers. Four journalists also came along for the ride, eager to cover the next chapter in the Kelly hunt. The train pulled into Benalla at 1.30am on Monday 28 June, picking up Superintendent Francis Hare, who assumed command, seven policemen and a plucky volunteer.

The gang's bold operation came unstuck when Ned made a fateful mistake. He allowed Curnow to leave the inn, wrongly believing him to be a sympathiser. As the special train finally steamed towards Glenrowan in the early hours of Monday 28 June, Curnow intervened: he flagged down the train with a candle and his sister's red scarf. Saved from disaster, Hare, O'Connor and their troopers laid siege to the gang in the inn. Clad in the improvised armour, which mostly proved more of a hindrance than a help, the gang fought the police for hours, with volleys of gunshot ricocheting back and forth. Hare was shot in the left wrist early on, sustaining a serious wound, and had to be evacuated back to the train station. A crack shot, Constable Charles Gascoigne got Ned through the left elbow. The police peppered the inn with shots, unintentionally wounding some of the hostages, including Ann Jones's son, Jack, who was hit in the hip.

Other police officers converged on the scene, including Superintendent John Sadleir, who assumed control of the chaotic police operation. Sergeant Arthur Steele galloped in from Wangaratta, intent on finally getting his man. Some hostages managed to escape the mayhem during several short ceasefires, scampering to safety.

Eventually it became clear to the gang that they were done for. Joe Byrne was the first to die, when he was shot in the groin while sitting at the bar taking a defiant drink. Leaving Dan and Steve Hart behind, Ned emerged from the bullet-riddled inn at 7am in his armour for one last stand. He was already badly wounded, but he was determined to go down fighting, trading shots with four officers and a gutsy railway guard. It was perhaps fated that it was Steele who finally brought down the most infamous outlaw of the day. Realising that the armour left the legs unprotected, Steele aimed low and hit Ned in the right knee with his shotgun, bringing him to ground. The Glenrowan constable, Hugh Bracken, stopped his enraged comrades from finishing off the bushranger as he lay prone.

Ned was conveyed to the railway station with a staggering twenty-eight wounds. It was astounding that he had survived. But the police operation had not finished; Dan Kelly and Steve Hart were still inside the inn. After the last twenty-five hostages escaped during a brief lull in the gunfire, Sadleir instructed his constables to set fire to the inn. Father Matthew Gibney plunged into the flames, emerging shortly afterwards to confirm that Byrne, Dan Kelly and Hart were all dead. He said he had seen the latter two lying side by side, apparently killed by police gunshots or poisoned by their own doing. As the fire consumed the flimsy structure, two constables dragged Byrne's body out of the inn; it was later put macabrely on display in Benalla, strung up on the lock-up door. The corpses of Dan Kelly and Steve Hart were burnt to a crisp. Commissioner Standish arrived by train at Glenrowan in the afternoon, after all the action was over.

Having chased the Kellys for so long, Anthony must have been devastated that he was so far away when the gang was brought to heel. Had he been present, he would have been unsurprised to see the familiar faces of the McAuliffe brothers, long-time friends of the gang, emerging from the inn at the end the siege.

Following a committal hearing in Beechworth, Ned was brought before Justice Redmond Barry in a special sitting at the Central Criminal Court in Melbourne on 28 October 1880. The charge was wilfully and maliciously murdering Constable Thomas Lonigan near Mansfield. The indefatigable Charles Smyth was the prosecutor. David Gaunson, a lawyer and a member of the Legislative Assembly, had taken up Ned's cause, but it was an Irishman, Henry Bindon, who had been a barrister for only six weeks, who defended the bushranger.

Armed police stood guard at the court's entrance to keep the scores of interested onlookers outside. Anticipation was high: one newspaper said the court was 'well filled long before the time fixed for commencing'.[3] Ned's older sisters, Maggie, Kate and Grace, and his purported sweetheart, Ettie Hart, took their seats in the public gallery. Eventually Ned was brought into the courtroom, wearing a borrowed Chesterfield overcoat.

The sole survivor of Stringybark Creek, Constable Thomas McIntyre, was the chief witness. During his long testimony, he recounted what had happened that night, not deviating from what he had passed on to his colleagues in October 1878. He stated unequivocally that Ned had killed Lonigan. He affirmed that Ned had told him, when they were sitting around the fire at the police campsite waiting for Kennedy and Scanlan, that he would like to roast four police officers alive if he could: Flood, Fitzpatrick, Steele and Strahan.[4] So Anthony made another ghostly appearance in the Kelly saga, even though he was almost certainly not at the trial and did not testify.

In all, sixteen people testified. There was little doubt about the verdict. On 29 October, the twelve-member jury took less than thirty minutes to find

Ned guilty. Given a chance to speak before he was sentenced, the fearless bushranger was defiant: 'Nobody knew about my case except myself, and I wish I had insisted on being allowed to examine the witnesses myself. If I had examined them, I am confident I would have thrown a different light on the case. It is not that I fear death; I fear it as little as to drink a cup of tea.'

Ned sparred with Justice Barry for some time, as the packed galleries looked on. At one point, he declared, 'A day will come at a bigger court than this when we shall see which is right and which is wrong.' But Barry was unmoved, underscoring the need to set a stern example: 'Foolish, inconsiderate, ill-conducted, unprincipled youths unfortunately abound, and unless they are made to consider the consequences of crime, they are led to imitate notorious felons, whom they regard as self-made heroes.' Contending that the jury's verdict was 'irresistible', he told Ned that he might envy the death his 'unfortunate and miserable companions' had found and handed down the death sentence. Ned's rejoinder has become legendary, though some have subsequently disputed what he actually said: 'I will see you there where I go.'[5]

Ned would not have to wait long for the gallows, but his fate continued to stir up much public interest, and no little anger in some quarters. Big crowds gathered in central Melbourne. At one point, Kate Kelly threw herself at the feet of the Governor, George Phipps, the Marquess of Normanby, begging for mercy.[6] Over 30,000 people apparently signed a petition asking for clemency, but the Executive Council ruled on 8 November that the execution would proceed in three days' time as planned.

On 9 November, another crowd, numbering as many as 2000, assembled in the evening on the reserve near the gaol. Some called out for justice for Ned. *The Argus* claimed, however, that 'it was observable both then and afterwards that the greater portion took no part whatever in either the cheers or groans that were uttered'. David Gaunson's brother, William, another lawyer, and several other fervent Kelly supporters arrived on a lorry drawn by a horse and flanked by 'several rough-looking persons bearing torches'. A large contingent of police moved in on the crowd.

After addressing the throng, first on La Trobe Street and then at the corner of Madeline and Queensberry streets in Carlton, William Gaunson and his companions proceeded to the Treasury Building on Spring Street to ask the Chief Secretary, Graham Berry, to reconsider the verdict. With the crowd milling around outside, a delegation, including Gaunson and Ned's uncle, Pat Quinn, was admitted to the Executive Council chamber. There, Gaunson asked Berry for a reprieve for Ned. He read out Quinn's affidavit, which portrayed Anthony as the villain who had threatened to shoot Ned like a dog. He said Quinn was now ready to sign the affidavit before the Chief Secretary himself as a justice of the peace. Quinn spoke up, although he declined at first to reveal who he was. He told Berry that he knew about 'the case from beginning to end' and claimed the police had only chased down his nephew because a reward had been offered. He declared that the people in the northeast wanted a royal commission to investigate the whole affair, saying he 'certainly was willing to speak his mind openly and fearlessly'.

Berry was unmoved. He noted that Quinn's affidavit was unsworn and stressed that the time to consider such a document would have been during the trial. 'It was all very well for [Quinn] to come forward now with the document, when it could not be at once answered,' Berry told the delegation. 'If the statements made in it had been made at the proper time, the officer who was referred to would have had the opportunity to reply to them.'[7]

Looking back on this exchange, it seems plausible to me that Ned's lawyers had not presented Quinn as a witness because they feared he would be exposed under cross-examination as a man who bent the truth. Had Quinn testified, the prosecution would have both grilled him and called Anthony to the stand to rebut his claims.

In the end, Quinn didn't sign his affidavit in the Executive Council chamber that night, despite Gaunson's protestations that he would. Perhaps Ned's uncle realised that there was no hope, or perhaps he feared signing a document that wasn't altogether true. Berry told the aggrieved delegation before him that the Victorian government had not placed 'any obstacles in the way of those who are acting to get a reprieve'. When Gaunson remonstrated one last time, the Chief Secretary was firm. 'Some people might talk about the condemned man and what he had suffered, but the many cruel murders he had committed, the widows he had made, and the lives he had destroyed, could not be ignored.' The delegation left the chamber, a disappointed Gaunson addressing the crowd from the steps of the Treasury.

Quinn's affidavit failed to sway Berry, but its contents were printed in full in *The Argus* on 10 November, meaning Anthony's colleagues and the general public could read its apparently damning accusations in full. Anthony must have felt humiliated.[8]

The Executive Council confirmed the sentence on 10 November. That night, Ned had his last meal: roast lamb, peas and a bottle of claret. Family and friends had been allowed to visit him earlier in the day. Refusing to take his breakfast the next morning, Ned was removed from his cell. *The Argus* described his final walk in sombre but triumphant terms:

> Immediately afterwards, he was conducted from his cell in the old wing to the condemned cell alongside the gallows in the new or main building. In being thus removed, he had to walk through the garden which surrounds the hospital ward, and to pass the handcart in which his body was in another hour to be carried back to the dead house. Making only a single remark about the pretty flowers in the garden, he passed in a jaunty manner from the brilliant sunshine into the sombre walls of the prison.

The warders escorted Ned to the drop, where Dean Charles O'Hea, who had baptised him twenty-six years earlier, and Dean Thomas Donaghy, the prison chaplain, waited to administer the last rites of the Catholic Church. The Governor of the Gaol and thirty or so policemen, doctors, justices of the peace and journalists looked on. His arms pinned behind his back and his head covered by the customary white hood, Ned was brought across to the drop. An *Argus* journalist recorded the condemned man's apparent last words, 'Ah, well, I suppose it has come to this.' Shortly afterwards, the executioner, Elijah Upjohn, a Ballarat chicken thief, pulled the bolt.

Edward Kelly died a few minutes after 10am. 'On removing the cap the face was found to be placid, and without any discolouration, and only a slight mark was left by the rope under the left ear. The eyes were wide open,' *The Argus* noted.[9] Max Kreitmayer, a waxworks owner, made the famous plaster death mask that is viewed with such interest to this day, housed at the National Portrait Gallery in Canberra.

A large crowd, perhaps 4000 strong, waited outside the walls of the gaol for confirmation that Ned was gone.[10] Ellen Kelly was weeping uncontrollably in a cell nearby, where she was serving her sentence for aiding and abetting her son's hotly disputed attempt to murder Constable Alexander Fitzpatrick. She had seen Ned one last time the day before his execution. With prison guards looking on, their final conversation was, according to Ian Jones, 'starchy and impersonal', but mother and son were determined to maintain their dignity. Ellen's grief ran deep.[11]

Ned's family and supporters claimed some retribution when Justice Barry, a diabetic, died twelve days later, an infection spreading from a carbuncle on his neck.

Anthony was far away in Rutherglen when the execution took place. He likely followed the last two weeks of Ned's life through the pages of the press. Had he picked up *The Ovens and Murray Advertiser* on 6 November, he would have been gratified to read about 'what a wretched ending is about to be made of a worthless and miserable life'. On 11 November, the very day Ned was escorted to the drop, Anthony wrote to Superintendent Sadleir in Benalla about a disputed bill for supplying forage to the Rutherglen police station.[12] It was somehow apposite that Anthony was preoccupied with an utterly mundane matter just as the life of his bête noire ended.

The board appointed to apportion the £8000 reward to 'those officers and civilians who assisted in the capture of the Kelly gang' met for the first time on 17 November. It had sensibly waited until after Ned's execution. Composed of three parliamentarians, the board placed advertisements in the press and government gazettes, calling for individuals to lodge a claim for a share of the reward and giving a deadline of the end of the year.

Anthony wrote up his application on Christmas Eve. He attested that he had been actively engaged in the hunt for the Kellys from the time he had led the Greta police party into the Wombat Ranges until three months before the siege at Glenrowan. He had searched in the 'wildest and most remote parts' of the northeast, lying in the frost throughout the night to surveil the houses of the friends and relatives of the gang. He had endured 'the greatest hardship' and injured his health, though he didn't specify how, requiring him to go to 'considerable expense to call in doctors'. The exigencies of the force had meant it was necessary to transfer him to Rutherglen, so he had not been present at Glenrowan at the time of Ned's capture, through no fault of his own. He insisted that he was as entitled to a share of the reward as those who had been at Glenrowan, many of whom had arrived at the scene at a late hour, when the danger had passed.

In total, ninety-two people, including many policemen, put in claims. The board needed help in assessing such a large number. Commissioner Standish had been forced into retirement in September 1880, so the board asked Nicolson, as the Acting Chief Commissioner, to 'report upon each claim, either personally or through such officer as he might consider best able to decide upon the merits of the claims'. Nicolson was hardly a neutral adjudicator given his strong opinions and rifts with other officers.

After considering the claims for some weeks, the board released its findings in mid-April 1881, dividing the claimants into those who were not entitled to a share of the reward (schedule A, 25 individuals) and those who were (schedule B, 67 individuals). Anthony was horrified to find his name in schedule A. This rebuff was humiliating, the more so because it appeared in the press. His sense of being wronged, even scapegoated, was exacerbated when some of his colleagues – Superintendent Sadleir, Sergeant Steele and Detective Ward – were given rewards. Why was he scorned? The board said it could not 'distinguish further between members of the force, all of whom appear to have done their duty', but it did not explain publicly why it had rejected some claims but accepted others.

In the board's confidential papers, Superintendent Hare acknowledged that Anthony 'did a lot of work in the search for the Kellys' but was some distance away from Glenrowan at 'the time of the destruction of the gang'. Sadleir made a similar comment. He agreed that Anthony had been active in 'the early part of the search' in 1878–79 but stressed that he had not been involved for some months and had not been present at the capture.

This assessment was hardly fair. Although he too had been absent from Glenrowan, Ward was rewarded because of his 'connection with the employment' of Aaron Sherritt, who had supplied vital information. Yet it had been Anthony, not Ward, who had introduced Sherritt to Nicolson and Sadleir following the abortive raids on the Byrne and Sherritt huts in November 1878.

Anthony wasn't the only apparently deserving person to miss out. Both Constable Thomas McIntyre, the key witness in Ned's trial, and the police informant Daniel Kennedy, who applied under a pseudonym to protect his identity, went unrewarded. But this was cold comfort for Anthony.

Among schedule A were some meritorious claimants acting in the service of the government, who were recognised in a schedule C. It was recommended that they were 'worthy of special recognition for the zeal displayed by them, at all times, in their several positions during the long period of the search for the outlaws'.[13] Anthony was further stung by the fact that six of those whose claims had been rejected – McIntyre, a second constable, the stationmasters at Benalla and Wangaratta and the postmasters at Benalla and Beechworth – were listed under schedule C. That left only nineteen claimants who had been rebuffed entirely. Of the fourteen police officers whose claims had been rejected, none had done nearly as much as Anthony over such a long period to bring the gang to justice. Had Ned's accusation in the Jerilderie Letter and Pat Quinn's last-ditch affidavit cruelled his prospects?

The reward board released its determinations a few weeks after the royal commission into 'the circumstances of the Kelly Outbreak and the present state and organization of the Police Force' had held its first hearings in March 1881. Composed of nine members and chaired by long-time parliamentarian Francis Longmore, the commission held sixty-six meetings and questioned sixty-two witnesses over the next seven months, asking nearly 18,000 questions. Although he was a central figure in the first year of the Outbreak, Anthony was not called to testify. Several witnesses, including Sadleir, Steele, Ward and Flood, referred many times in their own testimony to the role that Anthony had played at critical points, especially in the lead-up to and after Stringybark Creek. It is therefore inexplicable that he was not summoned. The surviving record doesn't reveal why this glaring omission came about. The royal commission visited Beechworth, Benalla, Glenrowan, Greta, Sebastopol and Wangaratta, all not far from Rutherglen, where Anthony was stationed. Pat Quinn referred to him six times in his evidence, always in a neutral manner. Tellingly, he did not mention, even obliquely, the contents of his affidavit. One might have expected him to lay much of the blame for what had happened to his nephews at Anthony's feet, but he did not.[14] This glaring silence cast yet more doubt on his affidavit's veracity.

The commission's proceedings had one stinging moment for Anthony. Commissioner Standish was the first witness to appear. When quizzed about various officers' fitness for duty during the Outbreak, he described Anthony as 'a blathering fellow'.[15] He didn't elaborate, but one would have to conclude that this damning comment harkened back to Pat Quinn's allegations. Standish would likely have read Quinn's affidavit in *The Argus*, or at least heard about its contents, which seemed to confirm what Ned had claimed in the Jerilderie Letter. Anthony had not had a chance to state his case in public, so the Kelly clan's pernicious claims stood uncontested, at least in the eyes of some.

Standish's damning character assessment was a horrible fall from grace for my great-great-grandfather in one sense. Standish had approved at least five rewards for Anthony in the 1860s and 1870s in recognition of his excellent police work, most notably for apprehending the perpetrators of the Wooragee Outrage. He had promoted Anthony to senior constable in 1874 and then personally selected him in late 1877 to take charge of the police station in Greta. He had in part pinned his reputation on my great-great-grandfather and felt let down: all that old high regard had evaporated by March 1881.

Ultimately, though, Anthony was fortunate the commission didn't drag him into the spotlight. Through the evidence of multiple witnesses, he appeared in a generally positive light. By contrast, the commission grilled some police witnesses with varying degrees of scepticism or outright hostility. Superintendent John Sadleir later accused the commission of using methods 'repugnant to all ideas of justice and fair play', claiming that 'Longmore was eminently honest and conscientious, but he went relentlessly for scalps'.[16]

When it released its initial findings in its second progress report in October 1881, the commission exposed flaws in the efforts to locate and apprehend the Kelly Gang. It was Standish, not Anthony, who came out of the proceedings badly. The commission described his evidence as untrustworthy and concluded that his conduct while in charge of the force 'was not characterized either by good judgment, or by that zeal for the interests of the public service which should have distinguished an officer in his position'. More damningly, it sheeted home the bad feeling that had often prevailed between the officers engaged in the hunt for the Kellys to his 'want of impartiality, temper, tact and judgment'.[17] This sweeping negative assessment wasn't entirely fair, forever staining Standish's reputation and clouding the positive aspects of his career. He died at the Melbourne Club at the age of fifty-eight on 19 March 1883.

Other members of the force were subjected to a dressing-down. The commission called for Nicolson and Hare to retire, blasted Brooke Smith's 'indolence and incompetence', criticised Sadleir for making 'several errors of judgement', reduced Ward by one grade for 'misleading his superior officers', decried Steele's 'impromptitude and poor judgement' and found the three constables in Aaron Sherritt's hut guilty of 'arrant cowardice'.[18] Many officers felt misunderstood, even victimised, by these scathing conclusions. It is notable that some of the policemen who received a share of the Kelly reward fund were criticised in stern terms by the commission

– including Nicolson, the Acting Chief Commissioner who was assessing the claims – creating a contradictory, if not absurd, outcome.

The commission would continue its deliberations over the next eighteen months in more temperate circumstances, releasing its general findings about the state of the force in April 1883. It formulated sensible suggestions about police reform, but it would be remembered mostly for its unsparing critiques of individual officers.

Even though Anthony's Greta posting lasted only one year, it defined much of his career and his reputation. Whether he liked it or not, he would never be free of that small town.

On my way to Melbourne from Canberra in August 2018, I pulled off the Hume into Greta West to see where my great-great-grandfather had been stationed during the Outbreak. I had driven past the Greta sign countless times over the years and never diverted. It was a crisp winter day, sunny and still. Greta's town centre had long ago moved 8 kilometres southwest of the original site. Today both locations, Greta West and Greta, are no longer recognisable as towns. According to the 2016 census, the population of the Greta district was 269, spread across a large area. As I entered Greta West, I tried to find the old police station, but didn't get far. I didn't even know if Bridget O'Brien's cottage had survived.

Next I drove towards Glenrowan, on the road that runs out to the remains of Ellen Kelly's hut. This was where my father had paid homage to Ned in 1963, two years before I was born, photographing Clem Christesen on 'the bellows said to have been used to forge the gang's armour'.[19]

I didn't come to pay homage. I do not regard Ned with hostility or see him as a psychopath. I recognise that he was shaped by larger social and economic forces. And I see some of what transpired during the Outbreak as the result of a series of cascading events that were to a great degree beyond the control of the participants. But I am sure Ned was a criminal who killed three policemen in cold blood and would have killed my great-great-grandfather if given the chance. Ned wasn't a demon, but nor was he a hero.

The remains of the Kelly hut are located on private land and the owners don't want people trampling over their property. There is nothing left of the hut now aside from two crumbling chimneys, which can't be seen from the road. I felt disappointed. The chimneys hidden, I couldn't feel the past rippling through the air.

That all changed when I drove across to the Greta Cemetery. In January 2013 Ned Kelly's remains were removed from Melbourne and reinterred in an unmarked grave in Greta, according to his dying wish, or so the press claimed. Under a white marquee, descendants watched on as Ned was buried close to the unmarked grave of his mother, Ellen. His new grave was deliberately deep, his remains encased in concrete to deter looters. When the marquee was removed, onlookers could see five mounds, another measure to thwart grave robbers. 'One tattooed bloke tipped beer on one of the mounds, presumably a gesture to the outlaw's legendary rebellious spirit,' observed journalist Benjamin Preiss. 'Others might have thought it disrespectful.' A lawyer said the Kelly family could lodge an appeal for a pardon on the grounds that Ned had not received a fair trial.[20] This was nonsense: Ned was convicted in a proper trial.

When I walked through the cemetery gate, I was confronted by the past in black letters chiselled into granite. A hip-high gravestone read: *Here within this cemetery in unmarked graves lie Edward Kelly, mother Ellen, sisters and brothers Margaret, Grace, James, Daniel & Anne buried nearby, along with their extended family & friends. May they rest in peace.* This inscription struck me as restrained and respectful, shorn of the grandiose claims of the Kelly legend. Perhaps no more needed to be said, for the site is suffused with the Kelly story by virtue of who is buried there. Steve Hart and Tom Lloyd, the unofficial fifth member of the gang, also lie here, adding to the place's aura.

With the winter sun crystalline, I walked through the cemetery and back towards my car, parked on the other side of the road, stopping at a small pavilion by the front gate. There on a dusty table I found a visitors' book. As I opened it, I remembered what Tom Griffiths had written in the mid-1980s about Ned Kelly's enduring reputation in the northeast: 'Many say that if you knock him publicly in Beechworth, you'll find a hundred defenders, and perhaps a punch in the nose. "They don't seem to grow to his stature now – I never heard a hard word about Ned," they say, and take pleasure in knowing someone who knew him.'[21] I knew such sentiment ran deep. I had recently read an article in the *Benalla Ensign* about the artist Ray Hearn and his show, 'The True Ned', staged at the Benalla Art Gallery. Hearn said he wanted to complicate the conventional Kelly story, as represented by the highway sign at Glenrowan, 'which depicts Kelly with two six-guns as a Wild West cowboy–style desperado'. Ned was wounded, Hearn declared, 'four times in his left arm (and foot) in the first exchange of gunfire' and could 'never have held those two pistols aloft'. Yet the bravado lives on. A friend picked up a bumper sticker in Beechworth in 2019. With a policeman and an armoured Ned standing either side of the courthouse, it simply read: 'Whose side are you on?'

If the inscription on the Kelly tombstone was unemotional, the messages in the visitors' book were anything but. People had come from all corners of Australia, from as far away as Perth and northern Queensland – and sometimes from other parts of the world, especially Ireland – to see Ned's grave. Most messages were passionately pro-Kelly – not surprising given that Greta is part of the so-called Kelly Trail. Some were simple positive remarks: 'RIP Ned', 'You will always be remembered', 'Never never dead', 'Proud to have visited here!' and, echoing Ned's purported words, 'Such is life'. Others were blokey or employed contemporary slang: 'It was good to have a beer with you Ned and family', 'Ned you rock', 'Awesome RIP'. One remark was incongruous and altogether too late: 'Best of luck Ned'. Another was inscrutable because it was written by a Dubliner in Gaelic.

A few visitors referred to Ellen or to the Kellys in general: 'I've come to say farewell to the Kelly family with love', 'Rest easy Ned and family' (from self-described 'West Oz Natives'), 'Mrs Kelly – a true gentlewoman'. Some adopted the mythology surrounding the Kellys: 'Misunderstood – life taken too soon', 'Ned was hard done by', 'You're our hero – God bless you

Ned and your mother'. Others saw Ned as a role model: 'There should be more out of his mould!!', 'You're a legend Ned. More should stand up for themselves', 'Let's hope a little bit of Ned lives on in all of us'. A conviction that Ned was victimised recurred. One pilgrim seemed to anticipate his own (premature) demise: 'I came here today to be buried near you. A hero. Not a villain.' Another highlighted an alleged incident at the heart of the Outbreak: 'They should have kept their hands off his sister.' Had he been alive, my dad would have written a passionate pro-Kelly message, rendered in his own quirky prose.

But no one referred directly to the gang's victims. No one named any policemen, though the police force was present implicitly in the remarks that Ned was persecuted. I thought about leaving a pointed message, but opted to write simply that I was 'the great-great-grandson of Senior Constable Anthony Strahan', gesturing towards the other side of the story. I felt this duty to my ancestor and to history. If subsequent visitors flicked through the comments and saw mine, most would not know how Anthony fitted into the Kelly story – but at least they would know he was important to someone.

I don't believe in ghosts. But for a small burial ground in an unremarkable place, Greta Cemetery brings close a powerful, vexed and lingering national story. Although he would live for years to come, Anthony would be haunted by Ned Kelly and by what he did – and didn't – do as a policeman during the Outbreak. He would never be free.

18

RUTHERGLEN DAYS

Anthony commenced duty in Rutherglen on 19 March 1880, a week after his fortieth birthday. The Strahans likely travelled from Wangaratta to Rutherglen by rail, catching a train along the line towards Wodonga before switching to the trunk track that ran from Springhurst through Rutherglen to Wahgunyah.

The railways symbolised how much Victoria had changed during Anthony's eighteen-year career. When he joined the force in the early 1860s, the colony's rail was rudimentary, with inland lines reaching only Ballarat, Bendigo and Echuca, leaving most of Victoria connected by rough dirt tracks through the bush. The 1870s saw a railway boom, linking much of the interior in a web of lines, with a track reaching Rutherglen in 1879, only months before Anthony arrived. It was good if the Strahans did move to Rutherglen in the comfort of a train because Anthony and Marion were now travelling with six small children, Anthony Oliver the oldest at eight and Francis, my great-grandfather, the youngest at six months.

The expansion of the railways was one sign of a retreating frontier society. The demise of the Kelly Gang was another. No one knew it yet, but Ned Kelly was among Victoria's last bushrangers; the bushranging era was coming to an end as social and economic conditions across the colony became more settled. The Rutherglen that Anthony and Marion came to in 1880 reflected this pattern. The population, which had swelled to a rowdy 10,000 during the 1860s goldrush, was a modest 500. Another 1900 lived in the surrounding shire, which stretched across 650 square kilometres, from the Murray in the north to Indigo Creek in the east,

Black Dog Creek in the south and the Ovens River in the west. Most of the fizz had gone out of goldmining. 'The once famous deep leads are now all forsaken,' remarked *The Ovens and Murray Advertiser* on 20 November, 'mining being only represented by a few quartz reefs and a solitary mill.' The area derived much of its income by this time from agriculture and from wine-making, which used the good soils and congenial climate. Ten vignerons were active in the district in 1865, planting 16 hectares of vines; by 1880, there were 400 hectares, with vineyards employing many locals during harvest season.

Rutherglen was an agreeable home for the Strahans. It boasted a railway station, a town hall, public baths, a courthouse, the police station, a post office and a telegraph station. There were also several churches, the Anglican St Stephen's the most prominent, and more than enough hotels – there were six dotted along Main Street, including The Star, The Shamrock, the Victoria Hotel and the Rutherglen Hotel, once known as the Golden Ball. A Bank of Victoria and an array of shops, including a bookseller, a druggist, an ironmonger, several grocers, a dressmaker and Mr Hunter's deliciously named general store, Hit or Miss, completed the picture. William Burrowes's grain warehouse purchased grains from around the district and sold flour, pollard and bran. Most children, including the two eldest Strahans, Anthony and Alicia, attended Rutherglen State School. Tree-lined streets radiated out from the town centre, forming 'long vistas or delightfully suggestive sylvan walks', *The Advertiser* wrote on 13 October 1881. Rutherglen Park, 65 acres in all, featured a triangular artificial lake, which supplied the town water; a plethora of elms, pines, cedars and blue gums; and a racecourse, of which Anthony would make good if controversial use. The town's calendar was bookended by the annual regatta in January on Lake Moodemere and the Rutherglen Agricultural Show in October. The Strahans arrived in Rutherglen just after a ball on St Patrick's Day, raising funds for Irish famine relief.

Anthony was again in charge of his own station, commanding a couple of foot constables. This would be his longest posting, stretching across fourteen years. His predecessor, Senior Constable Arthur Gribbin, had served in the district for eighteen years; the local newspaper praised him as 'an efficient, painstaking and zealous officer'. Anthony would work hard to earn the community's support. But he quickly confronted a familiar problem: a station requiring repairs, this time to leaking water tanks and a kitchen, 'blown down' by the wind. A new weatherboard skillion improved matters. As he had before, he assumed non-policing functions, serving as the inspector of slaughterhouses and nuisances, a truant officer under the *Education Act*, inspector of factories and a vaccinations officer. Although these roles diverted him from his policing duties, they generated much-needed additional income. The post of inspector of slaughterhouses came with an annual £10 stipend.

In contrast to the bushranging cases that had marked his career to date, Anthony would spend most of his time in Rutherglen on humdrum matters: petty larceny, common assaults and public-disorder offences such as drunkenness or using abusive language. The booty in many theft cases was paltry – Anthony arrested one fellow for stealing two shirts and a pair of socks from a clothesline. He and his constables often found themselves being asked to maintain law and order at public events, from rowing regattas, horseraces and football matches to balls, concerts and the annual show, even though the folk in attendance rarely stepped out of line, aside from imbibing too much liquor. But patrolling these events built trust between the township and the police.

Stock theft remained a problem, though on a less audacious scale than the Greta mob's operation. It was one case of horse-stealing that brought Anthony into indirect contact with one of his brothers. The prosecution of George Whitnell appears to be the only time Anthony ever came across any of his siblings in the discharge of his duties. Whitnell was suspected of stealing horses around Whorouly in 1878 but avoided justice by a mix of good luck and guile, including using aliases. This good run ended on 15 July 1880. The committal hearing in Wangaratta on 12 August revealed that Whitnell had taken the horses south to Wallan Wallan to move them on. He sold one mare to a farmer, asking the teacher at Wallan Wallan State School, Richard Strahan, to witness the receipt. There was no suggestion that Anthony's brother knew the horse was stolen, and he was not called to testify. Whitnell was undefended when a jury found him guilty in Beechworth in February 1881.

Although he gave evidence during Whitnell's committal, Anthony was unable to testify in Beechworth because a colourful character from his past, John 'Saucy Jack' Trembath, re-emerged to claim his attention. Anthony had arrested Trembath and another man, Charles Watson, in Eldorado a decade before for attempted highway robbery under arms. Found guilty, the two had been despatched to prison. Released from Pentridge in June 1876, Trembath had travelled to Gippsland, where he had taken up goldmining, working a claim on the Tangil River with Henry Wilkinson. Ever trouble-prone, Trembath fell out with Wilkinson, assaulting him viciously on 29 October – kicking him with hobnailed boots while Wilkinson was asleep. The cause of the dispute was contested on 9 February 1881 during Trembath's trial in Sale for malicious wounding. The prosecution alleged that Trembath had been attempting to convince Wilkinson to surrender his share in the claim when it had started paying good returns. The defence countered that Trembath had thrashed Wilkinson because he had broken into his house, stealing rum and attempting to rape his wife. Wilkinson had been rewarded, the defence opined, with 'no greater violence at the hands of the husband than British law would justify'. But the circumstances on 29 October were clouded by a session of heavy drinking involving Wilkinson, Trembath and his wife, and several other men.

After a short deliberation, the jury found Trembath guilty of a lesser offence, common assault. Determined to incarcerate him for a long stretch, the prosecution noted that Trembath had been convicted in Beechworth in 1872 of assault with attempt to rob. Trembath was irate, insisting he had never been in Beechworth and had spent the last twenty years in Gippsland. The Crown brought Anthony across to Sale to confirm that Trembath was the man convicted in 1872. Anthony was adamant the prisoner was the man he had arrested in Eldorado for attempted highway robbery. Characteristically forthright, he declared that he could pick Trembath out of a thousand men, no matter how he disguised himself, even though he had not seen him since his conviction. He said he also recognised Mrs Trembath because he had placed her in custody in Eldorado. Justice George Higinbotham referred Anthony's testimony to the jury as a matter of fact. After a brief discussion, the jury professed they were not convinced that Trembath was the same man convicted in 1872. Perhaps a bunch of Gippslanders didn't want to be told what to do by a trap from the northeast. Higinbotham sentenced Trembath to three months' imprisonment with hard labour, noting that he had already spent four months in custody awaiting trial.[1]

Anthony was unimpressed. His professional integrity had been impugned, and it had been taxing getting to Sale via a series of trains. His mood darkened when he returned to Rutherglen, for he had become entangled in a quarrel with William Burrowes, the grain merchant. Burrowes had held the forage contract for the Rutherglen police station for fourteen years. On 15 March, one of his employees delivered a consignment, which Anthony claimed was light by 28 pounds of oats and 111 pounds of hay. Burrowes rode down to the station to remonstrate, alleging that Anthony had knowingly used the station's faulty steelyards balance to weigh the forage. After a row, the men agreed to weigh one bag of oats from the consignment as a test on another set of scales. They set off together unhappily on a dray. Several stores weighed the bag, confirming that Burrowes was right in his calculations.

Anthony and Burrowes were cut from the same cloth: they were hot-tempered and good at holding grudges. Anthony retreated, writing to Burrowes on 18 March conceding his mistake. But Burrowes refused to relent. Anthony informed his commanding officer, Superintendent John Sadleir, that Burrowes was 'a man that will give all the trouble that he can'. He unwisely alleged that a portion of the consignment had been musty and poor quality. Upon hearing this, Burrowes went apoplectic, writing to Sadleir twice, first on 28 March and again two days later. The second letter ran for ten indignant pages. He vehemently denied that the forage was either underweight or shoddy. He insisted that he had been forced to speak out because the allegation that he had tried to cheat Senior Constable

Strahan had become known around the district. Damningly, he accused Anthony of being motivated by 'an interest in getting revenge'. The origin of this vengefulness was, he charged, a racehorse.

Anthony spent much of the 1880s trying to earn an extra quid. Although he should have thought twice about it, he purchased a racehorse soon after reaching Rutherglen, naming her Alicia, after his eldest daughter. He presented the mare at the Rutherglen Show in October 1880, later keeping her on the property of a local farmer. Alicia was good enough to win the Maiden Plate, for horses that had never won an advertised prize, in Rutherglen on 1 January 1881, claiming £4 for Anthony. But she flopped at Wangaratta on 17 February, running this time under the farmer's name. Burrowes had accused Anthony of refusing to pay for hay he had ordered to feed Alicia, and implied that Anthony had disputed the station's consignment in retaliation for the contested personal forage bill. He also suggested that Anthony was keeping Alicia on the police paddock. Policemen were demoted or dismissed for such transgressions. He made a broader point:

> Some years ago a general order was made to the effect that any constable selecting land would be removed from that locality. In my opinion it would raise the status of the force much more if a general order were issued prohibiting constables in charge of stations where forage is kept from keeping cattle of any kind as the temptation is very great to resist from giving a cow a handful of hay or the fowls a few grains of oats.

He demanded a board of survey to investigate the matter, insisting that no previous officer in charge of the Rutherglen station had questioned his deliveries.

Anthony was just as indignant, telling Sadleir that Burrowes's letters were 'nothing but lies from beginning to end'. He denied purchasing hay from Burrowes, noting that Burrowes had previously accused him of using government forage to feed his cows. He said he had never allowed his horse to remain in the police camp. He professed, disingenuously, that he could not 'conceive the motive' behind Burrowes's letters. Burrowes should summons him so he could secure a decision from the bench. Both men were now demanding a legal process.

Anthony had been in this place before, several times. And challenging Burrowes wasn't altogether smart. The merchant was well-established in Rutherglen, holding some sway in the district. He was a member of the shire council and served as a justice of the peace, sitting on the police court and the court of petty sessions.

Burrowes summonsed Anthony for not paying 8 shillings 4 pence for the forage for Alicia. The police magistrate, William Foster, and a justice of the peace, the bookseller Thomas Reeve, heard the case at the Rutherglen police court on 6 April. Anthony knew Foster, having appeared before him in the past, but Burrowes and Reeve were particularly well acquainted, serving on the council and hearing cases together as magistrates. During the proceedings John Mitchell, the farmer who was agisting Alicia, admitted to ordering the hay, saying he had offered to pay Burrowes the 8 shillings 4 pence in question. After what *The Advertiser* described as 'a patient hearing', the bench ruled in Anthony's favour, dismissing the case and ordering Burrowes to pay £1 10 shillings in costs. Anthony triumphantly informed his superiors that Foster had accused Burrowes of acting out of malice.

But Anthony's triumph was short-lived. Burrowes would not drop his demand for a survey board. On 12 May, Acting Chief Commissioner Hussey Chomley duly ordered that one be convened. He instructed Superintendent William Montfort, an experienced, capable officer who had taken over in Benalla from Sadleir after the Kelly royal commission, to ascertain if Anthony owned a racehorse and how many other animals were in his possession. Anthony responded quickly. He confirmed that he did indeed own a racehorse, but added that he had offered to sell Alicia for £18 and would dispose of her shortly for whatever price he could realise. He said he also owned two dogs; nine or ten hens; one milk cow; ten cattle pasturing on the Commons; another horse, which was grazing on a paddock at Black Dog Creek; and a boy's pony, which was on the Commons.

On 18 May, the survey board, which included Foster and Reeve, found the forage Burrowes supplied was correct in weight and of good quality, and ordered Anthony to pay the merchant in full. Montfort informed Chomley that Anthony had been 'perfectly candid' in his responses during the inquiry: 'I think the most objectionable part is he being the owner of a racehorse.' Having been snubbed by the police court, Burrowes was delighted that the survey board had backed him. He informed Montfort that he did not intend to take any further action, and the affair ended in a draw.[2] Anthony had made an early and controversial mark in Rutherglen.

As he was finishing up in Benalla, in May 1881 Superintendent Sadleir rated Anthony as 'a very zealous and willing sub-officer' who had been employed for nearly two years in 'very responsible and arduous duties in connection with the search for the Kelly gang'.[3] By now, Anthony had been in the force for almost twenty years. But so many years as a mounted constable, riding long distances, often in harsh weather, had exacted a heavy price. The force accepted his request in March 1883, as he was turning forty-three, to become a foot constable. He would still ride a horse at times in the course of his duty, but he was no longer required to undertake gruelling patrols. This was good news for Marion, as the Strahan family had continued to grow. Marion had given birth at the Rutherglen police station to her seventh and last child, Edward, on 23 June 1881.

Anthony's career in Rutherglen in the 1880s settled into a rhythm. Some local incidents had a theatrical, even comic, element. In 1883 Anthony apprehended a swindler who was wanted in New South Wales, preventing him from swallowing an incriminating letter by grabbing him around the throat and forcing him to literally cough up the document. On another occasion, *The Rutherglen Sun and Chiltern Valley Advertiser* noted that 'the usual dullness of Main Street was enlivened for a short time on Thursday' as Anthony tried to serve a summons on a local lady, who was seated in a buggy. Each time he approached the buggy, the horse skipped backwards, almost standing on his toes, to 'the intense amusement of the spectators'.

Anthony finally managed to hand the summons to the lady, with 'much danger to his extremities'. All to no avail. The lady cast 'that little bit of paper' to the wind and rode off 'very well satisfied'.[4]

Drunkenness caused plentiful public-order offences, with Anthony arresting men and women for behaving in an unseemly manner in public, using insulting or improper language or being generally rowdy. But he inevitably confronted grimmer events. Sometimes sheer bad luck was to blame. On 24 April 1882, two-year-old David Emms fell down a well. By the time Anthony arrived at the scene, 'the body was quite cold and [he could find] no signs of life whatsoever'. A year later, he told an inquest into the death of Ann Hansen, who had died around midnight on 11 April 1883, that the deceased had been 'drinking heavily and [was] shamefully neglected'. He testified that a police magistrate had ordered several local pubs not to sell her liquor, but he had nonetheless seen her drunk on the streets of Rutherglen on many subsequent occasions, concluding she had managed to get her hands on some grog across the Murray in Corowa. Attesting that she had died of disease of the liver, stomach and kidneys, a doctor said Hansen would have survived had she been given 'proper attention'. As I read the inquest transcript, I could feel Anthony's frustration and anguish.[5]

Hansen's demise was not an isolated occurrence, for women often seemed to cop a harsh deal in country Victoria. Anthony was regularly called in to handle instances of women who were in extreme distress or the victims of violence. Eliza Dixon was a case in point. After falling down a staircase, Dixon became prone to fits of suicidal intent. In 1882 she tried to hang herself on a fence outside the town but was cut down by a rider before she expired. She next drank poison. Attempting to commit suicide was an indictable offence and Anthony was forced to bring Dixon before the police court. Simple compassion thankfully prevailed and the police magistrate, Foster, decided not to proceed further 'in the interests of humanity' if Dixon promised not to re-offend. She was released into her father's care and placed under Anthony's watchful eye.[6] Poverty and mental illness lay at the heart of many such incidents.

Sometime in mid to late 1885, Anthony received news from Ireland that his mother, Anne, had died in Timolin on 27 March, at the age of seventy-three. She was buried in the same grave in Baltinglass Cemetery as her husband, Anthony senior, who had predeceased her by seventeen years, and her father-in-law, Edward. Anthony had not seen his mother for a quarter of a century, but her death likely made him feel his own mortality a little more keenly. His day job continued to remind him that life could be fickle, unkind and at times downright mean. Just before his mother's death, a pauper had drowned in a dam near Rutherglen. Anthony and his constables had fished the body out of the muddy water. Had the pauper succeeded where Eliza Dixon failed and taken his own life in desperation?

Anthony was affirming his reputation as a diligent policeman who could handle distressing cases professionally. He earned the trust of the district's superintendent, Montfort, and the two formed a close working relationship. In characteristic style, however, he incautiously risked losing Montfort's goodwill in 1884 by picking an unnecessary fight about broken windows at the Rutherglen station. When Anthony caustically refused to cover the cost of the repairs, Montfort rebuked him for being impertinent. Acting Chief Commissioner Chomley adjudicated, deciding that Anthony should not be asked to bear the costs. Montfort was not one to nurse a grudge: he gave Anthony strong assessments twice in 1885, recommending that he be promoted to sergeant.[7] These recommendations went nowhere.

Despite similar endorsements over the years, Anthony remained a senior constable for the rest of his career. It is unclear why the recommendations of an officer as well-regarded as Montfort were rejected. Had Anthony acquired a reputation for being difficult and argumentative? Was he dogged by his run-in with Pat Quinn? Likely both factors were at play. Age was also telling against Anthony. Ill health was taking an increasing toll. As a junior constable Anthony had barely taken a day off, but he began to flag. He was laid up by gout in June 1885 and later in the year by rheumatism, which recurred periodically. Two years later, a miscreant kicked Anthony hard on the right shin during an arrest. Anthony ignored the injury, and his leg 'swelled to a great size'. Dr William Lang had to lance the wound twice. Anthony was out of action for weeks.

Still on a modest policeman's wage, Anthony continued his efforts to find another source of income. In August 1885, he returned to his family's agricultural roots and applied for 277 acres of farming land abutting Black Dog Creek at Norong, 10 kilometres from Rutherglen. He was granted 147 acres, 3 rood and 18 perches in December 1886. He now faced the task of simultaneously running the station in Rutherglen and farming his land at Norong. He and Marion built a four-room weatherboard house close to Black Dog Creek. Despite his earlier difficulties, he hadn't given up on horseracing either. His horse Exile beat Mr Findley's Winnie in the Benalla Winter Stakes in July 1888, winning £1. Marion continued the gruelling work of bringing up seven children. The older kids were doing well at school, with Jessie claiming an art prize in 1884 and Thomas a Grade 3 prize in 1886.

The family unexpectedly grew in 1888 when Anthony agreed to take in John, his younger brother Simon's son. Simon had not fared well in his career with the Victoria Police. He was still a constable nearly seventeen years after joining when his 34-year-old wife, Jane, died in August 1886, after a painful illness. Jane had given birth nine times in twelve years and the family had been struggling. Jane's death sent Simon into a spiral. He was a widower with five children to care for (three had died at young ages). He didn't cope well. In December 1887, Simon's superior reported that he was 'an unreliable man without zeal or activity and quite unfit in other respects for the Force'. The medical board pronounced him unfit for duty, and he was discharged at thirty-nine. The force was not unkind, paying him out in full and adding a gratuity: £270 in all. Things didn't improve. On 10 July 1888 Simon was admitted to hospital in Melbourne, facing a long stay. He left his four sons in the care of a neighbour. Mary Condon kept the lads for as long as she could afford to, eventually surrendering them to the police. A court considered their fate on 10 September, asking Simon's brothers if they could assist. Edward, still a schoolteacher, was fifty-eight and had nine children of his own, aged between nine and twenty-five. *The Age* noted that he was 'said to be wealthy, but he refused to do anything for the boys'. Richard had good reason to hesitate. By then he was living near Castlemaine on more modest means with his second wife, Sarah, and providing for ten children. Anthony agreed to take in the eldest of the four boys, ten-year-old John. In the absence of further offers, the other three were sent to the industrial schools.[8]

Anthony and Marion were now caring for eight children aged between seven and seventeen. Did Anthony sometimes also ponder the fate of his eldest child, Nina, born out of wedlock in 1868?

Not long after taking in John, Anthony was confronted by a wrenching case that underscored the travails facing women caught in difficult circumstances. At 4.30am on 25 October, Margaret Price came into the station to confess that she had drowned her child in the town's reservoir. Anthony rode out and found the infant floating face down, 'quite dead'. He informed Montfort of the tragic situation, noting that Price 'could assign no reason' for drowning Rose, only ten months old. He had arrested Margaret's husband, Edward Price, six days before for stealing a plough in Bairnsdale.

Margaret and Edward were almost certainly unmarried. Born in Wales in 1841, Margaret was a widow twice over by the time she was forty-seven. She had given birth to ten children. Although her older children were adults by the late 1880s, Margaret was still caring for four kids aged six to fourteen. Losing two husbands and being alone for some years had been tough. It's easy to see why she ran off with Edward, a blacksmith twenty years her junior, leaving her younger children in the care of their siblings and relatives. Rose arrived in Albury in December 1887.

Margaret told a coronial inquest six days after her arrest that Rose had been restless on 25 October so she had decided to take her to the park. Retracting her apparent confession, Margaret claimed that she had become drowsy while sitting on a pier at the reservoir and Rose had rolled off her knee into the water. She insisted that she had tried to save her child but could not. Anthony rebutted this evidence. He said Rose had been found floating in the water with a shawl folded on her back; the shawl could not have stayed in place had Rose fallen from the height of the pier.

The jury concluded that Margaret should stand trial for wilful murder. The wheels of justice turned quickly, and Margaret's case was heard before the Supreme Court in Benalla on 6 November, before Justice Edward Holroyd. Anthony's long-time colleague, Charles Smyth, prosecuted, while another lawyer he knew well, Frederick Brown, who had defended Smith and Brady during the Wooragee Outrage, represented Margaret.

Anthony said he had found Rose floating around eight feet from the reservoir's bank. 'The prisoner was all wet up to the arm-pits and appeared to have been in the water herself.' He had seen Margaret three times before, when she had come to the lock-up to visit her husband; she was 'the worse for liquor' each time. He had asked Margaret why she had drowned her baby. She had replied, 'I don't know – what little money I had, it was taken from me by Williams for rent.' Anthony attested that Margaret had not been crying when she presented at the station; nor had she appeared much confused. Mounted Constable Michael Quinane agreed. He too had asked Margaret why she had drowned her child. 'If any of you had come to speak to me,' she had replied, 'I wouldn't have done it. I was left all alone and the landlord took the last few shillings I had in the house and refused me a jug of water to wash the baby.'

Dr Lang deposed that Rose had died from asphyxia, caused by immersion in water. He found no signs of violence, but Rose had been in ill health. Lang had also examined Margaret, finding her to be much excited and perhaps drunk. Mental illness, including post-natal depression, was not well understood at the time, but Dr Henry Fox, the medical officer at Beechworth Gaol, was nonetheless compassionate in his assessment. He attested that Margaret had been 'in a wave of insanity' when she drowned Rose, 'in an unconscious state of what she was doing'. It was not safe for her to be at large. The jury found the accused not guilty on the grounds of insanity. Holroyd sent Margaret to the Beechworth Asylum, where she would be kept until she became thoroughly sane.[9]

Margaret's fate tugged at the hearts of the most senior policemen. Even Chomley asked for an update. Edward Price received a paltry three-day prison sentence in Bairnsdale in the plough theft case, in part because the principal evidence came from 'only a Chinaman's unsupported testimony'. He returned to the Rutherglen area, working in Wangaratta and visiting Margaret regularly. In April 1889 he told Sergeant Steele that he believed Margaret to be 'quite sane and safe to be at large'. He said he would place her in a boarding house with someone to look after her. This hinted that he didn't intend to stay around for the long haul.[10]

As Margaret's well-being was being considered, the Strahan family was under intense pressure. Anthony Oliver came down with typhoid in March. The 'colonial fever' was a blight across the colonies into the late nineteenth century, as overflowing cesspits, contaminated waterways, poor sanitary habits and overcrowding allowed disease to spread. Three weeks after his son fell ill, Anthony developed an intense fever. It was suspected that he too had contracted typhoid, but Lang diagnosed a case of bilious attack. Anthony took a few days off work, while his son rebounded, defeating a scourge that killed many.

Although its wildest days were past, the northeast could still be turbulent, with cross-currents and animosities disturbing the peace. An incident in the Rutherglen police court on 17 December 1889 saw not one but three feuds play out before a good portion of the township, testing Anthony's policing skills.

Locals packed into the courtroom to watch Isaac Olcorn, a well-known grazier, face a charge of maliciously burning down the house and crop of a farmer, Patrick Seymour, on 21 November. A father of fifteen children by two wives, Olcorn was a colourful character, sometimes going by the name George Melbourne. One of Olcorn's daughters, Eliza, had sold 320 acres to Seymour a year earlier soon after marrying, aggravating her father. Anthony pressed an arson charge and the police court agreed that Olcorn should stand trial, setting a heavy bail. The situation was complicated by the fact that the fire had spread to an adjacent property owned by William Meehan, consuming his fences and 200 acres of land. Once on friendly terms, Meehan and Olcorn fell out bitterly over the fire, with the former believing the latter had set the blaze out of spite. Adding to the web of recrimination, Olcorn's bid to put a road through Meehan's land had been thwarted.

But it was not these festering grievances that ignited the trouble which exploded in the courtroom. Two other men, James Cockburn and Olcorn's brother-in-law William Emms, were standing side by side watching the proceedings when they set upon each other. Notorious around town for being belligerent, Cockburn loathed Emms. He spat in his face. Emms retaliated, knocking Cockburn down. Both men were immediately brought before the bench. Emms refused to enter the dock with Cockburn, fearing for his life. Anthony and one of his constables manhandled the two into the dock, with the bench swiftly dishing out penalties, £1 or seven days' imprisonment for Cockburn and 5s or three days for Emms. Still in the dock, an enraged Cockburn whipped out a butcher's knife and plunged it into Emms's chest, narrowly missing the heart. Standing nearby, Anthony leapt into action. He later told Superintendent Montfort that he could only restrain Cockburn after 'a severe struggle'. Meanwhile, the rest of the room erupted. Anthony and his constable held the crowd back from trying to attack Cockburn and took him off to the lock-up. Emms was only saved because the knife hit a rib.

These fraught matters resulted in three trials in 1889. His case delayed because Emms was in a precarious state, Cockburn finally came before the Assize Court in Benalla on 18 May and pleaded guilty to stabbing Emms with the intent to commit murder, relieving Anthony of the need to testify. Justice George Kerferd meted out a ten-year prison sentence, saying Cockburn should have gone to the gallows. Olcorn was next in the dock, appearing before Kerferd three days later in Beechworth. The old legal line-up was back in action, with Smyth prosecuting and Zincke and Brown defending. Anthony was laid up with rheumatism and could not testify, but his deposition was read out. He attested that Olcorn had admitted being at the back of Seymour's house on the day in question. Other witnesses gave conflicting evidence, some defending Olcorn and others accusing him of setting the fire. Meehan claimed Olcorn had been down on him, bitterly so, ever since he had witnessed the agreement transferring the land to Seymour. Olcorn had tried to injure him all he could. More damningly, he alleged that Olcorn had tried to keep him quiet about the fire, offering to pay him £50. In addressing the jury, Brown described the alleged bribe as preposterous and said the hearing had found no evidence against Olcorn's moral character. The judge admitted that proving arson was difficult, and the jury took only five minutes to acquit Olcorn despite Meehan's good standing in the town.

But Olcorn wanted revenge. He waited until Meehan had been elected for a third time as the Rutherglen Mayor before pouncing. Under Olcorn's instigation, Meehan was charged with perjury for having invented the £50 offer and brought before Justice Edward Williams in Beechworth on 21 September. In his evidence, Olcorn accused Meehan point-blank of lying. This was a risky gambit, and Meehan's lawyer, Sir Bryan O'Loghlen, set about destroying that very moral character that Brown had extolled in the arson case. Under a barrage of hostile questions, Olcorn admitted he had 'had the occasional tiffs with womenkind' but denied that he 'was in the habit' of hitting his wife. He fiercely rejected suggestions that he had cut the clothes off her on one occasion and dragged her home from the railway station on another. He likewise denied whipping another woman. Anthony's evidence was critical. Noting he had never received much trouble from Olcorn and none from Meehan, he said Olcorn had come to the police yard in July under the guise of buying a mare from him. It had soon become apparent that he had turned up to see if Anthony would back his claim about Meehan's mendacity. Anthony said he had rebuffed Olcorn, asking why Olcorn was saying bad things about the good people of Rutherglen and urging him to go home. Unsurprisingly, the jury took one minute to acquit Meehan.[11]

By the early 1890s, Anthony was reporting to a new superintendent in Benalla, James Rennie. Born in Scotland in 1830, Rennie was one of the force's true veterans, having joined in 1852. In addition to settling in with a new boss, Anthony's job became more taxing in other ways. In 1886, the discovery of gold at the Great Northern Extension, 5 kilometres east of Rutherglen, saw a small goldrush. Goldmining would continue at the Great Northern into the late 1890s, bringing an often raucous population of itinerant miners into the district. The local wine industry also continued to expand, with more and more acres under cultivation, requiring an ever bigger contingent of pickers. In August 1891, Anthony reported that most of the men employed at the mines were 'rough characters and generally visit the town in large mobs and get drunk'. Four months later, he wrote to his direct superior in Beechworth, Sub-Inspector James Irwin, to underline the challenges facing his station. With the Great Northern booming, 2000 people were living in the sub-district; the 736-strong populace of Rutherglen, less than 2.5 kilometres across, was growing daily. The grape-picking season would commence soon and Anthony was concerned it would be impossible to maintain order with only two constables. He summarised the station's workload in 1891: sixty arrests, thirty-seven warrants and 241 summonses.[12]

The constables at the station in early 1892 were not much chop. Constable Denis McCarthy was on the verge of being charged if he continued to fail to do his duty. George Braithwaite was even more trouble – on 31 January 1892, an anonymous resident wrote to Chomley under the nom-de-plume Believer in Reform to lodge a complaint about him: 'When a man on duty will go into hotels and get drunk after hours, who insults respected ladies on the streets, it is high time that the matter is investigated. On one occasion ... I noticed the person in question throw his arms around a well-to-do young lady's neck in the street while on duty, drunk, much to her disquiet.' When asked to make an apology, Braithwaite said 'he would apologise to no bloody woman'. The constable had insulted a dozen women besides; his bad behaviour was a daily occurrence. On 19 February, Anthony despatched a telegram to his superiors about Braithwaite's poor conduct. As a result, Braithwaite was charged with three offences: being drunk when returning off-duty at 6pm on 18 February; assaulting his superior officer by striking him in the chest and calling him a bloody tyrant; and being derelict in his duty by remaining in the Victoria Hotel until 10pm and being absent from his barracks overnight on 18 February. Braithwaite retaliated and lodged an assault charge against Anthony, alleging he had grabbed him by the neck in the police yard and tried to throw him to the ground.

These charges paralleled two episodes in Anthony's past. In 1864, he had accused his commanding officer in St Arnaud of being a tyrant and three years later he himself had been accused of drinking all night in a pub in Bealiba. The roles were now reversed, and the older man won. The force suspended Braithwaite and ordered him to go to Beechworth, deciding it was 'inadvisable' for him to remain in Rutherglen. Matters only got worse for Braithwaite while the charges against him were being investigated. On 4 April 1892, Superintendent Rennie informed Chief Commissioner Chomley that Braithwaite had ridden a troop horse into the ground, giving her a sore back due to his poor horsemanship. An 'exceptionally good and quiet horse' had been rendered unfit for further service.

Five days later, a board of inquiry convened in Rutherglen. The redoubtable Beechworth barrister Frederick Brown represented the defendant. Braithwaite pleaded guilty to the charge of refusing to return to the barracks, receiving a £1 fine or three days' imprisonment. But he lodged not-guilty pleas to the other charges, while Anthony pleaded not guilty to the assault charge. The two officers provided predictably contradictory accounts. The board dismissed the drunkenness charge, giving Braithwaite the benefit of the doubt because it was uncertain if he was 'drunk or excited'. It found him guilty, however, of assaulting and insulting Anthony, imposing a £4 fine or two weeks in gaol. The key witness against Anthony, a twelve-year-old boy, appeared to have been coached, but became confused nonetheless, contradicting Braithwaite's evidence. The charge against Anthony was dismissed. In addition to copping the fines, Braithwaite had his pay docked for the time he had been suspended. In a final indignity, he was dismounted and transferred to Melbourne.[13]

Now fifty-two, Anthony likely found the job increasingly difficult, especially when he had to put up with incompetent or unruly subordinates. And he was about to be dragged into a case that reminded him yet again that even quiet communities could be suddenly unbalanced by savage outbursts of violence.

19

A TERROR TO EVIL-DOERS

Trouble came Anthony's way in November 1892 from southern New South Wales. Although he did not know it at the time, what became known as the Pender Affair would be the last big case of his career, the final time he would feature in a gripping sequence told in newspapers across the colonies.

Thomas Prendergast, a labourer, and Hanorah 'Norah' McMahon, a domestic servant, struck up a relationship in the late 1880s. Both were Irish Catholic immigrants, he from County Wexford and she from County Clare. They had a daughter, Hanorah, out of wedlock in 1887, marrying in April 1889. It was the second marriage for both. Norah's first husband, George Wright, had died in September 1880. By the time she met Thomas, only one of her three children by George was still living. Thomas's first wife, Annie, had died in December 1884, leaving him with several children to look after. By 1889, one of his adult sons, 28-year-old James, was living in Eldorado with his own family. Norah was seventeen years younger than her new husband, a factor that likely contributed to the tensions which built up between them.

When they married, Norah was living in Adelaide and Thomas had no fixed abode. As a labourer and railway ganger, he moved from job to job. Norah gave birth to their second child, Sarah, at the Goulburn River irrigation works near Echuca in April 1890. Reflecting the variable spelling of names at the time and perhaps a desire to conceal his identity, Thomas often went by the surnames Prendergast, Pendergast and Pender.

In mid-1890, the couple moved to southern New South Wales. Norah began running a small boarding house at Quat Quatta, a settlement near the Murray River between Corowa and Howlong, and Thomas worked on the Corowa–Culcairn railway line. But the marriage was tumultuous and the couple sometimes lived apart. The unhappiness escalated in January 1892. Thomas headed to Molong, around 500 kilometres to the north, taking their eldest daughter, Hanorah, with him. He had threatened to kill Norah as he departed – but sent her a telegram not long after asking if she intended to join him. She, unsurprisingly, declined. Her boarding house was doing well. Perhaps more importantly, she had struck up a relationship with one of her boarders: Patrick Hourigan, another labourer working on the railway lines.

After Patrick moved west to work at Mulwala, Thomas returned to Quat Quatta with Hanorah, using the name Pender, in the hope that he could reconcile with Norah and reunite the family. But the rift was too deep and the couple's quarrels became bitter. The death of Norah's sole surviving child by George Wright exacerbated the ill feeling. Fearing he was on the verge of violence, Norah fled in a buggy to Mulwala, taking both children with her, to join Patrick. When she heard that Thomas had relocated to northeast Victoria, Norah unwisely returned to the Corowa area in mid-September, moving into a cottage on the river.

Thomas appeared on her doorstop a week later, claiming he had walked all the way from Wangaratta – a distance of around 45 kilometres. After a brief conversation, in which Norah likely refused to take him back, he exploded in a rage. He began to whack Norah with his stout walking stick. A neighbour intervened and wrestled the stick from him, but Thomas grabbed Norah by the hair, dragging her into the kitchen. She broke free, running for the door, yet Thomas knocked her to the ground. Jumping on her prone body, he pulled out a knife, yelling, 'You whore, I'll do for you now,' and plunged the blade into her face, inflicting a deep wound on one cheek and a cut on the other. 'I thought my eye was out,' Norah would say later. Another neighbour came to the rescue, grabbing the knife, but Thomas started biting his wife's right hand. Norah broke loose and fled.

The New South Wales police arrested Thomas and he faced the Corowa police court on 30 September on a charge of assault with intent to commit murder. Several witnesses gave ample evidence about his violent behaviour, but the local doctor, William Lang, downplayed the abuse. He thought 'the injuries were not such as he would have expected a determined man bent on murder to cause'. The defence lawyer stressed that 'there had been great provocation, inasmuch as the wife had confessed that she had misconducted herself'. He claimed Thomas also believed his wife had failed to care for Hanorah after she had fallen from a buggy and broken a leg. The bench was not swayed by such special pleading and decided that Thomas should stand trial for attempted murder, though it released him on bail. With her enraged husband at large, Norah fled south across the Murray to Rutherglen with Patrick and Sarah, finding a shanty at the Great Northern Extension.[1] It is not known where Hanorah was at this time. Perhaps she was already with Thomas's extended clan. Two of his siblings, an older brother, James, and an older sister, Sarah, were living near Myrtleford.

Thomas Pender's anger turned to fury when news reached him that Norah was again living with Patrick. He headed south. On 27 November, he boarded the afternoon train for Wangaratta armed with a six-chamber British Bulldog revolver, determined to exact vengeance. Missing the connection at Springhurst, he walked all the way to Rutherglen and then on to the Great Northern, a rage-fuelled journey of 24 kilometres. One innkeeper saw no reason not to give the seemingly respectable man directions to Norah's shanty.

At 7pm, Thomas knocked on the door of his wife's hut. When Patrick answered, he shot the younger man without warning, yelling, 'How do you like that Hourigan, you bastard!' The bullet passed through the collarbone and lodged near Patrick's lungs. Thomas charged into the hut, screaming at his wife, 'You bloody dog, I'll shoot you as well.' He shot Norah in the chest at point-blank range. Although bleeding profusely, Patrick grabbed Thomas by the throat and wrenched the revolver from his grasp, fleeing down the street with Norah in his arms and laying her on the grass 100 metres away.

A furious Thomas set the shanty alight. As the flames engulfed the hut, he realised Sarah was still inside and he dashed back through the front door, reappearing with the infant wrapped in his coat. But he didn't flee the scene. Instead he sat on a log to watch the blaze, coolly remarking to one spectator that the police were a long time coming.

Riding in from Rutherglen, Anthony reached the smouldering hut at 10pm with Constable McKenna. Thomas gave himself up without a struggle. He told Anthony that he had intended to kill Norah and Patrick and then shoot himself. Anthony informed Superintendent Rennie that both victims were in a bad way. Two doctors had extracted the bullet from Norah's chest, but she was too grievously injured to be moved to Rutherglen. She was left at T.H. Williams's store at the Great Northern, her chances of survival in doubt. Anthony enlisted a local woman to look after her. Little Sarah was left in the care of Mrs Williams. Although the bullet was still lodged near his lungs, Patrick was well enough to be conveyed by cart to the Victoria Hotel in Rutherglen. Anthony reported that he was not thought to be in immediate danger.

A day later, Rennie instructed Anthony to interview both victims: 'If the life of either of the injured persons is in danger, their deposition should be taken before a magistrate in the presence of the accused so that the latter may have the opportunity for cross-examining.' To a modern eye, it seems extraordinary that the victims of a terrible crime would be questioned in the presence of their attacker, who could, even more extraordinarily, quiz them.

Anthony informed Rennie on 28 November that Norah and Patrick had identified Thomas as their assailant. Moreover, the accused had admitted guilt. Anthony charged the labourer with arson and two counts of attempted murder.

The shootings at the Great Northern drew press attention across the colonies, with *The Advertiser* running its first report under the headline, 'Attempted Murder At Rutherglen: A Revengeful Husband Wounds His Wife And Her Paramour'. But no one thought Thomas Pender had right on his side, with *The Ovens and Murray Advertiser* describing him as 'a very violent character'.[2]

Norah died at the Williams's store on 30 November. Pender now faced a murder charge. Patrick, however, was on the way to recovery.

On 12 December, Rennie asked Anthony why he had failed to take Norah's deposition in the presence of a magistrate, as instructed. Anthony said it had been impossible: the closest magistrate was in Rutherglen, 5 kilometres away. Thomas had been drunk and 'in a very excited state' on the night of the incident. 'I took the prisoner with me to where Mrs Pender was lying and he became so violent that it took myself and Constable McKenna to keep him from doing her serious injury.' Anthony had asked Norah in the presence of her husband if she knew who had shot her. She pointed at her husband. Thomas used foul language: 'He asked no questions but was trying to get at the woman to kill her.' Anthony put him in the lock-up – given his ferocious behaviour, 'it was not considered safe to bring him into her presence'. The doctors cautioned that Norah might die if rattled, she was so weak.[3]

Thomas Pender stood trial for murder in the Supreme Court before Justice Holroyd in Beechworth on 2 March 1893. Charles Smyth was prosecuting and Frederick Brown acting for the defence. Several witnesses detailed Thomas's murderous violence, but Holroyd would not admit Norah's deposition, arguing that it was 'not made at a time when she believed her dissolution to be impending'. Although correct according to the letter of the law, his ruling was harsh and unreasonable. It severely weakened the prosecution's case.

Brown set about blacking Patrick Hourigan's name. Under cross-examination, the railway worker confessed that he had been in trouble with another man in Corowa because 'he had been in the habit of visiting his wife'. He admitted that he had been intimate with Norah for some time. Brown articulated many of the common notions of the day by painting Thomas Pender as the victim of the whole affair. Addressing the jury, composed entirely of men, in his closing statement, he said his unfortunate client had done:

> nothing more than any of them would have done under similar circumstances. For tedious months he had done his utmost to reclaim his wife from the influence of the man Hourigan. He had obtained

employment at various places and sent money to his wife in order that she might come to him, but by the evil influence of Hourigan she was kept from him ... in a frenzy of passion on seeing his wife's betrayer coming from her bedroom he shot him.

Brown did not paint Norah as the evil party, which was the common stratagem in similar trials of the day, but rather as the hapless victim of a predatory male. Yet his next contention was risible: he insisted that Pender had shot his wife by accident in a scuffle with Hourigan. The second shot had been intended for 'his wife's betrayer and the destroyer of his home and happiness'. His final point was absurd: 'Everything in his client's actions showed that he had done his utmost to save his wife.' Brown presented no evidence for this claim. No one mentioned that Thomas Pender had savagely bashed his wife only two months before shooting her. Despite this failure to go beyond mere assertion, Brown said the jury could only find the accused guilty of manslaughter, with a strong recommendation for mercy.

In his summation, Holroyd revealed he was of a mind with the defence lawyer. He noted that Thomas Pender had striven unsuccessfully to rescue his wife from her betrayer: 'There were some cases in which a murderer could be pitied.' The accused had entered the hut to encounter circumstances that caused him 'to think an unlawful intercourse had taken place'. In a moment, his blood rose. True, he had come to the hut with a loaded revolver, which 'could be proof of a malicious intent'. But it was 'open for the jury to say whether it was taken by the prisoner in anticipation of being called upon to defend himself'. True, also, that the prisoner had admitted that he had gone to the hut with the intention of killing Hourigan and his wife. But it must not be concealed that 'he made this heavy charge against himself'. Holroyd barely mentioned Norah, the person who had been killed. Reading this summation all these years later, knowing the mores of the day, I was still taken aback by his bias. But Holroyd was reflecting deeply rooted attitudes of the day, which were questioned by few. He had set his course: 'The jury, if they could honestly do so, would deal mercifully with the prisoner.' The jury concurred, taking only thirty minutes to find Thomas Pender guilty of manslaughter, not murder. They made a strong recommendation for mercy. Holroyd delivered a sentence of only three years' imprisonment with hard labour.[4]

Although they described Norah in sympathetic terms, the newspapers reported the sentence matter-of-factly. None complained it was too soft. Perhaps in the moral accounting of the day, which enshrined the sanctity of marriage but considered women to be the weaker sex and in need of protection, three years seemed about right for a man who had been betrayed by a love rival.

Anthony had witnessed Thomas's savage behaviour and Norah's suffering and could have been excused for feeling the convicted man had escaped lightly. The trial had one sour footnote for Anthony. On 20 March, Rennie sent a memo to Sub-Inspector Irwin stating that Anthony should have made sure that Norah's statement was complete. Irwin forwarded the memo for Anthony's 'guidance in the future'. Anthony held his tongue this time. He felt he had already explained himself.

Norah's death left a mess. She had died intestate and the Curator of the Estates of Deceased Persons decided to use her humble belongings – four gold rings, two silver lady's watches, one gold brooch, two gold earrings and one handbag – to defray some of the costs that Anthony had accumulated in providing Norah with medical care and having her buried in Carlyle Cemetery, outside Rutherglen. But Thomas wrote to the curator from his prison cell on 4 April, asking that Norah's estate be used to look after their daughters, who would otherwise be left 'quite destitute' and end up in the Asylum for Neglected Children. He said dividing the estate evenly between the two girls would allow one to go into the care of her stepbrother, James, and the other into the care of her aunt, Sarah. Thomas ended his letter with a line both pleading and accusatory: 'Sir, as this money is part of the £280 the deceased took from me, I hope you will see your way to apply it for the benefit of the poor children and not make paupers of them.' The curator was unmoved, however, and allowed Anthony to use the proceeds of Norah's estate, a modest £18 13 shillings and sixpence, to cover some of the police costs. The girls were still taken in by relatives, fortunately.

Thomas left Pentridge in July 1895, having served two years and four months, and took up a farm at Waterloo, near his siblings in the northeast. He died in 1910 at seventy-two, while milking a cow – Norah, had she lived, would have been fifty-five.[5]

Anthony Strahan was approaching thirty years of service in the force. The Kelly royal commission had concluded a decade before that police officers were 'unserviceable' at the age of fifty-five due to 'the debilitating effects of their duties'. But no compulsory retirement age was set until Chief Commissioner Chomley ruled in August 1889 that police of all ranks should retire at sixty-five.

Anthony was fifty-three. This meant he could theoretically serve for another thirteen years. But he was flagging. Some cases continued to confront him with life's harsh circumstances. On 6 October 1893, he rode out to a farm near Lilliput, south of Rutherglen, to retrieve the body of 22-year-old James Pevitt. A labourer well-known as a cricketer and a footballer, Pevitt had committed suicide outside his hut by shooting himself in the forehead with a shotgun, scattering his brain over the grass. Anthony told the inquest that he had lifted the body into a sitting position, checking the gruesome wound, and found no signs of a struggle. Several witnesses revealed that Pevitt had had improper relations with his stepsister and his foster sister, who were both fifteen. Charles Pevitt testified that when he had discovered what had transpired, he had told his son to leave the area and never return. He had not been impressed when James had blamed the two girls. Another young man, William Schluter, who had been saying for some weeks that he was feeling melancholic, shot himself with a double-barrelled breech-loader in his father's stable in Rutherglen. Anthony told the inquest that the shot had blown Schluter's skull to pieces.[6] How much carnage could he witness before he decided enough was enough?

However, it was sly grog that caused the most grief for Anthony in the early 1890s, leading in part to the end of his career. The pressure to crack down on sly grog had increased over the past decade as the temperance movement became more active across Victoria, with the Women's Christian Temperance Union, founded in the United States, stepping up its efforts from the mid-1880s. The consumption of alcohol wasn't prohibited, but the government limited the number of pubs that could be licensed. The Chief Secretary, James Munro – a dour Presbyterian and the president of the Total Abstinence Society – slugged beer with a heavy tax in 1892. All this pressure didn't deter Victorians, especially men, from drinking; it arguably only encouraged more sly grog shops. All sorts of buildings could be used as a front to sell grog on the sly: coffee shops, stores, lodgings. It was hardly surprising then that drunkenness became an even greater bugbear for the Rutherglen police following the opening of the Great Northern Extension mines. Sly grog shops popped up to meet the needs of thirsty miners, breaking council by-laws. It wasn't just about drink: grog shanties were often associated with prostitution. Anthony and his constables made 117 arrests in 1892, more than three per week. Although they carried out fifty-four arrests for being drunk and disorderly and another twenty-two for using obscene language or engaging in insulting behaviour, they only arrested three individuals for selling liquor without a licence.

Licensed hotels were pushing the police hard to shut down their illicit competitors. Some residents were angry about an apparently unchecked trade that was degrading the moral fabric of the community. In January 1892, one wrote to Chomley to complain about 'two low grog shanties being carried on with impunity in this place which is becoming a thickly populated township'. This illegal trade had been going on for at least a year and was on the increase: 'The quality of the drink is of the very worst and the men make disturbances and are very often delirious and fit subjects for the Lunatic Asylum.' Anthony rode across to the Great Northern to investigate but could find no evidence of the sly grog selling. The local excise officer reached a similar conclusion.

This official response looked weak or evasive. On instructions from Chomley, Anthony was ordered to return to the Great Northern to have another go at pinning down the illicit trade. In June 1892, he reported that he had made inquiries, but could find no person willing to give up information about the grog shanties. Rutherglen itself was quieter than it had been several months earlier, he said. True, larrikins from the mines came into town on Saturday nights and caused disturbances, but they were either locked up or pushed out of town. Anthony contended, oddly, that the police were powerless to act and suggested that an excise officer instead was 'the proper person to endeavour to put down the grog shanties'.

The heavy drinking continued unabated, sometimes resulting in more than just general rowdiness. Ann Ginnivan was dancing in a hut at the Great Northern with miners in June 1893 when her employer, an Italian who went by the name Rojeni, smashed her over the head with a bottle in a jealous rage. He fled, and Ginnivan was left on the floor for four hours, bleeding profusely, until Anthony arrived with a doctor. Luckily she survived, but Rojeni vanished without trace. Such incidents could not be ignored. In July, Sub-Inspector Irwin, based in Beechworth, told Superintendent Rennie that the Great Northern was 'a hot bed of shanty keepers and up to the present it has been impossible to suppress them'. The population was composed of 'all sorts of persons'. Edward McGeehan, a Wesleyan and a member of the Ancient Order of Foresters, sent an indignant letter to Chomley in September. On pay days, 'drunken fights are frequent and at them the filthiest and most obscene language is used to the disquiet of all decent minded people and to the contamination of the young', he said. He asked that adequate police protection be put in place. Irwin confirmed that the Great Northern was turbulent: during a recent visit he had found the town full of roughs even on a weeknight.

The situation was veering out of control. What on earth was Anthony doing? On 5 October, Chomley revealed he had lost confidence in him. He instructed Rennie to engage several officers to secure evidence against the shanty owners: 'All but the men employed should be kept in complete ignorance of the action. The local police should not be allowed to know anything about it.' Rennie was damning of Anthony, telling Chomley a week later that 'a great deal of the disorder at the Great Northern is due to the inaction of Strahan in not suppressing the numerous sly grog shanties ... The Senior Constable explains his apparent neglect by professing an ignorance of the provisions of the Licencing Act which is most unaccountable in a sub-officer of his experience'. He ordered officers from Rutherglen, Chiltern, Barnawartha and Wahgunyah to 'prevent any cause of complaint in the future'.

Anthony had had enough. On 20 October, he tendered his resignation. Noting he had served for thirty-one years, he wrote that he might leave the colony and asked if the force could provide a severance gratuity by 1 December. Chomley accepted this request, mandating that the resignation would take effect from 30 November. But Anthony changed his mind the next day, asking to withdraw his resignation and explaining that he had been in pecuniary difficulties when he had submitted his request. It seems odd he could have resolved those difficulties so quickly. Could he himself have become embroiled in the sly grog trade in some way? Chomley accepted the withdrawal, indicating that he still saw Anthony as an effective policeman.

But the sly grog problem was getting worse. On 18 November, Irwin reported that he had been unable to find additional officers to crack down on the shanties at the Great Northern, which likely numbered around a dozen. Although he noted that a customs official was endeavouring to detect the sly grog sellers, he insisted that the local police could easily obtain the necessary information if they exerted themselves. On 20 November an irate Great Northern resident wrote to Chomley to complain about Joseph Cardwell, a store owner who had applied for a wine licence a week earlier. He charged that 'it would be most absurd to grant a licence to a person who is defrauding the Revenue by keeping a shanty in disguise of a store'. Cardwell had been running his grog shop for eight months, he alleged, doing a trade 'equal to a good many hotels', and now wanted to 'get into more public favour by a wine licence, a hoax for his shanty'. He asserted that the police seemed to have no power in the matter: 'Well, sir, don't you think it is a great shame allowing things to exist in a colony like Victoria where there are so many police paid to put a stop to such things.'

It soon became apparent that Anthony had recommended Cardwell's application, attesting in a written endorsement on 16 November that he had known the store owner for twenty-four years and he was 'a most respectable man' who would conduct his business properly if the licence were granted. Irwin sent a memo to his superiors in Benalla and Melbourne on 24 November summarising where things stood. He agreed with Anthony that Cardwell had been 'a respected shanty keeper … for a long time'. But he revealed in addition that Cardwell had been 'the principal witness called to prove the charge of drunkenness preferred by Strahan against Sergeant Simcocks some short time ago at Rutherglen'.

Anthony and Thomas Simcocks had been working in the district side-by-side for a decade, Anthony commanding the Rutherglen station and Thomas the Chiltern station. The Great Northern lay between the two towns but fell under Rutherglen's jurisdiction. Bringing a charge against a colleague, a superior officer at that, was bold. Simcocks was a well-regarded policeman, but he seemed to have the occasional problem with drink – he received a fine in Wangaratta in 1874 as a constable for being drunk and disorderly. One source of tension might have been the fact that Simcocks was promoted to the rank of sergeant second-class in January 1893, something that had eluded Anthony for so long.

Was my great-great-grandfather resentful? Jealousy corrodes the equanimity of even the most even-tempered, and Anthony wasn't the most temperate man around. Simcocks, born in Kent, England, was nine years younger than Anthony. Indeed, he had joined the force in January 1872, only nine months before Anthony, already in uniform for almost a decade, was about to crack the biggest case of his career, the Wooragee Outrage.

Compounding the complications, Irwin reported that he had instructed Simcocks to search the Great Northern for reputed shanties, including the one owned by Cardwell. But this search had been a failure, resulting in only one conviction. This was allegedly because Cardwell had tipped off the other shanty-owners. Irwin did not say how Cardwell had known that Simcocks was on his way, though an obvious implication was left hanging. He was firm in his overall assessment: 'I have been unable to get Strahan to take any steps in the matter and I fear that while he is at Rutherglen very little will be done in that direction by the police. The Senior Constable is under the impression, which I cannot remove, that the police should not do this duty.'

Anthony was in increasing financial difficulties in the early 1890s. Was he in cahoots with shanty-owners like Cardwell, perhaps receiving small payments? No evidence of such shenanigans has come to light. He could have had other reasons for being uncooperative. He thought he and his officers already had too much to do. Was he pushing back against an impossible workload, arguing that the customs department should be responsible for enforcing the licensing laws? He and his two constables were certainly kept busy with other tasks, including a scarlet fever outbreak and the death of a prisoner, awaiting trial on a charge of careless use of fire, in the Rutherglen lock-up.

Chomley was at the end of his tether. On 7 December, he told Rennie that Anthony seemed unable to 'keep a proper restraint on the shanty keepers' and held 'peculiar views as to the carrying out of the Licencing Act by the police'. He suggested redeploying Anthony, perhaps by making a direct swap with Senior Constable Peter Nee, who oversaw Wodonga. Irwin agreed, noting Nee was in every way suitable for Rutherglen, and Rennie gave his stamp of approval on 27 December. This was a stinging result for Anthony, since he was making way in Rutherglen for a much less experienced officer (Nee had joined up in 1874, twelve years after Anthony), and Wodonga was nearly 60 kilometres away from his farm at Norong. Rennie gave him a good annual report that month, describing him as 'a well-conducted and active sub-officer', but this must have done little to dispel Anthony's sense that he was being punished.[7]

Anthony was leaving Rutherglen after nearly fourteen years of service. The Strahans had put down roots in the Rutherglen region. The children had grown up there: Anthony Oliver, at twenty-two, had done most of his schooling in the district, and Edward, the youngest at twelve, had been born there. Rutherglen had given Anthony's policing career stability, and he was well regarded by the community. On 5 January 1894, *The Rutherglen Sun and Chiltern Valley Advertiser* said many residents would regret to learn that Anthony was departing:

> Mr Strahan has been a very straightforward and honest officer, both to the Crown and the general public, he being an officer possessed with good sound common sense. Mr Strahan was not a man to overstep the bounds of duty, but worked his district with a strict yet not by any means antagonistic hand, and was always capable of judging the class of men which he had to deal with. As a private citizen the senior was always ready to lend his assistance to advance the interests of the town and district, which he had at heart, and we, with others, wish him the same success at his new station as he has gained at Rutherglen.

The paper described Anthony as 'a terror to evil-doers', noting that he had arrested notorious horse and cattle thieves. *The Ovens and Murray Advertiser* concurred, affirming that Rutherglen was losing 'a real good officer'. Senior Constable Strahan had 'always performed his duties, which were many times unpleasant, without fear or favour'. He was more than just a copper: *The Advertiser* said he was 'a genuine sportsman and a good giver to all cases of charity'. In light of the controversy that dogged my great-great-grandfather at times, I am struck by these affirming comments about other aspects of his life. Anthony could be tough-minded and obstreperous, but he was clearly liked and respected by many.

Twenty of the town's leading men, including no fewer than eight justices of the peace, shared a farewell glass of wine with Anthony at the Rutherglen Hotel on 4 January. They presented him with a breast pin and a magnificent certificate of appreciation in 'sincere friendship', which is reproduced on the inside back cover of this book. Resembling an illuminated manuscript, the certificate was festooned with images of introduced and native flowers, a bush stream, the town's reservoir and a small picture of Anthony standing in front of the police station and its attached living quarters. The signatories were unstinting in their praise: 'During the period extending over 14 years that you have been stationed at Rutherglen you have proved yourself to be conscientious and fearless in the performance of your duties and while displaying your zeal and activity in enforcing the Law have rendered an ever ready and willing assistance to those requiring its protection, and by the upright and honorable conduct of your Office have won the Respect and Esteem of all.' They trusted Anthony's future would be as honourable as his past, hoping he would 'long be spared to enjoy a continued and deserved prosperity'.

Joseph Pearce JP led a toast to Anthony, declaring that everyone present was aware that 'at the time of the Kellys anyone who was opposed to them was considered a doomed man, and Senior Constable Strahan was one who put terror into that gang'. George Graham JP concurred, repeating the local paper's claim that Anthony 'struck terror to the hearts of evil doers'. After another eight speeches by grateful townsfolk and a round of recitations and songs, Anthony rose to thank his well-wishers. Observing that he did not think he had 'so many friends as a policeman', he declared he had always endeavoured to have the 'respectable portion of the community on his side'. He had met many rough characters in his time, and although some thought Rutherglen a hard place, 'there were less larrikins in the town than any place' he knew of.[8]

Anthony went to Wodonga by train, arriving on 14 January, but he did not settle in well. Perhaps he knew the end of his career was nigh. He resigned from the force for good on 30 April 1894, not long after his fifty-fourth birthday. He had served thirty-one years and seven months. His commanding officer described him as 'an active and trustworthy member of the force' with an excellent conduct record. He had not incurred a disciplinary infraction since 1868, though he had sometimes sailed close to the wind. Commissioner Chomley said he should be paid a gratuity.[9]

Anthony could be forgiven for leaving the force with some disappointment, even resentment. He felt he had deserved more given his hard work on big cases. That promotion to the rank of sergeant, so long apparently within reach, never came.

Instead, he turned his attention to the farm. He had come full circle. His grandfather and father had been farmers in County Kildare. But Anthony had left the police force at an inopportune time. The slump that started in 1891 had by 1893 become a full-blown depression, as thirteen banks closed their doors. Victoria was hardest hit, with hundreds of bankruptcies. Savings vanished and unemployment climbed to a terrible 30 per cent. Compounding matters, five successive years of good weather ended in 1895, when drought gripped Victoria. This big dry would continue for several years.[10] Under these circumstances, farming proved tough for Anthony, and his licence was revoked and then reinstated.

More ill fortune may have struck on 20 February 1895. The Strahan family went to Rutherglen on 19 February to attend the annual show, staying overnight. They returned to the farm the following afternoon to find that the homestead had burnt to the ground. The house was insured with the Manchester Insurance Company for £200.[11] Perhaps this was no more than an accident, but that amount of insurance would help to clear Anthony's debts. An accidental fire brings to mind what might have happened to the International Hotel in Bealiba all those years ago. The company paid out, suggesting it didn't harbour any suspicions, at least none that could be proven. The fire had another deleterious impact, which made writing this book more challenging. It's likely that various family papers and photographs went up in smoke.

The insurance payout didn't end Anthony's pecuniary troubles. His debts continued to mount. By 1896 his position had become dire. He and the family had moved into a small house in Rutherglen, but all those cherished hopes of building a better life in the new country seemed to be evaporating – the bailiffs were chasing Anthony for unpaid debts. A solicitor in Wangaratta, Thomas Notcutt, lent Anthony £100 with the farm as security. The men had known each other for a decade, crossing paths in the courts when Anthony had overseen the Rutherglen station. But this loan failed to clear all his amounts outstanding.

Anthony might have felt proud when his eldest son, Anthony Oliver, gave up his profession as a wheelwright and joined the Victoria Police in August 1896, at the age of twenty-four. The fourth member of the extended Strahan clan to join the police, Anthony Oliver was posted to Wangaratta, not too far from Norong, and later, in September 1897, to Corryong. He might have contributed some of his wages to support his parents. Even if he did, it would not have been enough to support a family of nine.

Anthony took a desperate step in 1897. Like many before him, he turned to goldmining for salvation. The beginning of the depression had coincided with a new goldrush in Western Australia, first in Coolgardie and then in Kalgoorlie. At least 60,000 Victorians headed west in the 1890s to try their luck. Anthony joined this exodus at the age of fifty-seven, selling off his personal property, presumably to fund the trip. This move was risky, even foolhardy, given his health had not been good for some time. This last roll of the dice was almost bound to fail. One newspaper reported that the climate in Western Australia 'soon laid him low, so much so that doctors gave him very small hopes of getting away. The indomitable will which had ever characterised him, however, gave him sufficient strength to return to Victoria, where on his return the startling effects of his illness were very manifest to his numerous friends.'

Anthony rallied at first in Rutherglen. But he knew he was declining, and he drew up a will on 11 February 1898.

The sense of impending doom was alleviated fleetingly by a wedding. On 23 February, Anthony's second-oldest daughter, Marion, married a butcher, George Conisbee, in St Paul's Church in Chiltern. Anthony was too unwell to walk her down the aisle. Marion had been living in Mitta Mitta before the ceremony, perhaps with her aunt Margaret Neilson, most likely to avoid a very ordinary scandal, for she was pregnant. *The Advertiser* reported that Marion, 'who was prettily attired in white silk, with a large picture hat to match', was given away by Anthony Oliver, and attended by her sister Jessie, 'who was becomingly dressed in cream muslin'. While the couple headed off to Albury for the honeymoon, the rest of the wedding party drove to the Strahan residence for a wedding breakfast.[12] Perhaps Anthony was able to partake modestly. Given it was customary for the bride's family to pay for the wedding, the Strahans must have struggled to cover the costs. Did other members of the wider family network help out?

Less than three weeks later, on 11 March 1898, Anthony Strahan died in his house in Rutherglen, off Soles Street. It was the day before his fifty-eighth birthday. The cause was given as kidney failure. He was not known to be a big drinker, and alcohol seemed to play no part in his demise.

Anthony's death was met in the press by much sympathy and no little praise. 'The news of his death spread quite a gloom over the community,' noted *The Rutherglen Sun and Chiltern Valley Advertiser*. His policing career loomed large. Observing that 'the Grim Destroyer' had claimed another 'old resident', a second newspaper said Anthony had been 'a strict disciplinarian, but never made himself objectionable anywhere, by reason of over-officiousness or a straining after cases that did not require harsh measures'. *The Ovens and Murray Advertiser*, which had reported on his work as a policeman since the late 1860s, noted that Anthony had been 'stationed in the Kelly country at the time of the outbreak of the gang, and was one against whom the gang had sworn vengeance'.

An 'exceptionally long' funeral cortege left the family home at 2pm on 14 March. Anthony was buried in Carlyle Cemetery outside Rutherglen. Reverend Alma Howard conducted the lengthy service. Norah Pender's grave was nearby. People came from all quarters to 'pay the last tribute to one who was a good friend, a faithful servant and a kindly and goodhearted husband and father'. In the evening, the reverend addressed a large audience at St Stephen's Church in Rutherglen, referring 'in touching terms to the death of Mr Strahan'. A choir sang 'suitable hymns'.

Anthony left everything he owned – the house in Rutherglen and the 147 freehold acres at Norong, worth £500 – to his wife. Two mortgages against the house and land, amounting to £180, were left unpaid, as were other smaller debts, cutting into the estate.

Anthony missed the wedding of his eldest daughter, Alicia, to a widowed Cornish miner, Thomas Grose. They were married three months after his death at the Strahan residence in Rutherglen by Reverend Howard, indicating that the family remained tight. Marion and Anthony had been proud of their first-born daughter when she became a bank clerk in Melbourne. Alicia and Thomas settled in Rutherglen, reinforcing the Strahans' deep connections with the town.

One hopes Marion took comfort from her daughters' weddings, for she would experience another major personal loss in 1898. Her mother, the ever-feisty Eliza, died nine months after Anthony. Eliza and her de facto husband, John, had left Victoria for the Riverina in the late 1870s, settling close to Cootamundra, and later moving much further north to Nymagee. Their three children, Jane, Samuel and Jessie, had all married into farming families in southern New South Wales, creating a supportive wider family network. Despite her tough beginnings in London's East End, Eliza had lived until the ripe age of seventy-five. Unlike so many former Vandemonian convicts, she created an extensive lineage: all of her eight children lived into at least their middle years. Distance meant Marion had been able to see her mother less often during the 1880s and 1890s (Rutherglen and Nymagee were 500 kilometres apart), but they were close for many years, emotionally and geographically. At critical points, Eliza had been there for her daughter and son-in-law.

Marion was fifty years old when Anthony died. She was only halfway through her life: she was to live for another forty-one years. She never remarried and stayed in and around Rutherglen for the rest of her days. The northeast was very much her home. Between 1899 and 1904, four more Strahan children – Anthony Oliver, Edward, Jessie and Tom – married into local families, meaning Marion was surrounded by a strong extended family. My great-grandfather, Frank, born in Wangaratta in 1879 at the height of the Kelly Outbreak, was the only one of the seven children to leave the northeast. He married Martha Ward, the daughter of a carpenter, in January 1903 in Gippsland's Tongio West, 20-odd kilometres south of Omeo. Both Frank and Anthony Oliver described their father on their marriage certificates as a sergeant of police, claiming for him that elusive promotion. The youngest Strahan, Edward, married one of his cousins: May Winifred Boon, the daughter of Jane Frances Boon (née Ferguson), Marion's half-sister. May was only seventeen, and she was pregnant. This union brought together two of Eliza's grandchildren, one tracing back to Edward Evans, her convict husband, and the other to John Ferguson, her de facto partner.

After Anthony's death, Marion worked the old Strahan family farm at Norong with Edward and May. She continued to be active in Rutherglen's community affairs. In the first few years after Federation, a horse called Lady Strahan ran in the Rutherglen races. Given Anthony had owned several racehorses over the years, it is hard not to conclude that Lady Strahan was connected to the Strahan family. Had she been named after Marion?

Two of Marion and Anthony's sons joined the Australian Imperial Force during World War I. Anthony Oliver was too old for active service, but Tom was wounded as a private at Gallipoli (shrapnel hit an ankle). He returned to Rutherglen with some fanfare in May 1916. Had he been alive, Senior Constable Anthony Strahan would have been proud of his son's service.

By 1925, Marion had had enough of a life on the land. She leased out the farm and moved into Rutherglen. By the late 1930s, Marion was living with one of her granddaughters, Ada Conisbee, on Lake Road. Ada had married into a local farming family, the Taylors, who worked land at Brimin, close to Norong. Marion had many contented years in the Taylor family, the support of her granddaughter buffering the impact of her slow decline through her eighties. She was struck down by a heart attack at Ada's house on 8 June 1939 at the age of ninety-one, surrounded by three generations of her family. Senility had affected her in her later years.

By the time her death, the daughter of convicts had become a respectable grand old lady of the town. Identifying her as 'a native of the Mitta district', *The Rutherglen Sun* observed that she often related incidents from Rutherglen's past. Her death certificate also concealed her convict origins, declaring Melbourne, not Gravelly Beach, as her place of birth.

Eliza was fittingly listed on the certificate under one of her many false maiden names, Rose.

Underscoring the continuing power of the Kelly legend, *The Sun* noted: 'Her husband, the late Sergeant Anthony Strahan, was in charge of the police station at Rutherglen in the early days, and frequently had to go in search of the Kelly gang when they were at large.' So Anthony finally secured that promotion in the eyes of the reading public.

Marion left her estate to her seven children and her preferred grandchild, Ada, in equal shares. Alicia was her executor. Marion no longer owned any property: she must have transferred all real estate to her family some years earlier, which would have made sense, given her advancing years. Her personal estate, including 'money in hand or house', came to a modest £52, granting her beneficiaries a little over £6 each, a decidedly slim inheritance.

Marion was buried with Anthony in Carlyle Cemetery, outside Rutherglen. Today their grave has partly subsided, leaving the headstone on a tilt, but the lettering is still clear and strong.

CODA

When I visited Carlyle Cemetery in the winter of 2016, it was an appropriately overcast, even sombre, day – nothing like the blistering blue sky that greeted me when I walked into the Greta Cemetery in search of Ned Kelly. This time I came in search of my great-great-grandfather. And this time I wasn't alone. I came with my youngest brother, Keir, and my children, Joschka and Katya, and his Mirren, Coen and Annabel.

I found Anthony and Marion's grave in the middle of the cemetery. It was fitting that they were still resting together more than a century later. In the absence of any private family papers, a sense of Anthony as a husband and a father has proven elusive. One of my second cousins, Bruce Painter, told me that our ancestor was remembered somewhat harshly in his family line. By this inherited family memory, Anthony was known to be very hard on Marion and their children. His sons apparently hated him. I have nothing more to verify this account. It could well be true, at least in part. Anthony had a hard job in hard times. He came to the Victoria Police with a tough mindset as a young Irish immigrant. Across his long career, he witnessed considerable violence and hardship, quite possibly reinforcing a certain hardness. And some fathers can be tough on their sons, holding exacting and inflexible expectations. It seems that Anthony had a softer relationship with his daughters.

If he was hard on her, Marion seems to have retained an affection for her copper husband. A year after his death, in March 1899, Marion placed a notice in two Melbourne newspapers: 'In loving remembrance of Anthony, dearly loved husband of Marion Strahan, ex-officer of police, Rutherglen.'[1] This tender message underscored the strong affection that had bound Anthony and Marion together for nearly thirty years. Anthony had stood by her with that same uncompromising strength of character since the very beginning of their relationship. Marion would retell many times the story of Anthony sprinkling pepper on the floor of the Athenaeum Hall in Beechworth to avenge her when she was snubbed from the ball, either because she was pregnant but unmarried or because she was the daughter of convicts. When she retold the tale, she would throw her head back and laugh with glee.

It seems that Anthony and Marion might have disagreed about one key aspect of his career. Anthony came to hate the Kellys. He did so for at least three reasons, all for him compelling. He felt Ned and his family never treated him with the respect he deserved as a police officer. He was a proud man who took offence easily. And the Kellys certainly knew how to give offence. The Kellys were also nothing but criminals and cutthroats in his eyes. If they were not brought to justice, the broader community would have been in danger. The last reason for regarding them with antipathy was more personal: he believed, without a shred of doubt, that all those long patrols hunting the Kellys over many months, through tough country and often harsh weather, led to the breakdown of his health.

But Marion remembered the Kellys differently. She would tell people she had great sympathy for Ellen and her family, believing extreme poverty caused them to make decisions they might not have otherwise.[2] No one knows if she aired these views while Anthony was alive. Perhaps not, for she would have known that her husband would have reacted very badly to any soft or understanding words about the damned Kellys.

Given that their fates became so intertwined, it feels somehow just that Anthony Strahan and Ned Kelly were both buried in northeast Victoria, close but not too close to each other. The 60-odd kilometres between the two gravesites seems to encapsulate the divide between the Irish-born policeman and the Australian-born bushranger. One was on the side of the law and one broke it, but both were motivated by fierce loyalties and a certain hardness.

Unsurprisingly, my father never took his three sons to Carlyle Cemetery to see the grave of our ancestors. He paid homage across the years at various

Ned Kelly sites, but he could not bring himself to gaze upon the resting place of his own great-grandfather. He had in a way banished Anthony Strahan and all he thought the man represented, much as he had exiled himself from his own father. Ironically, had he known Marion's story better, Dad would have realised, perhaps with no small amount of surprise, that he and his grandmother shared a sympathy for the Kellys.

As I gazed on the grave my father had shunned, I felt I had completed a circle, discovering things about my family's past that had been blotted out, sometimes inadvertently and also, perhaps, deliberately. If Dad was still with me, I would tell him that our ancestor, the boy from Timolin, had come a long way, achieving much as a policeman during a turbulent time. He wasn't a hero or a villain. He was in the end ordinary, like most of us, with his own strengths and failings. Sure, his temper sometimes got the better of him, embroiling him in unnecessary and even petty stoushes, and he occasionally sailed close to the wind, particularly for a police officer, in his various endeavours to make a better life for himself and his family. But I felt sure, under that cloudy sky, that his life should not be defined by those few hot words reportedly uttered to Ned's uncle, Pat Quinn.

If Dad were still here, I would say to him that we now know much more about who the Strahans were, where they came from and what they did. I'd tell Dad that Senior Constable Anthony Strahan embodied, in his own ways, qualities that Dad admired. Our copper ancestor rarely took a backward step in the face of arbitrary authority; he liked a good yarn and had a way with words; he was not elitist, marrying a convict's daughter; and he stood by his family until the end. I'd say, Dad, the sins of your father don't need to be visited on your great-grandfather. History – of a nation, of a region and, especially, of a family – is sometimes more intricate and contrarian than we like to admit.

ACKNOWLEDGEMENTS

I've spent many solitary hours researching and writing this book, but I've only reached this point because many people helped me along the way. From the very first inkling that I may have found a story worth telling until the moment the printing press started rolling on *Justice in Kelly Country*, my wonderful wife, Lily, and our terrific children, Joschka and Katya, have supported me, sustaining me when I faltered, asking penetrating questions about Anthony's past and walking around some of the sites that feature in his story.

Modern writers can turn to two powerful tools their predecessors lacked. These tools have made the job of researching the past easier. The National Library of Australia's Trove database is indeed a national treasure, though I discovered I had to spell my family name many different ways to track down all the articles written about Anthony's exploits as a police officer in a plethora of metropolitan and local newspapers. Ancestry.com is a quite different tool, spanning continents and millions of users. It too contains a wealth of information for uncovering aspects of the past.

But in the end good history still has to be pieced together the old-fashioned way – by spending many dogged hours in archives. This can be tedious and frustrating as you hit dead ends and realise vital documents are missing, likely lost forever. Yet it's also wonderfully tactile, pungent work, as you feel the texture of old pages, brush off accumulated dust and sometimes mould, decipher ornate and quirky handwriting, and see the past emerging. This is the real stuff of original research, and it takes time. The tedium and frustration vanish in the blink of an eye when you find what you're looking for. More than a few times I laughed, even yelled, with glee when the eighth or twentieth box was the one I was looking for.

ACKNOWLEDGEMENTS

The ever-resourceful staff at the following institutions helped me navigate these vital primary sources: Public Record Office Victoria, State Library Victoria and the Victoria Police Museum (especially Caroline Oxley) in Melbourne; and the General Register Office of Ireland, the National Archives of Ireland and the Representative Church Body Library of the Church of Ireland in Dublin. The Avoca, Beechworth and Rutherglen historical societies filled in gaps.

Justice in Kelly Country is in part the story of the wider Strahan clan. Some of my cousins pointed me in the right direction at key points, shared their own inherited stories of Anthony and helped me chase down various leads: Alan Strahan, Rod Strahan, Karren Strahan, Melissa Traverso and Bruce and Kerri Painter in Australia, and Laura Daly in Ireland. John Fitzgerald helped me understand Cantonese names. A long-time colleague at the Department of Foreign Affairs and Trade who has always shared my love of good writing and well-grounded history, Mark Pierce, found unexpected nuggets. Russell Kelly showed me around Mitta Mitta. I would probably still be writing this book if Frances Adamson, as the Secretary of the Department, didn't allow me to take six months long-service leave in 2018 to get stuck into the task at hand.

I was able to refine my tale, avoid bloopers and think about aspects of Anthony's life differently because Frank Bongiorno, Ian Britain, Tom Griffiths, Jeremy Kruse, Janet McCalman, Phillipa McGuinness, Doug Morrissey, John Rickard and Karen Visser gave up their time to read the manuscript with care and wisdom.

A manuscript will remain in a desk drawer unless you can find someone who will back you and put it into print. The team at Monash University Publishing have brought *Justice in Kelly Country* into being with passion, good humour and expertise. Publisher Julia Carlomagno took on this book and edited the text with deft and unobtrusive skill; Sarah Cannon (who worked on my first book at Cambridge University Press, *Australia's China*, more than twenty-five years ago) put together a sensational marketing campaign; Jo Mullins handled the production with precision; Les Thomas

ACKNOWLEDGEMENTS

created a striking cover; and Sam van der Plank rustled various administrative and legal issues. Thanks also to Alan Laver, who drew up the maps, and Julia Farrell, who proofread the text and compiled the index.

NOTES

Introduction
1   Wright, 'Ned's Women'.

Chapter 2: Ordered Out Like a Dog
1   VPRS24 1863/297.
2   Haldane, p.44.
3   Coleman, Service Record, Victoria Police Museum.
4   Gaggin, McInnerney and Kilbride, Service Records, Victoria Police Museum.
5   Haldane, p.49.
6   VPRS, 937/P0 Unit 8.
7   *Avoca Mail*, 23 June; *The Age*, 24 July 1866.

Chapter 3: Swindle
1   VPRS 937/P0 Unit 8.
2   Haldane, p.22.
3   VPRS, 937/P0 Unit 8; *Avoca Mail*, 27 January 1866.
4   Morrissey 2018, pp.245–6.
5   Haldane, p.51.
6   VPRS 407/P0 Unit 5 Item 7.

Chapter 4: Tragedy and Vice
1   *The Talbot Leader*, 16 February 1867.
2   Broome, pp.91, 97.
3   Cahir, p.79.
4   VPRS 1867/137, 24, P000, Unit 200.
5   Quoted in Broome, p.98.
6   Broome, p.104.
7   Gibney, p.2.
8   VPRS 937/P0 Unit 9.
9   *The Bendigo Advertiser*, 30 December 1868; Augustus's death certificate, 7817/1868.
10 'Anthony and Marion Strahan of Rutherglen', p.2.
11 Morrissey 2018, p.275.

Chapter 5: The Convict Stain
1   Griffiths, p.12.
2   Woods, pp.75–8, 117, 119, 120; Griffiths, pp.15, 20, 38.
3   Haldane, p.111.
4   Woods, p.147.
5   *The Ovens and Murray Advertiser (OMA)*, 16 December 1869.

NOTES

6 McCalman, p.204.
7 *OMA*, 21 December 1869 and 21 April 1870.
8 VPRS 937/P0 Unit 412.
9 Woods, pp.59, 66–7.
10 Woods, pp.58, 64, 68.
11 *OMA*, 19 March 1870.
12 John Fitzgerald to the author 27 November 2018.
13 Woods, p.102.
14 Service Records 178 and 2006, Victoria Police Museum.
15 Alexander, p.1.
16 McCalman, p.25.
17 Bongiorno, p.9.
18 McCalman, p.68.
19 Alexander, p.63.
20 McCalman, p.7.
21 Cowley and Snowden, pp.1–6.
22 Alexander, p.37.
23 Alexander, p.63.
24 Morrissey 2018, p.46.

Chapter 6: Saucy Jack
1 Smith, p.21.
2 Eburn, p.80.
3 McLaren, p.454.
4 *OMA*, 15 February 1872.
5 Pike, p.110.
6 *OMA*, 17 April and 9 September 1872; VPRS 937/P0 Unit 414.
7 *OMA*, 18 October 1872; VPRS 937/P0, Unit 414.

Chapter 7: Something Wicked This Way Comes
1 *OMA*, 26 October 1872.
2 My account of the Wooragee Outrage is drawn from the near-verbatim transcripts of the inquest in October 1872 and the trial in April 1873, printed in *The Advertiser* (*OMA*, 28 October 1872 and 19 April 1873).
3 VPRS P264/P0 Unit 415.
4 *The Herald* (Melbourne), 16 October 1862.
5 VPRS P264/P0 Unit 415.

Chapter 8: Chain Reaction
1 *The Leader* (Melbourne), 23 Nov 1867; *OMA*, 18 July 1872.
2 *OMA*, 22 October 1872.
3 *OMA*, 24 and 26 Oct 1872.
4 *The Age*, 5 November 1872.
5 *OMA*, 26 October 1872.
6 *OMA*, 28 October 1872.
7 VPRS 937/P0 Unit 415.
8 VPRS 3991/P0 Unit 712.
9 *OMA*, 1 November 1872.

10   *The Argus*, 5 November 1872.
11   VPRS 937/P0 Unit 414.
12   *OMA*, 16 November 1872.
13   VPRS 937/P0 Unit 415.

Chapter 9: Judgement Day
1   *The Argus*, 6 May 1880; Miller, p.403.
2   Bongiorno, p.44.
3   *OMA*, 19 April 1873.
4   *OMA*, 19 April 1873.
5   Courtroom sequence based on information in Miller.
6   *OMA*, 18 April 1873.
7   VPRS 3991/P0 Unit 700.
8   *The Argus*, 2 September 1870 and 11 September 1873.
9   *Australasian*, 25 January 1873.
10   *The Queanbeyan Age*, 13 February 1873; *The Argus*, 17 March and 11 September 1873.
11   VPRS 24 P0 Unit 289 and 3991/P0 Unit 700.
12   *OMA* and *The Argus*, both 13 May 1873.

Chapter 10: Loose Ends
1   *OMA*, 13 May; *The Australasian*, 31 May 1873.
2   VPRS, 3991/P0 Unit 700.
3   *The Wagga Wagga Express*, 5 February 1873.
4   VPRS 937/P0 Unit 415.
5   VPRS 937/P0 Unit 415; *The Argus*, 22 July 1876.
6   *OMA*, 11 July 1873 and 8 October 1874.
7   *OMA*, 31 May 1873.

Chapter 11: A Master of His Own Domain
1   VPRS 937/P0 Unit 415.
2   VPRS 937/P0 Unit 416.
3   VPRS 937/P0 Unit 416; *OMA*, 30 May 1874.
4   *OMA*, 23 Oct 1873.
5   VPRS 937/P0 Unit 415.
6   VPRS 937/P0 Unit 416.
7   *OMA*, 13 February 1875.
8   *OMA*, 11 April 1875; *The Australasian*, 11 April 1875.
9   Blainey, p.60.
10   Blainey, p.121.
11   *OMA*, 26 June, 2 November and 25 December 1875.
12   *OMA*, 21 June 1873 and 16 December 1876; Pike, p.490.
13   *OMA*, 29 January 1875.
14   *OMA*, 23 Sep 1875.
15   *OMA*, 5 February 1876.
16   VPRS 937/P0 unit 418.
17   McQuilton, p.66; FitzSimons, pp.52–3; Clune, p.71.
18   Kieza 2022, vp.12; and Dufty, p.15.

NOTES

Chapter 12: The Greta Mob
1. Ellis, p.3.
2. Morrissey 2018, p.255.
3. Morrissey 2018, p.202.
4. Second Progress Report, Royal Commission of Enquiry into the Circumstances of the Kelly Outbreak, Melbourne, 1881, pp.46–8, 319–20.
5. Royal Commission, p.455.
6. Haldane, pp.96–7.
7. VPRS 937/P0 Unit 419.
8. Blainey, p.108.
9. Kennedy, p.56.
10. *OMA*, 16 February 1878.
11. Strangio.
12. VPRS 937/P0 unit 415.
13. *OMA*, 21 April 1873.
14. VPRS P0 unit 415.
15. Royal Commission, p.320.
16. McQuilton, p.67.

Chapter 13: Over the Edge
1. McQuilton, p.85; FitzSimons, pp.129–30.
2. FitzSimons, pp.130–1; Kennedy, p.86; Morrissey 2015, p.184.
3. Royal Commission, p.47.
4. FitzSimons, p.138.
5. MacFarlane, pp.58–9.
6. Kieza 2022, p.29.
7. 'Anthony and Marion', p.3 and Kerri Painter to the author, 8 May 2022.
8. FitzSimons, pp.140–1; Wright, 'Ned's Women'.
9. VPRS 937/P0 Unit 419.
10. Kieza 2022, p.30.
11. Royal Commission, p.160.
12. VPRS 937 P0 Unit 419.
13. *OMA*, 30 April 1878.
14. *OMA*, 4 and 7 May 1878.
15. Royal Commission, p.160.
16. 'Anthony and Marion', p.3.
17. *OMA*, 6 June 1878.
18. P937/P0 Unit 419.
19. Kennedy, pp.20–1.
20. Kennedy, pp.77–8.
21. McIntyre, p.7.
22. Kieza 2022, p.62.
23. *OMA*, 25 June 1878.
24. Royal Commission, pp.105, 609.
25. FitzSimons, p.154.
26. *OMA*, 12 Oct 1878.

Chapter 14: A Few Words

1. *OMA*, 1 Sept 1870; McQuilton, pp.73 and 196; Morrissey 2018, p.258.
2. Morrissey 2015, pp.219–21.
3. Clune, pp.54, 57, 60.
4. McQuilton, pp.99, 220.
5. McQuilton, p.62, 85, 183.
6. McQuilton, p.64.
7. Molony, p.120.
8. Jones, pp.158–9.
9. FitzSimons, pp.159–60.
10. Morrissey 2015, p.39.
11. FitzSimons, p.xii.
12. Dufty, pp.3, 58, 72, 82, 85, 110, 120, 138, 205, 232–3.
13. Wilson, pp.97, 100 and 117.
14. Kieza 2022, pp.28-9, 31, 40, 61, 96, 275.
15. MacFarlane, pp.217–19.
16. Morrissey 2015, pp.72–3.
17. Kieza 2022, p.216.
18. Royal Commission into the Kelly Outbreak, p.670; Kennedy, p.179.
19. Strahan, pp.42–4.
20. 'Anthony and Marion', p.3; and Kerri Painter to the author, 22 May 2022.
21. McQuilton, pp.127, 137–8, 171.
22. MacFarlane, pp.173–5.

Chapter 15: Stringybark Creek

1. Kieza 2022, p.40.
2. McIntyre, p.5.
3. McQuilton, p.96; Jones, p.161; FitzSimons, p.176.
4. Morrissey to Strahan, 25 March 2019.
5. Jones, pp.160–1; McQuilton, p.95; Carey, pp.272–3.
6. Utley, p.138.
7. Morrissey 2015, pp.73, 220; MacFarlane, p.69; Kennedy, p.102.
8. McIntyre, p.24.
9. Dufty, p.110; Wilson, p.187.
10. Dufty, p.114 and FitzSimons, p.185.
11. Kieza, p.55.
12. McQuilton, pp.69–70, 98–9.
13. Kennedy, pp.101–12; Morrissey 2015, p.82.
14. Royal Commission, p.106.
15. Royal Commission, p.164.
16. Royal Commission, p.164.
17. *The Herald* (Melbourne), 6 November; *The Mercury* (Hobart), 9 November 1878.
18. *The Argus*, 5 November; *The Herald*, 6 November; *The Leader* (Melbourne), 16 November 1878.

Chapter 16: The Endless Chase

1. *OMA*, 1 March 1870 and 4 February 1871.
2. Royal Commission, p.109.
3. *OMA*, 16 November 1878.
4. Royal Commission, p.500; FitzSimons, p.244.
5. Royal Commission, pp.670–2.
6. Kieza 2022, p.110.
7. VPRS 4965/P0 Unit 6 Item 489.
8. Morrissey 2015, p.62.
9. VPRS 4965/P0, Unit 6, Item 489.
10. *The Argus*, 10 November 1880.
11. VPRS 937/P000 Unit 365.
12. MacFarlane, pp.217–8.
13. *OMA*, 14 January 1879.
14. Royal Commission, pp.64–5.
15. Morrissey 2015, pp.205, 213, 219.
16. Royal Commission, p.65.
17. VPRS 937/P0 Unit 365.
18. *OMA*, 28 June, 30 September and 9 October 1879.
19. *OMA*, 28 August and 9 October 1879.
20. 'Anthony and Marion', p.3.
21. VPRS 937/P0 Unit 365.
22. *OMA*, 18 October 1879.

Chapter 17: One Last Stand

1. *The Argus*, 30 October 1880.
2. Jones, pp.176–7.
3. *The Ballarat Courier*, 29 October 1880.
4. *The Herald* (Melbourne), 28 October 1880.
5. *The Argus*, 30 October 1880.
6. Kieza 2022, p.259.
7. *The Argus*, 10 November 1880.
8. *The Argus*, 10 November 1880.
9. *The Argus*, 12 November 1880.
10. *The Argus*, 12 November 1880.
11. Jones, p.346.
12. VPRS 937/PO Unit 366.
13. *Weekly Times*, 16 April 1881.
14. Royal Commission, pp.670–3.
15. Royal Commission, p.12.
16. Sadleir, p.240.
17. Kieza 2022, pp.265-6.
18. Haldane, p.94.
19. *Overland*, 84 1981, p.42.
20. *The Age*, 21 January 2013.
21. Griffiths, *Beechworth*, p.90.

Chapter 18: Rutherglen Days

1. *Gippsland Times*, 11 and 14 February 1881.
2. VPRS 937/P0 Unit 366.
3. Strahan, Conduct Record.
4. *Rutherglen Sun*, 2 September 1885.
5. VPRS 24/P0 Unit 437, Item 1882/479 and Unit 452, Item 1883/447.
6. *Albury Banner and Wodonga Express*, 9 June 1882.
7. VPRS 937/P0 Unit 371.
8. *The Age*, 11 September 1888.
9. VPRS 937/P0 Unit 378, *The Argus*, 31 October and *North Eastern Ensign*, 9 November 1888.
10. VPRS 937/P0 Unit 379 and *Bairnsdale Advertiser*, 20 October 1888.
11. VPRS 937 P/0 Unit 378; *The Queenslander*, 22 December 1888; *OMA*, 25 May and 28 September 1889.
12. VPRS 937 P/0 Unit 385.
13. VPRS 937 P/0 Unit 385.

Chapter 19: A Terror to Evil-Doers

1. *Corowa Free Press*, 7 October; *Australian Star*, 8 October 1892.
2. *The Advertiser* (Adelaide), 29 November; *OMA*, 3 December; *The South Australian Chronicle*, 3 December 1893.
3. VPRS 937 P/0 Unit 387.
4. *The Argus*, 7 March 1893.
5. *Corowa Free Press*, 30 September and 7 October 1892; *Wodonga and Towong Sentinel*, 10 March 1893; *OMA*, 4 August 1900; VPRS 937 P/0 Unit 387, 28 P/0 Unit 653 Item 51/544 and 28 P/2 Unit 358 Item 51/544.
6. VPRS 24/P0 Unit 617 Items 1893/1196 and 1238.
7. VPRS 937 P/0 Units 386 and 387.
8. *The Rutherglen Sun and Chiltern Valley Advertiser*, 5 January 1894.
9. Strahan, Conduct Record.
10. Blainey, pp.148–9.
11. *The Age*, 22 February 1895.
12. *OMA*, 12 March 1898.

Coda

1. *The Age*, 10 March; *The Leader*, 18 March 1899.
2. Kerri Painter to the author, 8 May 2022.

BIBLIOGRAPHY

Author unknown, 'Anthony and Marion Strahan of Rutherglen', unpublished and undated memoir.

Alexander, Alison, *Tasmania's Convicts: How Felons Built a Free Society*, Allen & Unwin, 2014.

Blainey, Geoffrey, *A History of Victoria*, Cambridge University Press, Port Melbourne, 2013.

———, *The Rush that Never Ended: A History of Australian Mining*, Melbourne University Press, Carlton, 1963.

Bongiorno, Frank, *Sex Lives of Australians: A History*, Black Inc., Melbourne, 2012.

Broome, Richard, *Aboriginal Victorians: A History since 1800*, Allen & Unwin, Sydney, 2005.

Cahir, Fred, *Black Gold: Aboriginal People on the Goldfields of Victoria, 1850–1870*, ANU Press, Canberra, 2012.

Carey, Peter, *True History of the Kelly Gang*, University of Queensland Press, St Lucia, 2000.

Clune, Frank, *The Kelly Hunters*, Angus & Robertson, Sydney, 1980.

Cowley, Trudy and Snowden, Dianne, *Eliza Redman*, unpublished and undated memoir.

Dawson, Stuart E, 'Redeeming Fitzpatrick: Ned Kelly and the Fitzpatrick Incident', *Eras Journal*, vol. 17, no. 1, 2015.

Dufty, David, *Nabbing Ned Kelly: The Extraordinary True Story of the Men who Brought Australia's Most Notorious Outlaw to Justice*, Allen & Unwin, Sydney, 2022.

Eburn, Michael, 'Outlawry in Colonial Australia: The Felons Apprehension Acts 1865–1899', *ANZLH E-Journal*, 2005.

Ellis, Samuel E., *A History of Greta*, North Eastern Historical Society, Kilmore, 1972.

Fitzgerald, John, *Big White Lie: Chinese Australians in White Australia*, UNSW Press, Sydney, 2007.

FitzSimons, Peter, *Ned Kelly: The Story of Australia's Most Notorious Legend*, William Heinemann, Sydney, 2013.

Foster, R.F., *Modern Ireland: 1600–1972*, Allen Lane, 1989.

Gibney, John, *A Short History of Ireland: 1500–2000*, Yale University, New Haven, 2017.

Griffiths, Tom, *Beechworth: An Australian Country Town and Its Past*, Greenhouse, Richmond, 1987.

Haldane, Robert, *The People's Force: A History of Victoria Police*, Melbourne University Press, Carlton, 2018.

Jones, Ian, *Ned Kelly: A Short Life*, Lothian, Sydney, 1995.

Kelly, Russell J., *Mitta Mining*, Wombat Gully Productions, Mitta Mitta, 2007.

———, *Mitta Mitta: Photographic Memories*, Wombat Gully Productions, Mitta Mitta, 2015.

Kieza, Grantlee, *Mrs Kelly*, ABC Books, HarperCollins, Sydney, 2019.

———, *The Kelly Hunters*, ABC Books, HarperCollins, Sydney, 2022.

Kennedy, Leo (with Looby, Mick), *Black Snake: The Real Story of Ned Kelly*, Affirm Press, South Melbourne, 2018.

Kingston, Beverley, *The Oxford History of Australia, volume 3, 1860–1900: Glad, Confident Morning*, Oxford University Press, Melbourne, 1988.

MacFarlane, Ian, *The Kelly Gang Unmasked*, Oxford University Press, South Melbourne, 2012.

McCalman, Janet, *Vandemonians: The Repressed History of Colonial Victoria*, Miegunyah Press, Melbourne, 2021.-

McIntyre, Thomas, *A True Narrative of the Kelly Gang* (1900), Victoria Police Museum, victoriancollections.net.au.

McLaren, Ian, *Australian Dictionary of Biography, volume 5, K–Q, 1851–1890*, Melbourne University Press, Carlton, 1970.

McQuilton, John, *The Kelly Outbreak, 1878–1880: The Geographical Dimension of Social Banditry*, Melbourne University Press, Carlton, 1979.

Malcolm, Elizabeth and Hall, Dianne, *A New History of the Irish in Australia*, NewSouth, Sydney, 2018.

Miller, Robert, *Australian Dictionary of Biography, volume 6, R–Z, 1851–1890*, Melbourne University Press, Carlton, 1976.

Molony, John, *I Am Ned Kelly*, Allen Lane, Melbourne, 1980.

Morrissey, Doug, *Ned Kelly: An Unlawful Life*, Connor Court, Redland Bay, 2015.

———, *Ned Kelly: Selectors, Squatters and Stock Thieves*, Connor Court, Redland Bay, 2018.

———, *Ned Kelly: The Stringybark Creek Police Murders*, Connor Court, Redland Bay, 2020.

Musk, William John, *Hamlets in the Hills*, W. Musk, Stanley, 1993.

North Eastern Historical Society, *Rutherglen and Its History*, n.d.

Pike, Douglas, *Australian Dictionary of Biography, volume 3, A–C, 1851–1890*, Melbourne University Press, Carlton, 1969.

Russell, Roslyn, *High Seas and High Teas: Voyaging to Australia*, NLA Publishing, Canberra, 2016.

Sadleir, John, *Recollections of a Victorian Police Officer*, George Robertson, Melbourne, 1913.

Second Progress Report, 'Royal Commission of Enquiry into the Circumstances of the Kelly Outbreak', Melbourne, 1881.

Smith, Babette, *A Cargo of Women: Susannah Watson and the Convicts of the Princess Royal*, Allen & Unwin, Sydney, 2008.

Smith, Peter C., *The Clarke Gang: Outlawed, Outcast and Forgotten*, Rosenberg Publishing, Kenthurst, 2015.

Strahan, Frank, 'The Iron Mask of Australia', *Overland*, issue 84, July 1981.

Strangio, Paul, 'Black Wednesday', *eMelbourne: The City Past and Present*, July 2008, www.emelbourne.net.au/biogs/EM00200b.htm

Utley, Robert, *Wanted: The Outlaw Lives of Billy the Kidd and Ned Kelly*, Yale University Press, 2015.

Watson, Don, *The Bush: Travels in the Heart of Australia*, Hamish Hamilton, Melbourne, 2014.

Whitttaker, Max D., *Wangaratta*, Wangaratta City Council, Wangaratta, 1963.

Wilson, Rebecca, *Kate Kelly: The True Story of Ned Kelly's Little Sister*, Allen & Unwin, Sydney, 2021.

Woods, Carole, *Beechworth: A Titan's Field*, Hargreen, Melbourne, 1985.

Wright, Clare, 'Ned's Women: A Fractured Love Story', *Meanjin*, vol. 69, no. 2, 2010.

INDEX

A
Aboriginal people, 51, 151
   Djadjawurrung, 51
   perceptions of, 52–3
Ah Gow, 66–7
Ah Sing, 48
Ah Wah, 88–9, 124
Aitken, James, 164–6
Amphitheatre, 54
Avoca, 47

B
Bachelor, George, 34
Baker, William, 67
Bamford, William (executioner), 133–6
Barclay, Hugh Ross, Superintendent, 25, 62
   describes Wooragee Outrage offenders, 99
   promotion of, 148
   recommends rewards for Anthony, 86–9, 147–8
   by Watt's deathbed, 139
   and Wooragee Outrage, 100–1, 139
   and Wooragee Outrage arrests and trial, 113–16, 118–24
Barry, Redmond, Justice, 83
   death of, 252
   Ned Kelly murder trial, 248–9
   sentences Ah Wah, 88
   sentences Kennedy and Baumgarten, 200–1
   sentences Trembath and Watson, 86
   trial of Ellen Kelly, Williamson and Skillion, 199–200
Battle of the Boyne, 4
Baumgarten, Gustav, 193
Baumgarten, William, 193, 200
Beechworth, 61–3
   Chinese population, 66
   perceptions of Ned Kelly among community, 259
Beechworth Cemetery, 118, 147
Beechworth Gaol, 83, 88, 108, 121, 138, 148–9, 185, 273
   Ellen Kelly's time in, 194
   execution of Smith and Brady, 135–6
   Smith and Brady buried in grounds, 144
   Thompson, Charles, Governor, 132
Berry, Graham, Chief Secretary, 181, 250-1
Bindon, Henry, 248
Black Wednesday, 181
Bluecap Gang, 109
Bowler, Henry, 156, 162, 165–6
Brady, Peter snr, 102–4, 105–6
   arrest of, 113
   death of, 146
Brady, Peter jnr, 106, 120, 123–4, 146
Brady, Thomas, 102–4, 106, 154
   at Beechworth Gaol, 148–9
   burial at Beechworth Gaol, 144
   charged with robbery under arms and wilful murder, 119
   commits series of crimes, 112–13
   committal hearing, 118–22
   court appearances for Wooragee Outrage, 114
   execution of, 133, 135–6
   identification by witnesses, 116–18
   at John Watt coronial inquest, 116
   at John Watt murder trial, 126–32
   last declaration of, 137–43
   Wooragee Outrage committal hearing, 113–22

INDEX

Braithwaite, George, Constable, 277–8
Brooke Smith, Alexander, Inspector, 153, 164–6, 178, 186
   criticism by Royal Commission, 256
Brown, Frederick, 129–30, 142, 275–6, 283–4
Burke and Wills, 18
Burrowes, William, 265–8
bushfires, 162–3, 177, 180
bushrangers, 80
   public opinion of, 81
bushranging, 111–12, 261
Byrne, Joe
   attack on police camp at Stringybark Creek, 223–6, xv
   at bank robbery in Euroa, 234
   death of, 247
   family, 227
   joins Kelly Gang, 219
   Ned Kelly dictates Jerilderie Letter to, 237
   shoots Aaron Sherritt, 245
   see also Greta Mob
Byrne, Margaret, 231, 238

C

Campbell, Sarah Ann *see* Strahan, Sarah Ann
Campbell, William, 87–8
Captain Thunderbolt, 111–12
Cardwell, Joseph, 289–91
Cardwell, William, 157–8
Carey, Peter, 224, xv–xvi
Carlyle Cemetery, 300–2
Cartwright, George, 50
Catholic church
   role in community, 162
   in Sandhurst (Bendigo), 162
Catholicism, 5
   Catholic devotional revolution, 12
Catholics
   discrimination against, 14
   proportion of Ireland's population, 7
   proportion of Victoria Police officers, 21
cattle stealing *see* stock theft

Cawse, Mary Anne, 85–6
Chadwick, William, Sergeant, 68, 82–3, 102–4
chain migration, 14
Charge of Sebastopol, 231
Chemimi, death and inquest, 50–3
children
   attendance at school, 160
   high infant mortality rate, 10
   illness among, 19, 156
   premature death of, 156
   sexual exploitation of, 64–5
Chinese population in Australia
   in Avoca, 47
   in Ovens district, 66
   in Snowy Creek area, 151
   passion for gambling, 48
   perceptions of, 47–8, 49
   riot at Avoca, 49
Chomley, Hussey, Superintendent, 178–9, 194, 199–200, 267–8, 270
Christesen, Clem, 213, 257
Church of England, 4–5
Church of Ireland, 4–5, 7, 13
churches
   role in nineteenth-century Victoria, 160
Clarke, John, 80
Clarke, Thomas, 80
Clune, Frank, 167, 203
Cockburn, James, 275
Coleman, Bryan, Sergeant, 25–32, 41
colonisation, impact on Aboriginal population, 51
Conisbee, Ada (Anthony Strahan's granddaughter), 298, 299
Connell, Margaret *see* Cook, Margaret
Conniff, Mathew, Sergeant, 48–9
Connolly, Bob, 'the Mailman', 159, 171
convicts
   death rate among, 74
   female, 75
   and marriage, 73
   mistrust of, 74–5
   punishments for, 70
   transportation of, 69–70
   in Van Diemen's Land, 69, 74

INDEX

Cook, John, 35–46
Cook, Margaret (nee Connell), 38–9, 42–3, 45–6
Cooke, William, 193
County Kildare, 6, 53
Crawford, Victoria, 63–5
crime, 65–6
  Irish representation in statistics, 21–2
  in London, 71
  in Melbourne, 19
  in northeast Victoria, 174
  public-order offences, 22, 269
  rates, 174
  rates lower among Chinese population, 48
  serious violent, 22
Cromwell, Oliver, 5
Curnow, Thomas, 246

D
Daly, Laura, 8
Darvall, Charles JP, 184, 192
Deasy, Dennis, Senior Constable, 24
Declaration of the Republic of Northeastern Victoria, 245
Delaney family, 173
Denholm, Robin, 4
depression (economic) late nineteenth century, 294
Dixon, Eliza, 269
Djadjawurrung, 51
Dooley, Jane, 59
drought, 162, 177, 180–1, 294
Drummond, Archie
  death of, 156
drunkenness, 22, 65–6, 269
  among police, 29
Dufty, David, 209, 225

E
Eliza (ship), 13
Emms, William, 275
Evans, Edward, 69–71, 73–6
  as a convict in Van Diemen's Land, 69–70
  marriage to Eliza Redman, 71

Evans, Edward jnr, 75
Evans, Eliza (nee Redman), 71–7
  affair with John Ferguson, 75
  in Cascades Female Factory, 73
  death of, 297
  in Launceston Female Factory, 72–3
  marriage to Edward Evans, 73
  transported to Van Diemen's Land, 72
Evans, Margaret, 74, 77
  bitten by snake, 159–60
Evans, Marion *see* Strahan, Marion
Evans, Winifred Eliza, 73
executions, 80, 133–6, 251–2

F
Felons Apprehension Act 1865 (NSW), 80
Felons Apprehension Act 1878 (Victoria), 235, 241
Ferguson, John, 75–6
Fielding, David, 240
Fitzpatrick, Alexander, Constable, 186–9, ix, xi
  in Jerilderie Letter, 237
  Ned Kelly's alleged threat to, 224, 248
  trial for attempt to murder, 199–200
FitzSimons, Peter, 186, 207–8
flood
  in Mitta Valley, 163–4
  at Snowy Creek, 155
Flood, Ernest, 193, 204, 223–5, 248
Foster, William (police magistrate), 243, 267–9
Fox, Henry (doctor) 99, 114, 273
Francis, James, Chief Secretary, 118, 137

G
Gaggin, John, Constable, 28–9
Gale, Henry, 95–7
  marriage to Sarah, 147
  witness at Wooragee Outrage trial, 119, 127, 139–40
Gale, Margaret, 95–6, 127, 138–9
  death of, 146–7
gambling, 48–9
Gaunson, David, 248
Gaunson, William, 249–251

INDEX

gender imbalances in population in early colonial era, 73
Gidley, Thomas, 107–9, 140
Giltrap, Anne *see* Strahan, Anne
goldmining, 61, 151, 261–2, 276–7
  Anthony turns to, 295
  decline, 180, 262
goldrush, 150–1
  in Beechworth, 61
  and Chinese immigrants, 47
  in Eldorado, 67–8
  at Great Northern Extension, 276
  impact on Indigenous society and culture, 51
  in Lamplough, 50
  in Redbank, 24–5
  in Rutherglen, 261
  in Wooragee, 93
Goodman, Amelia, 185
Goodman, David, 185
Graham, George (magistrate), 99, 114, 116, 139, 143, 293
Greaves, Lucy, 153–4, 158, 159
Greta, 171–2
Greta Cemetery, 258–60
Greta mob, 172–5, 182, 241–2
  see also Byrne, Joe; Hart, Steve; Kelly, Dan; Kelly, Ned
Greta police station closure, 236

H
Hall, Ben, 80
Hall, Edward, Senior Constable, 202
Halloran, Bridget, 66
Hansen, Ann, 269
Happenstein, William, 104, 144
  arrest of, 113
  charged with robbery under arms and wilful murder, 119
  identification by witnesses, 116–18
  in last declaration of Smith and Brady, 141
  at Watt coronial inquest, 116
  witness at Watt murder trial, 128–31
  Wooragee Outrage committal hearing, 113–22

Hare, Francis, Superintendent, 81, 167, 176, 235, 238, 246–7
  on Anthony's work in search for Kellys, 254
  Royal Commission calls for his retirement, 256
Hart, Richard, 196, 242–3
Hart, Steve
  attack on police camp at Stringybark Creek, 223–6
  bank robbery in Euroa, 234
  death of, 247
  joins Kelly Gang, 219
  plan to derail Victoria Police special train near Glenrowan, 245–6
Hartley, John, 101–2
Harty, Francis, 235
Hayes, James, 175, 193
Hearn, Ray, 259
Henessey, Adelaide, 242
Henry VIII, 4–5
Higgins, John, 81–4
Holywell, Wales, 69
Holyroyd, Edward, Justice, 273, 283–5
Hopkins, Thomas, 240
horse stealing *see* stock theft
Hourigan, Patrick, 280–4

I
illness
  among children, 19, 156
  on ships, 13
International Hotel, Bealiba
  Anthony's alleged inappropriate conduct at, 35–42
  fire, 42–5
Ireland, 4–11
Irish Famine, 11
Irish migration, 12–13
Irish population in Australia
  over-representation in crime statistics, 22
  stereotypes of, 14
Irwin, James, Sub-Inspector, 277, 285, 288–91

INDEX

J
James II, 4
Jarvis, William, 95–6, 113–14, 116, 120–1, 127, 138
Jerilderie Letter, 26, 201–2, 203–4, 210, 224, 237–8, 239, xiv, xvi
Jones, Ian, 206–7, 223

K
Kelly family, 173–4
  brawl with Fitzpatrick, 187–8
  remains of hut, 258
  sympathisers, 192, 249
Kelly Gang, xiv
  armour, 245
  attack on police camp at Stringybark Creek, 223–6
  bank robbery and holding hostages in Euroa, 234
  bank robbery and holding hostages in Jerilderie, 237
  hideouts, 213
  holding hostages at Glenrowan Inn, 246
  low profile after Jerilderie bank robbery, 240
  plan to derail Victoria Police special train near Glenrowan, 245–6
  police search for, 185–96, 221–2, 228–9, 234–5
  siege at Glenrowan, 246–8
Kelly Outbreak
  media coverage of, 231–3
  research into, xvi–xviii
Kelly, Dan, 173–4
  attack on police camp at Stringybark Creek, 223–6
  bank robbery and holding hostages in Euroa, 234
  bank robbery and holding hostages in Jerilderie, 237
  death of, 247
  police search for, 185–96, 221–2, 228–9, 234–5
  siege at Glenrowan, 246–8
  see also Greta mob

Kelly, Denis, 38–9
Kelly, Ellen, 173–4, x
  arrest of, 189
  committal hearing, 193–4
  encounter with Anthony, 188–9
  Marion looked after, in lock-up, 189–90, 194
  at Ned's execution, 252
  trial of, 199–200
Kelly, John 'Red,' 173
Kelly, Kate, 173, 188–9, 191, 209, 249
Kelly, Maggie, 191, 235
Kelly, Ned, 173–4
  alleged shooting of Fitzpatrick at Kelly hut, 187
  alleged threat to kill police, 224
  on Anthony's alleged threat to kill him, 203
  appearance in Central Criminal Court, Melbourne, 248
  armour, 245
  arrest for horse stealing, 184
  attack on police camp at Stringybark Creek, 223–6
  bank robbery and holding hostages in Euroa, 234
  bank robbery and holding hostages in Jerilderie, 237
  capture at Glenrowan, 247
  charged with murder of Thomas Lonigan, 248
  committal hearing in Beechworth, 248
  death mask, 252
  encounter with Anthony and Shoebridge at Ovens River, ix–xii
  execution of, 251–2
  furious about Ellen's arrest, 190
  grave at Greta Cemetery, 258
  guilty verdict, murder of Lonigan, 248–9
  plan to derail Victoria Police special train near Glenrowan, 245–6
  police search for, 185–96, 221–2, 228–9, 234–5
  public interest in murder trial, 249

INDEX

reputation in the northeast, 259
research on, xvi–xvii
reward for capture of, 239, 252–5
sentencing for murder of Lonigan, 251
siege at Glenrowan, 246–8
writing on, 203–12
Kennedy, Daniel, 190, 254
Kennedy, Leo, 212, 224
Kennedy, Michael, Sergeant, 196–7, 199
    death at Stringybark Creek, 225
    leads Kelly Gang search party in Mansfield, 219–20
Kennedy, Samuel, 193, 200
Kieza, Grantlee, 189, 210, 246
Kilbride, John, Constable, 28–30
Kincardineshire, 4

L

Lamplough, 50
Larkan, Seymour, Constable, 55
Lavelle, Michael, 66
Lavelle, Thomas, 66
Lee Sin, 15
Lewis, John (Black Jack), 109–13, 115, 118–19
    committal hearing, 118–22
    identification by witnesses, 116–18
    trial of, 144–6
    at Watt coronial inquest, 116
Lloyd family, 173
Lloyd, John 'Jack' jnr, 185, 188–9, 192, 196, 228, 241
Lloyd, John 'Jack' snr, 173–4, 196
Lloyd, Thomas 'Tom' snr, 195
Lloyd, Tom jnr, 173, 185, 228, 258
Longmore, Francis (parliamentarian), 181, 255, 256
Lonigan, Thomas, 209, 210, 223–5, 237
    death at Stringybark Creek, 223–4
    joins Kelly Gang search party in Mansfield, 220
    Ned Kelly charged with murder of, 248
Lord Raglan (ship), 17

M

MacFarlane, Ian, 210, 217–8, 224, 236
Martin, James, 63–5
Mason, Joseph, Superintendent, 26–31
    conducts inquiry at Bealiba station, 36, 40–2
    recommends Anthony for leave, 56
    recommends Anthony for mounted constable, 33
    recommends reward for Anthony, 35
Mason, Robert jnr, 195
Mason, Robert snr, 195
McAuliffe family, 241–2, 248
McCann, Frances
    death of, 156
McCoy, James, 196
McInnerney, Thomas, Constable, 27, 28–9
McIntyre, Peter, 240–1
McIntyre, Thomas, Constable, 196–7, 220–5, 227
    chief witness in Central Criminal Court, 248
    in Kelly Gang search party in Mansfield, 220
    at Stringybark Creek, 227
McMahon, Hanorah 'Norah', *see* Prendergast, Hannorah 'Norah'
McMonigle, Jack, 234–5
McQuilton, John, 203–5, 212, 214
Meehan, William, 274–6
Meighan, John, 242–3
Melbourne, 18–19
mental illness, 269, 273
midwives, 154
Mitchell, Catherine, 119, 127, 138
Mitchell, Peter, 94–5, 119, 127
Mitta Mitta River, 150
Mitta Valley, 150–1
Molony, John, 206, 214
Montfort, William, Superintendent, 167, 267–8, 270
Morgan, Daniel 'Mad Dog', 80
Morgan, George, 76
Morris, William, 40
Morrissey, Doug, 36, 211–12, 223, 224, 226

321

INDEX

N
Nee, Peter, Senior Constable, 291
Neill, Ann, 76
New Model Army, 5
Nicolson, Charles Hope, Inspecting Superintendent, 167–8, 175–6, 187, 231
   on claims for reward for capture of Kelly, 253
   leads raids on Sherritt and Byrne huts, 231
   meets with Quinn, 233–4
   plan to capture Kelly Gang, 230
   Royal Commission calls for his retirement, 256
Nixon, John, Constable, 103–4
Nolan family, 241–2

O
O'Brien, Bridget, 172, 178, 190
O'Donnell, Michael, Senior Constable, 34, 35, 40–1
O'Donnell, Murthay, 67
Oatman, Billy, 142
Olcorn, Isaac, 274–6

P
Painter, Bruce, 300
Peck, Jane, 127–8
Pender Affair, 279
Pender, Thomas *see* Prendergast, Thomas
Pevitt, James, 286
Pewtress, Henry, Sub-Inspector, 227–8
police
   arms, 15
   conditions of work, 20, 24
   duties of, 62–3
   low morale, 182
   nature of work, 24
   role in community, 25
   threats to, 236
   training, 22
   uniform, 20, 197, 221
Police Regulation Act 1853, 14
Police Regulation Act of 1873, 20
Police Reward Fund, 34–5
political crisis in Victoria, 181
Portland, Victoria, 13
Power, Harry, 81, 167, 182
Prendergast, Hannorah 'Norah' (*nee* McMahon), 279–86
Prendergast, Thomas, 279–86
Price, Margaret, 272–4
prostitution, 51, 128, 287
Protestants
   in Ireland, 4–5
   proportion of Australian population, 13
   proportion of Victoria Police officers, 21

Q
Quinn family, 173
Quinn, Jimmy, 189, 202
Quinn, Patrick, 202–12, xiv
   affidavit at Ned Kelly's trial, 250–1
   altercation with Anthony, 203–12
   assault of Senior Constable Edward Hall, 202
   assisting police in search for Kelly Gang, 233–4, 235

R
railway system, Victoria, 261
Rajah (ship), 72
Rajah Quilt, 72
rape, 63–5, 217
Recovery (ship), 69–70
Redbank, 24–5
Redman, Mary Ann, 71–2
Reid, Curtis, 77–8
Reid, Robert, 77, 124
Rennie, James, Superintendent, 276, 278, 282–9
Rogers, William (Bill the Butcher), 35
Royal Charter (ship), 17
Royal Commission into the Kelly Outbreak, 175–6, 178, 182, 254–7
Royal Irish Constabulary (RIC), 14–15, 19
Rutherglen, 261–2
Ryan, Cornelius, Constable, 198–9, 219

INDEX

S

Sadleir, John, Superintendent, 198–9
  criticism of Royal Commission, 256
  on disarray at Greta police station, 239–40
  leading raids on Sherritt and Byrne huts, 231
  plan to capture Kelly Gang, 219
  at Royal Commission, 226
  search for Kelly Gang, 229, 234
  at siege at Glenrowan, 247
Sams, Edwards, 101–2
Scanlan, Michael, Constable, 220, 225, 227, 233
Schluter, William, 286
Schmidt, Augustus, disappearance of, 53–5
schooling, 160
  in Ireland, 12
Scotland, 3–4
Scott, John Irvine (Jack the Devil), 109–13
sex imbalances in population in early colonial era, 73
Seymour, Patrick, 274–5
Shakespeare (ship), 16
Shanklin, Thomas, Senior Constable, 35, 48–9
Sherritt, Aaron, 230–1, 237
  death of, 245
Sherritt, John, 230
Shoebridge, Edward, Senior Constable, 82
  encounter with Ned and Dan Kelly at Ovens River, ix–xii
  in Greta contingent to apprehend Kelly Gang, 219
Simcocks, Thomas, 290–1
Skillion, William, 189
  committal hearing, 193–4
  trial of, 199–200
Slocomb, Margaret, 127
sly grog, 287–91
Smith, Anne, 107
Smith, Hugh, 105, 107
Smith, James, 102–4, 107, 154
  arrest of, 113
  at Beechworth Gaol, 148–9
  burial at Beechworth Gaol, 144
  charged with robbery under arms and wilful murder, 119
  commits series of crimes, 112–13
  committal hearing, 118–22
  court appearances for Wooragee Outrage, 114
  crime spree, 108
  execution of, 133, 135–6
  fails to appear at Gidley trial, 108
  identification by witnesses, 116–18
  last declaration of, 137–43
  trial at Wagga Wagga, 111
  at Watt coronial inquest, 116
  at Watt murder trial, 126–32
  at Wooragee Outrage trial, 113–24
Smyth, Charles (prosecutor), 84, 107–8, 248, 273, 275, 283
  at John Watt murder trial, 126–30
Snowy Creek, 151, 160–1
St Arnaud Hotel, 27, 29–30
St Peter's Eastern Hill, 15–16, 58
Standish, Captain Frederick, Chief Commissioner, 22–3, 30–1, 239–40
  on Anthony recommendation, 34–5
  on Bealiba inquiry, 41–2
  chooses Anthony for replacement at Greta, 176
  damning assessment of Anthony at Royal Commission, 255
  death of, 256
  decides to relocate Anthony, 41
  forced into retirement, 253
  on Greta police, 176
  plan to capture Kelly Gang, 230
  promotion of Anthony to senior constable, 154
  promotion of Hugh Barclay, 148
  on recommendation and reward for Anthony, 33–5
  at Royal Commission into the Kelly Outbreak, 255
  and Wooragee Outrage, 118, 123–4
Stawell, William, Chief Justice, 64, 192–3

INDEX

Steele, Arthur, Sergeant, 175–6, 182–3, 185, 188–9, 224, 236
   criticised by Royal Commission, 256
   shoots Ned Kelly, 247
Stephen, Sir Alfred (NSW Chief Justice), 111–12
Stock Protection League, 185
stock theft, 174, 192–3, 204–5, 240–1, 263
Strahan family history, prior to migration to Australia, 3–11
Strahan, Alan, 4
Strahan, Alicia Maria, 153, 262, 266, 297, 299
Strahan, Anne, 9–11
   death of, 270
Strahan, Anthony, 125
   alleged threat to Ned Kelly, 203–4, 206–12, 237
   altercation with Patrick Quinn, 203–12
   altercations with Sgt Bryan Coleman, 25–30
   arrival in Melbourne, 18
   assumes care for nephew John, 271
   claim for reward for capture of Ned Kelly, 253
   cross-cultural encounter with Aboriginal people, 50–3
   cross-cultural encounter with Chinese, 48
   death of, 296
   dire financial position, 294–5
   duties in Rutherglen, 263
   encounter with Ellen Kelly, 188–9
   encounter with Greta mob, 242–3
   encounter with Ned and Dan Kelly at Ovens River, ix–xii
   encounter with Trembath and Watson, 81–3
   family memories and impressions of, 214–17
   farewell from Rutherglen, 292
   farming, 271, 294
   feud with James Aitken, 164–6
   grave of, 300–2
   Greta assignment reports missing, 210–11
   homestead burnt down, 294
   ill health, 270–1, 295
   indirect encounter with brother Richard, 263–4
   at inquest for Robert Strahan, 24
   investigations into Wooragee Outrage, 102–4
   involvement in Pender Affair, 282–6
   John Cook complaint and subsequent inquiry, 35–42
   joins police force, 19
   in last declaration of Smith and Brown, 143
   leads Greta contingent to apprehend Kelly Gang, 219
   at Lewis trial, 144–5
   marriage to Marion, 125
   meets Marion, 78
   meets with Patrick Quinn, 233
   migration to Australia, 17
   Nicolson's report on, 167–8
   and Pender Affair, 282–5
   poor living quarters, 153–4, 177–9
   posted to Avoca, 47
   posted to Bealiba, 33
   posted to Beechworth, 60
   posted to Belvoir, 59
   posted to Eldorado, 67
   posted to Greta, 171
   posted to Redbank, 24
   posted to Rutherglen, 244
   posted to Snowy Creek, 150–2
   posted to St Arnaud, 25–6
   posted to Wangaratta, 236
   posted to Wodonga, 291–3
   promoted to mounted constable, 34
   promoted to senior constable, 154
   purchase of a racehorse, 266
   quarrel with William Burrowes, 265–8
   raids in search for Ned and Dan Kelly, 231
   relationship with brother Simon, 59
   relationship with Catherine Tannim, 55–60

religious affiliation of officers, 21
research into his life, xvi
resignation, 293
rewarded by superiors, 34, 35, 87–8, 89, 124, 147–8
at risk at the Greta police station, 182
search for Kelly Gang, 185–96, 202, 234–5
search for shotgun used to shoot Watt, 123–4
at Stringybark Creek, 226–9
threat by Ned Kelly, 248
at trial of Lewis, 145
trip to New Zealand, 56
turns to goldmining, 295
unique position in search for Kellys, 230
view of Kelly family, 301
at Watt murder trial, 129
and Wooragee Outrage arrests and trial, 115, 119, 122–4
Strahan, Anthony Oliver, 78, 125, 150, 180, 261, 274, 292, 295, 297–8
Strahan, Anthony snr (Anthony Strahan's father), 7, 9–11, 57
Strahan, Anthony 'Tony' (Anthony Strahan's grandson), 215–6
Strahan, Deborah, 6, 9
Strahan, Edward (Anthony Strahan's brother), 10–17, 58, 271–2
Strahan, Edward (Anthony Strahan's grandfather), 5–10
Strahan, Edward (Anthony Strahan's son), 268, 297
Strahan, Francis 'Frank', 236, 241, 261, 297–8
Strahan, Frank, 3, 216, 218, xvi
  birth, 241
  marriage, 297
Strahan, Jessie, 177, 271, 297
Strahan, Marion (nee Evans), 68–9, 74, 78–9
  birth of, 74
  character of, 78
  conditions in Greta, 179–80

death of, 216, 298
life after Anthony's death, 297–8
meets Anthony, 78
snubbed by Beechworth community, 79
view of Kelly family, 301
Strahan, Marion jnr, 159, 295–6
Strahan, Mary, 16, 59
Strahan, Nina, 56–7, 60
Strahan, Richard, 58, 272
Strahan, Robert, 14–15, 24
Strahan, Sarah Ann, 16
Strahan, Simon, 58, 59, 271
Strahan, Thomas 'Tom', 271, 297, 298
Stratford family, 8
Stringybark Creek (events at), 222–7
Studders, John, 193
suicide, 158, 269, 286

T
Tannim, Catherine, 55–60
Tasmania see Van Diemen's Land
theft, 65, 69
  see also stock theft
Thom, Hugh, Constable, 174–6, 182–3
  in Greta contingent to apprehend Kelly Gang, 219–20
Timolin, 6–8, 10
Todd, Hamilton, 38
Traverso, Melissa, 216
Trembath, John, 82–7, 264–5

U
Ussher, Senior Constable, 110, 113

V
Van Diemen's Land, 69, 218
  convicts in, 74
Victoria Police, 14–15, 20
  arms, 15
  budget cuts, 20, 197
  change of uniform, 197
  changes in deployment, 181
  districts, 197–8
  funding cuts, 20
  make-up of force, 20–1

religious affiliation of officers, 21
reorganisation in 1878, 197–8
requirements for enlisting, 15
size of force, 15, 20
thinly stretched, x
a tight-knit organisation, 31

W

Walsh, William (doctor), 99, 113, 117, 129, 136, 146
Ward, Michael, Detective, 190–1, 193, 217–18
   meets with Quinn, 233–4
   reduced by one grade by Royal Commission, 256
   rewarded, 254
   at Stringybark Creek, 227
Warren, Richard, 137
Watson, Charles, 82–7
Watt, Ellen, 97–100, 113, 114, 116
   at Watt coronial inquest, 117
   at Wooragee Outrage committal hearing, 119–20
Watt, John, 97–100, 113, 115–20
   death of, 116
   murder trial, 126–32
Wellwood, Samuel, Constable, 68, 125
Whitnell, George, 263–4
Whitty, Charles, 193
Whitty, James, 184–5
Wilkinson, Henry, 264
William of Orange, 4, 8
Williams, Edward Eyre, Justice, 126, 130–2, 142, 276
Williamson, William 'Brickey,' 188–9, 193–4, 199–200
Wilson, Bowes, Superintendent, 59–60
Wilson, Rebecca, 209–10, 225
wine-making, 262, 276
women
   facing difficult circumstances, 272
   life in nineteenth-century Victoria, 179, 269
Wooragee, 93
Wooragee Hotel, 97–9, 116, 139
Wooragee Outrage, 101–2, 115, xvi
   aftermath, 147–9
   arrests, 113
   committal hearing, 118–22
   events of the night, 94–9
   impact on police careers, 147
   investigation into, 99–104, 113–16
   rewards for police involved, 147–8
   Watt murder trial, 126–32
Worsley, Leonard (coroner), 50, 51–2
Wright, Clare, 190, xvi

Y

Young, Robert, Constable, 48–9
Young, William, 16

Z

Zincke, William, 114–15, 140, 193, 199, 275

ABOUT THE AUTHOR

Lachlan Strahan is a historian and the Australian High Commissioner to Solomon Islands. His first book, *Australia's China*, has become one of the standard works on Australia–China relations. His second, *Day of Reckoning*, traced a series of crimes in Papua New Guinea after World War II and was shortlisted for the 2006 NSW Premier's Australian History Prize.

Lightning Source UK Ltd.
Milton Keynes UK
UKHW012217050922
408363UK00005B/378